Greenhill Books

ENGLAND IN THE SEVEN YEARS' WAR
VOLUME II: 1759–63

ENGLAND IN THE SEVEN YEARS' WAR

VOLUME II: 1759–63

by Julian S. Corbett

INTRODUCTION BY CHRISTOPHER DUFFY

Greenhill Books, London
Presidio Press, California

This edition of *England in the Seven Years' War
Volume II: 1759–63* first published 1992 by
Greenhill Books, Lionel Leventhal Limited,
Park House, 1 Russell Gardens, London NW11 9NN
and
Presidio Press, P.O. Box 1764, Novato, Ca. 94948, U.S.A.

British Library Cataloguing in Publication Data
Corbett, Julian S.
England in the Seven Years War - Vol.2
- New ed
I. Title   942.07

ISBN 1-85367-134-7

Library of Congress Cataloging-in-Publication Data available

Publishing History
England in the Seven Years' War was first published in 1907
(Longmans, Green & Co.) and is reproduced now exactly
as the original edition, complete and unabridged, with the
addition of a new Introduction by Christopher Duffy.

Printed and bound in Great Britain by
Biddles Ltd, Guildford and King's Lynn

CONTENTS

MAPS AND PLANS

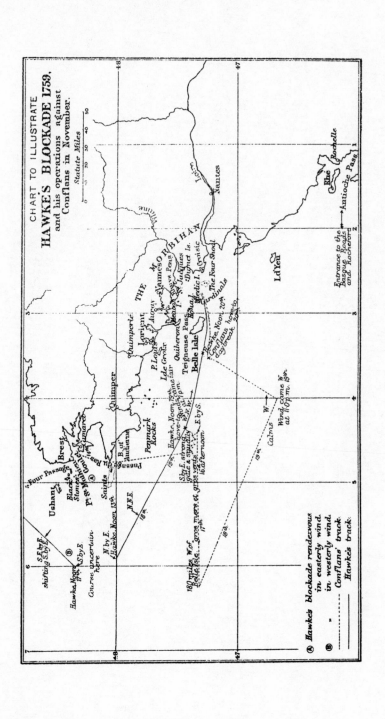

CHART TO ILLUSTRATE
HAWKE'S BLOCKADE 1759,
and his operations against
Conflans in November.

Statute Miles

Ⓐ Hawke's blockade rendezvous
   in easterly wind.
Ⓑ   ,,   in westerly wind.
.... Conflans' track.
———— Hawke's track.

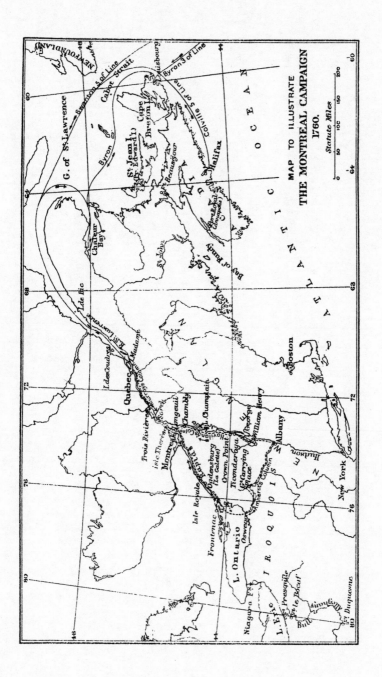

MAP TO ILLUSTRATE
THE MONTREAL CAMPAIGN
1760.

Statute Miles

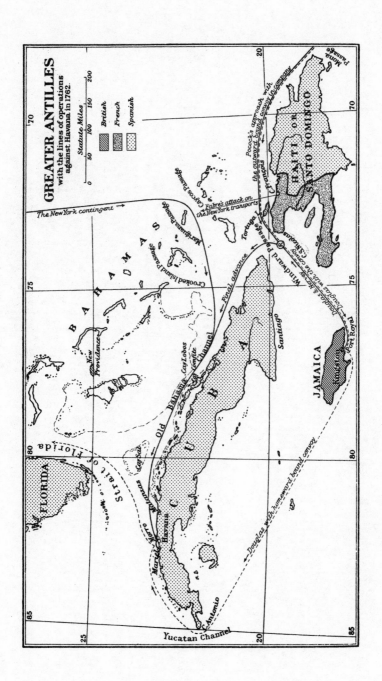

GREATER ANTILLES
with the lines of operations
against Havana in 1762.

Statute Miles
0   50   100   150   200

British
French
Spanish

FLORIDA

BAHAMAS

New Providence

The New York contingent →

Mayaguana Passage

Crooked Island Passage

Caicos Passage

Fabre's attack on the New York transports

Pocock's approach with the outward bound convoy in company

Caicos Passage

Crooked Passage

HAITI OR SANTO DOMINGO

Mona Passage

Turks Passage

Cironilos

Final advance

Old Bahama Channel

Cay Lobos

Cay Confite

Cay Sal

Williams's Bank

Marial

Morro

Havana

Straits of Florida

Yucatan Channel

Antonio

CUBA

Santiago

S. Nicolas

Douglas & party

Douglas, with the homeward bound convoy

Windward Passage

JAMAICA

Kingston

Port Royal

ENGLAND IN THE
SEVEN YEARS' WAR
VOLUME II: 1759–63

ENGLAND IN THE SEVEN YEARS' WAR

CHAPTER I

THE FRENCH COUNTER-ATTACK OF 1759

A STRIKING feature of the operations against Quebec is
that in spite of their extreme difficulty and the risk they
involved, and in spite of the decisive importance of the
objective, no direct attempt to interrupt or even to harass
them was made from France. The conditions which
produced this result have still to be dealt with, and are
well worth study.

In the first place, they introduce us to a fresh principle
of higher strategy which recurs in almost all great wars,
and above all others tends to strategical confusion in
their conduct. That law, or principle, is the tendency
of limited wars to become unlimited in character. The
process, as between two powerful and determined states, is
almost inevitable. In a limited war, correctly conducted,
a phase must be reached sooner or later in which one
party begins to predominate in the limited area—that is,
the area of the special object. The other party, as he
feels himself unable to retain his hold in that area or
shake that of his adversary, will seek to redress the
balance by striking him at the centre of his power. In

other words, the losing party will seek to destroy or
cripple his enemy's resources for war at their base, and
to inflict upon his home population suffering more intense
than the attainment of the special object is worth. A
war conducted on these lines is unlimited in character,
since by acting thus we seek, through general pressure
upon the national life of an adversary, to force him to
do our will or to abandon his own.

It is this stage of a limited war which most severely
tests the imperturbability of a government, and at the same
time exhibits the highest function of the defensive. And
here lies the second point, in which the home aspect of
the campaign of 1759 is so significant. Pitt's success in
the war, so far, had been due fundamentally to the clear-
eyed determination with which he had differentiated and
co-ordinated the offensive and defensive parts of his
scheme. The vigorous offensive in the limited area had
been given its utmost attainable intensity, and nourished
to the last available man and gun by a cool insistence
upon a rigid defensive at home, so far, at least, as
that defensive was compatible with diplomatic demands.
Though France had for a while hung back from the truth,
it had been her interest from the first to make the war
unlimited in character. She was so much the weaker in
the limited area and upon the common lines of passage
and communication, that general coercion was her only
real chance of fighting the war to a favourable peace.
It was with this object in view, as we have seen, that she
had attacked Hanover, but the connection between Hanover and England had not proved sufficiently intimate
to convert the character of the war. In Europe Pitt
stubbornly refused to go beyond the general defensive
attitude which was necessary to cover his offensive in
America; and France had been provided by diplomatic

means with preoccupations which as yet had made it impossible for her to break that defensive.

So far, the correct line for England to pursue had been comparatively clear and easy to follow; but when France, finding her first design for expanding the war ineffective, went a step further and decided to make a direct attack upon the British Islands, the case became more complex. The question at once arose whether the time had not now come for abandoning the defensive attitude which had hitherto sufficed. Pitt above all men was a believer in the supreme efficacy of the offensive. In our history he may be taken to stand for that faith, as Napoleon stands for it in France; and yet it was Napoleon who wrote, " The whole art of war consists in a well reasoned and strictly judicious defensive, followed by audacious and rapid attack." Such too was Pitt's faith. No man grasped more firmly than he the absolute dependence of the offensive upon a foundation of defence, and no one moreover knew better that where the offensive is not directed justly at the main object of the war, it is mere superstition and untutored instinct. To meet offence by quicker and more violent offence was the keynote of Pitt's method, but he never permitted the brilliance of the conception to blind him. He never forgot that to be tempted into taking the offensive in an area which was not the true area of the war, and in which the enemy was naturally the stronger, was not to show vigour, but to play stupidly into the enemy's hands. We have only to follow his handling of the new situation to see how true was his eye and how masterly his grasp of war.

That the French determined to resort in some form or other to their old deterrent device of an invasion, or at least a formidable demonstration, was known early in the year. Indeed they made no secret of it. Seeing that the whole object of the design was to divert British attention from America and to attract her main forces within reach of French weapons, she had every reason to sound her trumpets as loudly as possible. What she had to keep secret was not her intention, but the manner in which it was to be carried out.[1] Before ever Saunders and Wolfe had sailed for Quebec, our intelligence left no doubt that the French intention was at least serious enough to be reckoned with. Choiseul, who was now all-powerful at Versailles, had said they meant to play the Pretender again and make a serious descent upon England to ruin her credit, since in his opinion this was the only means France had left for maintaining the balance. It was English supplies that kept the war in Germany going, and they must be stopped. For it was only in Germany that France could secure the means of recovering the ground she had lost in America. There Frederick must be subdued, and the only way to subdue Frederick was to invade England, and so detach her from his alliance. Her eyes were not shut to the naval difficulties, but these she hoped to overcome by bringing in the other maritime powers, and particularly Sweden, who was as anxious as herself to see the horn of Frederick brought low.[2] The fleet was already arming, and forty thousand men were cantoned along the Channel coasts. Threats so definite as these had never failed to impress the peculiar tenderness of British strategy. The device had been tried again and again, and had always had the effect of attracting to itself the mass of British effort. But, unlike his predecessors, Pitt was unmoved. He saw the old net being spread before his eyes, and refused to walk into it.

---

[1] Choiseul to Havrincour, June 7, *Newcastle Papers*, 32,891.
[2] Information from Paris, *Newcastle Papers*, *Add. MSS.* 32,888, f. 252, Jan. 20, 1759 ; Scheffer to Höpken (intercepted), *Ibid.*, Jan. 20, 32,887.

The orders for Canada stood, and Pitt gave no more heed to the French threat than, as we have seen, slightly to strengthen his naval defensive by ordering Saunders to detach two of the line to reinforce Brodrick in the Mediterranean.

There was, however, one factor in the situation which caused Pitt real anxiety, and that was the uncertain and even menacing attitude of the neutral sea powers—Spain, Holland, Denmark, and Sweden. It may be taken as a law of maritime warfare, which cannot be omitted from strategical calculation with impunity, that every step towards gaining command of the sea tends to turn neutral sea powers into enemies. The prolonged exercise of belligerent rights, even of the most undoubted kind, produces an interference with trade that becomes more and more oppressive. But the process is usually accelerated as the sense of power inclines the dominating belligerent to push its privileges beyond admitted limits. In the present case the atmosphere was very highly charged, owing to the fact that the Dutch and those that followed them still claimed immunity for enemy's goods in neutral ships; while England asserted her traditional doctrine that enemy's goods were good prize everywhere upon the high seas. In the present war this old dispute received a special aggravation. For, as we have seen, France, in an effort to save her West Indian trade, had suspended her exclusive navigation laws, and had thrown open that trade to neutrals. Now, however willing England might be to relax the severity of her doctrine in order to keep well with her neighbours, this was a length to which she could not go. To permit neutrals, and above all the Dutch, to carry on for France her West Indian trade, was to render that trade almost invulnerable, and the islands themselves much more defensible. We argued that for a neutral in war time to carry on belligerent trade which was denied to her in peace was to better her position by the war, and to give illegitimate assistance to the belligerent. Our courts, therefore, had laid down from the first the famous " Rule of 1756 " that during war neutrals may not engage in a trade with the colonies of a belligerent which is denied to foreign vessels in time of peace.

On this rule our courts acted with legitimate severity, to the especial annoyance of the Dutch, whose commercial position had always owed so much to their inveterate practice of fishing thus in troubled waters.[1] Added to this was the further provocation that the Dutch were the most confirmed dealers in contraband of war, and the result was that their ships were seized ruthlessly and condemned in our prize courts without mercy, and often with a stretch of justice. Danes, Swedes, and Spaniards fared little better. What the King's cruisers did might possibly have been borne, but the action of our privateers was outrageous beyond endurance. Every year it had been growing worse, and it is not to be denied that at this time there was a swarm of smaller privateers in the Narrow Seas who were not to be distinguished from pirates. No matter from what innocent port the luckless vessels came, they seized them regardless of their papers, and in some cases went so far as to capture vessels which had just been released by our own prize-courts. To increase the danger of the situation, it happened that the Princess Royal, who had been regent in Holland, had recently

[1] For the serious extent of this trade see Governor Thomas to Pitt, Antigua, Nov. 20, 1750, *Chatham MSS.*, 98. He says three Dutch convoys under French escort had passed between Martinique and St. Eustatius in the last four months.

died, and we were deprived of her kindly influence. In Spain, too, the Anglophile King Ferdinand had sunk into imbecility. His end was obviously near, and the heir-presumptive was the Bourbon King of Naples, a strong partisan of France. Still General Wall maintained his ascendency over Spanish policy, but it was expected not to outlast the frail life of the King.

This, then, was the uncertain element in the situation, and it was the only one which caused Pitt any real anxiety. He was honestly doing his best to check the abuses, but the privateers were incorrigible. What oppressed his mind from the first was a vision of the three northern powers uniting to protect their trade. He saw how easily on such a pretence they might gather a powerful combined fleet to escort their convoys down Channel, and then, having seen them clear, it would be open to them to run into Brest, join hands with the French fleet, and declare war. We should then be unable to keep command of the Channel or the North Sea, and the threatened invasion would become a real danger.[1]

The vision does credit to Pitt's long sight and acute perception. It was far from fanciful. France was doing all she could at this time to tempt Sweden into taking a hand in her invasion project, and Denmark was actually approaching Holland as to the possibility of forming a maritime union and taking common action for the assertion of neutral rights. Pitt, who knew how to make concessions as well as to be bold, met the danger by

---

[1] Newcastle to Yorke, Dec. 19, 1758, and " Mem. for the King," Dec. 22. " Mr. Pitt's apprehensions that the Dutch and Danes may come into our channel without our having any certain knowledge of their object, and if the court of France should have any design to disturb us, these very ships may join and assist in it."—*Add. MSS.* 32,886.

bringing pressure to bear on the prize courts to release as many ships as possible, and by restraining the excesses of the privateers by administrative action. In May, as the complaints continued and the crisis became more acute, he went so far as to hurry a severe Act through Parliament to restrain and punish their abuses, and to facilitate the release of captured vessels, while licenses were almost entirely refused to small vessels, and the prize courts had a fresh hint to show every possible leniency. The resistance of the privateer owners was violent and formidable, but a few weeks after the Act came into operation means were found for reconciling them to the new measures, and at the same time of using their energy. The growing menace of invasion called, as it always did, for the formation of a defensive flotilla, and a number of them were taken into Government pay and attached to squadrons under the command of naval officers who could direct their energy into more profitable channels. By these means the air was cleared. The neutral powers were pacified, and the special danger passed.[1]

Still in spite of these measures as the spring advanced the seriousness of the general outlook only increased. Week by week signs that the French were in earnest

---

[1] Waddington, vol. iii. p. 425 ; Beatson, vol. ii. pp. 201–203. Beatson says : " Great numbers of these privateers were very small, and some of them were commanded by men remarkable only for brute courage and entirely devoid of every principle of honour or humanity, &c." They actually robbed the Marquis de Pignatelli, Spanish Ambassador to Denmark, on his way to Copenhagen in a Dutch ship. The new Act came into force on June 1, and was entitled, "An Act to explain and amend an Act of 29 George II. for the encouragement of seamen . . . and for the better prevention of piracies and robberies by private ships of war." Commissions were limited to ships of over 100 tons and 10 guns, with a discretionary power to grant them to smaller vessels made in favour of the Channel Islands, whose fishing craft had been doing real service against the French coastwise traffic.

grew in intensity. Troops were gathering about the Flemish ports, and a flotilla was being prepared in those of the Channel. Yorke, in Holland, assured the Government it meant nothing, but Newcastle's intelligence was too good, and he had no illusions. " The design," he wrote " of making an attempt here, and perhaps at the same time in Ireland and Scotland, goes on, but the particular time of its execution is not yet determined. These things are not given out to frighten us, but are under their serious consideration. You know, I suppose, that flat-bottomed boats are preparing all along the French coasts."[1] Yorke persisted in his scepticism, while at home the Government was acting on its convictions. The French were assuring all the allied courts that, owing to the great fleets which England had sent out to the West Indies and Canada, it would be impossible for them to be superior in European waters. But Anson's labour had never ceased. On April 5th he was able to promise the King that he would have thirty of the line ready for the Channel Fleet in May, and that the French between Brest and Rochefort would have no more than twenty-seven. He proposed to send Boscawen, who was still at home, to look into Rochefort with ten sail, and to order a cruiser squadron to Bordeaux to destroy a convoy of victuallers which had gone thither for provisions.[2] His cruisers upon the French coasts were supplying him with excellent information, and at the same time actively operating against the coastwise trade upon which the equipment of the French invading forces must principally depend. The effect of Anson's energy and Pitt's politic concessions to the neutral powers was that the control of the home waters was soon in little danger.

---

[1] Newcastle to Yorke, April 3, *Newcastle Papers*, 32,889.
[2] " Mem. for the King," April 5, *ibid.*, 32,889

The more immediate anxiety was from Toulon, where the French preparations were more advanced. The probable intention of the squadron was to seek to join the Brest fleet, and if this were carried out the control of the Channel would become more difficult to secure. It was therefore decided to give Boscawen three of the line and send him down to join Brodrick before Toulon and take command. In accordance with this plan he sailed on April 14th.

So far, it will be observed, the measures taken to repel, or rather prevent, the threatened disturbance were purely naval. Pitt refused to take the invasion seriously. For him it was but a menace, intended to cover some ulterior action by the French fleet, possibly in the West Indies, Canada, or elsewhere. The situation, in his eyes, was met by confronting it with a fleet capable of dealing with the threatened attack. Everything else was courageously ignored. Formidable as was the display of military movement along the French coasts, there was no calling out of the militia, no raising of volunteers, no issue of orders for driving the coast country, nor indeed any of the traditional measures by which governments had been used on these occasions to further the enemy's object by creating a scare at home and disturbing the current of national life. It was Pitt's conviction to make the defence purely active, to picture the country to itself as only waiting eagerly for the tortoise to dare to show its head. The army must, therefore, take its part in the play beside the fleet, and be deprived of any appearance of waiting to be attacked. So of land defence there was no sign, nor any considerable movement of troops, except the formation of another camp in the Isle of Wight.

It was his old device, and it had never failed him. With the Channel fleet getting rapidly ready for Hawke's flag at Spithead, the Isle of Wight force became a violent threat, and its effect had been immediate. The Duc d'Aiguillon, Governor of Brittany, had been pressing for leave to make an attempt to seize Jersey, but Marshal Belleisle, who was directing the whole of the operations, would not consent. " We must not permit," he wrote, " a secondary expedition, however interesting, to turn our attention from an enterprise of far more importance, the great project against England, which is on the eve of being realised." In justification of his discouraging attitude, he informed the sanguine governor that they were expecting an attack upon Brest in March, and that he must devote all attention to placing it in a state of defence. " The English Ministers," he said, " have learnt that all the batteries of the port, the haven, and the adjacent parts are unarmed, and a portion of the garrison withdrawn. . . . Success by the enemy at this point would give us a mortal blow." [1]

Nor was it at Brest alone the disturbance was felt. From all quarters as before, where it was possible for an expedition to strike, the same anxiety clogged the French preparations.[2] Even so, Pitt was not content. The threat must be made keener still, and once more Newcastle, whose nerves had already as much as they could bear with the risks that Pitt was calmly taking, was thrown in a flutter of despair. On the morning of April 17th, Anson received a note from Pitt, desiring him to receive the King's orders that very day for ten thousand tons of transport for five thousand men. Not a word was said of the objective, and Anson, who himself was still unreconciled to Pitt's fondness for combined expeditions

---

[1] Lacour-Gayet, pp. 302–3.
[2] Intelligence from Sluys, *Newcastle Papers*, 32,890, f. 70 ; Yorke to Newcastle, April 17, *ibid.*

went to Newcastle. The admiral assumed the King knew
Pitt's mind. Newcastle went to the King; but the King
knew no more than he, and refused to issue the order.
This was far from bringing comfort to Anson. When
Newcastle came out of the closet and told the admiral,
who was waiting in the antechamber, what had passed,
Anson, to the Minister's surprise, expressed regret at
the attitude the King had taken. Pitt, he said, would be
outrageous and blame them; and finally he persuaded
Newcastle to go back and tell the King the thing had
better go forward, and that he, as First Lord, personally
wished it to. Upon this the King agreed to sign the
order, on condition that Anson went to Pitt to find out
what service he intended. Newcastle tried to console
himself with the reflection that perhaps a mere alarm
was intended, as we certainly could not spare troops for
another expedition. But he was thoroughly upset, and
told his friend Hardwicke it was " a most abominable and
most unheard-of measure."[1]   To make matters worse,
Pitt was continuing to display a breezy disbelief in the
reality of the invasion. Next day Newcastle tried to
relieve his feelings by a long memorandum on home and
foreign affairs. He despaired of England's being able to
bear the expense of the war any longer, and lamented the
disposition which existed to despise the notion that an
invasion was really intended. It was certainly the French
aim, though it would probably be deferred till the autumn.
It would, of course, depend on the naval force they could
gather and the state of the war in Germany. But in
any case our policy, as he laid it down in italics, was not
to waste our land and sea forces with useless and expensive expeditions, but to collect an organised army for
home defence, and keep the home fleet superior to any-

[1] Newcastle to Hardwicke, April 17.

thing the French could bring against it. There was no knowing how long Spanish neutrality would last, and it was indeed a question whether they should not inform Frederick at once that they could not support the war another year.[1]

Meanwhile Anson had been to Pitt. He found him too ill to be seen, but his secretary explained that no new expedition was intended. The purpose was only to increase the defensive activity of the kingdom by giving complete mobility to the Isle of Wight corps. The effect would be to increase the French apprehension of a counter-attack, and at the same time to secure that a force could be dropped in Scotland or Ireland wherever the French might land.[2] Newcastle and his friends were quieted, but not for long. In the course of the next fortnight, intelligence came in, which made the prospect of invasion more formidable than ever. Newcastle had obtained information, which he regarded as certain, that the French corps in Flanders was intended for England, that it was to be reinforced by the Guards and a detachment from the army of the Rhine, and that Soubise himself was to command it.[3] There was also an assurance from our spies that thirty thousand men were assembling within twenty-four hours' march of Brest, and that they were suddenly to be thrown upon the west coast of Ireland.

Consequently Newcastle's nervousness returned with increased force, and to do him justice it was not without excuse. As he had said, the offensive action of the French would depend upon how the war went in Germany, and it was going very badly. Ferdinand, who had wintered

---

[1] *Add. MSS.* 32,890, f. 149, April 18–19.
[2] Anson to Newcastle, *ibid.*, April 18.
[3] Newcastle to Yorke, April 27.

on the line of Münster, Lippstadt, and Paderborn, found himself confronted by Marshal Contades in superior force. Added to this, his left rear was threatened by the French army of the Upper Rhine, which was based on Frankfort, and which, as Soubise had been called to command the army of England, was then in the far more capable hands of the Duc de Broglie. To free himself from the impossible situation, Ferdinand, with characteristic energy, before the campaign had really opened, made a dash at Frankfort ; but his attack on Broglie's position failed, and he had to fall back with considerable loss and no relief of his awkward situation. A secondary effect of this operation was to relieve the French of one serious uncertainty. Till Ferdinand began to move towards Frankfort, that is, eastward and away from the coast, they had to face the possibility that Pitt's force in the Isle of Wight foreshadowed a combination with him in Flanders.[1] This fear was removed, and though they were still anxious about Normandy and Havre, the army of Soubise in Flanders was left comparatively free for eccentric offensive action.

Still Pitt refused to believe in the reality of the French threat, while Newcastle's alarm grew in proportion to Pitt's assumption of confidence. Pitt was still confined to his room, and Newcastle was everywhere. The result was that by the first week in May he had worked the country into a regular scare, and on the 9th a Cabinet Council had to meet at Pitt's house to deal with it. Pitt was as contemptuous as ever. He told Newcastle that he and his friends had worked up the panic, and it was their business to allay it. The French, he affirmed, were in no condition to attack, and had made no preparation to do so. Newcastle and Hardwicke, whose information was

---

[1] Yorke to Newcastle, April 17.

often better than Pitt's, contradicted him. Holderness
held his tongue. Bedford urged the unprotected condition of Ireland. But nothing could be got out of Pitt,
except an order that in ten days' time Hawke was to
repair to Torbay with eighteen of the line to watch Brest,
and that a proclamation should be issued calling out some
of the new militia.[1] The force was still scarcely born,
and Pitt seems to have relied for military defence upon
his characteristic principle of giving the regular troops
their extreme mobility by providing them with sea
carriage. For at this time he ordered the ten thousand
tons of transport he had called for to be victualled for
three months, and a fortnight later he called for fifteen
thousand tons more to assemble at the Nore for immediate service.[2] What this last order meant is not known ;
but in all probability the intention was to frighten
Soubise and hold him in Flanders away from Ferdinand.

From this point the whole situation turned upon the
capacity of the home fleet to perform its defensive function. That function was to secure the lines of passage
and communication in the Narrow Seas so as to make it
impossible for any French invading force to get to sea—
or if by the hazard of war any part of that force did get
away and land, to ensure that we could quickly throw
troops upon its back and prevent the French supporting
it. It was in fact a problem as purely naval as any problem of war can be, and Pitt acted accordingly. We
have seen that in the offensive areas of the war, where
results depended upon the intimate co-ordination of
naval and military action, the admirals were receiving

---

[1] For the Cabinet see " Mem. for the King," May 9, *Newcastle Papers*,
32,891, and for calling out the militia the correspondence from May 17 to
27, *ibid*.

[2] *Admiralty Secretary, In-letters (Secretary of State)*, 4123, May 16 and
June 1.

their orders direct from him, but in this case it was different. Nothing is more eloquent of Pitt's grasp of war than his frank recognition that here his interference was uncalled for. Having determined the function of the navy in the home area he gave it a perfectly free hand, and the whole of the operations for discharging that function were left to the judgment of Lord Anson and his colleagues on the Board of Admiralty.

The energy which they had been displaying in turning what remained of the navy into a powerful home fleet fully justified Pitt's confidence. Hawke acted with equal promptitude. Three days after the decision of the Secret Committee he hoisted his flag at Spithead, where he was informed by the Admiralty that Bompart had left Martinique for San Domingo, and would probably be home shortly. He was therefore to try to intercept him by keeping a detachment down the Bay, and for this purpose he would shortly be reinforced.[1] Within the ten days specified he was at Torbay with his eighteen of the line : on the morrow he was stretching over to Ushant, and before the week was out he had struck the note which was to dominate the idea of naval blockade for a century to come.

His instructions had been framed on the traditional " observation " idea of watching Brest from Torbay. But once his flag was flying he determined to act on his own theory of what a defensive blockade should be. In his first two despatches he enunciates his ideas. On May 27th he wrote that he had arrived off Brest on the 24th, and found eleven sail out in the Road. His advanced cruisers reported four others ready for sea at L'Orient, and he had

---

[1] Hawke to Admiralty, with answer endorsed, *Admiralty Secretary, In-letters*, 92, May 14. In this volume and in *Out-letters*, 83–4 and 526, and *Secret Orders*, 1331, will be found the whole of the despatches relating to the Brest blockade hereafter quoted.

immediately detached Captain Keppel with five of the line to Audierne Bay to prevent their stealing round to Brest. In his opinion the eleven ships in the Road were not intended to proceed against Great Britain, but for the relief of the West Indies. He himself was going to stay where he was to watch them. "As the eleven in the Road," he said, "may be joined by others from the port, I don't think it prudent to give them a chance of coming out by retiring to Torbay." He therefore signified his intention of staying where he was unless their lordships recalled him, or strong westerly weather forced him to seek shelter. A week later, on June 4th, he reported that the ships from L'Orient must have got round before Keppel reached his station. There were no longer any to be seen there, and there were seventeen in Brest Road. He therefore reiterated his intention of staying where he was till further orders. On the morrow, however, a south-westerly gale was upon him; and on the 6th he was forced to run back into Torbay, and there he was held, in spite of every effort to get back, for the best part of a fortnight.

As ill-luck would have it, it was at this moment that the whole situation was intensified by a master-stroke of the intelligence department which seriously increased the agitation in London, and which for the first time opened Pitt's eyes to the magnitude of the French design. Neither Choiseul nor Belleisle concealed from themselves how desperate was their plan without further naval assistance. Except from Sweden there seemed no immediate chance of obtaining it, and, as we have seen, they were straining every device to induce her to turn her war with Prussia into a war with England as well. The Swedes, however, were sceptical as to the practicability of the intended invasion. To convince them, Choiseul decided to reveal to them practically the whole of Belleisle's plan, and on May 31st he sent to his ambassador at Stockholm a complete account of it.   About the middle of June a copy of this letter found its way into Newcastle's pocket.[1]

He could now rejoice in something to justify his attitude against that of Pitt : for, as he told Hardwicke, the French design was " not only serious but extremely well laid." [2] Few will deny that Newcastle's opinion was no more than the truth. The idea which the letter disclosed was a considerable modification of that which Belleisle had first put forward.   His original plan was one which Napoleon adopted—that is, a flotilla of flat-boats sufficient for the transport of fifty thousand men was to be assembled between Ambleteuse and Boulogne, under cover of formidable coast defences. The work was actually begun, but Belleisle, unlike Napoleon, when he came closer to the design rejected it as requiring too much time and being too costly.   In its place he adopted a plan which was far less amateurish and much more promising, and was entirely new.   It was based on a *coup-de-main* upon London from the army of Flanders.   Twenty thousand men were to march suddenly to Ostend, embark there, and land upon the coast of Essex at Maldon in the estuary of the Blackwater, where they would be within two marches of London.   So far all was simple and promising enough—but there remained the difficulty of securing the passage. It was approached in a thoroughly scientific spirit. Its seriousness was not shirked. Indeed the greater part of the whole design was devoted to a very ingenious method of securing what was wanted. Another army of twenty thousand men was to be assembled in Brittany under the Duc d'Aiguillon, whose

---

[1] Choiseul to Havrincour, May 31, *Newcastle Papers*, 32,891.
[2] *Newcastle Papers*, 32,892, June 14.

destination was the Clyde.   By a junction of the Mediterranean and Atlantic squadrons a fleet of from thirty-
five to forty of the line was to be concentrated in Brest.
Under escort of this fleet D'Aiguillon was to proceed to
his destination, and the fleet, after landing him at some
favourable point near Glasgow, was to proceed north-about
and run down to Ostend to cover the passage of the
Flanders army.   Meanwhile D'Aiguillon would have
marched across Scotland and seized Edinburgh, and as a
further source of confusion Thurot, the famous privateer
captain, would have sailed from Dunkirk with a cruiser
squadron and made a raid on Ireland.[1]

The design, it will be seen, was, as Newcastle said,
"extremely well laid."   So far as it was possible for such
an enterprise to succeed without previous command of
the sea, every chance was taken.   Nothing could be better
devised for confusing the enemy and concealing from
them what the real line of operation was.   But with all
its cleverness it was a soldier's plan, based, as such plans
always have been, on the analogy of an army protecting
its train in an enemy's country.   In the eyes of Belleisle,
the fleet while at sea was the active force advancing
against its objective, and the transports the train.   The
analogy is false, and the fact that the plan involved a
hybrid conception between a passage by force and a
passage by evasion shows that its falseness was felt, if not
quite realised.   If the French fleet was capable of defending an expedition of twenty thousand men against an
attack by Hawke, still more was it capable of dealing with
Hawke if it had no convoy to encumber it.   All it would
then have to do would be to fight a containing action,
while the two expeditions crossed freely under commerce
protection escort.   This had been pointed out.   At one

[1] Lacour-Gayet, *Marine sous Louis XV.*, 321-2.

time there had been a suggestion that D'Aiguillon ought to sail for Scotland under a small escort sufficient to keep off cruisers, and that the mass of the fleet should engage Hawke's attention in the Channel while the Flanders corps crossed. This idea was eventually rejected for the one which really rested ultimately for its success on evasion. For since by clogging the French fleet with a cumbrous convoy its sole chance of decisively defeating Hawke was denied it, the expedition could only hope to arrive safely by evasion. Yet at the same time nothing was so likely to attract Hawke's fleet, and reduce the chances of evasion, as the presence of the main French fleet with the invading corps.

The difficulty which brought so capable a strategist as Belleisle to adopt so faulty a design was probably a part of the British system of naval defence which has not yet been noticed. To confine the enemy's main fleet to port is not to command the sea. By so doing you may prevent the enemy gaining command, but your own fleet will be too much occupied to exercise the command itself. In demobilising the enemy's main fleet you demobilise your own to an even greater degree, for the blockading fleet must be superior. For the active control of the communications in the theatre concerned, secondary lines are necessary. No principle of naval warfare is so much ignored in ordinary discussion as that you cannot command the sea with a battle fleet. Without it, it is true, you cannot do so, if the enemy has one too. But even if your own battle fleet be not occupied and contained by the act of watching that of the enemy, it can never itself be numerous or ubiquitous enough to exercise the actual control. It is, and always has been, the third and the second lines of the fleet that actually control the lines of passage—particularly against transports—that is to say, it is, and always has been, the flotilla and its supporting cruisers and intermediate ships. The function of the battle fleet is to prevent the enemy's battle fleet from interfering with the function of your cruisers and flotilla. By corollary to it follows that you by no means necessarily lose control when your battle fleet is defeated, unless that defeat is so complete as to leave your enemy potent enough to remove your other two lines.[1]

All the great naval First Lords from Anson to St. Vincent recognised this principle, and in the present case secondary lines had been provided, for the special purpose of preventing the enemy's transports passing the Channel while the British main fleet was tied to Brest. The actual defence force took the form of a series of flotillas with supporting cruiser squadrons, disposed along our south-eastern and southern coasts. One, under Commodore Boys, was watching Dunkirk and the Flemish ports, and another, under Sir Peircy Brett, was stationed in the Downs. His special point of vigilance was Havre and the adjacent ports, where it was known that the French were massing a number of large flat-boats for the obvious purpose of transporting troops across the Channel. A third squadron, under Rodney, was being prepared at Spithead. The defence system was thus complete, and it was impossible for the invasion to take place till these squadrons were removed. A mere containing action would not enable the transports to avoid this danger, nor

---

[1] The "flotilla" of that time may be taken to include all vessels of sloop type and under, which regularly used sweeps as auxiliary propulsion. The "intermediate" ships had also battle value, and corresponded to the armoured cruisers of to-day. They were mainly "fifties" and light-armed "sixties," whose normal function was to support cruisers in the regular duties of commerce protection and the like, though they were frequently diverted to assist battle squadrons.

did the presence of Hawke permit of its being removed by anything less than the whole fleet. It all, indeed, comes back to the old story that the defeat and disablement of the British main fleet was the sole expedient which could bring the enterprise within the limits of a sound military risk. Still, given the fact that the enterprise had to be undertaken as the only chance of saving the general situation, it was as well laid as it could be with the given material, and far more likely to have succeeded than was the alternative rejected plan which was the one Napoleon most obstinately favoured.

In London it was received at least with respect. As divulged to Sweden by Choiseul it differed slightly from the above design. Havrincour was told that twenty-four battalions and a regiment of dragoons would sail from Brest under the escort of Conflans and the main fleet, and that, having seen this force to its destination, the admiral would then proceed north-about into the North Sea to cover the passage of fifty thousand men from Flanders and Dunkirk. Marshal Contades meanwhile would prevent Ferdinand from interfering. Of the naval concentration nothing was said, but Newcastle assumed that La Clue would join Conflans from the Mediterranean if he could escape Boscawen, and that Bompart would come in from the West Indies. He was, therefore, for ordering home eight or ten large ships from the West Indian squadrons as soon as Bompart left, but he feared Pitt would not consent. He was getting more and more anxious, and had no faith in Hawke's blockade. " My chief dependence still," he wrote, " is that our little light squadrons in the Downs and Spithead [that is, Boys's, Brett's and Rodney's] will prevent or harass them extremely, on their landing." If they failed, he did not see how we could oppose thirty thousand men, or half that number, unless the militia were used to guard the thousands of French prisoners that crowded our jails. The comfort was, there was time to prepare. It was known the French were still pressing Sweden to assist the Scottish enterprise, and that they could take no final decision till they got a definite answer. Anson therefore did not look for the attempt for two months, and Newcastle accepted his view, but only as a reprieve from the terrors he saw ahead.[1]

Pitt, on the other hand, continued breezily confident. At Anson's suggestion he had sanctioned a secret blow against the French preparations, with which he hoped to teach them a severe lesson. His gaiety even irritated Newcastle, who complained to Hardwicke that Pitt ridiculed the idea of the French being able to make any serious attack, though he had no doubt they would be mad enough to try. The difficulties Hawke was encountering in the Brest blockade increased the anxiety of those who could not share Pitt's security. No sooner did he get to sea again than another gale drove him back to Torbay. "I never saw," he wrote, "so much bad weather in summer since I have been at sea." So seriously disturbed was Newcastle that he now determined to show Pitt the Swedish correspondence he had intercepted. Hitherto it had been kept from him; for ever since the days of Elizabeth it had been the practice of Ministers who were not too sure of themselves to increase their importance with the Crown by getting intelligence and keeping it from their rivals in power. How far Pitt was affected by the disclosure is difficult to say. The immediate effect was that Ligonier was ordered to form

[1] Choiseul to Havrincour, June 7, *Newcastle Papers*, 32,891 ; Newcastle to Hardwicke, June 14, *ibid.*, 32,892.

camps in England and in Ireland, or, as we should say
now, to mobilise the army.   It was now too that the
privateers, who were just then growling over the operation of the new Act, began to be taken into navy pay
to increase the flotilla, and Anson's project was pressed
on with all vigour.

His idea was one after Pitt's own heart.   For the
project was a vigorous counter-stroke with Rodney's
squadron against the flat-boats at Havre.   It was in this
manner he proposed to use the respite of two months
which he believed he had in hand.[1]   Bomb-vessels and
fireships were brought forward for Rodney's flag, and in
hope of keeping the objective secret his own orders and
those of all his captains were made out for proceeding to
Gibraltar to reinforce Boscawen.   But as Rodney at the
same time had to institute inquiries for pilots for Havre,
the attempt was not very. successful.   The admiral
said his officers were already talking of Havre, and before
the weather would permit him to sail the newspapers
were doing the same.[2]   By June 19th the weather had
moderated enough for Hawke to return at last to his
station off Brest, and what with this and the newspapers
Rodney was burning to be off; but all who knew the
Norman coast said it would be useless, since with the
winds that prevailed there would be such a seaway off
Havre as would make it impossible for bomb-ketches to
be used.   June passed away before the weather changed,
but on July 2nd Rodney was able at last to sail. with his

---

[1] The evidence that the project was Anson's is that he was giving all
the orders from the Admiralty, and that on June 8, two days after Rodney
received definite instructions, Newcastle noted in his " Memoranda for the
King," " Lord Anson's project."—*Add. MSS.* 32,891.

[2] Rodney to Cleveland, June 6, 16, and 18, *Admiralty Secretary, In-
letters,* 93.   The sham orders are in *Out-letters,* 83, dated June 8.   The real
ones are in *Secret Orders,* 1331, June 26.

flag in the *Achilles* (60) and a squadron of four "fifties,"
five frigates, and six bomb-ketches.[1]

The next day he anchored before Havre, and during
the night proceeded to get the bomb-ketches into position. There was considerable difficulty in doing so, for
as usual the pilots proved quite useless. But Samuel
Hood and two of the other frigate captains undertook
the work themselves, and by the following morning had
them all arranged in the Honfleur channel within range
of the town, the docks, the flat-boats that were finished,
and the extensive magazines for making the remainder.
Under support of the frigates a furious bombardment
was commenced, Rodney directing it in person from
Hood's ship, the *Vestal*. For fifty-two hours it lasted,
and then only ceased because the mortars were no longer
serviceable. The actual extent of the damage done was
never ascertained. The French, of course, minimised it.
Rodney reported that the town was on fire several times,
that the magazines were burning for six hours, and that
"many of the boats were overturned and damaged by the
explosion of the shells." Also that the consternation was
so great that all the inhabitants forsook the town. The
probability is that the material damage was not very great.
In any case, that was unimportant beside the moral effect.
In that respect all that was wanted had been achieved.
For Rodney had demonstrated to the most nervous and
sceptical that his light squadron was quite sufficient to
prevent the Havre flotilla ever putting to sea without a
fleet escort, and on July 8th he was back at Spithead to
refit for renewing his attack.[2]

[1] Among his officers were several who afterwards achieved distinction.
Samuel Hood and Thomas Graves commanded frigates under him, as they
did squadrons in the fatal year of the next war. Hyde Parker also
commanded a frigate, and Rodney's flag-captain was Barrington.

[2] The most impartial account of the damage done was afterwards
obtained from a Spanish officer who was in the place at the time. He

The real anxieties, however, of the Ministers were far from being allayed. Ferdinand, with the whole force of Contades's army pressing on his left, was persistently retreating, and no one could see where the retreat would end. Frederick had refused to move to his assistance. For the first time in the war he was showing a tendency to act on the defensive, and to adopt any desperate means rather than his wonted activity in the field. Amongst other expedients he was deep in a negotiation with the Sultan, to try to get him to fall on the back of the Austrians. It was an unscrupulous policy, which others had tried before him and some have tried since. The only result that has ever come of it is to make the perpetrator a pariah in Europe. By the end of May he had got so far that Newcastle was officially informed that the Grand Vizier had promised a treaty of alliance if England would also affix her seal. Newcastle, with characteristic levity, was delighted, but Pitt refused to be a party. He knew too well the folly in war of taking measures, however plausible, which must have the effect of raising up fresh forces for the enemy, and he knew that the effect of Frederick's barbarous plan would be to turn Russia's lukewarm interest in the war into fierce and fiery earnest. For this reason alone he would give nothing but an equivocal promise of his good offices for securing the execution of the treaty when made. The Porte at once drew back, and for the time the subject dropped.[1]

During July the situation in Germany went from bad to worse. On the 9th the Duc de Broglie seized Minden, and there appeared no possibility of Ferdinand's being

said about 600 shells and carcases fell in the town, of which he counted 100 in the basin and harbour. He also said the magazine of plank, pitch, and cordage was entirely destroyed. See *Admiralty Secretary, In-letters*, 93, Sept. 21, 1759.

[1] Waddington, vol. iii. p. 113.

able to retain even the line of the Weser.   Hanover again
seemed doomed.   A fortnight later, the Prussian general
Wedell was defeated by the Russians at Poltzig, and the
way was open for a junction between them and the
Austrians at Frankfort.   Nothing, therefore, stood in the
way of the French devoting a very considerable force to
the invasion of England, and it was known that at the
end of June Conflans had left Paris to hoist his flag at
Brest.   At the same time came intelligence that the
Toulon fleet was to sail for Brest on July 15th, and that
at Bordeaux, Nantes, Bayonne, and Rochelle they were
arming ships *en flûte* for the same port.   All these circumstances, coupled with the information which Newcastle had
obtained as to the real nature of the French design exer-
cised a marked reaction on the system of naval defence.
Hitherto the primary objective, or, as the technical phrase
then was, " the principal object," of the home fleet was
the French main fleet, but now it tended to become what
it really was, the French invading armies.   The first indication of this is seen in Anson's activity in strengthening
the light squadrons.   At the end of June he was taking
up more privateers and small craft right and left, and to
reinforce the cruiser squadrons he was arming some of the
transports which had now served Pitt's purpose in alarming
the French, and for which he had no longer any use.[1]

The most interesting reaction, however, is seen in the
changed nature of Hawke's blockade.   It was on June
21st that he succeeded in reaching his station.   The port
had been open a whole fortnight, but to his great relief
he found that nothing had stirred out.   He was able to
send home a list of the French fleet, showing twenty of
the line ready, or almost ready, to sail, which Duff, one
of the best of his cruiser captains, had obtained.   The

---

[1] Newcastle to Hardwicke, June 27.

dispositions he then made related almost entirely to this
fleet, in accordance with a design which he had already
sent to the Admiralty. " Except I shall be drove off,"
he had said, " by winds and weather, I shall keep them
constantly in view, so as either to prevent their coming
out or doing my utmost, in case they should, to take or
destroy them." [1] His idea was that for this purpose
he required a battle squadron equal to, but no stronger
than, that of the enemy. This main squadron, whenever the wind was easterly, that is, offshore, and fair
for the French to come out, he kept off Point St. Mathieu,
inside the Black Stones, and practically in the entrance
to the harbour. In advance of this was an inshore
squadron of two of the line and two frigates, under
Commodore the Hon. Augustus Hervey, who in the
course of this command was to clinch the reputation
he had already established as one of the most brilliant
officers in the service. Whenever the weather rendered
the St. Mathieu station unsafe, Hawke moved out to a
rendezvous fifteen leagues W. $\frac{1}{2}$ S. of Ushant, while Hervey
took his place off St. Mathieu, and a chain of connecting
ships of the line was formed between the two squadrons.
This arrangement, with the three ships of the line which
remained over and were stationed in Audierne Bay to
watch L'Orient, constituted the naval blockade. The
commercial blockade was completed by frigates at both
ends of the Passage du Four, one in the Passage du Raz,
and one right in the Goulet. It was thus rendered effective enough, in Hawke's opinion, to entitle him to turn
back any neutral that tried to enter, and to seize every
Swede on suspicion of carrying contraband.[2] His task,

[1] To Cleveland, " Off the Start," June 12.
[2] To Cleveland, July 16. Danes were allowed in and out, Dutch as a
rule were merely warned off. In Hawke's view a strictly effective blockade
did not entitle him to seize neutrals except under suspicion of contraband.

however, did not end with watching the Breton ports.
For about this time the Government received definite
news that Bompart was about to come home from the
West Indies with seven or eight sail, and Hawke was
ordered, so soon as he had ships enough, to throw out a
squadron down the Bay to intercept him.[1]

So far, it will be seen, Hawke's attention was entirely
devoted to the enemy's battle fleets and their supplies.
It was not till he had been nearly a month on the station
that he seems to have thought it necessary to attend to
the transports and the army that were gathering to the
southward of him. In the middle of August, however,
whether upon fresh information or upon a hint from
home, he seems to have suddenly awakened to the danger
of the French transports evading him, while the presence
of Conflans's fleet compelled him to concentrate before
Brest. The first idea apparently was that the transports
which had assembled in the ports between L'Orient and
Nantes were about to attempt to steal round to Brest.
On August 15th Captain Roddam was ordered to cruise
with the Audierne or southern squadron as far as
L'Orient, with instructions that if he met a convoy he
was to attack it and not its escorting frigates. "The
convoy," he was told emphatically, "is your principal
object." A week later the anxiety grew more serious.
It was thought the troops might sail direct for Ireland
—perhaps even that they had already done so. The
southern squadron was therefore increased, and on August
26th Commodore John Reynolds was given the command, with orders to extend the blockade as far down
as Nantes. If he found no transports there he was
immediately to take the whole squadron to Ireland in
search of them, and to remember particularly that the

[1] *Out-letters*, 526, Aug. 13.

transports were his "principal object." If he found them
still in Nantes, he was to keep them there, and see if
they could not be destroyed with bombs.[1]

On his arrival Reynolds found the transports had not
moved, and with the force at his command, viz. one ship
of the line and a dozen cruisers, he established a strict
blockade. So far then all was well, and just then came
news that ashore things were even better. While
Reynolds was closing Nantes, Hawke was standing in
to St. Mathieu on special orders from home to fire a
feu-de-joie in the face of M. de Conflans. The French
fleet could not mistake its meaning. It was for the
famous victory of Minden. After the Duc de Broglie's
brilliant seizure of the town, which finally threw Hanover
open to the French, Ferdinand had turned in his apparently hopeless retreat. Marshal Contades was busily
and successfully engaged in enlarging the hole which
Broglie had pierced. All Westphalia and the whole
line of the Weser were practically in his hands, when
Ferdinand had suddenly fallen upon him at Minden and
completely defeated him. As all allowed, the victory
was mainly due to the daring attack of the British
infantry, but the honour of the exploit was overshadowed
by Lord George Sackville's refusal to charge with his
cavalry when Ferdinand had called upon him to complete the rout the infantry had begun. Every one now
knew him for the man he was; at last it was clear
enough how little chance a combined expedition ever
really had with him as its moving spirit. But for his
cowardice—for it could be called nothing else—Minden
must have been one of the most complete victories in
history. As it was, it was sufficient to save Hanover for

---

[1] Hawke's orders to Roddam, Aug. 15; to Reynolds, Aug. 26; Hawke
to Cleveland, Aug. 28, *Admiralty Secretary*, *In-letters*, 93.

another year, and the defensive part of Pitt's system ashore was restored almost as completely as it existed at sea.

This aspect of Minden must never be forgotten if we would keep a clear understanding of the development of Pitt's system. We naturally connect the battle almost solely with Sackville's disgrace of the British cavalry and that unsurpassed attack of British infantry on the un-shaken horse of France. But the magnificent resolution of Ferdinand, the cunning with which he prepared his success against heavy odds, and his eye for the moment to turn upon his enemy, rise above it all. But for his victory Hanover must have been lost, and the efforts of Saunders and Wolfe, of Boscawen and Hawke, would have been of little avail. If the navy was able in the end to secure the object of the campaign, it was because Ferdinand kept the ring intact at Minden. No finer example exists of the use of counter-stroke, of the function of attack in defence.

The victory could not have been more timely. For, as Marshal Contades was preparing to sweep Ferdinand before him and reoccupy Hanover, the great French naval concentration had begun. Bompart we know was on his way home to Brest; Conflans was making his final preparations; and on August 5th, four days after Minden was fought, La Clue put to sea from Toulon. There was nothing to stop him, and ten days later, just when Hawke was extending his blockade to meet the expected movement of D'Aiguillon's transports, he was able to pass out of the Straits untouched.

For the moment, then, the fate of the great French counter-stroke lay between La Clue and Boscawen. What had happened was this. It was now nearly three months since in the middle of May Boscawen had found Brodrick

off Toulon and had taken over the command. The
secret orders he brought out reflected the spirit that
prevailed at home when he had sailed. There was no
suggestion of an invasion to be stopped. In the time-
honoured form he was instructed that the principal
intentions of the Government in sending him out were
to annoy the enemy, secure Gibraltar, and protect the
trade.[1] His method of performing these functions was
from the first moment he arrived, to establish a close
blockade of Toulon and Marseilles, while his cruisers
were distributed at all the well-known focal points, or
escorting the convoys along the well-known routes. It
was the direct and obvious way to carry out the Government's intentions, and the annoyance to the enemy was
all they could wish. So close was Boscawen's blockade,
so daring the activity of his fireships, that the Toulon
squadron had retired into the inner road under the guns
of the fortress. Captured letters told him the people
were fearing a descent at any moment. Besides his
dozen cruisers he had thirteen of the line and two
"fifties," and they could not believe so large a fleet
meant only a blockade. The disturbing effects of Pitt's
previous descents were still working, and between Toulon
and Marseilles there were no less than ten battalions
of regular infantry, besides the militia.[2] Boscawen's
movements seemed to have threatened attacks in various
places, and the troops were constantly marching to oppose
them. On June 7th a very daring piece of service increased the effect. Two French frigates trying to get
into Toulon had been forced to anchor in a small bay,
now known as the Anse de Sablettes, immediately south
of the entrance of the port. Like all the coast, the

[1] *Secret Orders*, 1331, March 28.
[2] *In-letters*, 384, May 30 and June 1.

place was bristling with batteries, but Boscawen sent in the *Culloden, Conqueror*, and *Jersey* to try to destroy the frigates. For an hour they had to endure the fire of nine batteries, and then, with their mission unaccomplished, they had to come away in such a condition that the *Culloden* was sent to Gibraltar to refit.

Till the end of June his activity kept the coast in perpetual alarm, but then it became necessary to carry the whole squadron to the coast of Spain to water, and thence to Gibraltar to revictual. Till nearly the end of July he lay in Salou Bay, close to Tarragona, which he describes as the best watering-place in all the Mediterranean. Then he moved on to Gibraltar, where he arrived on August 3rd. Here he received a modification of his original instructions, which had been sent off at the end of June after the discovery of the formidable nature of Belleisle's plan. The new orders reveal the new anxiety about a naval concentration upon Brest. He was told that, notwithstanding any former order, if the Toulon squadron got out of the Straits and he heard it was bound for Brest, Rochefort, or any Atlantic port, he was to detach part of his squadron to England or to come home himself, at his discretion, leaving behind him at least seven of the line and all the frigates for the protection of Gibraltar and the other Mediterranean services.[1]

It was at this moment that La Clue had completed his crews, and on August 5th, by which time he must have known that Boscawen had just sailed to Gibraltar to refit, he put to sea. His force was ten of the line, two "fifties," and three frigates, quite enough to force the Straits when Boscawen's fleet was more or less disabled

---

[1] *Secret Orders*, 1331, June 29 ; Boscawen to Cleveland, *In-letters*, 384, Aug. 8.

in the process of refitting. For ten days or so it was actually in this condition, and practically out of action. But so soon as it was nearly ready for sea again Boscawen sent out the only two frigates he had with him to watch for La Clue's coming. One was to cruise off Malaga and the other across the entrance to the Straits between Estrepona and Ceuta. Boscawen had thus changed his close blockade for an open one; that is, he left La Clue free to come out, and was waiting for him at the point of his line of passage, where contact was practically certain. Whether it was a mere result of his necessities or the outcome of mature calculation, no strategy could be sounder. So long as his object was to secure trade and annoy the French, the close blockade and the threats to the coast were the best method of attaining it; but when the object was to demonstrate to France the futility of her trying to recover her position by an invasion, the actual destruction of La Clue's fleet was indicated. A decision was wanted, and open blockade was the best way to secure one.

If Boscawen had indeed opened the blockade deliberately, he had certainly calculated his time much too narrowly. When on August 17th La Clue appeared on the scene the British refit was not complete, and there was every chance of his getting through. His idea had been to make the Barbary coast, steal along it to the entrance of the Gut, and then run through under a press of sail in the night. The game was well played, and only detected when it could not be stopped. It was already nightfall when one of Boscawen's scout frigates came flying in to report the French fleet just east of Ceuta. It was eight o'clock before she could give the alarm, and nothing was ready. Boscawen's flagship, the *Namur*, had her sails still unbent; other ships were equally unprepared, and all of them had parties of men ashore. To make matters worse, the admiral and several of the principal officers were away dining with the Governor of San Roque. Somebody in the flagship, however, was bold enough, possibly by previous orders, to make the signal to unmoor. It was seen from San Roque, and broke up the governor's party in a moment. From all sides there was a stampede for the fleet, officers and liberty men getting on board any ship they could fetch. The excitement and confusion were intense. Yet such was the discipline that by ten o'clock Boscawen was able to slip and make sail with eight of his own division. Brodrick, who had been lying further in, followed not long after with the rest. By eleven Boscawen was clear out off Cabritra Point, and there he had to bring-to to hoist in his boats and clear-ship. It was a splendid feat of seamanship, such as only seamen who know the Rock can fully appreciate. In less than three hours a fleet of the line, moored in a difficult harbour, with sails unbent and the admiral absent, had got to sea at night. It would be hard to surpass it in all our annals.[1]

Meanwhile La Clue, with a fine easterly breeze behind him, had been pushing through the Straits in sailing order and unhindered. His plan was to rush past as fast as possible with all lights extinguished, and then to make for Cadiz in order to rally his fleet, which was sure to have got scattered. About midnight, however, he changed his mind. He had seen the frigate signal his presence and knew she was shadowing him. He had all his fleet together, and instead of hauling up for Cadiz he resolved to carry on as he was, direct for Cape St. Vincent, while

[1] See Admiral Sir Edward R. Fremantle, *Boscawen* (*Twelve Sailors*), p. 266; Ekin, *Naval Battles*, p. 36; *Journal of the Flag-Captain*, printed in Colomb's *Naval Warfare*, p. 139.

the wind held fair, and accordingly he made a signal to that effect.[1] This signal was either not seen or disregarded by the rear ships, which had presumably fallen somewhat astern. Still it appears they held on after La Clue till about two in the morning. Up till that time La Clue says his poop-lanterns were still burning, and the whole squadron could be counted. Between two and three, however, Boscawen's van began to come up and fire upon the rear ships of the French. Thereupon, seeing their admiral had extinguished his lights, they thought best to act on their original orders and steer for the Cadiz rendezvous.[2]

Boscawen, with fine decision, made no attempt to follow them. Without wavering a moment, he too held on direct for St. Vincent. Whether it was by instinct or reason we cannot tell. Possibly his frigate was calling him on ; he does not say. Whatever his motive, his action could not be more correct. He was engaged in an open blockade. He had failed to get actual contact at the first likely point on the enemy's line of passage. The next thing to do was to hurry on to the second. That was St. Vincent, and there he reaped his reward. At daybreak he saw seven of the line lying-to to leeward of him, about thirty miles short of the Cape. It was La Clue with all the best ships of his fleet. He had just discovered that his rearguard was not with him. Boscawen's fleet also was split into two divisions. Brodrick was still out of sight, and La Clue was hoping the eight sail that were with Boscawen were his own lost rearguard.

---

[1] The French had no night compass signals at that time. Some French authors say he signalled "W.N.W.," others "westerly." He probably signalled to "sail large on the starboard tack," which, as the wind then was E.S.E. to E., would give a course about W.N.W., straight for doubling St. Vincent. See Colomb, *Naval Warfare*, p. 139, n.

[2] Lacour-Gayet, *Marine sous Louis XV.*, p. 285 ; Waddington, vol. iii. p. 361.

However, as some of Brodrick's division began to appear he grew suspicious and made a private signal. Boscawen of course could not answer, and La Clue held away in line ahead under a press of sail. It was then about eight o'clock and broad daylight, and Boscawen immediately signalled for a chase to the north-west.[1] Then hour after hour it went on; but one of La Clue's ships was a slug; Boscawen, moreover, got the best of the breeze; and the French were fast being overhauled. By one o'clock they were abreast of Lagos, and though the wind was dying away it was clear an action could not be avoided. Both fleets showed their colours, and twenty minutes later Boscawen made the signal to engage.

It was not, however, till half-past two that the *Culloden*, who was leading, got into action with the *Centaure*, the rearmost French ship. As the others came up they, too, tackled the rearmost ships, doubling on them, and bringing about a formidable concentration. This apparently was not what Boscawen wanted. With Brodrick's division rapidly coming up, he could now make certain of the enemy's rear. He wanted to get at the van, and prevent any escaping. As yet there was no Additional Instruction to meet the case. He could not perform the manœuvre of attacking in inverted order, by which each ship as she came up passed on under cover of the one already engaged and got alongside the next ahead, till all the enemy from rear to van were tackled in succession. All he could do was to keep signalling to individual ships ahead of him to make more sail. But they did not understand, and it was not till four o'clock that he him-

---

[1] The "Instructions" under which these chasing signals were made are lost. They are not contained in the "Additional Fighting Instructions" of the time. See *Fighting Instructions* (*Navy Records Society*), p. 204.

self got up and engaged La Clue's flagship.[1] His reception was worthy of a French flagship, and after a hard
fight he had to fall away with his mizzen-mast and main
and fore topsail-yards gone.[2] In doing so, he came abreast
the rearmost Frenchman—the obstinate *Centaure*—which
had been battered to pieces by four other ships, and now
at last surrendered. Meanwhile La Clue was trying to
make off to the north-east. The "General chase" signal
had already been altered for " Chase to the north-east,"
and Boscawen, thirsting to renew his action, shifted his flag
to the *Newark* (80). All through the night the chase
went on, guided by the little *Guernsey* of 50 guns, who,
having understood Boscawen's meaning, had tried to
tackle the enemy's van ship and was now far enough
ahead to keep them in sight.[3]

At daylight they were seen again a few miles ahead,
making for Lagos. But now there were only four of them.
Of the original seven, the *Centaure* had struck, one was
making for Rochefort, and another for the Canaries. For
the rest there was no escape, and La Clue knew it well.
Determined not to surrender, he ran his splendid flagship
straight on the rocks, with every sail set and his flag

[1] Boscawen had issued a set of Additional Fighting Instructions when
he came on the station, but they contained nothing to meet the case
except a signal for the leading ships to form line, but this was far from
being the same thing. Subsequently the following instruction was introduced, and appears in the Additional Instructions used by Rodney in
1780 : "If the commander-in-chief should chase with the whole squadron
and would have those ships that are nearest attack the enemy, the headmost
opposing their sternmost, the next passing on under the cover of her fire
and engaging the second from the enemy's rear, and so on in succession,"
&c. This was the form of attack which Hawke used against L'Etanduère,
Oct. 14, 1747, but there the engaging in inverted order of coming up
seems to have taken place naturally.

[2] Boscawen in despatch (*In-letters*, 384, Aug. 20) says this happened in
"half an hour." The flag-captain's log says his action with the *Océan*
lasted till 7.15.

[3] The *Guernsey* was commanded by Lieutenant M. Kearney, her captain,
Millbank, being absent on a diplomatic mission to Morocco.

flying.   The captain of the *Redoubtable* followed his
example.   The other two, the *Téméraire* and *Modeste*,
anchored under some Portuguese batteries.   But blood
was up.   The chase was too hot for neutral rights or
neutral batteries to stop.   Boscawen could not hold his
hand.   Against each of the doomed vessels a ship was
sent in, and they all struck.   The *Océan* and the *Redoubtable* were burnt; the *Téméraire* and *Modeste* were brought
out as prizes; and La Clue's fleet had ceased to be a
factor in the situation.[1]

This fact, however, was not clear immediately.   All
Boscawen knew was that half La Clue's fleet was still
unaccounted for, and immediately after his work at Lagos
was finished he took up his station off St. Vincent.   After
watching there a couple of days and seeing no sign of
the missing ships, he felt there was a possibility of their
having gone northward, and that therefore the situation
contemplated by the last modification of his instructions
had arisen.   The Toulon fleet had passed the Straits
bound for the French Atlantic ports, and seven of them
were still at sea.   Accordingly on August 20th he sent
home an account of the action, and informed the Admiralty that it was his intention to return to England in
accordance with his last instructions, leaving Brodrick
on the station with the seven sail they had ordered.[2]   At
the same time he despatched to Hawke a laconic note
saying exactly what he had done, and giving him details
of the number and force of the ships that were missing.
" I heartily wish," he wrote, " you may meet with them.

---

[1] All the English authorities state that La Clue died of his wounds
shortly after the action.   Really he returned to France, and was so far
held guiltless for the loss of his fleet as to be retired, April 1, 1764, with a
lieutenant-general's pension.—Lacour-Gayet, pp. 261, 469.

[2] Boscawen to Cleveland, *In-letters*, 384, Aug. 20, "Off Cape St.
Vincent."

I hope to make sail this evening, and as I am bound
home will endeavour to fall in with you." [1]

This resolution was entirely in accord with the state of
opinion at home.   Indeed it so happened that the force
which he was taking was even less than Anson wanted.
For on July 25th, when it was no longer possible to doubt
that the French really intended to make their desperate
attempt to invade, an order had been directed to Boscawen
to bring home ten of the line instead of six.[2]   Before it
could reach him, however, he had repaired the damages
of the action, and on August 26th, therefore, the two
admirals parted company, Brodrick going back to Gibraltar to take up the ordinary duties of the Mediterranean station, while Boscawen stood north with his
three prizes.

The news of what had happened reached home in a
good hour.   Newcastle was getting thoroughly frightened,
An intercepted letter from the Danish Minister in Paris,
who had always disbelieved the French would try anything so mad as Belleisle's scheme, showed that even he
was now convinced they would, as a counsel of despair.
Yet Pitt would not hear of a man or ship being called
home from the West till Quebec was taken.   The militia
was proving a broken reed ; the nervous Prime Minister
had confirmation that Thurot from Dunkirk would strike
at one place while Conflans struck at another, and he was
wailing to Hardwicke that if La Clue once got to Brest
nothing could stop the invasion.   On September 5th the
Danish Minister's letter was discussed in the Cabinet.
Next day came the glorious news.   " Now," wrote Newcastle to his friend, " Boscawen will come back with seven
ships and three French ones, and two regiments from

---

[1] Burrow's *Life of Hawke*, p. 379.
[2] *Secret Orders*, 1331.

Gibraltar." "I own," he added, "I was afraid of invasion till now." [1]

The news was sent off as soon as possible to the fleet before Brest, where things by this time were at high tension. During August, while Boscawen was refitting in Gibraltar, Hawke's fleet also began to show signs of breaking down under the continued strain, and he told the Admiralty he could not last unless drastic measures were taken to send him relief ships to keep up his strength. How weak a form of war is a prolonged close blockade we have seen in La Clue's almost successful attempt to evade. Hawke himself had failed too often not to know the danger well. His importunity was not understood. At home it was thought he was asking for unnecessary superiority, and some friction ensued. He quickly replied that he had never asked, and would never seek, more than simple equality with the enemy. "I never desired," he said, " or intended to keep more line-of-battle ships than equalled the number of the enemy, which is now augmented to twenty-two." With an equal number he did not doubt of success, when a seasoned fleet was pitted against one fresh from port. But he insisted that his fleet must be kept in battle trim by constant reliefs. Not only did ships want cleaning, but what was more important, crews wanted rest and refreshment. So the friction passed, and everything was done as Hawke wished.

In addition to these anxieties, we have seen that the harassed admiral had been forced during the last half of August to extend his blockade to all the Breton ports as far down as the Loire. His last move, it will be remembered, had been to send Captain Reynolds with a cruiser

[1] Newcastle to Hardwicke, Aug. 31 and Sept. 6, *Newcastle Papers*, 32,895.

squadron before Nantes, with orders if he found the transports gone to pursue them to Ireland, and to blockade them if he found them still there. He had only just heard that Reynolds had them safely blockaded in the Loire, when on September 7th an express reached him from the Earl of Bristol, our ambassador at Madrid, that La Clue had passed the Straits. The news seems scarcely to have disturbed him, at least outwardly. Either then or the next day he must have received Boscawen's letter, for he contented himself with sending word to Reynolds that he feared some ships which escaped Boscawen might have got into the Basque Roads, and that he was to send a frigate or two to see.[1]

It is interesting to note that Hawke's main objective and his chief anxiety seems still to have been the transports and not the battle fleet. We have seen how he was constantly increasing the blockading cruiser squadron. His correspondence is full of minute directions for the conduct of the transport blockade and the distribution of the ships. By the middle of September he had even resolved to attempt the destruction of the transports where they lay, and for this purpose he once more changed the southern command 'and gave it to Duff over Reynolds's head.[2] Before the new commodore could take over the command, Reynolds had to report that the Nantes division of transports had come out of the Loire, and had stolen northward to join those at Vannes. He had chased them in Quiberon Bay, but had only succeeded in driving them into Auray.

---

[1] Hawke to Cleveland, Sept. 7; Hawke to Reynolds, Sept. 8. In his letter to Cleveland of the 8th he does not mention Boscawen's victory, and it is not till the 12th he says definitely he has heard of it (*In-letters*, 92). He probably received Boscawen's letter, therefore, on the 8th, between his letters to Cleveland and to Reynolds.

[2] Hawke to Duff, Sept. 17, *In-letters*, 92.

He had held a council of war to consider an attempt to destroy them, but the decision was that the operation was impracticable.

A few days later the impression that the French movement was about to begin was further increased. Three or four of the Brest fleet made a demonstration of coming out. Hervey engaged them in Camaret Bay, and drove them back. Such signs of activity could not be ignored, and Hawke sent an urgent order to Duff to go in person to Quiberon and see if nothing could be done with the transports. Duff had already forestalled the order. Having decided to give Reynolds the division watching L'Orient, he himself had gone into the Bay, and with Reynolds and another of his captains had actually landed on the island of Méaban, at the entrance of the Morbihan Gulf, where he got a clear view into the Auray River. But he could only endorse the decision of the previous council of war. He assured himself, however, that by leaving the bulk of his squadron in Quiberon Bay he could make it impossible for either the transports or their escort to come out. This accordingly he did, returning himself with his fastest frigates to the Isle de Croix to watch L'Orient.

With this Hawke had to be content, as he now could well be. For he had just heard that Brodrick, on his way back to Gibraltar, had located the remainder of La Clue's squadron in Cadiz, and was blockading it there. Hawke therefore had nothing more to fear from that quarter, and having received some fresh ships, he felt himself able to deal with Bompart, who was daily expected. Accordingly Admiral Geary was detached down the Bay with seven of the line, with orders to lie off Rochefort so as to prevent Bompart getting into that port, while at the same time he was to keep close touch with Duff so as to support him in case of need.[1] This bold conception was, however, disapproved by the Admiralty. No sooner had Hawke announced what he had done than Anson informed him that their lordships considered he was devoting too much force to Bompart and Rochefort. He was reminded that "the particular object of attention at this time" was "the interception of the embarkations of the enemy at Morbihan, and the keeping of the ships of war from coming out of Brest." He was therefore recommended, with some asperity, to station his ships accordingly.[2] Hawke, who believed he was fully strong enough to deal with Bompart as well as Conflans, was nevertheless forced to comply, and he immediately recalled half Geary's squadron to his own flag and sent the rest to reinforce Duff. It is difficult to judge between Anson and Hawke. Had Hawke been at Whitehall, saturated with the highly charged political atmosphere, he would probably have been as eager as Anson to see a rigid concentration of the fleet upon the main object. Had Anson been in Hawke's place, he would probably have felt the same breezy mastery of the whole situation. It is a case where it is almost impossible to decide whether the man at headquarters or the man on the spot was in the better position to decide.

At Versailles the tension was no less high than at Whitehall. When the news of La Clue's disaster had come, Belleisle and his supporters had only set their teeth the harder and adopted a still more reckless plan. Conflans must do what was no longer in La Clue's power. He was told to form a division of six of the line under Bigot

---

[1] For the above details see Hawke's Correspondence during September, *In-letters*, 92.

[2] Hawke to Cleveland, Sept. 28, with minute endorsed, *In-letters*, 92 ; Cleveland to Hawke, Oct. 5, *Out-letters*, 526. Compare a similar rebuke administered to Cornwallis in July 1803.—*Blockade of Brest (Navy Record Society)*, vol. i. pp. 82-3.

de Morogues and send it down to Morbihan to set the
Duc d'Aiguillon free and escort him to the Clyde.   In
vain Conflans protested against the viciousness of a
scheme which divided a fleet already far too weak for
its work.   In vain he lamented the soldiers were permitted to direct what was purely a naval operation.   In
the middle of September the final orders arrived.   We
have seen what came of them.   The moment Morogues
showed his nose outside he was driven in again by
Hervey and the inshore squadron.   Conflans continued
his protests.   Possibly the fiasco of Morogues's attempted
sortie was only intended to demonstrate their justice.
In any case no way could be found of disputing his
arguments.   He pointed out that the only possible
chance of success was to keep the fleet united.   Let him
retain Morogues under his flag, and he himself with the
whole fleet would go down and set the transports free.
Choiseul and Belleisle were forced to adopt his view, and
in the middle of October he was authorised to put it
in operation.   "I leave it," wrote the King, "to your
experience and courage to profit by any circumstance
you may think favourable to go out and attack the
squadrons and vessels blockading at Ushant and at
Belleisle.   Then, whether you decide to return to Brest
for a fresh sortie or whether you keep the sea, I give you
full authority to go yourself and escort the Morbihan
flotilla so soon as it is ready to sail.   I only bind you
never to forget that the main point of all our present
operations must be the greatest safety of the Morbihan
flotilla."   Finally he was told that if he decided to return
to Brest he was to detach six of the line and some
cruisers to convoy D'Aiguillon to his destination.[1]

These orders left Conflans no further ground for

---

[1] Lacour-Gayet, *Marine sous Louis XV.*, ch. xx.

protest. His own plan of operation had been adopted,
and there was nothing left but for him to go out and
execute it. The moment, too, seemed favourable. It
was on October 14th that Louis signed the new orders,
and that very day, to every one's consternation, Hawke
reappeared at Plymouth. A gale from the west-south-
west had forced him to run for shelter and to leave Duff
clinging alone to the transports at Morbihan. It was an
unhappy hour. For that same day there reached London
Wolfe's desponding despatch in which he announced to
Pitt the breakdown of his health, the failure of his plans,
and the small hope he had of eventual success. The
despatch plunged every one into a serious fit of depression.
As Horace Walpole says : " In the most artful terms
that could be framed he left the nation uncertain whether
he meant to prepare an excuse for desisting or to claim
the melancholy merit of having sacrificed himself without a prospect of success." [1]

Newcastle believed the game in Canada was lost. He
told Hardwicke that Pitt was of the same opinion, and
said so openly. Anson still maintained stoutly that
Quebec would fall. But then he had not seen Wolfe's
despatch. " If he had," wrote Newcastle, " he could not
be of that opinion." The old First Lord was equally unmoved at Hawke's being driven off.[2] Nor would Hawke
himself hear a word of the croaking. He assured my
lords that Conflans could not stir in such weather. His
enforced absence was therefore rather a stroke of luck, for
he could fill up with water for three months. There was
no foundation, he protested, for the present alarms. Duff
would be able to ride out the gale where he was and
prevent the transports moving; and so long as the

---

[1] *Memoirs of George II.*, vol. iii. p. 218.
[2] Newcastle to Hardwicke, Oct. 15, *Newcastle Papers*, 32,896.

weather kept his own fleet from resuming its station, it must also prevent Conflans from moving his. So confident indeed was he in his ability to deal with the situation that, so far from agreeing with the alarmists, he did not scruple to express his chagrin at having being ordered to call off Geary, and begged, as there were now plenty of ships at home, that he might be reinforced sufficiently to extend his blockade to Rochefort. As for himself, he did not mean to set foot out of the *Ramillies*, his flagship, and expected to be at sea again in a few days.

Still, there were other causes of anxiety at sea which the landsmen could not shake off. Rodney had found it impossible to make any further impression on the flat-boats at Havre. So active was the French defence that the bomb-vessels could no longer get near them, and it was only with the greatest danger and difficulty he could even maintain the blockade. Then in the depth of the depression came the news that the blockade of Dunkirk had been broken. Boys had been driven off in a violent storm. No one knew what had become of him, and Thurot had seized the opportunity to make his escape with his whole squadron.

This last stroke, however, had hardly been realised when the whole scene was changed. The widespread depression disappeared as by magic, and the sturdy confidence of Anson and Hawke was echoed in a shout of triumph from end to end of the country. Three days after Wolfe's melancholy letter had been received, and the very night of the news of Thurot's escape, Pitt, just before midnight, was breaking open Townshend's despatch, which announced that Quebec had fallen. No such reaction had ever been seen. "The incidents of dramatic fiction," says Walpole, "could not be conducted with more address to lead an audience from despondency to sudden exultation, than accident prepared to excite the passions of a whole people.   They despaired — they triumphed—and they wept—for Wolfe had fallen in the hour of victory !   Joy, grief, curiosity, astonishment, were painted in every countenance ; the more they inquired, the higher their admiration rose."

In the enthusiasm of the moment the alarms of invasion were forgotten.   Indeed all immediate danger quickly ceased.   In a few days it was known that Boys and his squadron were safe and in hot chase of Thurot. A squadron had been sent to head him off from Emden, which was believed to be his most likely objective.   That important post was safe at any rate, and Thurot was known to be speeding north for Sweden.[1]   Rodney about the same time sent in word that the flat-boats at Havre seemed to be on the point of starting ; but no one cared. For—best news of all—on the 20th Hawke had been able to resume his station off Ushant, and the French enterprise looked more desperate than ever.   Conflans had not stirred.   He was still bombarding the Ministers with requisitions.   Crews, stores, ships, everything was defective, and he practically refused to take his fleet to sea in the condition it was, without victuals or seamen.   The truth was that trained sailors were no longer to be had, and a convoy of storeships on which Conflans depended for victuals had been driven into Quimperlé by Hawke's cruisers.   Its escape was out of the question.   The stores had to be landed where they were, a hundred miles from the fleet, and laboriously carried by the almost impassable Breton roads to Brest.[2]

Under the circumstances Hawke continued to press his

---

[1] Newcastle to Hardwicke, Oct. 26.
[2] Hawke to Admiralty, Oct. 10, *In-letters*, 92.

idea of extending the blockade to Rochefort, so as to intercept Bompart. Anson approved, but at the same time he sent out a very serious piece of intelligence which must have rejoiced Hawke's heart. On October 11th Choiseul, still bent on inducing the Swedes to co-operate with D'Aiguillon's attack on Scotland, had sent to the French ambassador in Stockholm details of the final arrangements, and particularly the heroic resolution that, desperate as it was, "the essential enterprise" was to proceed in the teeth of the British fleet, and that Conflans had positive orders to go out and fight Hawke, in order to cover the sailing of D'Aiguillon's transports. This letter was intercepted, and its material contents immediately sent on to Hawke. He was therefore warned that the Admiralty was sending him every ship it could lay hands on, but that, until he had enough to make sure of Conflans, he was to send no detachment to Rochefort.[1]

Still, October passed into November and neither Conflans nor the transports moved. Hawke clung to his station, battling with incessant heavy weather. The strain was terrible. Hervey completely broke down: ships were continually reporting dangerous leaks, and Hawke began to grow anxious. He warned the Admiralty he might at any time have to let go, and if so it would now be a case of running for Torbay, as Plymouth Sound was no place for three-decked ships in winter. Two days after he had penned the warning the expected gale was upon him, and on November 10th he reported himself in Torbay. He had received at last the Admiralty's full approval of his design to intercept Bompart, but the arrangements he had been on the point of making had now to be abandoned. Nevertheless he had still little

---

[1] Choiseul to Havrincour, Oct. 11, *Newcastle Papers*, 32,896 ; Hawke to Admiralty, Oct. 24, with answer endorsed, Oct. 29, *In-letters*, 92.

anxiety except for the two ships of the line that were supporting Duff's cruiser squadron at Quiberon. He advised that they should be immediately called off. "If," he wrote, "which is very probable, the enemy should escape me and make their push there with their whole squadron, these two ships will be of little avail, and without them the five 'fifties' and nine frigates would be a much more manageable squadron, and therefore better able to preserve itself till my arrival." In view of what afterwards occurred, the letter is interesting as showing how clearly he shared with Anson the view of what was the main objective, and what the point on which his eyes must be fixed. For the present he had no fear. "It blows," he said, "a mere frett of wind from the north-west. Bompart may get in, but nothing can come out."[1] He had taken every precaution for locating Conflans the moment the weather changed; and he knew exactly what to expect. Before he was driven off Duff had procured for him, through a Portuguese skipper, information of the exact position of the Morbihan transports and D'Aiguillon's troops, and that they were not to sail till the Brest squadron came round to raise the blockade.[2] Accordingly Duff had received standing orders, in case Hawke were driven off by a gale, to cruise with his own "fifty" and two frigates before Brest, so soon as the weather would permit. If anything came out that he could not deal with, he was to send a frigate into Torbay and himself to shadow the enemy till he was certain of their objective, and then to report to the Admiralty.[3]

On November 12th the weather moderated a little, and Hawke at once put to sea. But it was only to be driven

---

[1] "Mere" is here used in the old sense of "unmitigated"; "Frett"= squally storm.

[2] Duff's report to Hawke, Oct. 18, *In-letters*, 92.

[3] Hawke to Admiralty, Nov. 10, enclosing Duff's orders of the 3rd *In-letters*, 92.

back to Torbay again next day, with the *Ramillies* in such
a condition that he had to condemn her for winter work
and shift his flag to the *Royal George*. On the morrow,
the 14th, he was out again laboriously trying to resume
his station. On the 16th, as he was then still short of
Ushant, he grew seriously anxious about Duff, and decided
to send him orders to leave only four frigates with the
fireships and bomb-vessels in Quiberon Bay: to station
three frigates off L'Orient, and himself with the rest of
the squadron to cruise off Belleisle in such a position as
best to cover the Quiberon detachment, and at the same
time have sea-room to escape being surprised by Conflans.

The fate of these orders is well worth recording. They
were entrusted to a favourite young officer of Hawke's
called Stuart, who had been his second lieutenant in the
Ramillies, and who, when she was condemned for the winter,
had been given the command of the *Fortune* sloop. On
his way to Quiberon he fell in with the *Hébé*, a French
forty-gun frigate belonging to Conflans's squadron. She
was under jury-masts, and, eager to flesh his new commission, he immediately attacked her. The recklessness
and obstinacy with which for several hours he clung to a
ship of three times his force compels a certain admiration, but nothing could be more unsailorlike, and scarcely
anything deserves more serious reprobation. In the end
he was killed, his ship reduced to a wreck, and his
message—on the prompt delivery of which hung, for all
he knew, the fate of the whole of Duff's squadron—never
reached its destination. As it happened, it did not
matter. An hour or two after the orders were despatched
Hawke knew they must be too late. The crisis had come.[1]

---

[1] For the *Fortune* episode see Hawke's Despatch, Nov. 24, *In-letters*, 92,
and Lacour-Gayet, p. 338. The *Hébé* had been dismasted in a collision on
the 18th.

What he had anticipated had happened. On November 5th, as he was battling with the weather, Marnière, returning from an unsuccessful cruise, had slipped in with a ship of the line and a frigate, and two days later as Hawke, in a westerly gale, was vainly trying to double Ushant in order to run into the Channel, Bompart had arrived with seven of the line and another frigate. None of these vessels, it would seem, were fit to take the sea again, but some of their crews were. Conflans was thus able to complete his companies with good seasoned men, and, having no further ground for delay, on November 14th he put to sea with twenty-one of the line and five cruisers.

Duff, not having received any fresh orders, was still clinging tight to his station in Quiberon Bay, The L'Orient division was also there, having run in presumably for shelter during the gale, though they sailed to resume their station the day Conflans came out.[1] His exit, however, had been seen by Captain Ourry of the *Actæon*, who all through the gale had clung to his post off Brest.[2] He immediately sent word to Hawke's rendezvous, but the message missed him, and for a good reason. Before the rendezvous was reached he had received later and better information. Late in the afternoon of the 16th, some forty-five miles west-north-west of Ushant, he fell in with four victuallers returning empty from Quiberon. One of them, the *Love and Unity*, informed him that the previous afternoon at two o'clock they had sighted the French fleet about seventy miles to the westward of Belleisle, working to the eastward. By the skipper's report, it consisted of eighteen of the line, besides three frigates, which were

---

[1] Duff to Hawke, Oct. 18, *In-letters*, 92; and Log of the *Rochester* (Duff's flagship), Nov. 14.—*Captains' Logs*, p. 792.

[2] Captain Ourry's Intelligence, Oct. 14, *In-letters*, 92.

chasing the *Juno* towards Quiberon.[1] The *Juno* was
one of the L'Orient blockading squadron who had left
Quiberon after the rest.[2] On her way to her station she
had fallen in with the *Swallow* sloop, who reported that she
had just seen the French fleet. Both vessels attempted
to get back to warn Duff; but, whether from being chased
or from the change in the weather, they both failed,
and the *Juno*, getting clear of the chasing ships, hurried
north to Hawke's rendezvous.[3] But she also missed him,
for Hawke had already acted on the information he had
chanced to get from the *Love and Unity*. Leaving word
for Geary, whom he had sent into Plymouth to land the
sick and bring out what ships were there, to take his
station off Brest, he had then and there made for Quiberon
as hard as he could go, with the twenty-three of the line
he had with him. Writing to the Admiralty next
morning, the 17th, he says, " I have carried a press of
sail all night, with a hard gale at south-south-east, in
pursuit of the enemy, and make no doubt of coming up
with them at sea or in Quiberon Bay."

Much has been written of Hawke's profound strategic
insight in taking this decision; but in truth insight had
little to do with it. It was something better. The
correctness of his move was not due to inspiration, but to
sober preparation beforehand, combined with the excellent
work of the intelligence department at home. Acting on
this basis Hawke was able, by well thought-out cruiser
work, to ensure that if Conflans put to sea he would
immediately know for certain on which of his possible
objectives he was bent. It is true a lucky chance had

[1] Log of the *Royal George, Captains' Logs,* 811 ; Admiral Geary to the
Admiralty, Nov. 17, *In-letters,* 93.

[2] Log of the *Rochester*.

[3] Admiralty Advices, Nov. 19, *Newcastle Papers,* 32,898 ; Hawke to
Admiralty, Nov. 17, *In-letters,* 93.

enabled him to anticipate by some hours his cruisers'
information. But apart from this, as to what Conflans's
objective would be, and what in any case was the main
danger to go for, there was no room for doubt at all, and
had been none for at least two months. It was just no
more and no less than a piece of just appreciation and
admirable organisation, and it requires no false colour of
inspiration to make it glow in naval memory.

The *Juno* not finding Hawke at his rendezvous, and
having heard apparently what he had done, held on to
carry the news home. Thus, so far from causing any
panic, it seems to have been received with elation. There
had been some alarm for Ireland. Pitt had recently told
the Duke of Bedford, the Lord-Lieutenant, plainly that at
this season of the year it was impossible to maintain a
strict blockade, and that the enemy might at any time
elude Hawke and appear on the Irish coast. Ireland
must therefore make ready to defend herself till assistance
could reach her. The announcement was received with
enthusiasm in the Irish Parliament, but there the matter
ended and very little was done.[1] In England every one
was now certain Conflans must be caught, and Newcastle
wrote in high spirits to reassure Bedford. It was thought,
he said, impossible for Conflans to escape, and as to fighting, Anson treated it as the idlest notion. Moreover,
they were in a very strong position at home. The day
after Hawke had been driven into Torbay, both Holmes
and Durell had reached Spithead with the bulk of the
Quebec fleet, and they reported that Saunders with the
rest was close behind them.[2] Newcastle therefore continued to write in the same triumphant strain. He told

---

[1] *Newcastle Papers*, Nov. 1, 32,898.
[2] Holmes to Admiralty, and Durell to same, Nov. 11, *In-letters*, 481.
They made the passage from the Gulf of St. Lawrence in sixteen days.

Yorke, at The Hague, that they were looking forward to a
battle which would give the *coup de grace* to the French
marine and decide the whole war, nor were they in the
least uneasy about it.

But this was not all. For now came news which raised
the prevailing elation to real enthusiasm. " We are in the
highest spirits from expectation," Newcastle wrote to
Yorke. "Sir Edward Hawke is now joined by Geary and
the brave and judicious Admiral Saunders in pursuing
Monsieur Conflans." It was true. On the 19th Geary
had got to sea with three of the line before Hawke's
order reached him, and instead of proceeding off Brest,
he too had held away for Quiberon.[1]   On the same
day Saunders, with Townshend in his flagship, and
accompanied by two other ships of the line, had reached
within about fifty miles of the Lizard, and there, within
a few hours of the repose and honours which he and his
men had so richly earned, he fell in with Captain Phillips
of the *Juno*, whom Geary had sent out again to try to
find Hawke. On hearing his news, Saunders, without a
moment's hesitation, had made up his mind, and in a
stirring little note which he sent off to Pitt, he laconically
informed him of his meeting with Phillips and his news.
" I have therefore," he wrote, " only time to acquaint you
that I am making the best of my way in quest of Sir
Edward Hawke, which I hope his Majesty will approve
of." [2] So soon as his resolution was known, a shout of
applause went up from every side. Even Hardwicke was
moved. "The part," he wrote, "which Admiral Saunders

---

[1] For Geary's movements and orders see Hawke to Admiralty, Nov. 15;
Geary to same, Nov. 17, 18, and 26, *In-letters*, 93.

[2] Saunders to Pitt, Nov. 19, "Lizard N.W. by W. 17 leagues," and
Nov. 24, "Off Isle Groas," *S.P. Colonial (A. and W. I.)*, 88 ; *Chatham MSS.*
79. He had with him *Somerset* (flag), *Devonshire*, and *Vanguard.—Townshend's Life*, p. 251.

has taken voluntarily is, I think, the greatest I ever heard of." [1]

So across the stormy waters of the Bay the squadrons were gathering for the final act of that immortal year. And as day by day went by and no word came from Hawke a reaction set in at home, and the first feelings of elation began to give way to nervous anxiety. Yet Hawke was playing his part with a directness that left nothing to be desired. Conflans's conduct is less easy to explain. Ten days before putting to sea he had told Berryer, the Minister of Marine, that his intention was to avoid action so as not to bring the Morbihan project to nothing. If, however, an action were forced upon him he would fight with all the glory possible. What was really in his mind is hard to say. On the balance of evidence, the French incline to the belief that he meant to avoid action at all costs, but the case is far from clear. [2]

On the eve of coming out he wrote to D'Aiguillon that his main object was to join hands with him, and then to escort his transports out with all the security that was possible. [3] On the other hand, there exists a remarkable memorandum or general order which he issued on coming out, from which it would appear the recent gale had made him more hopeful. At any rate it is clear that in this order he intended to persuade the fleet he was eager for battle, and thought his chances good. The document shows considerable tactical ability. He hoped, he said, to find the British fleet broken up into detach-

---

[1] *Newcastle Papers*, 32,899, Nov. 21–23.

[2] His latest French critic is of this opinion. See Lacour-Gayet, *Marine sous Louis XV.*, p. 329. Conflans's letter, given in Beatson, vol. iii. p. 247, is apocryphal, a burlesque written by an officer of Keppel's ship, the *Torbay*. See Burrow's *Life of Hawke*, p. 412.

[3] Waddington, vol. iii. p. 368.

ments, and to be able to crush them in detail. If, however, he found it all together, he meant to attack from to-windward as close as possible. If the British had the wind and would not come to close action, he meant to keep away and then suddenly haul to the wind, which would certainly bring the fleets together. He impressed the tactical importance of concentration, and of trying to reduce the enemy unit by unit in the most modern style. He was absolutely determined, he said, to fight at musket-shot or closer. For this purpose he formulated a method of oblique approach identical with that which Byng had attempted at Minorca, in order to keep the broadsides bearing as the fleet ran down to attack, and to avoid being raked. Disabled ships of the enemy were to be left for the frigates to secure. Finally he noted that board-ing in line was an almost impossible manœuvre, but that if he saw it was desirable he would make the signal, and all were to board their opposite number simultaneously.[1]

It is of course possible that this spirited order did not represent his real mind, but was rather intended to enhearten his desponding fleet. Moreover, whatever his real intention, he has always been accused of executing his movement on Morbihan with unpardonable slowness and hesitation. Here again it is doubtful whether the accusation is just. Owing to various accidents, it was not till the 15th that he got the whole fleet to sea. By midday on the 16th he was already half-way to his destination, that is, about seventy miles west of Belleisle. In the afternoon, however, the wind veered east-by-south, and then it was Conflans was seen by the British victuallers from Quiberon, trying to work against it to the eastward. But his efforts were in vain. The wind rapidly increased to a gale with heavy seas, and he was

[1] Troude, *Batailles Navales de France*, vol. i. p. 382.

forced to bear up and run; nor could he stop before he was a hundred and twenty miles west of Belleisle.[1] It was not till early on the morning of the 18th that he was able to begin reaching back, and even then he could not hold a true course. The wind had settled in the north-north-east, so that to make his easting he had to stand far to the southward, and when on the afternoon of the 19th the breeze died away he found himself becalmed seventy miles south-west of Belleisle, and no nearer to his destination than he was when the *Juno* sighted him on the 15th. It was not till nearly midnight that the wind came again. It was now fair from the westward, and he was able to signal to fill and hold away for Morbihan.[2]

It was really not a bad performance. Hawke, with all his skill as a seaman and his highly trained and homogeneous fleet, had been able to do little better, but being well to northward of his destination the northerly winds had lost him nothing, and he had been able to gain a day on his adversary. The easterly gale had struck him soon after he received the victuallers' report, but, being nearer inshore than Conflans, he was better able to hold up to it, and by noon on the 18th he had gained to the eastward, and was reaching on the north-north-east wind parallel to Conflans, and on what was for him his true course. Thus when the fair wind failed he too found himself only seventy miles from Belleisle, and at noon was lying-to west-by-north of it under double-reefed topsails in heavy squalls from south-by-east.[3] By seven

---

[1] Conflans to D'Aiguillon, Nov. 21, Troude, vol. i. p. 401.

[2] Conflans's Official Despatch, *ibid.*, p. 386.

[3] Hawke's noon positions were: 16th, Start N.E. by N. 30 leagues; 17th, Ushant E. by N. 18 leagues; 18th, Penmarks E. by S. 30 leagues; 19th, Belleisle E. by S. 23 leagues; 20th, Belleisle E. by N. ¼N. 5 leagues.— *Captains' Logs,* 811.

in the evening, however, he felt the westerly breeze, four
to five hours, that is, before it reached Conflans. With
the first breath of it Hawke signalled to send up topgallant masts, shake out reefs, and fill, and so under a
press of sail he bore away direct for Morbihan. At the
same time Howe in the *Magnanime* was ordered ahead to
make the land, and with him were two frigates that had
recently joined. All that night Hawke held on as he
was. He seems to have read clearly in the face of the
skies what must have happened to his enemy, and was
in hourly expectation of getting contact. At daybreak
on the 20th he had reached a point some forty miles
west of north of Belleisle, when sure enough at half-
past eight one of the ships ahead made the signal for
a fleet. So Hawke's conviction that he would come
up with Conflans at sea or in Quiberon Bay proved
correct.

Early in the night, as the fair wind had rapidly
increased in strength, Conflans had ordered the fleet to
proceed under easy sail, so as not to make the land
before daylight, and shortly before dawn he hove-to. In
this position, a little more than twenty miles west of
Belleisle, he sighted at daybreak seven of Duff's squadron.
It was but the evening before that Duff had received any
warning, and then it was by the *Vengeance,* another of the
frigates belonging to the L'Orient division. He was then
still in Quiberon Bay watching the transports dropping
down the Vannes River, and joining the frigates in Auray
in anticipation of Conflans's arrival. It was blowing hard
from the west-north-west, but during the night Duff
managed to get the whole of his squadron to sea. So
soon as they were sighted Conflans signalled for the fleet
to close and clear for action. But as the light grew he
saw he had only Duff before him, and signalled to fill

and give chase.[1] Duff divided his squadron and stood
inshore, half to the north and half to the south. The
French van stood after one, the centre after the other,
while the rearguard held the wind to watch some strange
sails which were appearing to seaward. The French fleet
was thus getting badly scattered when, just as the chase
was growing too hot to last, Duff saw the enemy haul
off. Ignorant of the reason, he seized the opportunity
to send a cutter away to Hawke's rendezvous, which
reached Plymouth five days later without ever having
seen his fleet—to the great increase of the anxiety at
home.[2]

The fact was that just at this moment Conflans had
found that the strange sails to seaward were the British
fleet. Directly Hawke's look-out frigate had reported
Conflans's presence he made the signal for line abreast,
"in order," as he says, "to draw all the ships of the
squadron up with me," for, being in cruising order, that is,
in no particular formation—the *route libre* of the French—
the admiral would be leading the body of the fleet. As
this movement began to bring the whole fleet into
sight, the astonishment of Conflans was profound. So
soon as he realised the truth, he signalled to cease chasing
and to close on the flag. His position was very difficult.
In face of a superior fleet bearing down on him, he had
to take a prompt decision whether to give battle where
he was or to continue his movement into Quiberon Bay.
He decided on the latter, and making the signal for order

[1] Conflans's signals were: 1. Ralliement (Close on the admiral); 2. Faire
le branlebas (Clear for action); 3. Attention aux signaux de combat
(Preparatory for battle signals); 4. Prepare for action; 5. General chase.
[2] Commodore Hanway to Cleveland, Nov. 18 and 25, *Newcastle Papers*,
32,898–9. The fact that the *Vengeance* did not reach Quiberon till the
night of the 19th shows that Conflans must have done very well to get his
fleet there by the morning of the 20th, and acquits him of the slowness
with which he is usually charged by his countrymen.

of sailing in single line ahead, he wore and led the way for the entrance.[1]

His idea, so he reported, was that he would be able to haul to the wind as he entered and form line of battle on the weather side of the Bay. In view of his inferiority and what his object was, he believed it was the best thing thus to take up a defensive position and defy Hawke to touch him in the labyrinth of shoals and reefs that would surround him if he tried. Seeing how the French ships were manned, and how great an advantage Hawke's seasoned fleet would have in an engagement in the open on a lee shore and in boisterous weather, it is difficult to say he was not right in assuming the defensive. It was thus he put his case. "The wind was then," he wrote in his report, " very violent at west-north-west, the sea very high, with every indication of very heavy weather. These circumstances, added to the object which all your letters pointed out, and the superiority of the enemy . . . determined me to make for Morbihan. . . . I had no ground for thinking that if I got in first with twenty-one of the line the enemy would dare to follow me. In order to show the course, I had chosen the order of sailing in single line. In this order I led the van; and in order to form ' the natural order of battle' I had nothing to do but to take my station in the centre, which I intended to do, on the second board, so soon as the entire line was inside the bay."

Nothing really could be more correct. He would at least have gained an important point in getting the fleet and the transports united in one port. Had they been together in Brest it is obvious that the whole expedition

---

[1] His signals were : 1. Lever le chasse ; 2. Ralliement ; 3. Ordre de marche sur une ligne ; 4. Preparatory for battle signals ; 5. Prepare for action.

would have eluded Hawke at least for a time, and that is all that was hoped. Once in a good defensive position in Quiberon Bay, all he had to do was to wait till the next westerly gale blew Hawke off and then proceed to sea with his charge in company, and with every possible chance there was of getting it clear away north. On the other hand, if he had turned and, with everything against him, had fought Hawke, no good could have come of it, even if he had sacrificed his own fleet to put Hawke's out of action. This is what his critics, and especially those of his own country, seem to think he ought to have done. But they forget that the force which had held D'Aiguillon's transports so long was still there. Duff, with his six cruisers, was even then in the act of joining Hawke, and the whole coast was swarming with the rest of his frigates and their supporting ships. How many men in such circumstances would have come to a different decision from that which Conflans had to take so rapidly ? As a piece of pure strategy it cannot be found fault with seriously. If it failed, it was because Conflans had failed to calculate a factor that was really incalculable. He could not calculate that Hawke in such weather would continue to carry the press of sail he did and hurl himself on a lee shore bristling with every kind of seen and unseen danger. He did not know the new English manœuvre which would double the rapidity of the attack; nor could he tell how desperate was the man that was tearing after him out of the west on the wings of the rising gale. He could not have in mind the ill luck that had dogged Hawke's splendid efforts without one break from the first shot of the war; how time after time he had missed fleets by the skin of his teeth, in spite of unprecedented tenacity and unsurpassed strategical cunning till it seemed some curse had doomed him to failure for ever. Du Guay, De la Motte, Galissonière, he had missed them all, and Bompart only a fortnight before. Was Conflans, too, to slip through his fingers? If Hawke was desperate, who can wonder? He had to break his luck, and there was a demon in him that wild winter day that knew no rule or risk.

About nine Hawke had sight of Conflans, and seeing he was making away, he hauled down the signal for line-abreast and substituted that for general chase, quickly adding one which possibly was now made for the first time in action.[1] It was a modification of general chase—a comparatively recent introduction into the "Additional Fighting Instructions," and possibly of Hawke's own invention, as a result of his action with L'Étanduère in 1747. It enabled the admiral while in general chase to direct the five or seven ships nearest the enemy to form line of battle ahead of him as they chased, without any regard to their regular stations in the order of battle, and to engage as they came up with the enemy, the rest of the fleet to support as soon as they could, also without regard to their regular stations.[2] The signal Hawke made

[1] For Hawke's preparatory movements I have followed his despatch. The log of his flagship (*Captains' Logs*, 811) puts them differently, thus: "At 8.0 made signal for the line of battle abreast, two cable's length asunder. At ½ past *Magnanime* made signal for a fleet. Made the general signal to chase at ¾. *Magnanime* made signal for the fleet being an enemy." From this it would appear that Hawke signalled "General chase" the moment the enemy was signalled. Hawke is confirmed, however, by the *Warspite* (*Captains' Logs*, 4004) and the *Magnanime* (*Master's Logs*, 935). The point is of interest as determining whether Hawke's first impulse on getting contact with the enemy was to get his fleet well in hand or to let it loose upon them at once. There can be little doubt he took the steadier course.

[2] Articles IX. and X. of the "Additional Fighting Instructions, 1759." The manœuvre first appears, so far as is known, in a MS. Signal-Book in the United Service Institution, dated 1756.

Article IX. is: "And if I should chase with the whole and would have a certain number of the ships that are nearest the enemy draw into a line of battle ahead of me, in order to engage till the rest of the ships of the

was for seven ships, and he could give the order with the lighter heart, owing to his having some hours earlier sent Howe forward to make the land. Howe was therefore nearest the enemy, and would lead the attack. Such was the compliment which in that great moment Hawke paid the man of whom he had so much reason to be jealous.

As the admiral made the signal he hoisted his flag, and, in spite of the weather, set his topgallant sails. Following his example, the rest shook out their topsail reefs. Keppel carried so much sail that the water poured into his lee ports, and he had to come up into the wind. So when Duff saw them he describes them as bearing down under a crowd of sail.[1] Conflans, in his report to the King, said he thought he could well get all his ships inside before the enemy; but he had not counted on the nerve of his pursuers, hardened in the long and stormy blockade. In the rising gale the movement was taking shape with a rapidity beyond all his calculation. " All the day," wrote Hawke, " we had very fresh gales at north-west and west-north-west, with

squadron can come up with them, I will hoist a white flag with a red cross on the flagstaff of the main topmast-head and fire the number of guns as follows [one gun for five ships, three for seven].

Article X. " Then those ships are immediately to form the line without any regard to seniority or the general form delivered, but according to their distances from the enemy, viz. the headmost and nearest ship to lead and the sternmost to bring up the rear, that no time may be lost in the pursuit ; and all the rest of the ships are to form and strengthen that line, as soon as they can come up with them, without any regard to my general form of the order of battle." See *Fighting Instructions* (*Navy Record Society*), pp. 208, 221.

This whole set of " Additional Fighting Instructions" had probably been printed and issued in 1757, for on May 28 in that year Commodore Moore, on his way to the Leeward Islands station, entered in his Journal that he issued to his captains " The Sailing and Fighting Instructions, with the printed Additional Signals and Further Additional Signals."—Moore's Journal, R.O. *Admirals' Journals*.

[1] The logs of the *Royal George, Warspite, Torbay, Rochester,* &c.

heavy squalls. M. Conflans kept going off under such sail as all his squadron could carry and at the same time keep together; while we crowded after him with every sail our ships could bear." Before them lay the narrow entrance to the bay between the La Four shoal to starboard and to port " The Cardinals," the last of the long range of rocks and islets that continue the Quiberon peninsula; beyond it a lee shore bristling with reefs. Yet no one faltered, and hour after hour the wild chase went on.

At half-past two Conflans made the entrance, and hauled round The Cardinals preparatory to forming line inside. Just then, far in the rear he heard guns, and knew that, as will nearly always happen when the admiral leads, he had misjudged the speed of his rear. It was, in truth, the *Warspite* and one or two other of Hawke's ships firing without orders at random range upon the rearmost ship of the enemy. It was immediately stopped, and the chase went on in silence.[1] Howe, in the *Magnanime*, held on, trying to reach as far towards the enemy's centre as he could before attacking. Hawke had made the signal to engage so soon as the first shot was fired, and it was not long before it was obeyed. The French van and centre got clear in, but with the rear it was different. They were in no formation, and the leading British ships were quickly all amongst them like a pack of wolves. Still there was no pause, and Conflans, as he says, could see them all crowding into the bay pell-mell together.

All that could be done the French rear-admiral, Du

---

[1] It is for this reason it is usually said the *Warspite* was leading. Her captain, Sir John Bentley, in his log says fire was opened without his orders, and he did not begin again till within musket-shot. He had been with his ship at Lagos, and had recently been knighted for his conduct in that action.

Verger, did.   But he was battered to pieces by ship after
ship, and as Hawke himself, just before four o'clock,
rounded The Cardinals, he struck to the *Resolution*.[1]   At
the same time Keppel, after recovering himself, had
engaged the *Thésée*, and after a couple of broadsides she
suddenly went down, a victim to the danger he himself
had so narrowly escaped.   Two other vessels, the *Superbe*
and the *Juste*, shared the same fate, while a fourth, the
Héros, struck to Howe.

Meanwhile the wind had shifted into the north-west
and thrown Conflans's half-formed line into complete
disorder.   Before the impetuous rush of the British fleet
the van and centre were huddled in an almost helpless
throng in the depth of the bay.   Seeing it was impossible to form line where they were, Conflans made a
signal to wear in succession, in order to clear the tangle;
but it seems only to have increased it.   "The confusion
was awful," wrote a French officer, "when the van, in
which I was, tried to go about.   Part could not do it.
We were in a funnel, as it were, all on the top of
each other, with rocks on one side of us and ships on
the other.   So we anchored." [2]   As for Conflans he had
made one attempt to get into his station, and seeing it
was now impossible to take the defensive position he
had intended, his idea was to lead the fleet out to sea
again.   With this object he bore up for the entrance.
But here he encountered Hawke coming in.   Even in
the gathering dusk the *Soleil Royal* was unmistakable.
Through the murk of the storm Hawke saw a chance of

---

[1] At this point there is a curious entry in the log of the *Royal George:*
"Fired a shot at the *Burford* for her to make sail and engage the enemy."
Her captain was James Gambier, uncle to Lord Gambier. He had been at
Louisbourg in 1758, and had just come home from the capture of Guade-
loupe.

[2] Waddington, vol. iii. p. 371.

raking her, and in spite of his master's anxious protest made a determined push to get across her stern. Seeing the flagship's danger, the *Intrépide*, a 70-gun ship that had followed closely the admiral's movements, thrust herself gallantly in between the two giants, and received the *Royal George's* fire. Though she had baulked Hawke of his purpose, Conflans's movement was stopped. In endeavouring to avoid Hawke's bold attempt to rake, the *Soleil Royal* had fallen to leeward, and in trying to tack to recover her position she fouled two ships that were following her lead. The result was she fell still further away, and being no longer able to weather the Four Shoal, she had to run back and anchor behind it off Croisic, at the opposite end of the bay to the bulk of the fleet.[1] By this time it was five o'clock and nearly dark. It was blowing harder than ever; the sea, even in the bay, was running high; an unknown shore was roaring just under their lee; the narrow waters were crowded with bewildered shipping. There was no more to be done, and Hawke made the signal to anchor.

So that famous day came to an end. Darkness settled down, and all through the night signals of distress could be heard above the din of the gale. Whether they came from friend or foe no one could tell. It was not till the morning broke, dark and stormy as ever, that any one knew what had happened. Then it was seen that the *Resolution* was ashore and dismasted on the Four Shoal, and the *Héros* beside her. The bulk of the British fleet had anchored about three miles from Dumet Island, which lies off the mouth of the Villaine River. The *Soleil Royal* was in the midst of them, and only eight of the French fleet were to be seen, anchored beyond and inshore of the British line. The rest, including

---

[1] Conflans's Report.

Bauffremont, the vice-admiral, and Bigot de Morogues, had succeeded during the night in doing what Conflans had tried in vain. They had got to sea, and were seen making for the Basque Roads and Rochefort. One other vessel, the *Juste*, after suffering severely in the action, had made for the Loire, and in getting in was lost with all hands.

The position of Conflans was indeed desperate, and the moment he realised it he slipped and tried to get into Croisic Road, where there were batteries to protect him. Hawke immediately signalled the *Essex* to follow her, with the result both vessels brought up hard on the Four Shoal beside the *Héros*. At the same time Hawke made the signal to weigh and attack the rest of the French fleet that was lying in the Villaine estuary. But his blood had cooled, and he quickly saw it was madness to move. "It blowed so hard," he said, "from the north-west, that instead of daring to cast the squadron loose I was obliged to strike topgallant masts." The French vessels seized the respite to escape. So soon as the tide began to make, they set to to work into the Villaine River, and by dint of jettisoning all their guns and gear, and having the wind in their favour, they managed to get over the bar. Only three of them, however, were ever fit for service again. The rest broke their backs on the mud.

All that day the gale continued to rage and nothing more could be done. But on the morrow it moderated a little, and three of Duff's ships were sent in to destroy the *Soleil Royal* and the *Héros*. Conflans thereupon set fire to his flagship, and Duff's people burnt the other. Meanwhile Hawke worked the fleet into the Villaine estuary, where the French ships had been lying. Here he found a more sheltered anchorage, but no means of attacking the ships in the river. An attempt with fire-boats proved impracticable, and so the long-sought encounter ended. It was not till the fourth day after the action that he sat down to write a report of his immortal victory. He had lost two ships and between three and four hundred men. The French had lost six, one the *Formidable*, Du Verger's flagship, a prize, two, including the *Soleil Royal*, burnt, and three driven ashore, besides four as good as wrecks in the Villaine, together with about two thousand five hundred men. It proved indeed the *coup de grâce* of the French navy, but Hawke was far from satisfied. " In attacking a flying enemy," he wrote apologetically to the Admiralty, "it was impossible in the space of a short winter's day that all our ships should be able to get into action, or all those of the enemy brought to it. . . . When I consider the season of the year, the hard gales on the day of action, a flying enemy, the shortness of the day, and the coast we were on, I can boldly affirm that all that could possibly be done has been done. As to the loss we have sustained, let it be placed to the necessity I was under of running all risks to break this strong force of the enemy. Had we had but two hours more daylight, the whole had been totally destroyed or taken."

And if he had not fallen in with the victuallers, if he had waited till his cruisers gave him the news, what then ? He would have arrived probably the next day and found Conflans snug in the bay. Before the gale had blown out he would have been joined perhaps by Geary, certainly by Saunders, who was only just too late to share Hawke's triumph. Then he would have gone in with perhaps thirty of the line. As the wind was he would have got to leeward of Conflans and prevented all possibility of escape, either out of the bay or into the Villaine.

Then there must have been another Battle of the Nile, but yet more terrible and destructive, since the numbers were so much greater, and the waters more confined.

Still it was enough. The catastrophe had come, yet Hawke could not tear himself away from the scene. In his eyes the triumph which awaited him at home was nothing compared with the chance of completing his work. A flying squadron was organised under Keppel to follow the ships that had fled to the Basque Roads. He returned in a few days to say that they had all got up the Charente, and were as inaccessible as those in the Villaine. Meanwhile Hawke, after engaging in an angry interchange of notes with D'Aiguillon over a question of prisoners, had been making the French feel the penalty of their abandonment of the sea. Croisic was bombarded for firing on working parties that were trying to salve the guns of the *Soleil Royal*. Isle d'Yeu, half-way down the coast to Rochefort, was seized, its defences destroyed, and its cattle carried off to refresh the fleet. In short, the movements of his squadrons kept the whole coast in alarm, with the effect that, though the English invasion was at once abandoned, D'Aiguillon's army remained unavailable, for it had to be cantoned along the threatened shores to save them from attack.

By the middle of December Hawke recognised that he had done his work. On December 9th he had written home recommending a division of the fleet into two squadrons, one for Quiberon and one for the Basque Roads, and the distribution of the frigates and fifties at the usual points from Brest down to Bordeaux. At the same time he ordered Geary to send home all the ships which had been specially ordered out as reinforcements. A week later he asked to be relieved, and early in the new year he was permitted to take the rest which he had so hardly earned.

CHAPTER II

THE SECOND PHASE OF THE WAR

It is recognised as a fundamental principle that lies at the root of the higher strategy that wars tend to exhibit two successive phases—phases not always very distinct, yet always existing, and so important in their differences that unless they be kept firmly grasped the conduct of any great war is sure to go astray. There is firstly the phase in which we seek to destroy the armed forces of the enemy, to overcome his means of attack and resistance, so that he is no longer able to gain his own object or to prevent us from gaining ours. If we are successful in this phase, then follows the second, in which we seek to exert our ascendency over him by bringing to bear upon his national life a general pressure in order to force him to accept our terms. In other words, our main objectives are no longer his armed forces, but what may be called the sources of his vitality; we direct our efforts to inflict upon him or to threaten loss and suffering which he shall recognise as harder to endure than the terms of peace we offer.

In the Seven Years' War, so far at least as England was concerned in it, this change—this transition from the first phase to the second—began to take place at the point we have reached. The complete failure of the desperate attempt of France to recover the situation by direct counter-attack demonstrated how irrevocably the armed forces of England dominated the situation in the main theatre of the war. It was clear that for all purposes of serious attack or resistance the French sea power had been reduced to impotence, and seeing the nature of the contest and its real object, it was the only kind of force that could directly affect the end. It is true Canada was not yet completely conquered. There remained upon the St. Lawrence a residue of potent armed force that, as we shall see, was destined to exhibit an unexpected power of resistance. But that made no inherent difference. For purposes of war-direction Canada was rightly regarded on both sides as lost. With the naval force of France destroyed, the destruction of her power of attack and resistance across the ocean could only be a question of a few months. The utmost the Canadian forces could do was to prolong the transition from the first phase to the second.

By no one was the decisive character of Hawke's victory more clearly recognised than by Frederick. "This naval battle," he wrote in the lowest depth of his fortunes, "is admirable, and comes to us as from the Lord."[1]

In France the point of transition was recognised by the collapse of her credit. The financiers saw too well that the pressure which England would now bring to bear would be mainly against her trade and against the Colonies, from which her resources could no longer be replenished. It was obvious that her finance was shattered, and the Government had to declare itself unable to meet its engagements.

A still more striking indication of the point which had been reached is the fact that, as almost always happens, there began to appear feverish attempts to patch up a peace and end the war. Hawke and his officers were startled

---

[1] To Finchenstein, Dec. 12, *Politische Corr.*, vol. xviii. p. 693.

to find themselves face to face with the movement immediately after the battle. During the course of the angry discussion that ensued between Hawke and the Duc d'Aiguillon over the question of exchanging prisoners, Howe had been sent ashore to conduct the negotiations. While thus engaged, he was surprised one day by D'Aiguillon's broaching the subject of a separate peace between the two countries without any regard to "Madame d'Hongrie," as he called the Austrian Empress. He said that his abortive irruption into the British Islands had been intended to secure peace, and that he had been given full power to treat so soon as he should have established himself in Scotland. These powers, he asserted, were still good, and he set himself to cajole Howe by all kinds of flattery to act as an intermediary between him and Pitt. Howe of course refused, but Hawke thought it best to send him home at once. He reached London at Christmas time, and as soon as he had reported himself Anson sent him on to Pitt.[1]

It was a thread of a very tangled skein which Howe had found so strangely in his hand. In every court in Europe they were pulling at it, and no one could quite tell how far his neighbour was committed. It was the outcome of a clever idea of Choiseul's to extricate France from the war by inducing Spain to mediate for a separate peace between France and England. If such a negotiation could be set on foot it would be sure in any case to breed mistrust between England and Prussia. Moreover, it was no part of Choiseul's policy to leave Austria without a rival in Germany, and if the negotiation succeeded, France would be able to withdraw from the war before Prussia was entirely crushed, without openly breaking her engagements with Vienna. On the other hand, if

---

[1] Anson to Newcastle, Dec. 27, *Newcastle Papers*, 32,900.

the mediation were refused, it was very likely to provoke Spain into declaring war upon England. The matter was put in hand directly after the battle of Minden, when, on August 10th, Ferdinand of Spain opportunely died, and was succeeded by his brother Don Carlos, King of the Two Sicilies, who had the reputation of being a devoted partisan of France, and a man of energy and character. The new king, eager to cut a figure in Europe, embraced the idea with alacrity. It was shortly after the news of the fall of Quebec had come home that the subject was definitely put before Pitt by Don Carlos's representative in London. He received it with a haughty intimation that the time had not yet come for thinking of peace. The Spanish agent replied that his master only wished to testify his goodwill, but at the same time he was bound to add that Spain could not sit still and see the balance of power in America entirely upset. The idea came on Pitt with disturbing suddenness. He saw in a flash the danger of the game that was being played on him, quickly recovered himself, and returned a soft and temporising answer.

But the news of Quebec, which hardened Pitt's heart, only drove the high spirit of Don Carlos further on the fatal path. It was the first thing he heard on landing in his new kingdom, and he vowed it froze his blood. If France were broken by England, it would be Spain's turn next. He was minded, he told the French ambassador, to act at once, but he must have time to arrange his finances, reorganise the army and navy, and repair the Colonial fortifications. All this, of course, was behind the back of General Wall, who was still at the head of the Government and as staunch as ever as to the insanity of breaking with England. He was determined not to play the new king's ambitious game, and Pitt

quickly offered him the means of checking it. Before
Carlos reached Madrid, Pitt's answer arrived. It was to
the effect that when there was a question of a number
of allies the difficulties of mediation were very great,
and for this reason his Britannic Majesty, while highly
appreciating Don Carlos's good intentions, had decided
to propose a Congress of the Powers with a view to a
general peace.

This clever parry had been originally the idea of
Frederick. Early in the year he had suggested that
England and Prussia should jointly propose such a
congress. It had been the outcome of one of his periods
of depression, when he saw no way of continuing the
struggle. After the disastrous day of his defeat at
Künersdorf on August 12th by the Austrians and Russians
and the consequent loss of Dresden, Frederick had re-
curred to the idea. The fact that not only Spain but Denmark also was being pushed forward by France to mediate
for a separate peace, made the suggestion welcome in
London. Pitt waited only for the news of Quebec to
act, and then rushed it through. On October 30th a joint
declaration in favour of a congress was transmitted to
Prince Louis of Brunswick, Prince Ferdinand's brother,
and commander-in-chief of the Dutch army, with a request that he would place it before the representatives of
France, Russia, and Austria at the Hague. He accepted
the mission, and proceeded to arrange for regular *pourparlers* to open.

Such was the diplomatic situation while France was in
the act of hazarding her desperate throw. On November
25th, before the news of Quiberon had been received at
the Hague, Prince Louis had delivered the declaration,
and it had been fairly well received. The French
ambassador went so far as to tell the Prince that his

court was in sore need of peace. He would not say that the sortie of M. de Conflans was their last effort, but he must own it was one of the last. Choiseul, though he quite understood the proposal for a general congress was meant to check his game of mediation and a separate peace with England, could congratulate himself that it also indicated mutual suspicion between England and Prussia. In his eyes the anxiety of both powers for every one to play with his cards on the table in open congress meant that neither power could trust the other. He consoled himself with this further reflection: "We know that a congress is not always the road to peace, but experience tells us it is very difficult for it not to become a cause of coldness between allies and soreness with the mediators." In any case it was diplomatically impossible not to entertain the suggestion, and accordingly the negotiations were opened at the Hague under the conduct of General Yorke. There month after month they continued, with ever-growing insincerity, while the exhausted armies lay still in winter quarters. The King of Spain, who disliked the Anglo-Prussian move as much as France, was still trying to insinuate his mediation in some form or other, in spite of Wall's efforts to keep him quiet. In line with him France was continuing to play for a separate peace with England, to save what colonies she had left, and as a step to stop the war before Frederick was crushed. Austria and Russia, on the other hand, were equally bent on the continuation of the war till Prussia was wiped from the map of Europe, while Pitt was absolutely inflexible in standing by his ally and in refusing even to consider any form of peace in which Frederick was not included.

The overtures which the Duc d'Aiguillon had made to Howe were the first attempt of France to shake Pitt's attitude—the first overt act, as Newcastle put it, of her desire and hope of a separate peace. No one but Wall seemed to believe in England's loyalty to Prussia. The French ambassador at Madrid assured him that there were clear indications that she was about to abandon her ally. " Oh," said Wall, " when you begin to think that, I have no more to say to you." Wall was right. The negotiations went on actively, but to every trick and turn Yorke opposed a blunt insistence on the participation of Prussia. Frederick, after some back-hand negotiations directly with Versailles, through the medium of Voltaire, became as confident as Wall, and finally placed the whole of his interests in the hands of the British Cabinet. In vain Choiseul went on scheming to open direct communication with Pitt. The attempt only produced, early in April 1760, an ultimatum which led quickly to a complete rupture of the negotiations. By the middle of May the *pourparlers* came to an end, and there was no doubt a new campaign must be opened.

It was in the black prospects of this campaign on the Continent that lay the complication of the British position. It has been said that the point of transition between the " armed force " phase and the " general pressure " phase had been reached in all but one area of operations. Though generally true of the war between France and England—the maritime war, as it was called—throughout the negotiations it was not true of the Continental sphere. There neither side had achieved a real domination, and it was still reciprocally a question of destroying armed forces. Yet everything pointed to the probability that those of Frederick could not possibly endure another campaign, and if he succumbed it would be out of the power of Ferdinand to continue the defence of Hanover. Soon after the opening of the negotiations for the congress, Ferdinand had made "a most secret and private" appeal to Pitt on the subject. "The army of the King of Prussia," he wrote, "has melted away to half what it was at the beginning of the campaign. I have good reason to doubt whether he can possibly recruit his regiments and mend everything for the next campaign. . . . What is more, the enemy, remaining masters of Dresden, can open the campaign when they will, that town serving them as a *place d'armes et d'appui*. If the Russians reappear at the same time, I don't know what will happen." The only salvation he saw was in making peace with France before the campaign opened. Mitchell, our ambassador with Frederick, sent home an equally desponding account. He spoke of the ten months' arduous campaign, the exhaustion of the troops, the two battles, Künersdorf and Maxen, lost, with twenty-one battalions, forty-five squadrons, and all the best officers taken prisoners. To make peace with France and hold back Russia was the only way to save Frederick from being lost beyond hope. The picture was not exaggerated. Frederick himself, in his secret correspondence, was painting it in still blacker colours. But for Ferdinand's victory at Minden all would perhaps have been lost already. The whole foundations on which Pitt's war-plan had been built were shaking, and something must be done to save them, or it would be impossible for England to garner the fruit of her late glorious campaign.

It was but natural, therefore, that a feeling should arise for drawing on the favourable balance of the maritime war to redress the Continental default. Accordingly, at the end of December, as the time drew near for settling the distribution of the fleet for the coming year, Newcastle broached the old idea of a Baltic squadron. He told Hardwicke that nothing could now hurt us

except Russian action, and that a British fleet was what
Russia most feared, and what Prussia most ardently
desired. It would have, in his opinion, the additional
advantage of checking the negotiations which France
was carrying on in Denmark and Sweden for a Northern
coalition against us. As to the Swedish navy, it would
be able to offer little opposition, since it was only twenty-
two sail strong, of which six had been disarmed to provide France with guns, and four others already had their
hands full with the Prussian privateers that were operating from Emden.[1] At Newcastle's request, Hardwicke
communicated these ideas to Anson. Anson replied in
a guarded manner that he generally agreed with Newcastle about a Baltic squadron, if it should be possible
to spare ships, but that must depend on the final attitude
of Spain, which at present was very uncertain. He also
begged to remind Newcastle that the statement of our
naval force upon which he relied as showing a Baltic
squadron was possible, exaggerated the number of ships
that would be at home ; for over and above Hawke's
squadron, which he regarded as a division of the home
fleet, they had then thirty of the line employed on
different foreign stations. Hardwicke threw further cold
water on the idea upon his own account. When the
King of Prussia, he said, originally asked for a Baltic
fleet, it was to protect Pomerania and his ports on that
side, and, secondly, to terrorise Russia. Now he said
nearly all the Baltic shore was in Russia's hands, and
what remained Sweden was too weak to take. Moreover,
Russia had already sunk back into her old half-hearted
attitude to the war, and a Baltic fleet was more likely to
provoke her into fresh activity than anything else.[2]

[1] Mem. on the Swedish Navy, *Newcastle Papers*, 32,900, f. 416.
[2] Newcastle to Hardwicke, Dec. 29, and Hardwicke's answer, Dec. 30,
Newcastle Papers, 32,900.

Though Pitt does not appear to have countenanced the idea, it must have been talked of somewhat freely. The French ambassador in Stockholm assured the Swedish Government the squadron was coming, but this may have been merely a move against the strong Anglo-Prussian party that was growing up out of jealousy of Russia's conquest of Pomerania. Still Höpken, the chief Minister, professed to be seriously alarmed. He said that the Swedish fleet would certainly be beaten, and that an English Baltic squadron would have the most serious consequences. Still Pitt gave no sign. There was, indeed, a very special reason for not proceeding with the idea. For at the moment Frederick was engaged in an attempt to gain the Russian court by offering a bribe of a million crowns to a certain Grand Duke, and a demonstration in the Baltic was the last thing that was wanted.[1]

The truth was that Pitt's mind was working in quite a different direction. From the first, with the unerring instinct of the great War Minister he was, his eyes were fixed on Spain. At the end of January he had consented to send to Prince Ferdinand two more regiments of horse and three of dragoons, but there was never a hint of entangling the fleet in the Baltic when Spanish arsenals were awakening. So concerned indeed was he with the outlook in the southern danger area, that he had sent the Earl of Kinnoul on a special mission to Lisbon, to apologise for Boscawen's breach of neutrality in destroying La Clue's ships on the Portuguese coast.

By April, when it had become clear that the negotiations for the congress must break down, and that another campaign would be necessary, the idea of a Baltic squadron seems to have been entirely dropped. Newcastle had a

[1] *Chatham Corr.*, vol. ii. pp. 27–31.

stormy interview with Pitt upon the prospect of a renewal of the war, in the course of which he said he did
not see how we could carry on another year. Pitt, he
says, "flew into a violent passion." That kind of talk, he
said, was the way to encourage the enemy. We were a
hundred times better able to continue than the French.
"In short," says the Duke, "there was no talking to him."
As to the Continental situation, Prince Ferdinand, whose
Prussian contingent had been recalled by Frederick, was
still pressing for further reinforcement. Here Pitt took
a curious attitude. He said he personally would send no
more troops to Germany, but if others wished it he would
not oppose. Newcastle's circle thought this meant a fresh
outbreak of combined expeditions. "Anson," the Duke
wrote to Hardwicke, "suspects there is some new project
of an attempt on some part of the coast of France carrying
on unknown to him," which he said was "monstrous and
insufferable." Hardwicke replied that he too had his
suspicions, and though Anson certainly knew nothing of
any such expedition, he fancied that Howe did.[1]

There is some reason to believe that these suspicions
were not without foundation. No indication is found,
however, that what was in Pitt's mind was any operation
against the French coast. An expedition does seem to
have been on foot very secretly, but the cotton clothing
ordered for the troops and the sheathing of the ships gave
an impression that it was intended for tropical seas.
Keppel, moreover, was mentioned for the naval command,
and he was best known for his brilliant conduct of the
little expedition which had inaugurated the great year of
victory by the capture of Goree, the French slaving
station on the West Coast of Africa, and had finally established the British position in that quarter. The im-

---

[1] *Newcastle Papers*, April 9 and 10, 32,904.

pression was that his mission was to do in the East Indies what he had done on the West Coast by the seizure of the French naval bases in those seas at Mauritius and Réunion. The military force was considerable, said indeed to amount to eight thousand men under General Kingsley; and those who knew were aware that orders had been sent out to the admiral on the East Indian station to meet the expedition with his whole force at Madagascar.[1]

How far Pitt had really committed himself to devoting so large a force to what we have called the "general pressure" phase of the war is uncertain. The idea was very likely strongly in his mind, but his behaviour at this time suggests that his instinct for strategy was forcing him against his inclination to continue the process of striking at the section of the enemy's armed force that was still confronting him undominated. It is as though he felt intuitively the necessity of breaking it down before he could move freely in the second phase of the war. We know for certain there was growing in his mind a conviction that, in view of the overtures of France, a decisive blow in Westphalia by Ferdinand was the shortest road to peace. Such a blow would bring home to Versailles the hopelessness of trying to regain in Hanover what had been lost beyond the seas. How coercively this idea possessed him will appear later. There can be little doubt it was correct. On the Continent the second phase had not been reached—there armed forces still remained to be struck, and in spite of his antipathy to Continental operations, and in spite of his anxiety to reap the harvest of the sea, he could not resist the promptings of his unerring instinct for war.

It was such considerations as these that were almost certainly at the bottom of the striking change of attitude

[1] Beatson, vol. ii. p. 420.

which compelled him, as we have seen, to relax the stubbornness of his antipathy to sending British troops to Germany. Upon Lord Hardwicke's suggestion, he and Newcastle had come to a compromise on the point. On condition that Newcastle would not oppose Pitt's contemplated Bill for the continuance of the militia, Pitt would not oppose sending more troops to Germany.[1] Newcastle promptly ordered away four battalions of infantry. Pitt protested against such a step without the consent of the Secret Committee. He insisted on its being convened, and thereupon consented to the despatch of six battalions and another regiment of horse. But it was on condition that they were to be recalled at the end of the campaign, or if a new invasion were threatened, and that the best of the militia were to be embodied " to make the face of an army at home "; all of which is suggestive of his longing to free the regular army for offensive operations abroad.

In less than three weeks " the glorious reinforcement," as Newcastle called it, had sailed from the Nore, this time for the Weser instead of Emden. It reached Ferdinand's camp by the middle of June, just in time for the opening of the campaign. The British troops, now under the Marquis of Granby in place of Lord George Sackville, numbered about twenty thousand, which, with the German troops in British pay, were calculated as giving Prince Ferdinand an army of eighty-eight thousand men, without counting Prussians and Hanoverians. It was a force which, in view of the diversion caused by the presence of the fleet on the French coasts, could be relied on to keep Hanover intact. But this was not enough, and here arose a question of the deepest strategical interest, and one which is still amongst the most difficult to answer.

[1] " Mem. for the King," April 24, *Newcastle Papers*, 32,904.

Hitherto the function of Ferdinand's army in relation to the whole war had been defensive—to cover Hanover while our main offensive proceeded elsewhere.   But now that something more was required of it—some positive, definite gain, and not merely prevention—its function became positive, and defensive action no longer sufficed. To achieve a positive gain leading by direct pressure to peace the offensive is always essential, and somebody, probably Pitt, regarded it as a matter of course that "the glorious reinforcement" was to enable Ferdinand to pass to the offensive.   It was an implied if not an express condition of the reinforcement that this should be done. Newcastle, however, appears to have raised the plausible but more than doubtful objection that the general on the spot must be the judge.   Others were certainly determined to dictate the nature of his operations, and Newcastle could not understand their attitude.   He referred as usual to Hardwicke, and the shrewd old lawyer laid down the strategical principle as lucidly as though it had been a knotty point of equity.   "Last year," he wrote, "the question was whether he should fight a battle.   Of that nobody could judge but the general on the spot.   But whether the general plan of a campaign should be offensive or defensive is a political consideration and to be determined upon a great variety of circumstances, of many of which the King and his Ministers are the most proper judges, though of many others of them the commander-in-chief of the army must first determine." [1]   It would be difficult to carry this thorny problem further.   Certainly no one has ever done so, and in this case it settled the question.

The point once determined against Newcastle's view, we find Pitt going still further on the new line.   It was

[1] Hardwicke to Newcastle, June 6, 1760, *Newcastle Papers*, 32,907.

never his way to do things by halves, and, moreover, it
was his inflexible rule that where you take the offensive
and seek to obtain some positive advantage, there you
must concentrate every unit you can come by. In June,
owing to Frederick's finding it necessary to recall his
cavalry from Ferdinand's army, two more regiments of
horse were ordered out to fill the gap. But even this
did not satisfy Pitt. More must and could be spared.
Ferdinand's offensive opening which was directed against
Homburg failed, and thereupon Pitt himself took the lead.
The moment was favourable. A new ambassador from
Spain, the Conde de Fuentes, had arrived, and was making
so good an impression in London that an alliance with
Spain, or at least an *entente cordiale,* began to look as
likely as war. At any rate it was clear that Spain was
not nearly ready for hostilities. The ambassador had
dropped the question of mediation, and was devoting his
attention in a very amicable tone to settling the long
outstanding differences as to our right to cut logwood in
Spanish Central America. Towards the end of July,
when Ferdinand's check was known, all looked well, and
Pitt surprised Newcastle by proposing to send out three
battalions of guards so as to ensure the campaign being
decisive. Even the King was staggered. At first he
strongly objected ; but in the end Pitt prevailed, and the
brigade was promptly sent.[1] Meanwhile on July 21st
Ferdinand had fought and won his brilliant little action
at Marbourg, mainly by the daring and endurance of
Granby's troops, and had thereby snatched the initiative
from his adversary. A fortnight later Frederick stumbled
on his lucky victory at Liegnitz, at which no one was
more astonished than himself. What he had struggled

---

[1] Newcastle to Hardwicke, July 21, *Newcastle Papers,* 32,908 ; Ferdinand
to Holderness, Aug. 28, *ibid.*, 32,910.

for in vain with all his art, Fortune suddenly threw into his lap; and thus at the end of August, when the Guards reached Ferdinand's camp, everything looked promising for a vigorous prosecution of his offensive operations.

Such, then, after the first two months of the campaign, was the condition of affairs in our Continental theatre of the war. Shortly, it may be said that our operations there, which had been originally of a purely containing or defensive nature, had now been complicated with a true offensive intention, and were taking on themselves the characteristics of a great attack. True, it was an eccentric attack, for though aimed directly at the main forces of the enemy, it was not aimed at the main object of the war or at the forces in the main theatre. It partook, by its very nature, rather of the second phase, and was aimed not at acquiring anything more for ourselves, but of forcing the enemy to accept the situation, and to agree to abandon what she had lost beyond the seas.

Bearing all this in mind, we are now in a position to study the manner in which naval action in European seas was related to the new development ashore. In general design it was a military blockade of the whole French coast from Dunkirk to Marseilles. The operations opened with what were really the dregs of the last campaign. At the beginning of the new year there remained, besides the ships of Conflans's fleet in the Villaine and the Charente, two other fragments of the French naval force that had escaped destruction. In the south was the division of La Clue's fleet which had taken refuge in Cadiz, under the command of its senior captain. In the north was Thurot, with the squadron he had got out of Dunkirk. The former had been engaging Brodrick's attention ever since Boscawen's action. The same after-noon that he had parted with his chief off St. Vincent he had ascertained from a Glasgow merchantman it was in Cadiz. In those days there was no question of interning or disarming belligerent vessels which had taken refuge in a neutral port. Brodrick, therefore, sat himself down to cruise before Cadiz, and his action was quickly confirmed from home by orders to blockade. For three months he held the station, picking up a number of valuable prizes from the West and East Indies, and living in constant hope that the French would put to sea. But not once did they offer to stir. This state of things continued till the first week in December, when a heavy south-westerly gale forced the British squadron to take refuge in Cadiz Roads in an almost disabled state. The *Prince* (90), Brodrick's flagship, was so much injured that he had to shift his flag to the *Conqueror* (74) and send the *Prince* to Gibraltar. Two others of the line had had to cut away their masts, and all the rest were short of spars. But General Wall was still supreme at Madrid, and the Spanish governor showed himself complacent in providing masts and spars and all facilities for a refit.

Brodrick, left with only three of the line and a fifty fit for service, was now inferior to the French, who had three sixty-fours and two fifties. De Castillon, their acting commodore, saw his chance to escape, and formally demanded assurance from the governor that the British should not be allowed to sail for twenty-four hours after he left. Thereupon Brodrick, to put a good face on the matter, boldly demanded a reciprocal privilege for himself, and eventually it was agreed that each side should have the right to put to sea on alternate days. Occasionally the French showed signs of getting under weigh, and it is said the English did their best to assist them by passing warps and the like. But nothing came of it, and on Christmas Day Brodrick himself got out. Scarcely was he off the port again when another gale struck him, and on December 30th forced him into Gibraltar in almost as bad a state as before. Once more he had to devote all his energy to repairing his ships. Then at last the French commodore hardened his heart to come out, and Brodrick had not been in Gibraltar two days before the French stole through the Straits at night unseen by the British cruisers. So cleverly had they managed that it was not till January 16th, the day before Castillon got safely into Toulon, that Brodrick knew for certain they had escaped him. Shortly afterwards he received orders to return home with all his ships of the line, leaving his senior frigate captain in command of the cruisers to perform the ordinary commerce protection duties of the station. From all that France had in the Mediterranean there was little to fear. Castillon's squadron was paid off and dismantled, and in view of the changing attitude of Spain it was necessary to use the respite gained by Hawke's and Boscawen's victories to overhaul the whole fleet as completely as possible in readiness for a great effort.[1]

The squadron of Thurot, well known as he was to the Baltic trade as a daring and redoubtable privateersman, caused the Government even less anxiety. After eluding the blockade of Commodore Boys in the gale off Dunkirk, he had been forced by bad weather to run to the coast of Sweden, and Boys ever since had been at Leith watching for his reappearance. He was heard of at Göteberg, and towards the end of the year near Bergen. Boys had cruisers out off Peterhead, but in council of war with the authorities in Edinburgh it was decided that it was best for him to remain on the Scottish coast cruising between Buchanness and St. Abb's Head till Thurot's where-

---

[1] For Brodrick's Despatches see *In-letters*, 384.

abouts was definitely known. He had indeed already
left Bergen, and the first day of the new year he was
forced to anchor at the Faroes. There he remained
unreported for a month. It was not till the end of
February that news came of how three vessels had
appeared at Islay, off the Argyle coast, and were
plundering the island for fresh meat. Still Boys did
not move. It was known that Thurot had sailed from
Dunkirk with five frigates of from forty-four to eighteen
guns, and a sloop. The general impression at Edinburgh
was that the strangers must be part of La Clue's squadron,
and that if Boys went to the West Coast Thurot might
appear on the East at any moment.

But it was indeed Thurot, with all that the winter
weather had left of his squadron. Sailing from Islay so
soon as his wants were satisfied, on February 21st he
appeared in Belfast Lough, and landed about a thousand
men at Carrickfergus. Thurot had wished to attack
Belfast itself, but Flobert, the military officer in command
of the troops, refused. Indeed relations between the
two services were by this time strained to a point that
made substantial success impossible. The little town,
which was without walls, and whose castle was in ruins,
resisted two half-hearted attacks; but the small detachment that garrisoned the place then found its ammunition
was exhausted, and unfortunately decided to surrender, a
course for which there was no need. Flobert had been
seriously wounded, and the flag of truce found the French
cowering behind walls with apparently no idea of renewing the attack. They naturally jumped at the capitulation, and so the sorry affair ignominiously ended. Thurot
then sent a flag of truce to Belfast to demand victuals,
and General Strode, who was in command, and the
gentlemen of the place were weak-kneed enough to

comply.[1] Upon this Thurot disappeared, but into seas which were soon so thickly swarming with cruisers as to leave him scarcely a chance of escape.

The news reached the Admiralty on the 26th, five days after the landing and the day after the re-embarkation. Boscawen was then at Plymouth about to take Hawke's place on the French coast, and orders to meet the situation were sent him the same night. They are of considerable interest as showing how speedily the organisation of the time could deal with a raid. One ship of the line and two frigates were to cruise off Cape Clear in such a way as to intercept Thurot if he came down St. George's Channel. A similar squadron was to cruise west of Cape Clear to catch him if he came down the West Coast of Ireland, while a third was to proceed off Brest to be ready for him if he escaped the other two. Yet a fourth squadron, after picking up the Milford guardship, was to proceed direct to Carrickfergus. By the evening of the 29th all these ships were away : yet all were forestalled.[2]

While Thurot and his troops were still at work there was lying in Kinsale Captain Elliot of the *Æolus* (32), who had been forced in there from Hawke's fleet to revictual. There were also in the harbour two 36-gun frigates, the *Pallas* and *Brilliant*, which were then on a cruise in the Soundings on commerce protection duty. In Cork was Captain Scott, whose station for similar duty extended to sixty leagues west of Cape Clear. Both these officers received the news on the 24th, that is, the day before the French re-embarked. Scott immediately ordered the

---

[1] Provost of Glasgow to the Admiralty, Feb. 21 and 26 ; Duke of Bedford's Despatch with Strode's Report, Feb. 23. Copies of all these are collected in *Newcastle Papers*, 32,902.

[2] *In-letters*, 520 (Boys); *Out-letters*, 84, Feb. 26–27 ; *In-letters*, 90 (Boscawen), Feb. 28–9.

Kinsale frigates to join him. His order was never delivered. Elliot was already away, waiting for no man. On the 26th, as the news reached the Admiralty, he was reporting himself off Dublin. Without pausing, he held on straight for Belfast Lough, being informed Thurot was still there. Arrived off the Lough, he tried in vain to beat in. A contrary and violent wind kept him out. But it was all to the good. At daybreak on the 29th he had sighted the enemy under sail and gave chase. Thurot had then the *Maréchal de Belleisle* (44), the *Blonde* (36), and the *Terpsichore* (24). Elliot's force was practically equal. Coming up with him off the Isle of Man, he closed at once, and in an hour and a half Thurot was dead, and all three ships had struck.[1]

So in a smart display of cruiser control ended the dregs of Belleisle's great attempt at a counter-stroke, showing how little such a raid could do even in days of slow communication on a coast wholly unprepared, where officers behaved badly and citizens without spirit. The opinion of the French military officers on the whole conception was expressed in stinging terms. "A madman," wrote one of Thurot, "puffed up with the favour and confidence of a Minister whom he has abused with chimerical projects. . . . Happy is he to have found a glorious death in action, when he ought to have found it on the gallows."[2]

By the second week in March all the ships that had joined the hunt were on their stations again, and Boscawen sailed to take up the Great Blockade. Holmes was given the Jamaica station, which he had so earnestly

---

[1] For copies of Elliot's Despatches see *Newcastle Papers*, 32,902, Feb. 24, 26, and 29, and Beatson, vol. ii. p. 413. The *Blonde* and *Terpsichore* were taken into the navy under the same names.

[2] Lacour-Gayet, p. 350 *n.*

desired. To Saunders fell the Mediterranean. The recall
of Brodrick and his ships of the line did not mean the
suppression of the squadron for long. The persistence
of Spain in her equivocal attitude rendered a strong
display of force within the Straits as necessary as ever,
and in May Saunders sailed with thirteen of the line and
a number of frigates, which brought his cruiser squadron
up to a dozen. While he kept his eye on Toulon he
devoted a large part of his force to the destruction of
French Levant trade. " The diligence of Admiral
Saunders was such," says Beatson, " that from the time
he made his appearance in these seas the enemy's trade
was reduced to a state of stagnation," and all the evidence
available tells us this was no exaggeration. His sagacious
feeling for a general situation enabled him also to play
an excellent stroke in support of Lord Kinnoul's mission
to Portugal. Hearing that a number of influential
Portuguese had been expelled from the Papal dominions,
he sent a frigate to Leghorn to carry them to Lisbon.
The step had an excellent effect, and no doubt contri-
buted substantially to Kinnoul's success.

With Saunders thus active in the Mediterranean, the
Great Blockade extended from Marseilles to Brest, and
thence it was carried onward by Rodney and Boys as
far as Dunkirk. It was, of course, not a true commercial
blockade; that is, it was not regarded as binding on
neutrals except for contraband of war. It was aimed at
preventing any reunion of the fragments into which the
French navy had been broken, as well as at covering
the operations in Canada, and paralysing the French seaborne trade. Several home-coming ships of war were
taken, and many privateers and rich merchantmen,
while the coastwise traffic, according to French local
accounts, was almost completely stopped. The pressure,

added to that which Ferdinand was exerting on the northern frontier, was very severe.

Nor did it end here. Up and down the coast threats of attack kept the local forces in constant alarm. In July Rodney, in pursuit of some flat-boats that were being used to transport naval stores to Brest, destroyed the forts of Sallenelles and Ouistreham, at the mouth of the Orne, and then bombarded Port-en-Bessin, where some of the chases tried to take refuge. He also destroyed all the fisheries about Dieppe. In August, when Hawke relieved Boscawen and again took command of the blockade, the pressure became still more severe. The island of Dumet, off Morbihan, commanded the best anchorage in the bay. He resolved therefore to seize it, and as soon as he arrived he entrusted its capture to Howe. He performed the work as neatly as usual. The island proved of great value for fresh vegetables, and so excellent a watering-place, that thenceforward water transports could be dispensed with, greatly to the ease and economy of the blockade. Having secured this advantage, Hawke, full of renewed vigour after his rest ashore, forthwith proceeded to work out a bold plan for seizing the ships that were still lying beyond his reach in Morbihan and the Villaine. His idea was to establish himself on the mainland at a point from which, with his marines and landing-parties, he could operate at little risk against Auray, Vannes, and the Villaine. The little peninsula of Rhuys, which is cut off from the interior by a narrow pass, called by Hawke the "St. Jacques Neck," seemed to offer an ideal position. In the admiral's opinion he would be able to hold it against anything the enemy could bring to bear upon him, and thus secure a perfectly safe base and point of retreat. The operation seems to have been designed in the soundest style, and to afford an excellent example of the kind of territorial pressure which is legitimately open to a purely naval force in complete command of the sea. Few things in the whole war would be more interesting than to know how such an extension of the naval arm would have worked; but unfortunately, as Hawke's scheme was ripening for execution, he received a communication from home which brought everything to a standstill.

As though by the working of some inevitable law, the strategical necessities of the shore operations against the armed forces of the enemy began to assert themselves over the secondary operations of the fleet. We have seen how rosy was the outlook for Ferdinand's taking the offensive when at the end of August Hawke had resumed the command in Quiberon Bay. So threatening, indeed, was the prospect for France that Marshal Belleisle saw that a further effort must be made to save the situation. Accordingly he ordered a fresh army to be formed upon the Lower Rhine to check Ferdinand's advance by operating against his extreme right. As the new move became known, Ferdinand redoubled his efforts to get a decision in the field. In England from day to day every one was hoping to hear a battle had been fought, and nobody was so eager as Pitt himself. As the days went by and Ferdinand's enemy continued to evade him, he grew anxious. Pitt knew that a decisive victory and that alone would serve his turn, and for that and nothing else he had consented to let the "glorious reinforcement" go. He was specially annoyed by a despatch from the commissary of the British troops, in which it was said that if Ferdinand could make the French retire it would be a great campaign even without a decisive battle. "I don't think so," said Pitt to Newcastle in discussing the letter. " That won't do our business. I declare, for one, that without a battle I will not be for the continuance of the measures in Germany another year." [1]

September was passing to its end, and still there was no news of the battle. Instead of it came growing expressions of anxiety about the new French army. The best intelligence reported that the bulk of the troops were to be drawn from the coasts of Flanders, Picardy, Normandy, and even Brittany. It was a clear case for the kind of diversion with which Pitt had inaugurated his conduct of the war. At the beginning of the difficulties which Ferdinand was encountering he had pressed for still further reinforcements, and had been refused with some asperity. Now therefore came, as before, a cry for another diversion by sea. On the last day of September Pitt and Newcastle talked it over. Pitt suggested as an objective Boulogne, which seemed the most obvious way to stopping the new French movement, and Newcastle was inclined to agree as it had a distinct Continental flavour. But, says Newcastle, Pitt also " flung out Belle-isle, which he has always harped upon." To Newcastle it was anathema. The idea had been suggested to Pitt as early as 1756 as a reply to the loss of Minorca. In the view of the author of the design the occupation of Belleisle would enable us effectually to blockade the French coast and force them to keep fifty or sixty thousand

---

[1] Newcastle to Hardwicke, Sept. 13. Hardwicke's answer is interesting as showing that he had made a serious study of strategy. He doubted the absolute truth of Pitt's strenuous theory of the decisive battle which has since become current coin. He quoted against it a saying of the great Duke of Alva : " It is the business of a general always to get the better of his enemy, but not always to fight, and if he can do his business without fighting so much the better." This was certainly the accepted theory of war at the time, and there were few besides Pitt and Frederick who would then have questioned it. See *Newcastle Papers*, 32,911, Sept. 13 and 14.

men in the neighbourhood. They would, he said, be even more afraid of us than our people had been of them.[1]

It was at any rate too good an idea not to recur now. The news that Montreal had fallen was expected any day, and the main object of the war was practically attained. The secondary phase of general pressure was declaring itself more emphatically, and what could be better for the work than the capture of Belleisle? As a base for the great blockade, and for such attacks as Hawke even then had in his mind, it was ideally placed. In Pitt's view the presence of a number of troops in so perfect a *place d'armes* would expose all the coast of the Bay of Biscay to sudden raids, and force the French to detach a considerable section of their forces for its protection. As a diversion in Ferdinand's favour it would be almost as powerful as an attack on Boulogne. But in Pitt's mind there was almost certainly a very different motive. The troops that were to form the new army on the Rhine were already in motion from all parts of France, and Ligonier and most other people were of opinion that by no possible means could the expedition be organised in time to be of use to Ferdinand. This difficulty only inclined Pitt still more strongly to prefer Belleisle as an objective, for he saw in it a means of securing compensation for a failure he could not prevent.

It happened that the negotiations with Spain had once more taken an ugly turn. The ambassador had just presented a new claim about the Newfoundland fisheries which was regarded as absolutely groundless. But this was not the worst. In presenting his note the

[1] "Project by Thomas Cole for taking Belleisle," Aug. 11, 1756. Whoever Cole was, he seems to have taken himself seriously as a strategist. He supports his idea thus: "To carry on war to the greatest advantage would be always to invade the invader. Queen Elizabeth did so with Philip II., and soon found the good effect of it."

ambassador stated that it had been communicated to
France. Pitt had very firmly expressed his surprise at such
a provocatory proceeding, and demanded an explanation
of what Spain meant by bringing into the negotiations a
court at war with England. Fuentes replied with two
" extraordinary pieces" which reiterated both claims and
only made things worse.[1] In Pitt's eyes it was a clear
intimation that Spain intended to make common cause
with France in order to secure her own Colonial possessions, and to save herself from the results of a peace
which would leave England mistress of North America
and predominant in the West Indies.

Here, then, it was that lay the supreme value of Belleisle, which no one but Pitt seems to have thoroughly
appreciated. Great as was the naval and even the
military importance of its capture, both were outweighed
by the diplomatic value. Nothing within the scope of
our forces could so surely strengthen our hand when it
came to making peace. Its retention would place us in
a position to dominate the maritime activity of France
that was unsurpassed by Minorca itself. It gave us a
post in the gateway of French Atlantic commerce; it
placed us astride of every avenue of their seaborne
trade. From every point of view it created a situation
which was unendurable for France, and 'nothing we
could demand could well be too high a price to pay
for its retrocession. It was not unlikely that Spain
would demand Minorca as a condition of her assistance,
but so long as we held Belleisle France would not be
able to grant it. It was an absolute pledge for our
recovery of the lost island, while as for its special strategical value, if Spain declared war it gave us a naval base
interposed between the French and Spanish fleets.

[1] Hardwicke to Pitt, Sept. 29, *Chatham Corr.*, vol. ii. p. 68.

Such at least was Pitt's view of the strategical value of Belleisle. Others thought differently, and, like Choiseul himself, regarded, or affected to regard, its capture as a pin-prick of no importance. Still, the reasoning which weighed with Pitt was undeniably strong, and if he was convinced, and in his masterful assurance carried away all opposition, it is no wonder. The day after his talk with Newcastle he went to the King, and the King "was violently for it." From the royal closet he went to the Admiralty to order ten thousand tons more transport to increase the expedition that was already on foot. Newcastle thereupon went in indignation to the King to protest. He also asked Anson to dinner, and Anson, he says, was "extremely against it." Ligonier, too, expressed his doubts. The question was therefore referred to the Secret Committee. But there, to Newcastle's disgust, no one would support him. Ligonier, it is true, pronounced the troops could not be ready for six weeks, and Pitt wavered a little. Anson in his turn declared the weather would be good till the middle of November. In the end nothing was definitely decided except that the expedition designed for the Mauritius was to be reinforced, and that it would act somewhere on the coast of France instead.[1]

Next day came the news that Montreal had fallen and Pitt appears to have made up his mind. The expeditionary force at Portsmouth was quickly brought up to seven battalions of the line. At the same time two more regiments were ordered to embark from Ireland, while a battalion of the guards, a regiment of dragoons, and a great siege-train were set in motion for the coast.

Every one could see the objective was no longer in the

[1] Newcastle to Hardwicke, Oct. 3, *Newcastle Papers*, 32.912.

East Indies. "Where they go, God knows," wrote Newcastle to Hardwicke, as troops and guns and stores began
to file down the Portsmouth Road past his house at
Claremont in endless procession. "I write treason.
Not a word!" For him it was all another bit of
Pitt's mania, and he was almost in despair. For such
an army to be risked on the sea in a November expedition was madness, and Anson himself was ill at ease.
The only hope of Newcastle and his friends was that
Pitt could not be really in earnest, and that the whole
thing was intended to operate as a threat only.

It was a view for which there was some colour. The
objective was still not decided officially. It had been agreed
to refer the matter to the Secret Committee, and Keppel,
who was to command, was called home to attend it. He
had personally reconnoitred Belleisle during the summer,
and when he arrived it was clear to the committee that
he was by no means sure the operation was practicable.
He was in doubt whether the ships could approach
within gunshot of the only landing-place, and whether
the citadel did not command it. Pitt himself was
shaken, and thought the point serious enough to refer
to Hawke before anything was finally settled. This step
was regarded by the doubters as meaning the abandonment
of the expedition, and Hardwicke predicted that no clear
opinion would be got from Hawke, "whose character," he
said, "I take it, is to be diffident and balancing."[1]

It was the receipt of a despatch from Anson informing Hawke of the project on foot and the points
he was to report on that interrupted his arrangements
for a landing on his own account. Naturally he did not
receive the idea with any great favour, being wholly

[1] Newcastle to Hardwicke, Oct. 11, and Hardwicke to Newcastle,
Oct. 12, *Newcastle Papers*, 32,913.

wrapt up in his own promising design. A fresh reconnaissance was made, and upon it Hawke made his report.
He began with a strictly professional protestation of his
readiness to carry out any enterprise that was commanded, and then, without very definitely answering the
questions that had been referred to him, he proceeded to
throw cold water on the whole project. Full weight was
given to the undoubted difficulties of the enterprise, but,
worse still, he criticised Pitt's strategy in terms that came
near to ridicule. He could not see, he said, how you
were going to affect the mainland by occupying an island,
and he then went on to explain his own project and to
point out how superior it was to Pitt's. He took no pains
to conceal his disappointment, but said that, as something
so much more ambitious was on foot, his own scheme
would be abandoned.[1]

A week later Hawke's answer reached Anson, and he
carried it straight to the King. In the interval the
opposition had been growing. Ligonier declared the
troops would be fit for nothing for three months after
they returned. Anson could not forget November
weather in the bay, and Pitt, bending before the storm,
had declared himself ready to drop the whole thing if
Hawke reported unfavourably, or if the Council was against
it. When he knew the report had come he hurried to
the palace. Newcastle describes the scene. Pitt was
thoroughly out of temper that the report had been taken
to the King before he saw it, but Hawke, it will be remembered, was not directly under his orders. Anson
came out of the closet to say that the King declared the
thing impracticable, and would not permit his troops to
go. Pitt was used to overcoming such opposition. He

---

[1] A copy of the despatch, dated Oct. 17, is in *Newcastle Papers*, 32,913,
also in Lord Donoughmore's *Beaufort MSS*. (*Hist. Com. Rep.*), p. 122.

was the last to go in, and presently came out "very disturbed." Presumably there had been something like a scene. Pitt gave vent to his feelings in the anteroom by attacking Hawke "most bitterly." He was "a very good sea officer," he said, "but no Minister." Not only had he stopped the Belleisle plan, but he had dropped his own, and the angry Minister declared he would have no more to do with it. He was, in short, furious with Hawke and his report. "From this letter," concludes Newcastle, "I date poor Sir Edward's fall and Admiral Boscawen's rise."[1] Newcastle was probably right. In the defective statesmanship which in Pitt's eyes Hawke had exhibited, and which the great War Minister regarded as so essential a qualification for high naval command, we see at least one of the reasons that so long denied the ill-starred admiral his reward. It was without doubt the origin of Pitt's well-known remark to Boscawen. "When," he is reported to have said, "I apply to other officers respecting any expedition I may chance to project, they always make difficulties: you find expedients."

But the episode was to have a catastrophe far more forcible than the marring of Hawke's career. The tension and heart-burning it caused culminated in a tragedy that distorted, no one can tell how profoundly, the whole course and result of the world-wide struggle. For early next morning, a few minutes after the harassed old King had risen, his valet found him dead.

The tragic end of a reign that was culminating so gloriously was wholly unexpected. No one was prepared. Nothing had been decided, and while every one was forced to be securing his position under the new sovereign nothing could be done. The expedition remained in suspense, while Ministers schemed and

[1] Newcastle to Hardwicke, Oct. 25, *ibid.*

intrigued. Still it was not abandoned. The Irish regiments were already marching, and advices kept coming in of the disturbance the armament was causing in French counsels. Ferdinand himself sent in a report, for the truth of which he could not vouch, that it had stopped the troops ordered against him from Flanders. The regular intelligence agents sent in information to the same effect, and Hawke obtained from a Dutch skipper an assurance that the marching orders of the troops in Southern Brittany had been countermanded.[1]

It is possible these reports had their effect. Within a fortnight of the young King's accession Pitt had established his ascendency; he was on the best terms with the new favourite, Lord Bute; and Newcastle's party, which included Anson, Hardwicke, and Mansfield, were in the shade. In the second week of November the Cabinet met to decide the fate of the Belleisle enterprise, and Pitt was able to obtain a resolution that it should proceed. Nor was this all. On November 14th Anson sent Hawke full details of the expedition that was coming, and orders to despatch a frigate for the Irish units, but that was the last he had to do with it. For Pitt, according to his usual practice where combined operations were concerned, obtained from the King an order that Hawke was to take his instructions from him, and not from the Admiralty.

On the 17th he sent off his secret orders. Practically they relegated Hawke to the position he had so deeply resented in 1757. He was simply told he was to afford every assistance to Keppel and Kingsley, and cover their operations with his fleet.[2] That Hawke would have done

<hr />

[1] Ferdinand to Holderness, Oct. 10; Advices from Versailles, Oct. 31, *ibid.* ; Hawke to Admiralty, *In-letters*, Nov. 6.

[2] Burrow's *Life of Hawke*, p. 433; Hawke to Admiralty, Nov. 26, *In-letters*, 92 ; Newcastle to Hardwicke, Nov. 7, *Newcastle Papers*, 32,914.

his duty in a situation that can hardly have been easy for him no one will doubt, but he was destined not to be put to the proof. In less than a week after Pitt had given the secret orders he was convinced that it was too late for the expedition to proceed, and on November 22nd he told Hawke he was to send back the Irish regiments, and that the expedition had been postponed.[1]

For some time longer it continued in France to cause anxiety for Rochefort, L'Orient, and Belleisle, and everywhere to exercise the ingenuity of the embassies. One was certain that it was going to combine with Amherst against Martinique. Another guessed Belleisle or the French coast. The Spaniards were sure it had been intended for Ostend if Ferdinand could have held his ground, and were equally certain it was now going to Minorca. "Every one," it was said at the Hague, "is impatiently watching for news of the great expedition." [2] Keppel himself was kept in ignorance of its postponement up to the last moment. On November 28th he informed Pitt the expedition was ready to sail, and the Admiralty that he meant to take the first fair wind. A few days later he dropped down to St. Helens to await his final orders. The movement caused a fresh outbreak of alarm along the French coast. As late as the middle of December they were trying desperately to pass troops across to Belleisle in the face of Hawke's light cruisers; the colonels of all the coast regiments were ordered to remain with their colours; troops were passed from Normandy to Brittany; Brest and Bordeaux were in a feverish state of alarm. Till the last possible moment Pitt kept up the threat that could no longer be executed, and it was not till December 11th that

---

[1] Hawke to Admiralty, Dec. 30, *In-letters*, 92.

[2] See *S.P. Foreign* (*Intercepted Letters*), Nov.–Dec., vol. 89.

Keppel was informed that he was not to proceed to sea till further orders, and that he was to disembark the troops at once.[1]

Nothing could illustrate better the importance which Pitt attached to the peculiar deterrent effect of troops upon the sea. Far away in India, as we shall see, it had been felt as keenly as in Europe. There it produced a marked and lasting effect, but at home it was all too late to save the situation in Westphalia. The decisive battle never came. The new army of the Lower Rhine was formed, and though not as strong as had been intended owing to the threat of Keppel's expedition, it sufficed to drive in Ferdinand's right under the young Hereditary Prince of Brunswick. The consequence was that Ferdinand was forced to retire and finally to take up winter quarters, which abandoned Hesse to the French, and left in their hands all the chief passes into Hanover. True, Frederick had balanced the situation somewhat by his costly victory at Torgau, which gave him back the greater part of Saxony; but on the side of Hanover the outlook for the next campaign was very dark. "For God's sake," wrote Newcastle to Yorke in the depths of his depression at the coldness of the new court, "don't name the expedition any more. I don't believe it ever frightened or alarmed France. I thank God it is now unanimously stopped."

---

[1] Paris Advices, Dec. 12, French Intelligence, Dec. 17, *Newcastle Papers*, 32,916; Pitt to Commodore Keppel, Dec. 11, Keppel, *Life of Viscount Keppel*, vol. i. p. 295; Hawke to Admiralty, Dec. 15, *In-letters*, 92; Keppel to same, Nov. 28 and Dec. 14, *ibid.*, 91.

CHAPTER III

MAIN ATTACK, 1760—MONTREAL

IF the operations in Europe had failed to achieve all the secondary effects that had been hoped, in their main function they had been an entire success. Behind them the conquest of Canada had been proceeding smoothly and without interruption. It might even be dismissed as little more than a military promenade, but though no feat of arms like that of Wolfe at Quebec distinguished it, it is still noteworthy as a piece of well-adjusted organisation, and as an example of the overwhelming force of a concentrated attack scientifically conceived, resolutely maintained, and adequately covered.

Amherst, in spite of his failure to penetrate to the St. Lawrence in the previous campaign, had far too great a power of administration, and too fine a talent for working with the Colonial authorities and troops not to be continued in command. His general orders for the conduct of the campaign were sent him by Pitt on January 7th. They gave him practically a free hand. He was instructed to push operations for the invasion of Canada with the utmost vigour. His objective was to be Montreal, but it was left to him to proceed by one or more lines of operation as he deemed best. He was also instructed to have a constant and particular care for Quebec, to inform General Murray, the officer in command, of the operations decided on, and to give him such directions as he thought expedient. Further, he was directed to undertake from Pennsylvania, in the southern area of his command, such operations as he thought necessary for removing all future dangers.[1]

Upon these instructions he proceeded to work out one of the finest combinations ever carried through by British forces. As before, the plan was based upon a convergence of three lines of operations, but with this important modification of the last year's design. His own main attack was no longer to be by Lakes George and Champlain, but by the westerly route which Prideaux and Johnson had opened for him by the capture of Niagara. Upon the old line he would merely employ a minor covering force under Colonel Haviland, one of his most trusty lieutenants, which would confuse the enemy, hold them to Montreal, and prevent a counterstroke upon his base at Albany. The advance on both lines was to be simultaneous, and to complete and emphasise the design a third advance in time with the other two was to be made by the Quebec garrison under Murray. The strategy was excellent, and obviously directed at dealing a decisive blow from which there could be no escape. For some time past Vaudreuil, in his more heroic moments, had been informing the French court that his intention was never to give up the struggle, but as a last resource to retire into the interior, either towards the Great Lakes or the Mississippi, so that when it came to negotiations for peace the King of France could maintain that he still had a footing in Canada. How far this was known to Amherst is uncertain. But it will be observed how nicely his change of plan was calculated to foil such a game, for by his very first move he would seize the proposed line of retreat, and advance along it to deliver his attack. When we consider how often so-called British victories, and not

[1] Pitt to Amherst, Jan. 7, printed by Thackeray, vol. i. p. 465.

only our own, have in similar theatres of war merely resulted in driving the enemy further and further into the
wilds, and only making a decision more and more difficult
to obtain, there seems much to justify the high place
which has been claimed for Amherst as a general.

His line was not chosen because it was the easiest.
It involved enormous difficulties, and amongst them the
descent of the famous St. Lawrence Rapids. To pass a
force of over ten thousand men, for that was the number
of his active column, with its stores, baggage, and artillery
through such a series of obstacles in the face of an active
and desperate enemy, was an enterprise at that time probably without precedent. This is a consideration that
should never be forgotten. Only the strongest military
character could have faced the risk. Yet for the sake of
a decision, Amherst faced it without flinching. Nor was
this all. His plan also demanded the naval command of
Lake Ontario, and his first care was to secure it. At
Niagara he ordered two fine sloops to be built. At
Oswego, which was to be his final point of departure, he
established a royal dockyard, and commenced the con-
struction of half-a-dozen row-galleys, besides collecting
the great flotilla, amounting to some eight hundred boats
and canoes, which his force would require.

While this inland fleet was being prepared in the Far
West, upon the Atlantic there was equal activity. The
naval force which was to assist Amherst upon the ocean
and cover his wide operations, was in three divisions.
There was firstly a squadron of five of the line and four
frigates, based at Halifax, under Commodore Lord Colville,
which on Pitt's orders Saunders had left behind him
to winter on the station in the usual way. A similar
squadron under Commodore Swanton sailed from England
in the early spring direct for Quebec with a convoy of

storeships for the garrison. And about the same time a third squadron of three of the line and two frigates under Captain the Hon John Byron proceeded to Louisbourg with engineers and miners to destroy the fortifications. For "after serious and mature deliberations" it had been decided that it was inexpedient to maintain the place as a fortress.[1]

Such a concentration of force, consisting as it did of thirteen of the line, was more than enough to secure all that was wanted. Indeed, in the strain of the continental struggle, every one at home had dismissed Canada from his mind, when early in June, just as all hope of peace was at an end and Ferdinand was opening his offensive campaign, came the news that Wolfe's conquest was in the sorest danger of being lost. At the moment it was a severe shock. "Who the deuce," wrote Walpole, "was thinking of Quebec? America was like a book one has read and done with, but here we are on a sudden reading our book backwards."

It will be remembered that at the close of the last campaign General Murray had been left with some seven thousand men, more or less fit for service, to establish himself amongst the ruins of Quebec. With so large and well seasoned a force, with a long winter in which to recover its strength, and abundantly supplied as it was with guns and ammunition, no anxiety for his safety was felt. No one had rightly calculated the effects of a Canadian winter under such conditions. The last frigates fired their parting salute; the ice closed in behind them; and the terrors of that frost-bound prison began quickly to declare themselves. To begin with it was found impossible to throw up the outworks which the state of the fortress imperatively demanded. The garri-

---

[1] Pitt to Amherst, Feb. 9, 1760, Thackeray, vol. ii. p. 472.

son, moreover, could not be housed properly or even clothed; fresh provisions were unobtainable, and scurvy added its terrors to the rigour of the merciless cold. Instead of recovering the men began to drop in scores, and it was only continual successes against hovering parties of the enemy that kept the garrison from despair.

Everything that passed within the crazy walls was known at the French headquarters. There Vaudreuil was still governor, and De Lévis commander-in-chief, with Bourlamaque and Bougainville for his chief lieutenants. They knew well enough what to expect in the coming campaign, and saw their only chance was to crush Murray before a new combined attack could develop. This at least they judged was the best chance of being able to keep a footing in Canada till the peace, which they like every one else were expecting, brought the war to an end. Fired with this idea, De Lévis took the extreme step of mobilising his forces in the depth of winter, determined to stake all on a desperate attempt to take Quebec by escalade. Everything was prepared. But the difficulties proved too great. The militia was dismissed, and the regulars returned to Montreal to resume their winter quarters, with outposts at Jacques Cartier, Deschambault, and Pointe-aux-Trembles. They could well afford to wait. Their daily reports from Quebec told them how the winter and the scurvy were doing their work. By March, Murray had not five thousand men fit for duty, and the sickness was increasing. Till April it was left to shatter the garrison still further, and by the end of the month the French began to move. By this time Murray's effective strength was barely three thousand, and he recognised how desperate was his situation. On April 21 he took the ruthless step of expelling the whole of the French citizens, and two days later, the river being now partly open, he sent off one of the sloops that had been left with him to Halifax to hasten Colville to his rescue.

Meanwhile the Chevalier de Lévis was falling down the river with the four cruisers Holmes had been unable to destroy, a whole flotilla of armed vessels and smaller craft, and over seven thousand men, besides Indians. On the evening of the 27th he began to appear on the heights about Sillery and St. Foy. The situation was now desperate. With the enemy once established on the heights of Abraham, Quebec was untenable. It had been Murray's intention to occupy them himself. All the material was ready for constructing an entrenched camp, but the soil was still iron-bound with the frost and field works were out of the question. Murray saw no way out of the difficulty but a bold attack. It was a remedy as desperate as his condition; but, full of confidence in the superiority of his troops, he decided to fling his whole force upon the French advanced guard before their movement was complete. After leaving the necessary guards in the town, he had barely two thousand men available: yet he thought he saw his only chance, and without hesitation delivered a furious onslaught. At first success seemed to justify the boldness of his counter-stroke, but overwhelming masses began gradually to pour round both his flanks, his advance had entangled him and his guns in a morass of melting snow, and in two hours he was forced to beat a retreat with the loss of about a thousand men. The blow meant the annihilation of a third of his potent force, including most of his best men, and for three days the garrison was reduced to such a state of demoralisation that an immediate assault could hardly have failed to carry the ruined city. But De Lévis had suffered almost as heavily, and had to content himself with securing his position on the heights of Abraham.

Murray seized the respite to send another sloop away to communicate his situation to Amherst. He told him he had still hopes of being able to hold out till the fleet arrived to relieve him, and that in the last extremity he should retire to Wolfe's first position on the island of Orléans and there await reinforcements. His despatch was opened by Colonel Lawrence at Halifax, and the news sent direct home with the startling effect we have seen. Amherst did not receive it till the middle of May. He immediately ordered transports to be requisitioned at Boston to carry the Louisbourg garrison to Murray's relief, and supplied their places with labourers for the work of demolition.[1]

Meanwhile De Lévis had sat himself down to a formal siege. It was no part of his plan to risk further loss in an assault. There was still plenty of time to take the place by regular approach if only the stores he was expecting from France could reach him. If they did not, then everything was lost, and the recapture of Quebec was useless. He knew a convoy was coming out with the idea of forestalling the British blockade, as had been done the year before. Its safe arrival would ensure a bloodless success. If, on the other hand, it failed to arrive, there was no hope but to fall back into the interior and concentrate the whole of the Canadian forces at Montreal. So while his army tried to entrench itself and commence its approaches in the frozen ground, his ships were brought down to the Anse de Foulon, and his guns and stores hauled up the cliff by the way the British had made. The process was slow, for Murray had

---

[1] Amherst to Pitt, May 19; Murray to Amherst, April 30; Pitt to Lawrence and to Amherst, June 20.—Thackeray, vol. i. p. 472, *et seq.*

quickly restored the spirit of his stricken force.   All was
activity once more, and the French siege works were soon
being galled by a fire of a hundred and fifty guns.   Still
the weakness of the defences, which there was no means
to strengthen, made the case scarcely less desperate,
and every eye was turned down the river.   At last, on
May 9, a frigate was seen standing up the Orléans
channel.   For a while there was breathless suspense in
both armies.   Was she French or was she English?
Every hand and gun was still, watching for what was
to come.   It was not till she was well in the Basin that
the British flag fluttered out to decide the question.   A
roar of triumph went up from the shattered ramparts;
for every one knew the fate of Canada was decided too.

It was Captain Deane in the *Lowestoft*.   He had
separated in a fog from Swanton's squadron, but he
could promise Murray his chief was close behind.   In
less than a week Swanton himself appeared in the
Vanguard (74) with another frigate.   On the morrow,
amidst a scene of the wildest excitement, he dashed at
the French squadron and drove it with heavy loss from
its moorings.   Ordering his frigates to chase and complete the destruction, which they did in thorough style,
he himself took up a position to enfilade the besieger's
trenches.   It was more than the French could endure.
The game was lost; De Lévis's well-played stroke had
failed; and that night, without striking his camp, he stole
away, leaving all his siege-guns behind him,.   Then, day
after day, the relief-transports kept crowding into the Basin.
On the 18th, Colville and his squadron came in, and
then the happy news was hurried home.   In London, the
drama of Wolfe's year was repeated.   For only ten days
after the first alarming report had reached the government, Murray's despatches came to hand, and all was

once more bonfires and festivity. "Join, my love, with me," wrote Pitt to his adored wife, "in most humble and grateful thanks to the Almighty. The siege of Quebec was decided on May 17, with every happy circumstance. The enemy left their camp standing, abandoned forty pieces of cannon, &c. Swanton . . . destroyed all the French shipping, six or seven in number. Happy, happy day! My joy and hurry are inexpressible.[1]

Pitt had cause enough to feel the relief with elation. The danger had been real and pressing. For, as we have seen, a convoy with stores and drafts for Canada had left Bordeaux early in April, and in spite of the vigilance of Boscawen, who was then commanding on the station, had cleared the blockade with the loss of only three sail. On May 14th they reached the mouth of the St. Lawrence, but only to find that a British squadron had just got in six days before them.[2] To enter the river was now impossible. They therefore ran into La Chaleur Bay, the deep inlet just south of the St. Lawrence estuary. Their hope was to be able to communicate with Vaudreuil over land, but their presence was soon known. Captain Byron, who by this time was at Louisburg assisting in the demolition, heard of it, and immediately left the work of destruction in search of them. At the same time Colville at Quebec sent down a detachment on the same quest. The two squadrons met in the bay, and in a few hours all the French stores of value were on board the British ships, and a score of transports and the frigate that escorted them were in flames.

The same day, July 9th, that the efforts of this devoted convoy were brought to so disastrous an end, Amherst

---

[1] Pitt to Lady Hester Pitt, *Chatham Corr.*, vol. ii. p. 45.
[2] See a captured Journal of the Voyage in *Newcastle Papers*, 32,911, f. 379.

reached Oswego. On June 21st, after seeing Colonel Haviland off with the centre column of some 3500 men upon
the old line of attack northward, he had left Albany, and
his army was streaming over the Great Portage down
to the shores of Ontario. The same week he reached
Oswego, Murray started up the river from Quebec with a
force of 2500 men, which he had been able to form from
the ruins of his garrison. His flotilla and its escorting frigates, sloops, and floating batteries, were under a
Captain Deane. The only serious obstacle in his path
was the Richelieu rapids, which it will be remembered
had been the limit of Holmes's operations in the previous
campaign. They could only be passed at flood-tide and
with a fair wind; the channel was intricate and defended
by batteries, while a little below them was a regularly
entrenched position on the heights of Jacques Cartier.
This was the main outpost of the French, and presumably
it was hoped that its reduction would delay the British
advance. But Murray had learnt from the last campaign
the secret of such riverine warfare, and finding a channel
under the south bank out of range of the French works,
he coolly passed them by and anchored immediately
below the rapids. Owing to persistent contrary winds
the passage of them proved a lengthy affair. Under
cover of the fire of the floating batteries and of perpetual
diversions and raids ashore the force was gradually passed
up in fragments, but it was not till July 26th, ten days
after the operation commenced, that the obstacle was
passed.

Ahead of him at Trois Rivières, where the St. Lawrence
leaves the St. Pierre Lake, lay another entrenched position, but Murray would not be stopped. It was treated
with the same contempt as Jacques Cartier. The troops
were passed by under the south bank, where the French

guns could not reach them, while the Canadians on that side were kept in check by landing parties. So Murray advanced, and as all obstacles seemed to melt before him, parish after parish submitted. By August 9th he had entered the St. Pierre Lake. At Sorel at the lake-head was the main position of the French, for here fell in the Richelieu River from Lake Champlain, the line of Haviland's advance, and it was at this point Bourlamaque was concentrating his force. On August 12th Murray was joined by Lord Rollo with the Louisbourg battalions, and was thus ready to push home his attack well up to time.

Two days earlier Amherst, without waiting for the completion of all his galleys, had left Oswego with his vast flotilla punctually to the day, and at the same moment Haviland began his voyage up Lake Champlain from his advanced post at Crown Point. Nothing could have been prettier. Murray was, of course, somewhat ahead of the other two columns, but the effect was excellent. It forced Bougainville to fall back before Haviland from post to post, for although his forces numbered about 2000 men, he dared not risk any serious resistance for fear of being cut off from the final concentration at Montreal. At the same time it held Bourlamaque at Sorel and prevented De Lévis drawing on that division to reinforce the positions above the city, which were to bar the advance of Amherst. The most advanced of these posts was a little below La Galette, the present Ogdensburg, where on Isle Royale a strong fort had recently been erected and named Lévis, after the commander-in-chief. Had Murray been in command he perhaps would have passed it by, but Amherst was too correct a soldier to permit himself such an irregularity. Nor must it be forgotten that when Murray passed Trois Rivières the dangers of the river were behind him. For

Amherst they were immediately ahead, and it was moreover only by capturing Fort Lévis he could hope to secure pilots for the rapids. Although, therefore, he did not reach the place till August 19th, ten days after Murray was safe in Lake St. Pierre, he decided to invest it, and so gallantly was it defended that it was a week before it was in his hands, and not till August 31st was he able to resume his advance.

It was upon such a delay that De Lévis had counted to enable him to crush Murray or Haviland in detail. But apparently Amherst had counted on it too, and the rhythm of his fine combination was in no way interrupted. Neither Murray nor Haviland were to be drawn. Murray, after landing his force at Sorel and trying to tempt Bourlamaque out of his entrenchments, re-embarked, and slowly pursuing his way up stream as the wind permitted, he forced Bourlamaque to follow him in fear of his joining hands with Haviland. The moral effect at least was excellent. Regulars began to desert by scores, and the militia by hundreds. By the end of the month trustworthy intelligence came down that Amherst had taken Fort Lévis; whereupon Murray seized Isle Therèse, just below the great island on which Montreal is built, and there stood fast. Haviland was equally cautious. Bougainville had fallen right back from the hills into the St. Lawrence valley, and was now in junction with Bourlamaque. Instead, therefore, of advancing direct upon Montreal, as he might have done, Haviland moved farther down the Richelieu River to his right and seized Fort Chambly, the last French post that lay between him and Murray's column. Thence he proceeded to feel for his colleague away to his right, and on September 3rd he succeeded in getting into communication. Murray now lost no time in acting. Two days later, finding Bourlamaque and Bougainville were again falling back, he crossed from his island camp to the south bank with his grenadiers, light troops, and rangers, and on the 6th joined hands with Haviland at Longeuil, the point where the road from Chambly reaches the St. Lawrence, opposite the island of Montreal.

On the very same day Amherst began to land at its upper end.   In five days he had overcome the terrors of those famous rapids with the loss of some fifty boats and less than a hundred men.   It was a feat of which he might well be proud.   True he had not been opposed. The Canadians who, under a tried partisan leader, had been told off to harass the passage, for some reason did next to nothing.   Probably they knew the game was up, as indeed it was.   Halting but a day at the foot of the rapids to repair his shattered boats, Amherst had pushed forward immediately with the utmost vigour.   The same day he landed on Montreal island saw him encamped before the walls of the city.   Murray as promptly hurried back to Isle Thérèse, landed his column on the lower end of the great island, and next morning encamped just below the city.

So, like the striking of a clock, Amherst's wide-flung movements chimed together at the appointed hour.   When we think of the distance the columns had had to travel, the wildness of the solitudes they had to pass, the obstacles to be overcome, and the difficulty of communicating one with the other; if we add the diversity of the troops with which Amherst had to deal, and the skill of the commanders he had to oppose—we seem to have before us one of the most perfect and astonishing bits of work which the annals of British warfare can show.   In the long struggle we had blundered enough—blundered in every conceivable way—in strategy and tactics, in training and organisation; but the national adaptability had told at last. The lesson had been learnt to perfection, and so in the end Canada was cleanly cut from France by a masterstroke of the art of war.

For won it was. The noose had been thrown too dexterously to admit of resistance, and drawn too tightly for surrender to mean dishonour. Lévis and the veteran battalions of France clamoured indeed to fight it out, but Vaudreuil would not permit the sacrifice, and harsh as were the terms on which Amherst insisted as his right, on September 8th all Canada was signed away to the British Crown.

CHAPTER IV

TRANSITION FROM COMMERCE PROTECTION TO ECCENTRIC ATTACK IN THE EAST INDIES

AMERICA was now indeed "like a book that is read and done with." Our object in the war was attained, and the transition from the primary to the secondary stage was complete. France, as we have seen, was still refusing to acknowledge her defeat. She was pushing on more vigorously than ever against Hanover in order to counter our success, and it remained for us to force the energy of our general pressure upon her in order to compel her to accept the situation before she could achieve a counter-vailing advantage.

The passing effort to clinch the pressure continentally by bringing up Ferdinand's force to offensive strength had failed. The attempt was false to Pitt's system, and but for the political and diplomatic exigencies of the case he probably would never have sanctioned it. The true sphere for such supplementary operations, as he knew well, was where our fleet could add its overwhelming impulse to our slender military force—on the coast of France and in the East and West Indies.

In the latter theatres the effect of the changed conditions of the war, which had been inaugurated with the fall of Quebec, are highly interesting. In both areas the operations were originally based on the idea of commerce protection. In the West Indies we have already seen how, as the transition began to make itself felt, this idea

of commerce protection began to be transformed into
an extension of the general offensive, with a view partly
of acquiring guarantees against possible successes of the
enemy in Europe, and partly of coercing her into peace.
In the East Indies the influence of a similar transforma-
tion is now to be observed.

It will be remembered that in the autumn of 1758
D'Aché, the French naval commander, had insisted on
returning to Mauritius in the usual way.   In spite of
General Lally's protests, who, eager to carry out his
orders for seizing the coast factories of the British Company, and fired by his success at St. David's, was burning
to lay siege to Madras, D'Aché absolutely refused to risk
another action with Pocock.   The British admiral, on his
part, after vainly trying to intercept the French squadron
on the way to its base, had also returned to refit at
Bombay on the approach of the monsoon.   This was
Lally's opportunity.   So soon as he knew Pocock was
really gone, he moved against Madras, and on December
12th sat down before the place in form.   The force his
energy had collected was formidable, but the resistance
offered by Governor Pigot and his officers was no less.
For nine weeks the struggle went on without Lally's being
able to make any serious impression.   Still the situation
was very critical; it could not last.   It began indeed to
look as though Madras must share the fate of St. David's,
when, on February 16th, long before Pocock's return
could be looked for, Kempenfelt, who was flag-captain to
Steevens, the second in command, appeared with a couple
of frigates and half-a-dozen transports carrying troops and
stores.   Pocock, unable to move himself without ruining
his fleet and risking the whole situation for the coming
season, had hurried him off from Bombay at the earliest
possible moment.   And he was in time.   As Kempenfelt

anchored in the road, Lally knew that his chance was gone, and in deepest exasperation he broke up the siege and withdrew to Pondicherry.

Meanwhile Clive had so firmly established himself in Bengal that he felt strong enough to send down an expedition under Colonel Forde into the Northern Sirkars, the district lying half way between Calcutta and Madras, which Lally had succeeded in bringing entirely under French domination. Clive had just sent home his secretary to persuade Pitt to extend his offensive to India. He urged how easy was the conquest of Bengal, and that it was in the East rather than the West that England should look for her Imperial destiny. It was full of this faith that he had sent Forde down to the Northern Sirkars, and fully did the expedition justify his conviction. Forde achieved a signal success. On April 8th Masulipatam, the chief town and port of the district, fell into his hands, and Lally found his province confined to Pondicherry and its immediate neighbourhood. It was plain throughout India that the tide was turning against France, and Lally felt his retention even of Pondicherry depended on D'Aché and his fleet.

It was an asset on which he could count with some confidence, for it had been considerably increased. At Mauritius D'Aché had found Captain Froger de l'Éguille with three of the line and several of the Company's ships. They brought his fleet up to eleven of the line, but it was a force greater than the resources of the island could bear. He had to send a dozen ships away to the Cape to get supplies from the Dutch. It was not till July 17th that he was able to put to sea, and then he had to go to Madagascar for rice. In India no one could tell why he lingered. Pocock, determined to be beforehand, had left Bombay with seven of the line the day after Masulipatam had fallen, and had established himself off Ceylon before D'Aché's ships had returned from the Cape. There he cruised week after week, knowing how much stronger D'Aché was, but determined not to let him pass unscathed. At the end of June he was joined by two more of the line from England, bringing out five Indiamen. They contained part of a new King's regiment which Colonel Eyre Coote had raised for service in India, and Pocock, knowing what odds were against him, kept the troops to reinforce his shrunken crews.

But now came a fresh complication. The Dutch, after their manner of fishing in troubled waters, had sent out a powerful armament to increase their own influence, and it was feared they meant to oust Clive from Bengal. As soon as Pocock knew of the danger, he, with his characteristic devotion, sent the troops on to Madras with a strong recommendation that at least part of them should go forward to Clive.

Still there was no sign of D'Aché, and fearing he had missed him, Pocock early in August sailed for Pondicherry. There he remained cruising before the port till the end of the month, when want of water forced him to go back to Trincomalee. As he lay there D'Aché appeared off Batticaloa, twenty leagues to the southward. His presence was unknown to the British, for on September 1st, so soon as his water was complete, Pocock sailed again to resume his station off Pondicherry. D'Aché did the same, and on the morrow the two fleets sighted each other. Pocock after his manner, regardless of the enemy's superiority, immediately signalled General Chase, and all that day and the next strove vainly to bring the French to action. But this was no part of D'Aché's strategy. In his eyes his duty was to throw supplies into Pondicherry, and he felt that if he prevented Pocock from stopping him he won the round. L'Éguille, his new colleague, was a man of different temper, but it was the abiding misfortune of France that most of the admirals she chose could never free themselves from the bonds of her defensive strategy. Excellent in its place, it was certainly out of place in India. The whole problem was one of commerce protection emphasised and made clearer by the vital necessity that France should get quickly into her hands something England could not afford to part with. It depended absolutely on getting command of the sea; D'Aché's force thoroughly justified a bold and sustained offensive; and yet his eyes were closed.[1]

In justice to D'Aché it must be said that there is one possible explanation of his apparently faint-hearted behaviour. According to a sailor who was in the fleet he had ordered seven of his largest ships to board, and had provided the men with "caps and breastplates for the purpose." It is conceivable, therefore, that his tactics may have been designed to secure a certain chance of executing this manœuvre, but the same authority says the whole object of his voyage was to land stores and money at Pondicherry.[2]

Pocock, as though he divined the object that was in his opponent's mind, was not to be beaten, and without making any further attempt to keep contact, gave up trying to engage him away from his port, and pushed on boldly to cut him off from Pondicherry. The stroke was well played. He was off the port on September 8th. D'Aché had not arrived, and it was not till next day

---

[1] D'Aché's force was two 74's and two 64's of the King's, and one 68 and six 54's of the Company's, or eleven capital ships in all (Lacour-Gayet, p. 515). Pocock had seven of from 60 to 68 guns and two 50's.

[2] " Report of a Man who was in the French Fleet," enclosed in Pocock's Despatch of Oct. 12, *In-letters*, 161. Pocock believed this report was substantially correct.

that he appeared. It was now impossible for him to get in without fighting, and he did not refuse the action. Early on September 10th Pocock saw him some eight or nine miles to leeward standing towards the land on the starboard tack in line ahead, with the wind at north-west by west. He at once bore down in line abreast on the enemy's centre. As he approached D'Aché wore on the opposite tack, and Pocock hauling into line ahead brought the two fleets parallel on the same tack in the orthodox manner. The usual action ensued, greatly to the disadvantage of Pocock, for D'Aché's movement had thrown his two rearmost ships out of action, and they were not able to engage at all. From eleven till four the action lasted, seven ships against eleven, so that the British were constantly fighting two to one. Still even so the superior British gunnery told its tale. One by one, as the French received the rapid fire into their hulls, they were beaten out of the line. At last, with D'Aché severely wounded and his flag-captain killed, the flagship herself hauled out. The rest that were still in action followed her lead, and by five the whole French fleet was bearing off south-south-east away from Pondicherry. So far it was a fine victory for the British. But as usual the French had cut our rigging to pieces, and Pocock, being unable to follow, could do no more than lie-to where he was, between the enemy and their destination. Next morning they were seen again, but were soon out of sight, and as Pocock was scarcely able to move, still less to beat back to the northward, they easily worked round him, and while in the far St. Lawrence the French flag was being hauled down on the walls of Quebec, they got safely into Pondicherry.

Thus D'Aché achieved his object, but at tremendous cost. While the British lost about five hundred and seventy men in killed and wounded, the French, according to the report Pocock received, lost about fifteen hundred, L'Éguille losing no less than a hundred and eighty in his own ship alone.[1] Allowing for all exaggeration it was for the numbers engaged a very sanguinary battle. But Pocock was not yet satisfied. On the 12th he anchored at the Dutch factory of Negapatam, and sending thence to Madras received a small reinforcement of men. Thus recruited, on the 20th he put to sea again, and began to work up to Madras in order to cover that place. To reach it he had to pass Pondicherry, and the French fleet was lying in the road. He might easily have run past in the night or have given the danger a wide berth, but that did not suit his spirit. It was liable, he thought, to misinterpretation. So in the true Elizabethan manner he chose to saunter past in broad daylight and in battle order just out of range of D'Aché's guns, with the wind straight off shore. Laying his main topsails to the mast he just kept steerage way, till towards evening the French officers could bear it no longer, and they forced D'Aché to weigh. By the time they were under sail it was of course too late to engage, and as night fell they returned ignominiously to the anchorage, leaving Pocock to continue his way in high contentment.

Angry as the garrison was with D'Aché for the insult he had suffered, their feelings rose to fury when he announced his intention of returning to his base as soon as he had landed the stores and treasure. In vain they protested. D'Aché said the season was too far advanced for further operations, and that he knew a British reinforcement of four of the line was close at hand. Accord-

---

[1] "Report of a Man who was in the French Fleet," *In-letters*, 161, Oct. 12.

ingly on September 19th he sailed. Thereupon there
was a solemn meeting at the governor's, where it was
unanimously resolved that D'Aché's conduct meant the
loss of everything in India, and they held him responsible
for the death-blow of the French power in the East. The
resolution was sent after him by a ship that had been
detained. It overtook him, and he came back. But
still he would not stay, and still protested his mission
was fulfilled. All they could even then obtain from him
was five hundred Europeans and four hundred natives,
and having landed this reinforcement on September 27th
he finally sailed for Mauritius.

It was indeed the death-blow to the French position in
India, as Lally and his officers had protested. It is easy
to exaggerate the effect of the command of the sea upon
Continental power, but in this case it meant nearly everything. The end might be far or near, but if the English
were left in control of the Indian seas there could be but
one end. Above all was it fatal at a moment when the
war was changing to its second phase, and England was
free to turn her commerce defence into a coercive offensive, which the French in the East were left powerless to
resist. What D'Aché the sailor could not see, Lally the
soldier saw too well: and Pocock saw it too.

For some days he had hovered to windward of Pondicherry, but when D'Aché put to sea and went southward
he penetrated the whole situation. Convinced that it
meant a return to Mauritius, and being wholly unable to
chase, he went north to Madras. There he heard that
Cornish was at hand with the rest of his reinforcements,
and after watering he decided he might safely go round to
the Malabar coast to refit. On his way he met the new
squadron with Coote and the rest of his regiment. All
was therefore secure, and sending the troops to Madras he

carried on round Ceylon with the whole fleet till the monsoon should be passed.

So ended Pocock's command. Cornish had brought out his recall, couched in highly complimentary terms, by which he was authorised to hand over the station to Steevens, his capable second in command, and come home for his health.[1] Still he tarried. For as he lay at Bombay refitting his squadron news reached him that the Dutch armament had actually struck at Clive in Calcutta, and he wrote home to say that, until he knew the extent of the danger and how far it was likely to be supported by the governor of Batavia, he meant to remain. The danger was real enough; but Clive knew how to deal with danger. Two Dutch transports arrived in the river from Batavia, bound for their chief factory, which was at Chinsura, some twenty-five miles above Calcutta. Clive promptly sent down word that he could not permit the troops they carried to proceed to their destination. The officer in command submitted, with a request that he might land his men for refreshment at the mouth of the river. It was granted, but he had no real intention of being stopped. He was only waiting for the rest of his force to persist in his mission. Five more ships quickly arrived, and he began seizing all the British vessels he could lay hands on. An Indiaman, under a Captain Wilson, dropping down the river homeward bound, was stopped and told she would be sunk if she tried to pass the squadron. Wilson promptly returned to Calcutta. Two more Indiamen were lying there, and Clive ordered the three to go down together and clear the river. The Dutch were seven to three, but the Company's captains, being better armed, did not hesitate. On November 24th they boldly engaged, and in two hours

---

[1] "Secret Orders," *Out-letters*, 1331, March 30, 1759.

they had captured all the Dutch squadron except the second in command. He escaped down the river, but only to be captured by two other Indiamen that had just come in from home. On shore Clive was equally successful. Before the action the Dutch troops had been landed to march to Chinsura. Forde, the hero of the recent success in the Sirkars, was ordered out to intercept them, and after a sharp engagement he practically annihilated the Dutch force. So the British position and prestige in Bengal were more firmly established than ever, and the Dutch eventually disowned the action of their officers and paid the Company compensation.

It is eloquent of the strategical difficulties of the Indian station that the news of these successes took nearly three months to reach Pocock in Bombay. It is the fashion now merely to deride his battle tactics, which after three actions in eighteen months had failed to secure a real decision, though the tactics which would have secured a decision against a superior force determined to avoid one are never very clearly indicated. More just it would be to praise his vehement "general chases," the daring and resolute attacks which in manner yielded nothing to Hawke's, and above all for the strategical insight and courage which enabled him to dominate a sea which it was practically impossible for his inferior force to command. Thus it was his conduct was justly regarded at the time. In April 1760 he sailed for England loaded with the praises of the Company's officials. At home the King received him with promotion and the Bath, and the India-House with the fullest honours they could confer. He had been sent out "to protect the East India Company's trade and settlements," and well had he done his duty. In one place only did he fail. While he was helpless after his last action, the Comte d'Estaing, a general officer who had broken his parole, struck behind his back with a small expedition from Mauritius at the defenceless factory of Gombroon in the Persian Gulf, and forced it to capitulate. But so small a loss was scarcely seen in the mass of Pocock's success.

It was not till he had seen the fleet ready for a new campaign, and on its way to the Coromandel coast, that he left the station. By his able arrangements Cornish was in position off Ceylon at the opening of the new year with his fresh squadron. Shortly before his arrival Coote had on January 22nd, 1760, completely defeated Lally at Wanderwash, a victory second only in importance to that of Clive at Plassey. Its effect was to enable him to re-duce all the French minor positions in the Carnatic, till at the end of March he was able to combine a joint attack with Cornish on the important port of Carical. It fell on April 5th. As it was the outlet for the rich country of Tanjore, to which Lally had to look for his supplies, the loss was very severe. Accompanied with the British successes in the interior, it meant that Lally had nothing left but Pondicherry, and that his retention even of his capital depended absolutely on the return of D'Aché. But of D'Aché there was no news. At the end of April, Steevens, the new commander-in-chief, joined Cornish from Bombay, and as Coote began to close in methodi-cally upon the last French foothold, Steevens estab-lished a vigorous blockade of the port. In July he was joined by two more of the line, which had been sent out in hot haste at the end of 1759, when it became known how strong D'Aché was.[1] In August Coote completed the investment by land, and still D'Aché did not come.

---

[1] " Secret Order to Captain (Hyde) Parker of the *Norfolk*." The second ship was the *Panther.—Out-letters*, 1331, Dec. 10.

So late in the season he was scarcely to be expected
now. Some unknown cause, it was felt, must have kept
him at the Mauritius. Yet the situation was by no
means easy. The time was close at hand for Steevens to
retire to the Malabar coast, and Coote found himself too
weak to deliver an assault. To starve Lally out was the
only chance, and if Steevens abandoned the blockade
this could not be done. Contrary, therefore, to all precedent the admiral received from Governor Pigot an
urgent request to hold his position despite the stormy
season. Was it the inspiring influence of Hawke's
winter blockade of Brest reverberating to the distant
East ? Who can tell ? All we know is that Steevens
consented. Early in October, when there was no longer
any reasonable fear of D'Aché's appearing, he held away
to Trincomalee to water and refit as he could, leaving five
of the line to continue the blockade, and by the end
of December he was back again in person. Still Lally
stubbornly held his ground, and day by day his devoted
garrison strained their eyes, almost without hope, for the
sails of a relieving squadron. Why did it not come ?
The answer to the question is one of the most striking
points in the war. It brings home to us more forcibly
than ever the far-reaching effect of Pitt's favourite
strategical device, and reveals how coercively the war
was changing its character.

Clive's urgent appeal to Pitt had reached his hands
just after he had received the inspiring news of Quebec.
In this letter Clive told how all in vain he had be-
sought the Company to put him in a position to seize
a country which by an easy conquest would bring them
a revenue of two millions. Possibly, he said, so large a
sovereignty as all Bengal was too great for a mercantile
company, but he urged it was well worthy of the British

government to take such a conquest in hand, and that it might be brought about without draining the mother country of her resources, as had been too much the case with our possessions in America. On November 26th, while Pitt was in hourly expectation of hearing Hawke had destroyed Conflans's fleet, he had an interview with Walsh, Clive's secretary, who had brought the letter home. Pitt received him very cordially, but though he declared he regarded Clive's project as quite practical, he made difficulties. There was doubt, he said, whether under the charter the Company would not be entitled to the conquest, and although the country might easily be taken, he did not believe it could be retained except by such "a genius as Colonel Clive." His successors would probably not be equal to the task.[1]

There the matter rested. Walsh could elicit no further encouragement, but it may be that a seed had been sown. It will be remembered that in April 1760 Newcastle was troubled with suspicions of a new combined expedition, of which Anson knew nothing but to which Hardwicke believed Howe was privy. Earlier in the year Pitt had certainly been bent upon carrying out his long-deferred project against Belleisle. At the time it was suspected that Soubise meant to occupy Flanders, and that possibly the movement portended another desperate attempt to invade. For Pitt it was a reason for renewing his old policy of counter-attack by attempting Belleisle, but the idea filled Newcastle and his friends with alarm. Boscawen apparently had been consulted and had reported against the enterprise, but Pitt was not to be deterred, and according to Newcastle he refused even to look at Boscawen's report, since he knew naval opinion regarded the capture of the island as use-

---

[1] *Chatham Corr.*, vol. i. pp. 387–392, and *note*.

less.[1] However this may have been, the thing was dropped, partly, no doubt, because the information of the intended invasion was soon found out to be false, and partly because Pitt was persuaded to give way and send the "glorious reinforcement" to Ferdinand in order to enable him to take the offensive and get a decision in a more orthodox way.

It would seem, however, that the idea of a combined expedition was not entirely laid aside, but it was now to be directed to a colonial sphere. The contemporary historian of the war, who was usually well informed, asserts that such an expedition was certainly being prepared, and that its objective was the islands of Mauritius and Bourbon.[2] This authority is not, of course, unimpeachable, and no trace of such an intention is to be found in official papers. This, however, counts for nothing when the secret was Pitt's own. In any case, it is certain something of the kind was in his head, and that he communicated it to the East India Company. In April the Company wrote out to the Council in Bengal a long and formal answer to Clive's unending complaints that his importunity for troops was ignored. They showed, on the contrary, that they had done their best, but that hitherto it had been impossible to move the government. Pitt's hands had been too full, but now things had changed. "The force," they wrote, "which went abroad last year and is now destined for India will show how we are working for you."[3] Hence it would seem quite clear that Pitt at this time was certainly planning to extend his offensive to the Indian

[1] Newcastle's "Mem. for business with Hardwicke, &c.," Feb. 18, 1760, *Stowe MSS.*, 263; and Newcastle to Yorke, Feb. 8, *Newcastle Papers*, 32,902.

[2] Beatson, vol. ii. p. 420.

[3] Auber's *British Power in India*, vol. i. p. 71.

Ocean. But there came a cry from Ferdinand for a diversion in his favour. In spite of the "glorious reinforcement" he had been unable to make head, and we have seen how at the last moment the secret expedition had to be reorganised and strengthened with the intention of directing it against the original objective, Belleisle. How it eventually fared must be told later. For the present the effect in India suffices.

There it had already done its work. The menace was enough to upset the whole position of the French in the East. By some means or other they must have got wind of the design almost as soon as it was conceived. For on June 8th a warning reached Mauritius from Versailles that an attack was coming. And not only a warning. For the French government in its alarm felt compelled to order the fleet on which Lally's position in India depended, to devote itself to defending its own base. D'Aché had not yet sailed for Pondicherry when the fatal order arrived. Early in the year a terrible cyclone had overwhelmed both fleet and island with misfortune. Ever since that time he had been busy repairing damages, and now that he was at last ready to try conclusions once more upon the Coromandel coast, he was stopped. For the warning from France of the intended attack brought him strict orders that on no account was he to quit the islands, and that even if he had left them he was to return immediately.[1]

So this is why, on the walls of Pondicherry, Lally strained his eyes in vain for the sails of the fleet which alone could save him. This is the answer to the question why D'Aché did not come. It was another startling result of Pitt's favourite weapon—one more striking

---

[1] Barchou de Penhoën, *Hist. de l'Empire Anglaise dans les Indes*, vol. ii. p. 247 ; Lacour-Gayet, p. 385.

example of the far-reaching disturbance of troops upon the sea. "I don't believe," wrote Newcastle of the abortive expedition, "it ever frightened or alarmed France." He could not tell that even if the threat had not availed to achieve what was hoped in Europe, yet far beyond his ken in the Indian seas it had caused so grave an alarm as to tear from Lally his last hope of retaining his hold for France.

So soon as the fatal order reached D'Aché he sent away two frigates, the *Hermione* and the *Baleine*, to inform Lally that he must now rely on his own resources. Both vessels managed to get into Pondicherry; and so, as Coote and Steevens closed him in, Lally knew the succour on which he had been relying as his only chance would never come. He did his best to keep the sentence of death to himself; he gave out that a great fleet was shortly to be expected; but the end of all was staring him in the eyes. To emphasise the impotence of his position, Steevens one night, by a daring piece of boat-work, cut out both the *Hermione* and *Baleine* from under his guns.

Once and once only there was a gleam of hope. Coote's lines drew closer and closer and his batteries galled more shrewdly, and it looked as if nothing would loose Steevens's hold in spite of the risk he had run in remaining on the coast. But as the old year passed there was a change, and the first hours of 1761 brought down upon the fleet such a cyclone as D'Aché had suffered just a year before at the islands. The havoc was terrible. At the moment the blockading force consisted of eight of the line with a couple of frigates and some storeships. Of these four of the line were dismasted, one driven ashore, two foundered, and the smaller craft fared no better. Steevens alone succeeded in getting to sea in the *Norfolk*, his flagship, and shortly returned all standing. He found Lally had sent far and wide notices that the blockade was raised, and urgent invitations for the despatch of provisions at any cost. But Steevens only set his teeth the harder. In a day or two he was joined by Cornish, who had fortunately been at sea with two of the line, and three more came in a little later. Thereupon Steevens sent out counter-notices to Dutch and Danes that he still had eleven of the line and two frigates, and the blockade remained effective.[1] For the French to hold on longer was useless. The reappearance of the dogged force which even cyclones could not shake off quenched the last spark of hope, and on January 15th Pondicherry capitulated.

So in the end the splendid fabric which the ill-requited sons of France had erected for her in India, fell to fine seamanship. We duly honour the great example which Hawke had set before Brest; his bold institution of the winter blockade has won its true place in our annals; but there is no reason, when we feel the glow of his achievement, why we should forget how the tempests of the changing monsoons were faced triumphantly by Charles Steevens.

Thanks to his courage and the tenacity of Coote, all was lost to the French on the mainland of India. But there yet remained their base in the islands, from which their position had been nourished, and from which it was still open to them to harass our Indian trade. While Mauritius and Bourbon remained in their hands the work was unfinished, and it so happened that the very day Pondicherry surrendered, orders were being issued for the final stroke.

---

[1] Steevens to Admiralty, Feb. 6, 1761, *In-letters*, 162.

In spite of the diversion of the secret expedition
for a European objective, the original intention had not
been lost sight of for a moment. Directly Keppel's
orders were changed for Belleisle, it had been
taken up by the East India Company on their own
account, and at the end of November 1760, when it
was still believed that Keppel was going to Belleisle,
they sent out instructions for the purpose to Madras.
The idea, as they put it, was that as soon as the French
were driven from the coast of Coromandel, the blow
should be followed to the Mauritius and Bourbon; but
the Madras council were given clearly to understand
that the Company had no intention of increasing their
responsibilities by retaining the islands permanently.
The object of the expedition would be to destroy the
fortifications and to ruin the harbours, so that the
French could never use them again. The caveat is
important, for it certainly suggests that Pitt's idea,
while it lasted, had been a permanent occupation. As
to the means, the Indian provincial authorities were
informed that the King's government had procured
twelve hundred men for the enterprise, and that the
Company was raising recruits of its own. At the
moment they were trying to get from Pitt a definite
order for the admiral to co-operate with his whole
fleet, and they assured their officers that success at the
islands was certain if they would do their part.[1]

The efforts of the Company at home fared even better
than was hoped. For no sooner was the Belleisle
project abandoned, as it was too late in starting to
succeed, than the matter was again taken in hand by

---

[1] Secret Committee of E.I.C. to Select Committees of St. George and
Bombay (Extracts), Nov. 23, 1760. Enclosed in Cornish to Anson,
June 21, 1761, *In-letters*, 1761.

Pitt. The completion of the conquest of Canada made an attempt on Mauritius and Bourbon more than ever legitimate as a form of final pressure to bring France to terms. It was exactly suited to the secondary phase which the war had now entered. Consequently, within a fortnight of Keppel's being ordered to disembark his troops at Portsmouth, the original idea was laid before the new king,[1] and a fortnight later again, as Pondicherry was surrendering, secret orders for carrying out the enterprise were drafted and placed in a sealed packet to be taken out to Steevens by Captain Hughes in the *Seaford* frigate.[2] The plan was on a scale that the seriousness of the operation warranted. By the sealed orders Steevens was informed that in March Keppel would sail with a fleet of the line, besides frigates, transports, fireships, and victuallers, that the troops would number ten thousand, besides an artillery train, that they would be victualled for eighteen months, and that Mauritius was the objective. He was, accordingly, to do all he could to co-operate. After detailing a fully sufficient force to protect the interests of the Company in India, he was to send or take the rest of his fleet to St. Augustine Bay in Madagascar. There he would find a frigate sent forward by Keppel to inform him when his force was to be expected off Mauritius, and the two admirals were then to rendezvous eastward of it at the island of Diego Rays.[3] The original idea

[1] *Newcastle Papers*, Jan. 1, 1761, "Mem. for the King. The Two Operations in the East Indies and in Martinico, &c."

[2] "Secret Orders," Jan. 15 and 16, *Out-letters*, 1331.

[3] "Secret Orders," Jan. 16, 1761, *Out-letters*, 1331. Professor Laughton informs me that "Diego Rays" was the name given in Queen Anne's time to "Rodriguez," which lies to the eastward of Mauritius. It is also so called in the *East India Pilot*, 1796. The movements of Cornish and Tiddeman show it cannot have been the present "Diego Rays" which lies to the south of the Maldives.

had been that Pocock should command the whole, but since he had come home Steevens was informed a little later that Keppel was to do so, and that he himself was to remain on the Coromandel coast and merely send his spare ships to Diego Rays.[1]

These orders Steevens never received. He died in May, leaving the command to Cornish. No sooner was the new admiral in office than he found himself entangled in what he regarded as a wild and ill-digested scheme for seizing Mauritius and Bourbon with the forces which the Company had at its disposal. The scheme was the result of the orders which the India-house had sent out in the previous November, when Keppel's expedition was first abandoned. The condition for action on which the Company's plan was based, was fulfilled by the fall of Pondicherry, and Pigot felt himself bound to begin. The idea had already been mooted at the beginning of March between Pigot and Colonel Monson, the officer who had taken Carical with Cornish. In communicating with Steevens the two officers said nothing about the Company's orders. The proposal came as an idea of Pigot himself, and there was a good deal of misunderstanding and delay, especially as Clive was clamouring for the troops intended for the expedition to be sent to Bengal instead. The fact is, that when Pigot first broached the project, the orders from the India House cannot have reached him. It was an idea of his own, but this, apparently, Cornish did not know. He felt that something had been held back from his former chief and from himself. Still, believing Pigot had no real wish to undertake the enterprise, and that he was only trying to entrap him into refusing on naval grounds, he gave a sullen assent,

[1] "Secret Orders," March 4, *Out-letters*, 1331.

and in no pleasant humour went round to Bombay to prepare his part, leaving Commodore Tiddeman in command on the Coromandel side.

The acrimonious correspondence that ensued, boded little hope of success. Fortunately, it was not put to the trial. In July Pitt's secret orders reached Madras. Tiddeman opened them, and, without telling Pigot their contents, he got him to forward them to Cornish at Bombay. He himself took the responsibility of acting on them at once, and sailed with his squadron for St. Augustine Bay. It was not till the end of August that the orders reached Cornish. He, too, was as eager as Tiddeman. Delighted to be rid of Pigot's scheme, he wrote to the governor that he was now proceeding on the King's affairs, and immediately sailed direct for Diego Rays.[1] There the two squadrons met. Tiddeman had not been into St. Augustine Bay, because he had met the frigate which was bringing out Pitt's latest order that Keppel was to command and Cornish to remain on his station. From the same source Tiddeman had also learnt that Keppel would be at the Cape early in September, and he had therefore come on to Diego Rays direct. Still Cornish was too eager for action to go back. He resolved, having come so far, to stay and see, as he said, if there was anything he could do for Keppel.

So, in spite of the last order, the two waited together in keen expectation week after week. October passed into November and still there was no sign of Keppel and his fleet. December came and with it a message

---

[1] Cornish to Anson, June 21, 1761, with its enclosures ; same to Madras Council, Aug. 22 and 31, and to Admiralty, Aug. 31 ; Pigot to Cornish, July 30, *In-letters*, 162. Colonel Monson to Colonel Draper, March 2, *Newcastle Papers*, 32,919.

from our Consul at Aleppo, by way of the Persian Gulf, that the expedition had been again diverted to Belle-isle, and that a peace congress was to meet in July. Though only half willing to believe the tale, Steevens and Ṭiddeman could remain no longer where they were. Provisions were giving out, and in deep disappointment they sailed back to Madras.   There they found the *Terpsichore*, Thurot's old frigate, which they had missed by not going to St. Augustine Bay, and in her were orders eight months old cancelling the whole project.[1] The Consul at Aleppo was right.   Again at the last moment the expedition had been diverted to Belleisle, and a congress was once more on foot.

1 Cornish's Despatch, Dec. 6, 1761, and April 5, 1762, *In-letters*, 162; "Secret Orders," May 18, 1761, *Out-letters*, 1331.

CHAPTER V

THE RESUMPTION OF COASTAL PRESSURE—
BELLEISLE

THE reasons for the second diversion of the Mauritius expedition lie deep in the tangled politics of the war. Since Pitt had first conceived the idea the situation had completely changed, and was twining itself into fresh complexities, which profoundly influenced his strategy.

At the end of 1760 the war had reached a crisis at which it occurred to every one that a balance might be struck. With the completion of the conquest of Canada England had attained her object, and with the other securities she had in hand was in a position to claim all she had fought for. Prussia was nearly exhausted, but had more than held her own. France was in a deplorable condition internally, and quite incapable, with the destruction of her navy, of recovering what she had lost to England. Moreover, she was persuaded she had nothing to gain by pursuing the quarrel of Maria Theresa with Frederick to the death. It was obviously not her interest to leave Austria without a rival in Germany. Every one, indeed, was weary of the cause of " Madame d'Hongrie," and no one but Austria, at least none of the combatants, could discern any advantage in the war being prolonged.

Frederick, with his usual penetration, saw it was the moment to act, and saw what the moment required.

With the new year there came from him a proposal
that England should open communications with France
with a view to negotiating a separate peace without regard
to his own quarrel with the Austrian coalition. The idea
was thoroughly worthy of his ingenuity. The previous
attempt at stopping the war had demonstrated the
clumsiness and indeed the futility of trying to secure
a general peace by means of a congress. The situation
was too complex and the various interests too diverse.
But as between France and England they were plain
and simple, if Frederick himself chose to give England
a free hand. This he could well afford to do, for he had
no illusions as to the real nature of the war. The clear-
ness of his political vision told him that if France once
made peace with her real and original enemy she would
soon find means of forcing Austria to follow her example.
With France and England at one and the great imperial
struggle finished, the minor European superstructure
must quickly collapse. Thus from Frederick's own lips
we have a striking confirmation of the British view of
the war. Like Pitt he saw the Prussian struggle for
existence, with which in modern times the Seven Years'
War has been too freely identified, as a sub-plot of the
world-wide drama in which France and England were
the protagonists. So dispassionate a sense of proportion
is the rarest of political virtues. Pitt's view of the war
could want no stronger endorsement.[1]

In London the proposal was received with mixed
feelings. Pitt held back, and kept finding excuses for
not receiving Frederick's envoys. In his eyes enough

[1] *Newcastle Papers*, 32,917. "Mem. for the King," Jan. 1, 1761, "Precis
of the King of Prussia's Letters"; Newcastle to Hardwicke and Hardwicke's reply, Jan. 3. For the text of the letters to which Newcastle
clearly refers, see Frederick to Knyphausen from Leipzig, Dec. 19 and 21.
Politsche Corr., vol. xx. pp. 156 and 162.

had not been done. He had firmly fixed in his mind that it was his duty to put it out of the power of France ever to resuscitate her navy, and that more must be torn from her before she would consent to the terms he wished to impose. His expedition against Mauritius was almost ready to start, and he was already preparing another for the complete destruction of the French power in the West.

Already in the middle of December he had warned Amherst to prepare to support it by placing the North American garrisons in the hands of provincial troops in order to free the greater part of the King's forces for an expedition " either against Mobile and the Mississippi, or Martinique and the other French islands in the West Indies." The first week in the new year after Frederick's proposal had been received, Amherst was informed more definitely that the expedition was to be directed against Martinique. Such an attempt, however, could not be made until after the hurricane months—that is, not till the end of September or the beginning of October. " In the meantime," Pitt wrote, " as it would be highly expedient for the good of his Majesty's affairs if some interesting attempt could be made with success during the earlier part of the year, the impression whereof could not but have a very beneficial influence in Europe both at home and abroad," he was to endeavour to get away two thousand troops at once, and in co-operation with the governor of Guadeloupe and Sir James Douglas, who was commodore on the Leeward Islands station, to seize Dominica, and, if possible, St. Lucia.[1]

With these projects on foot it was natural Pitt had no desire to treat till the results were in his pocket. Perhaps,

[1] Pitt to Amherst, Dec. 17, 1760, and Jan. 7, 1761, Thackeray, *History of Lord Chatham*, appendix iv.

too, his acute penetration permitted him already to perceive the deep and dangerous game with which the proposed negotiations were likely to be entangled—for which, perhaps, they were only a cloak. On the other hand, the King and his favourite, Bute, were ready to seize any opportunity of escaping from the German war. Newcastle and his friends, together with the powerful Bedford influence, were even more eager for peace, partly from a genuine belief that enough had been done, and that it was bad policy to secure too great a domination of the sea, and partly because nothing but peace could rid them of the detested domination of Pitt.

More powerful, perhaps, than all these ministerial influences were the rise and growth of a serious revulsion of public opinion against the war. It had been aroused during the past year by the publication of a pamphlet entitled " Considerations on the Present German War." With the exception of Swift's " Conduct of the Allies," no such work had ever produced so deep an effect in England, and no history of the war can afford to ignore it either on political or strategical grounds. It was issued anonymously, but was known to be the work of a nonconformist schoolmaster, called Israel Mauduit, who had already come forward as a clever pamphleteer during the controversy over the loss of Minorca in 1757.[1] Coming from such a source, the work displays astonishing ability and understanding. With a full grasp of modern military history, the author makes an ordered attack on the whole system of Continental war into which Pitt had been reluctantly forced. With merciless cogency he points out the political folly of a country with a weak army and a

---

[1] *A Letter to the Right Hon. Lord. B——y* (Blakeney), *being an Enquiry into the Merits of his Defence of Minorca.*

powerful navy engaging in a war between Continental
States, and in an area where the nature of our national
force had everything against it—and all for the integrity
of a small German province in which England had no
real interest. We had already spent upon it, he said,
more than all the cost of Marlborough's war both by
land and sea, and were only sinking deeper and deeper
into the mire. The whole is a frank and forcible appeal
to the insular national spirit. No adequate justice is
done to the place which the Continental operations held
in Pitt's system, but it is not ignored. The necessity of
covering Hanover is met by the argument that that
country, from its geographical position, was not one that
France would care or could afford to hold permanently—
an opinion which shortly afterwards was expressed by
Choiseul himself.[1] The argument was plausible, and to
some extent sound, though it certainly does not cover
the other complex diplomatic considerations which had
forced Pitt's hand, and which the public was not likely
to recall.

Most remarkable, however, of all Mauduit's conten-
tions is the strategical argument with which the latter
part of the pamphlet is occupied. "Every one," he
writes, "who has thought on the subject of war, must
have considered the three different kinds of it—a war
of offence, a war of equality, and a war of defence. And
every one knows that of these the last is the most dis-
advantageous and the most difficult. When an army
is to defend itself only, a general will find employment
for all his attention; but if it be to defend a large tract of
country, unless the attacking general be greatly inferior
in his art, he will usually prevail. The reason is that

---

[1] To Hans Stanley. See Stanley to Pitt, June 12, 1761, Thackeray,
vol. i. p. 523.

the general who acts offensively has it in his own choice
when and where to direct his main force, while the
defender must equally divide his." Further, he points
out that, if the attacking party fails, it merely means that
he must try again, whereas if the defender be defeated,
it means disaster. So in the long run defensive war
has scarcely a chance of succeeding. In dyke countries,
like the Netherlands, where fortified lines can be used
effectively, he admits defensive war may be strong, but
shows that even there the Duke of Marlborough had
always been able to penetrate any lines the French
could make. Now, our whole war in Westphalia was
in conception a defensive war. Ferdinand's army was
in theory an army of observation, a defensive army,
to cover Hanover and Frederick's right. Recently, it
is true, by the late "glorious reinforcement" an effort
had been made to enable it to pass to the offensive.
But Mauduit argues that even this idea is fundamentally
unsound, because in the Westphalian theatre we must
always be inferior, for no matter how many troops we
sent, France could always send more. Consequently
to adopt the offensive was bad, because we could never
be in sufficient superiority to push it to its logical conclusion by invading France itself. From this undeniably
good point he proceeds to develop on the most modern
lines the whole theory of the supremacy of the offensive,
rounding up with the conclusion that our right line of
action was upon the sea against the enemy's oversea
possessions, since in that way we could employ the arm
in which our supremacy was overwhelming, and which
enabled us to take the offensive legitimately and with
resistless power. From beginning to end, it is the doctrine
which sees the British army as a sword in the hand of
the fleet.

The weak point of the argument of course is that it treats the Continental operations as a separate war instead of as the defensive part of the whole. Still it remains the most striking criticism of Pitt's war-direction that exists. Where the learning and the very modern exposition of the theory of war came from is hard to say.[1] The hand was the hand of the dissenting schoolmaster, the mind was Lord Hardwicke's. Every one at least understood the pamphlet was issued with his countenance, and as we have seen his letters at this time are full of sound and advanced strategical thought.[2] It was, perhaps, hard that he should turn Pitt's own cherished theory against him. But the case was serious; politics are pitiless; and no one can expect to sin against the inexorable laws of war, however courageous the motive, without finding the sin come home to roost. It was Pitt's own system that the pamphlet developed, and the wound was the deeper for the true temper of the weapon. The power and clear conviction with which the case was reasoned, the obvious mastery of the question which it displayed, were irresistible. Attempts were made to answer it. By the army men still devoted to *la grande guerre* it was ridiculed in the way we know so well. "These are sounds," they mocked, "drawn from speculation, paper-staining warriors, and castle-building politicians, but they are disclaimed by

---

[1] It does not occur in Puységur's *Art de la guerre*, 2nd ed., 1749, nor in the *Rêveries* of Marshal Saxe, published in Paris in 1757, and at The Hague by M. de Bonneville, capitaine ingénieur de campaign in the Prussian service in 1758. Comte Turpin de Crissé has something like it in his *Essai sur l' art de guerre*, 1754, and still more in his commentaries on the *Memoirs of Montecuculi*, but this was not published till 1770. Nowhere is found at any rate the important distinction of the middle term, "war of equality," meaning where the two belligerents are equally balanced enough for each to seek to attack the other.

[2] See *ante*, p. 84.

practice and experience. Every war in its own nature becomes offensive, whatever the pretences may have been upon which it was originally founded. If an army of defence can offend the enemy, the means of offence becomes the most effectual principle of defence." [1] All this, though of course perfectly true, was beside the point; it missed the fundamental distinction between major and minor strategy, and displayed an incapacity to understand the eternal conditions of the offensive and the whole theory of the classification on which Mauduit's argument was based. Naturally, it failed to convince. In spite of the mockery of the Continental school, its influence continued to spread. In a few months it went through six editions, and Mauduit eventually received a Government post from Bute. Pitt, of course, entirely shared Mauduit's views, and would gladly have gone back to his old system had it been possible at the stage the war had reached. "If the King," he said to Bute at this time, "is not for the war on the Continent, I am ready to abandon it, though I think it a right measure." [2] Here he was probably correct, given the fact that the best chance of tiring France of further resistance was to support Frederick, and Pitt's instinct for concentration of effort justified his feeling that now was the time to throw all the weight we could into that particular scale. For him to do things by halves was the one unpardonable course.[3]

With such a weight of opinion behind Frederick's proposal for bringing the war to an end, it was impossible

---

[1] *A Full and Candid Answer*, &c. (Brit. Mus. 8132, a. 51, p. 71).

[2] Newcastle to Duke of Devonshire, Mar. 13, 1761, *Newcastle Papers*, 32,920.

Newcastle to Hardwicke, Jan. 3, 1761, and Hardwicke's reply, *Newcastle Papers*, 32,917.

to resist it. Secret negotiations were opened through The Hague, and proceeded so fast, that by February 22 an intimation had come from Versailles, that if a British agent were sent to Calais in a fortnight, Choiseul would simultaneously send an agent to Dover, and pourparlers could begin in both capitals at once.[1]

To all appearance France was as sincere as she was eager. But this may be doubted. At this time Marshal Belleisle, who was regarded as the strongest advocate of peace at the French court, fell ill. Choiseul, the firmest believer in his country's power of recovery, was dominating the situation, and when, on February 25th, the Marshal died, Choiseul took his place at the War Office, with practical and partly direct control of foreign relations as well. That Choiseul was already engaged in a subtle game with Spain is certain. It was a game which, if successful, seemed sure to place him in a good position either to continue the war or to insist on easy terms for peace. It was this game which Pitt had possibly detected. He saw the old shadow of Spain across the path, and by the sudden change in the objective of his expedition, he was making ready to deal with the lurking antagonist.

On March 4th, it will be remembered—about ten days that is after the French had agreed to open secret relations—the last order about the attempt on Mauritius had been signed for despatch to India. At that time, therefore, and indeed for some days later, Pitt's intention must have been that the enterprise against the French islands should go forward. Yet in ten days more, on March 25th, the King had signed secret orders for Keppel to make Belleisle his objective.[2] What had

---

[1] Newcastle to Hardwicke, Feb. 22, *ibid.*, 32,919.
[2] Keppel, *Life of Viscount Keppel*, vol. i. p. 302.

happened in that three weeks' interval? Nothing that
can be detected, except the interception of some highly
confidential Spanish despatches that were in a bad code
and easily deciphered.

To grasp all that these compromising documents said
to Pitt, it is necessary to understand exactly how our
relations stood with Spain. First, it must be recalled
how at the end of September in the previous year, the
tone of the Conde de Fuentes, the Spanish ambassador,
had suddenly changed. The claims he had been sent to
settle related to certain ships seized during the war, in
the exercise of our belligerent rights over enemy's goods,
but mainly to the settlements which our West Indian
colonists had made in Honduras for cutting logwood, and
to an alleged right to complete freedom of fishery on the
Newfoundland coast and in the Gulf of St. Lawrence.
Wall, who had never swerved from his Anglophile policy,
honestly believed that Pitt would eventually settle these
matters in a liberal spirit for the sake of Spanish friendship; and hitherto Fuentes had been urging the matter
in a friendly and equable tone. That Spain had much
reason to complain of our dilatoriness is not to be denied;
but when Fuentes suddenly assumed a peremptory tone,
and at the same time made the extraordinary statement
that the Spanish claims had been communicated to
France, it could only be interpreted as a threat that was
not to be endured.

The notorious Marquis of Ensenada, the arch-Anglo-
phobe in Spain, had been recalled to court by Charles the
Third. In 1754 he had been banished for instructing
the Spanish governors to make a piratical attack on the
British in the West Indies, such as John Hawkins had
suffered at San Juan de Luz two hundred years before.
The natural inference was that Wall's friendly influence

was waning and Ensenada's taking its place. But the truth was that Wall himself was losing patience, and the real motive force was the energetic and not too wise King himself. Pitt answered in the firm and high tone that was natural. "I must observe to your Excellency," he said, "that we are quite unable to understand the motive and object of so extraordinary a communication to a court at war with England, and which in any case or on any consideration has not any business to interfere with Spanish claims on us to the Newfoundland fishery." He referred the matter to Hardwicke, and even the level-headed, peaceable old lawyer was staggered. "I own," he wrote, "I never was more surprised in my life than at the style and turn of these two extraordinary pieces, so different from what there was reason to expect from the mission of M. de Fuentes; but what could not fail to strike most was the previous and unprecedented appeal to the Court of France avowed in the memorial relating to the Newfoundland fishery;" and he heartily approved Pitt's dignified and forcible answer. As to the Honduras and other claims, although, as he said, the manner and tone of their presentation disgusted and offended him, he wished parts of the claim were not so well founded upon the merits. But he warmly applauded the step which Pitt had taken in the matter, which was in a very temperate despatch to instruct Lord Bristol in Madrid to confer confidentially with Wall.[1] Since then relations had only been going from bad to worse. The Spaniards continued to arm both by sea and land. At the end of January, the Marquis de Grimaldi, a protégé of Ensanada's, who had also been in Wall's confidence, was called from

---

[1] Hardwicke to Pitt, Sept. 29, 1760, *Chatham Corr.*, vol. ii. pp. 68–72, and *notes;* Pitt to Lord Bristol, Sept. 26.—Thackeray, vol. i. p. 487.

The Hague to take the Spanish Embassy in Paris.[1]   On
December 23rd and January 3rd Fuentes again presented
his claims, and Pitt absolutely refused to listen to him.
Wall kept pressing him to get an answer, and on January
23rd he wrote to say it was useless.   Pitt would add
nothing to the despatch he had written to Lord Bristol.
At the same time Fuentes gave Wall to understand that
Pitt's inexorable attitude was not generally approved, and
that a strong party, headed by the Duke of Devonshire,
were bent on unseating him.   This letter was intercepted,
with what effect upon Pitt can be imagined.[2]

Meanwhile Grimaldi had arrived in Paris and continued his correspondence with Fuentes.   The whole of
this was also intercepted.   Grimaldi opened on February
15th, with information that, although there was an
ardent wish for peace in France, he was officially informed no direct negotiation had begun.   Choiseul was,
however, trying to get Russia and Austria to agree to
terms which he believed England and Prussia could not
fail to accept.   Grimaldi enjoined absolute secrecy, because
he meant to try to get some advantage out of it.   "I do
not know," he concluded, "whether our court will come
to it, but I think it my duty to propose what may be
useful to us and I judge it necessary without exposing
the King."   Ten days later another letter was intercepted, saying that France was resolved to make peace
on the basis of *uti possidetis*, and that Vienna and St.
Petersburg had assented.   It was absolutely necessary
to keep this from the English court, for, as he said, "In
consideration of this and of our situation, I begin working

---

[1] Grimaldi to Fuentes, Jan. 30, *S.P. Foreign* (*Intercepted Letters*), 91.

[2] Fuentes to Wall, Jan. 23, 1761, *Newcastle Papers*, 32,918.   See also
Chatham Corr., vol. ii. p. 89, where only the latter part of the letter is
given.

in order to see if we can make some alliance with France which may protect us from those accidents we ought to fear."

So far then it would look as if Grimaldi thought peace certain, and had hovering in his mind the idea which was to develop into the famous " Family Compact," to secure Spain against the maritime domination which the peace would confirm to England. On March 5th he wrote a third letter, saying he had begun his intrigue and had informed Madrid for approval. " It appears to me," he wrote, " of the utmost importance for us to assure ourselves of France, and engage her before she makes peace : for afterwards I do not know what inclination she may have to go to war again for our sake. I return your excellency a thousand thanks for your advices about the English expedition. . . . The notion of making proposals to England for a congress continues, and I believe will be made ; but for all this peace is not yet." On March 10th Fuentes replied in terms which showed he thoroughly understood that Grimaldi's game was to deter France from consenting to peace by offering to make common cause with her, and thereby to drag her into the Spanish quarrel. In a week Fuentes wrote to Paris again to say amongst other things the expedition was about to sail, but that he had nothing to add about its destination. He was delighted with Grimaldi's progress. " If," he concluded, " we behave with proper resolution—as I hope we shall—and if the Court of France thinks and acts as it ought, I promise myself great satisfaction, and the greatest of all will be to reduce this nation to proper limits, and to reason, which they do not know." On March 20th he wrote in the same strain to Wall. " If France," he said, " continues the war, we shall be able to operate more at our ease. However, the blow will be none the less certain if the King is willing to strike alone."[1] On the top of these stirring discoveries there was received on March 17th a formal intimation from Paris that the French secret agent had been appointed and was about to start for England.[2]

With all this information before him, Pitt had reason enough to make Belleisle and not the Mauritius the objective of his expedition. If war with Spain was coming, it would not do to send so considerable a part of our force into the Indian Ocean. There would be demand and use enough for it nearer home. Again, if we were really on the brink of peace with France, it was desirable to improve our position at once by a telling stroke before negotiations began. Success in the Indian Ocean would have no effect, for, as Hardwicke had pointed out at the first, the result could not be known for a year.[3] On March 18th the instructions for our diplomatic agent, Hans Stanley, were settled, and they conclude with a significant direction that he was " to give watchful attention to the conduct and motions of the Spanish ambassador " in Paris.[4]

Pitt thus saw the country committed to negotiations for peace ; but for him that was only a reason for pressing the war to its utmost energy. The week that followed was devoted to this end. On March 24th he wrote again to Amherst to tell him that " an early impression on the enemy in America would not fail to have the most material, and probably a decisive, influence on the Court of France." He was therefore to endeavour to deliver

[1] See *Chatham Corr.*, vol. ii. pp. 89–101. Fuentes's letter of March 10 is also in *Newcastle Papers*, 32,920, and is endorsed as having been read the same day. None of this correspondence is amongst the "Intercepted letters" in the Record Office, *S.P. Foreign.*

[2] Hardwicke to Newcastle, March 17, *Newcastle Papers*, 32,920.

[3] Hardwicke to Newcastle, Jan. 3, 1761, *Newcastle Papers*, 32,917.

[4] Thackeray, vol. i. p. 509.

the attack on Martinique the moment the hurricane months were passed, and to the six thousand troops he had been told to despatch, he was to add every man who, in his opinion, could be spared. Further, he was to take up transports on the spot, to prevent the possibility of delay from the failure of a sufficient tonnage coming from home.[1] It was the day after this letter was penned that Keppel's secret instructions for Belleisle were signed, and four days later the expedition had sailed.

Still no countermand was sent to India. Possibly Pitt believed that a quick success would clinch matters with France, and that he would be able, with Bristol's help in Madrid, to get ahead of Grimaldi's intrigues in Paris. Such an impression must have been strengthened ten days after Keppel was gone. For on March 31st Pitt received from Choiseul a memorandum concerning the peace, assuring him of his good faith and of his intentions to treat the King of Prussia in a liberal spirit in the proposed congress, and confirming the retention of conquests as the basis of negotiation.[2] More probable, perhaps, is the view that Pitt, knowing what he did from the intercepted Spanish correspondence, read in Choiseul's memorandum a mere device to gain time till he could gather the fragments of the French navy into some show of a fleet, and till Spain had completed her armament. It is, at any rate, certain he was for adopting a very high tone for the answer to the memorandum, as though he wished to unmask the Franco-Spanish game by forcing Choiseul's hand, and so be in a position to strike before the enemy had time to concert their measures for the revival of the war.

---

[1] Pitt to Amherst, March 24.—Thackeray, vol. ii. p. 499.
[2] Copy in *Newcastle Papers*, 32,921 March 26.

Three days after the receipt of Choiseul's memorandum, Pitt had a talk with Newcastle, in which he formulated his views. In answer to Choiseul, he proposed to say that the British Government would not entertain the idea of making any compensation for the evacuation of Hanoverian territory. He was ready, he said, to defend it, but not to purchase its restitution. On our own account he would insist on retaining the whole of Canada and Cape Breton, and the exclusive right to the Newfoundland fisheries; and he was for giving the French agent to understand at the outset that on no consideration would these demands be abated. Newcastle objected that Spain would never consent to a monopoly of the fishery, even if France would; but Pitt was unmoved.[1] He must have believed as firmly as Newcastle that his attitude would in all probability break off the negotiation at once, and this was apparently his real desire. For everything points to the fact that his keen intuition had already convinced him that France would not suffer us to gather the fruits of the war while she had Spain to fall back upon, and that Spain, moreover, was determined to intervene.

A few days later he had an audience of the King, in which he pressed the same course of action. He urged that he was far from hopeless about the war in Germany, where Ferdinand had opened the campaign with a brilliant if desperate stroke at Soubise, and had forced him to retire out of Hesse and fall back on Frankfort. As for the rest of the war, our successes in the East and West, the prospects of the coming expedition against Martinique, on the heels of that against Belleisle, would place us in a position to make the demands he had formulated. But the King was unconvinced. He argued

---

[1] "My Conversation with Pitt," *Newcastle Papers*, 32,921.

strongly against any peremptory declaration, and so the matter had to rest.[1]

To add to Pitt's vexation, his rebuff was followed immediately by news that Keppel had failed at Belleisle. It was scarcely surprising. The constant reconnaissances that had been going on, and the long postponement of the enterprise, had given the French warning and time enough to reinforce the garrison and greatly strengthen its defences. Moreover, the military part of the expedition was far from what Pitt had intended. At the outset the King had vetoed the despatch of two old regiments, because, as he said, to Pitt's disgust, our safety at home was endangered in several quarters.[2] The influence was probably the old Duke of Cumberland, to whom the young king was showing marked deference and attention.

To the same influence, at least partly, must have been due the appointment of General Hodgson as commander-in-chief. He had been one of Cumberland's numerous aides-de-camp both at Fontenoy and Culloden, and was a thorough Duke's man. Writing to his friend Lord Albemarle, the commodore's brother, he says, " Amongst other flattering things his Majesty was pleased to say, he told me he should always have a partiality for the officers bred under the Duke: he looked upon that as the best school." [3] In the present war he had commanded the first brigade at Rochefort, and been one of the famous council of war which, as Wolfe put it, decided unanimously " not to attack the place they were ordered to attack, and for reasons 'that no soldier will allow to be sufficient." Still, times had changed since then, and with

---

[1] Newcastle to Hardwicke, April 17, *ibid.*, 32,922, and see Albemarle's *Memoirs of Rockingham*, vol. i. p. 23.

[2] Barrington to Newcastle, Jan. 2, *Newcastle Papers*, 32,917.

[3] Keppel, *Life of Keppel*, vol. i. p. 298.

them the whole spirit of the service. Keppel at least must have approved his colleague's appointment, for he was an old and intimate friend of his family ever since he had served as aide-de-camp to the commodore's father at Dettingen. Pitt, too, expressed his confidence handsomely, gave him *carte blanche*, and kissed him when he said good-bye.[1] It was the composition of the force that was wrong. To begin with, it was far short of the designed ten thousand men. Though nominally comprised of twelve battalions, it mustered only seven thousand. Most of the regiments were quite unseasoned, and two of them in so disgraceful a condition of discipline and equipment that Keppel wanted to leave them behind. To complete the trouble a large proportion of the officers were absent.[2]

The transports for the force numbered about a hundred sail. The escorting fleet consisted of ten of the line, all of the lighter kind except one, and eight frigates, besides sloops, bomb-ketches, and fireships. Keppel had also a covering squadron off Brest, consisting of three or four sail, so little was the old danger point to be feared.[3] It was under the immediate command of Commodore Matthew Buckle, who had been Boscawen's flag-captain throughout the war. As such he had been present at the capture of Louisbourg, and had brought home the despatches from Lagos. He also had had the luck to fight at Quiberon. Boscawen himself had died suddenly of typhoid fever early in January as the squadron was being brought forward for sea, but the influence of "old Dreadnought" was in the ascendant, and was evidently great enough to secure the command for his most trusted officer.

---

[1] Keppel, *Life of Keppel*, vol. i. p. 298.   [2] *Ibid.*, pp. 300-1.
[3] Keppel to Admiralty, May 21, *In-letters*, 91.

Hawke's unlucky star, as Newcastle had foretold, was waning. His peerage was still denied him. Pitt, who had never liked him, had been exasperated, as we have seen, at his failure to grasp the possibilities of the situation at Quiberon, and his original patron, the old king, was dead. This scant recognition of the admiral's services, however, was by no means confined to Pitt. There certainly existed a general dissatisfaction. To all appearances his last command had been entirely barren and inactive. No service had been done of a kind to touch the popular imagination. It was forgotten how little the completeness of his victory left him to do. Still it was not to be denied that the ships which had escaped into the Charente and the Villaine remained in the security they had reached, and no attempt had been made to destroy them. In January two of them, with a couple of frigates, actually got away to Brest under the charge of a few brilliant young officers, who had volunteered for the service. It could hardly be argued in Hawke's favour that their destruction was impossible, for he had been in the act of attempting a carefully elaborated operation to that end when he had received the first intimation that Keppel's expedition was coming. Later critics have supported the opinion of the time in severely censuring his inactivity. There is, however, this in support of his attitude. The operation he contemplated was essentially one for a military force, and if he had reason to expect that a military force was coming, it was at least correct not to hazard the fighting efficiency of his fleet and his power of keeping control of the sea by exposing a large part of his crews ashore. Moreover, when he abandoned his own scheme, he was only told that the expedition was postponed—not that it was abandoned. All, indeed, that can fairly be laid to his charge is that his genius for using the command of the sea was not equal to that which he displayed in obtaining it; or, as Pitt succinctly put it, he was a fine sea-officer but no minister.

At the end of January, when the menacing attitude of Spain could be ignored no longer, Anson had ordered him to send home all his three-deckers. A week later he was told to bring them home himself, and in March, just as Pitt decided finally to send Keppel against Belle-isle, he struck his flag at Spithead. Now, therefore, he was enjoying the repose that his long winter blockade had earned, and took no part in the revival of the coastal warfare which had been inaugurated under his flag at Rochefort.

Pitt's resumption of his original policy is worth close study. That policy has come to be judged by the Rochefort expedition. Its real exemplification was at Belleisle. It is there in its ripest form we should look not only for the strategical power of such designs, but also for the character and spirit of the operations they demand. For though the force, both in its units and in its commander, seemed tainted with the old Rochefort sickness, its performance was in every way the antithesis of that unhappy fiasco. It is true the first attack of Keppel and Hodgson proved, as has been said, a failure, but it was just this failure that marked how great a change had been wrought in the spirit of the services since Pitt first took the war in hand.

Owing to adverse weather it was not till April 6th that they were off Belleisle, but six frigates had already been thrown forward to cut off its communication with the mainland. Working in during the night, the fleet rounded the south end of the island at daybreak, keeping close inshore so that a reconnaissance could be made as it passed. The inspection was not encouraging. Every accessible point was well entrenched and guarded by batteries. Still, at an inlet midway upon the south-eastern shore, known as Locmaria Bay, both Keppel and Hodgson thought they saw a chance. They were for

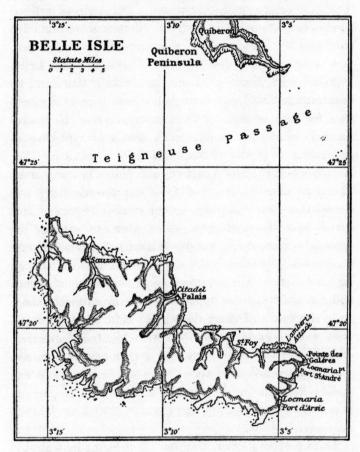

attempting it on the spot, but the wind was southerly, almost dead on the landing-place, and it put an attack out of the question. They had to pass on, and at noon the whole fleet anchored in the road opposite Palais, the chief town and fortress of the island, which lay on the

north-eastern shore facing the mainland. Not to waste
time while the flat-boats were being prepared for the
troops, the two chiefs at once proceeded together in a
cutter to reconnoitre the extreme north end, where stood
the little fishing port of Sauzon. But here, as everywhere, they found the garrison alert and formidably
entrenched. " The coast," wrote the general, " is the
most inaccessible I ever saw, the whole island is a fortification." To both of them the task looked almost
desperate, but no longer was that a reason, as at Rochefort, for not trying. " The enemy," wrote Hodgson,
" have been at work upon it ever since Sir Edward Hawke
appeared here in the winter, but all this is nothing. The
fashion of the times required extraordinary measures.
Therefore when we returned from our reconnoitring we
agreed that Port St. Andro, on the south-east part of the
island, was the most practicable place to attempt a
descent." Here surely was Wolfe's spirit burning. Again
we can hear the echo of the words he wrote in his shame
for Rochefort : " The greatness of an object should come
under consideration as opposed to the impediments that
lie in the way." Indeed the whole conduct of the enterprise was in exact accordance with his trenchant and
soldierlike criticism. Here was no council of war, no
considering whether an attack was feasible or not, but an
instant decision by the admiral and general in perfect
harmony to try, and try hard, where the thing looked
least ugly.

From Keppel's letter it appears Port St. André was the
same little bay they had reconnoitred the previous day
near Point Locmaria, and here on the morrow they set
to work. To ease the difficulty of the task, Captain Sir
Thomas Stanhope of the *Swiftsure*, who had been knighted
for his conduct in Boscawen's action at Lagos, and had also

fought well at Quiberon, was ordered to make a demonstration to the north against Sauzon with two battalions
and the marines. With the rest of the troops in the
flat-boats Keppel went southward, sending forward two
of the line to destroy a battery that commanded the
beach at Port St. André. This was quickly done, and
the troops were at once pushed forward for the strip
of sand that had been marked for a footing. Above it
rose the hills in an amphitheatre, where the enemy were
entrenched up to the teeth. Under a destructive fire
the troops moved in, and effected the landing with boldness and precision. But it was only to be brought to
a hopeless standstill. The foot of the hill had been so
cleverly scarped away that it was impossible to reach the
enemy's breastworks without scaling-ladders. Desperate
attempts were made, but all in vain, and Generals Crauford and Carleton, who were in command, decided to
retreat. Meanwhile a party of sixty grenadiers, who
landed at a little distance from the rest, succeeded in
climbing up beyond the entrenchments, and formed on
the top. Could they have been supported all might
have gone well, but unfortunately their success was not
seen in time, and before anything could be done all but
twenty were killed or taken prisoners.

It was a gallant but unhappy beginning. Though the
retirement had been well covered by the ships and bomb-
vessels, the loss was about five hundred men. To make
matters worse, as the troops were getting back to the
fleet a severe gale blew up, lasting all night and all next
day, and in the end half the flat-boats on which a landing depended were lost. Both commodore and general
became seriously discouraged. At first Keppel, in announcing the defeat to the Admiralty, had quietly
informed them they were going to find a better place

and try again.   But that proved not so easy.   After careful reconnaissances they could find no spot which gave any hopes of success, and a few days later both of them wrote home to Pitt that they regarded it as quite impracticable to make good a landing.[1]   Seeing the situation Pitt was in at the moment, the repulse was a serious blow to his influence, but it does not seem that he lost heart for a moment.   Instead of repining, he immediately ordered off four more battalions with a fresh supply of boats and military stores.   So determined was he to succeed that, even at the risk of delaying the Martinique enterprise, he devoted to the Belleisle reinforcements some of the transports preparing to go out to New York to carry Amherst's troops to the West Indies, and for their escort he called for five more ships of the line.[2]

He knew his men.   With such a war-seasoned band as they were despair did not last long.   A week later they were joined by a number of transports bringing on four troops of light dragoons which had not been ready to sail with the fleet.   They at once decided to try again, since the new-comers would enable them to support a fresh attack with two feints instead of one.   This was important, for the attempt was to be on a new plan, modelled apparently on Wolfe's great exploit.   Both the commanders were still of opinion that all the ordinary landing-places were impregnable; but it was thought, says Keppel, "that by attempting a place where the mounting of the rocks was just possible," and where the enemy consequently had not thought of entrench-

[1] Keppel to Admiralty, April 13, *In-letters*, 91 ; Hodgson to Pitt, April 12 and 18, and Keppel to same, April 18—Albemarle's *Life of Keppel*, vol. i. pp. 306–310.

[2] Pitt to Amherst, June 18—Thackeray, vol. ii. p. 500.

ing, they might succeed. Such a chance seemed to offer at a point just to the southward of Port Locmaria, where stood a small work called Fort d'Arsic. Here was to be the main attack, and Crauford, the second in command, was again entrusted with it. He was to be assisted by a feint, under Brigadier Hamilton Lambart, upon the little village of St. Foy, which stood on the opposite or northern side of Point Locmaria, the eastern extremity of the island.[1] This demonstration was to be supported by Stanhope from the sea with three of the line and a "forty-four." At the same time the demonstration against Sauzon to the northward was to be repeated by the newly-arrived dragoons, with two of the line and some frigates.

By April 22nd all was ready. At daybreak the ships were in position and at work with the batteries, while the troops gathered at their stations. By three o'clock the enemy's guns, not without considerable damage to the ships, were silenced, and the attack began. Crauford made for Fort d'Arsic, where he found the enemy ready and in great strength to meet him. Lambart, however, reached the shore without a shot being fired, and finding himself unobserved, landed his force about half-way between St. Foy and Point Locmaria. There was not a soul to oppose him, but above his head towered cliffs that the French regarded as defence enough. Lambart was of a different opinion. He had been told he might push home his feint if he saw a fair chance, and he thought he did. It was a case of the Heights of Abraham over again, and he had at least one good precedent to justify his daring. The grenadier company of

---

[1] Keppel to Admiralty, April 23, *In-letters*, 91; Engineer Welsh's Survey, *King's Drawings, Brit. Mus.*, $\frac{\text{LIX.}}{73}$.

the 19th Foot led the way and succeeded in reaching
the summit, still unobserved. A detachment of marines
followed, and before the enemy, whose attention was
absorbed in watching Crauford's column on the other
side of the Point, could recover their surprise, more
troops had joined the advanced parties. At last, from
the height upon which the enemy were watching Crauford, they were attacked by half a battalion of regular
infantry, but posting themselves behind a low wall, they
held their ground with a steady fire till Lambart himself
joined them with another grenadier company and the
rest of the marines. He immediately ordered an advance, attacked the enemy in flank, and forced them
to retire under their guns at the top of the hill they
had come from. Below Captain Stanhope had been
eagerly watching the brilliant feat of arms from his
ship, and the moment he saw the advance he signalled for all his boats, manned and armed, to support
Lambart's attack. The movement attracted Crauford's
attention. With quick perception he saw what it
meant, and promptly followed suit. Abandoning his
own attack on Fort d'Arsic, he hurried back round Point
Locmaria to his colleague's assistance. Thus, thanks
to the quick appreciation of Stanhope and Crauford,
Lambart soon found himself strong enough to press
home his attack and supplant his opponents in their
commanding position. By five o'clock the whole of the
troops were landed, and before night Hodgson was
securely posted with all his force on a height three miles
in the interior.

There, as they lay upon their arms all night, they saw a
great beacon fire reddening the sky in the centre of the
island. It was the signal of Monsieur de Sainte Croix,
the gallant and capable officer to whom the defence of

the island had been entrusted, for all the troops and inhabitants to concentrate on Palais. He had at his command three regular battalions and one of militia, numbering probably at this time nearly three thousand men. The Duc d'Aiguillon, at the first alarm, had arrived at Vannes, and was gathering a large force on the mainland. His intention was to throw in more troops, but the vigilance of the cruisers which Keppel had pushed forward put it out of the question. With a strength numbering barely half what the British could land, it was useless for Sainte Croix to try to hold the whole island, but it was a force quite capable of a prolonged defence of the fortress. Hodgson quickly overran the island as the French retired, seized all the defenceless ports, and so soon as the weather permitted the necessary stores and material to be landed, he sat down to besiege Palais, securely covered by Keppel's fleet.

The news of the British success came as a serious shock to Versailles. The exact extent to which it modified the French plans is as usual difficult to determine. By heroic exertions Choiseul was collecting a vast force of a hundred and twenty thousand men, which was to form two armies under Soubise and Broglie, and finally crush those of Ferdinand and the Hereditary Prince of Brunswick. Such numbers were of course overwhelming, and Ferdinand had been forced to retreat again out of Hesse, but not before he had destroyed all Soubise's advanced magazines. Such a loss must necessarily delay the opening of the campaign, and on the top of it came the news of Belleisle. According to our most trustworthy intelligencer the Court was very anxious about it. It was seen, he said, that once the island was entirely in British hands, it could be used as a *place d'armes* to alarm the whole coast from Brest to Bayonne. To increase the trouble there was

serious discontent in Brittany, and it is said there was a
proposal to recall at once thirty battalions from Germany.[1]
This was certainly not done. It seems, however, that it
was found necessary to provide D'Aiguillon with twenty-
two battalions and eight squadrons, and Pitt received
from the Dutch ambassador at Paris intelligence "that
the whole line of Soubise's corps was altered." That is
to say, that the Normandy troops had to be moved into
Brittany, those of Picardy into Normandy, those of
Flanders into Picardy, and these, finally, had to be
replaced from Soubise's active army. We also know that
an inquiry was held as to why D'Aiguillon had too few
troops to reinforce Sainte Croix while the sea was open,
and the answer was that Choiseul, in order to swell Soubise's army, and in spite of the protest of the War Office,
had recalled troops which Marshal Belleisle, while he was in
office, had considered absolutely necessary for the defence
of the coast. The one hope of relief now was to get a
squadron to sea to engage Keppel's attention, and the
result was that, instead of being able to devote all his
resources to answer Pitt on land, Choiseul had to order
the most strenuous efforts to be devoted to the ships at
Brest and Rochefort.[2]

These last preparations Keppel soon detected for
himself. He heard that seven of the line were being
brought forward at Brest and eight at Rochefort, and the
news was confirmed from home. The danger naturally
caused him some anxiety, and drew from him a highly
interesting expression of what he regarded as the correct
strategy to meet the occasion. Assuming the two French

---

[1] Cressener's Intelligence, May 4, *Newcastle Papers*, 32,922.

[2] Memorandum in Newcastle's hand, May 13, *Newcastle Papers*, 32,923;
Cressener's Intelligence, May 16, and other Paris advices, May 22 and 24,
ibid.

divisions were under orders to combine against him, he
said he intended to keep practically his whole force concentrated at Belleisle; but as soon as the expected reinforcement which Pitt had ordered arrived, he would
send a squadron to Rochefort to stop that division
mobilising. He could not, however, conceal his apprehension that the French ships might get to sea before
he could blockade their ports effectually. " Indeed," he
added, " the confining them at Brest is so very precarious
that it cannot be depended upon, and therefore I should
imagine Captain Buckle and his ships being called here
would answer the purpose better than his remaining
there—unless ships could be spared to make him as
strong as the Brest ships, while the King's squadron,
[meaning his own], after despatching one to Rochefort,
remains equal to both the enemy's squadrons at Brest
and Rochefort." He concluded by saying he was going
to order Buckle to fall back on him if the French came
out and were superior.[1]

The principle that was guiding him was practically
that on which Pitt had been acting all along. Where a
military force was engaged in coastal operations from a
sea base, it was not a just risk to trust to the blockade
of the enemy's fleets at their points of departure. The
covering fleet itself ought to be equal to them, or so disposed as to ensure concentrated equality with any concentration which the enemy might be in a position to
make at the point of operation.

On this principle therefore he acted till, at the end of
May, his reinforcements began to arrive. Six of the line
joined him by April 31st, and he at once detached
Stanhope with a division of six, besides fireships and
bombs, to prevent the Rochefort ships getting out into

[1] Keppel to Admiralty, May 21, *In-letters*, 91.

the Basque Roads, and also to keep his eye on Bordeaux. During the next week two more ships of the line joined him, and he thereupon sent away to Ushant five to bring Buckle's blockading force superior to that which was said to be in Brest. Though only a captain, Keppel now had some twenty of the line and as many cruisers under his broad pendant, so that, with eight left for himself, he was able to enjoy the disposition he wanted. With the landing of the fresh regiments, which arrived simultaneously with the ships, the position of Sainte Croix was therefore hopeless. The wall of Palais was breached; relief was impossible; and the gallant French soldier knew it as well as any one. Accordingly, on June 8th, he capitulated, being allowed, as he richly deserved, to march out through the breach with all the honours of war, and was conveyed to L'Orient with all that was left of his force.

CHAPTER VI

SPAIN AND THE FALL OF PITT

THE great news reached London on June 13, and the country was once more ablaze with bonfires and illuminations as in the intoxicating days of 1759. The effect, of course, was greatly to increase the strength of Pitt's attitude on the terms of peace; and he certainly needed all the support he could get. Things had been moving fast. Not only were the negotiations for the separate peace between France and England proceeding apace both in Paris and London, but all the Powers had accepted the proposal for a general Congress, and plenipotentiaries had already been named. Lord Bute had replaced Holderness as Secretary of State for the Northern department, and thus had the continental war and its diplomacy in his hands. At present, it was true, he showed a strong inclination to act with Pitt, but at any time his own instability and Pitt's domineering might shift him to the opposite camp. There the peace forces were closing up, and had received a powerful addition in the person of the Duke of Bedford. He had recently resigned the Lord-Lieutenancy of Ireland, and was attending the Cabinet, where he quickly earned the reputation of being the only man bold enough to face Pitt.

Nor was it only in the dignity and power of its members that the peace party was strong. The arguments by which they supported their views were states-

manlike and widely convincing. By no one were they
so cogently put as by Bedford, and from the mouth of
no one did they come with greater weight, for his
unwilling admiration for Pitt was evident to all. Though
he has not lived in history as a statesman of mark, his
utterances at this time are instinct with a political
wisdom and insight that, whether his own or not, are
little short of prophetic. What troubled him most was
not the continental war, though that he believed to be
beyond the resources of the country, both in treasure
and manhood. His firmest opposition was to Pitt's
determination to crush the French sea power out of
existence by refusing them the right of fishery in Newfoundland and the St. Lawrence Gulf. To exclude
France from the fisheries, Bedford argued in a letter to
Newcastle, would give umbrage to Spain and the other
maritime powers; for it would be a great step to the
monopoly of a trade which was the source of all maritime power, "and which," as he said, "would be as
dangerous for us to grasp at as it was for Louis XIV.
when he aspired to be the arbiter of Europe, and might
be likely to produce a grand alliance against us." France
would never acquiesce for long in a peace concluded upon
such terms, and to make a peace that could not last was
emphatically bad policy.

Nothing could shake his well-reasoned convictions.
They grew stronger as time went on. " Indeed, my lord,"
he wrote to Bute two months later, " the endeavouring to
drive France entirely out of any naval power is fighting
against nature, and can tend to no one good to this
country; but, on the contrary, must excite all the naval
powers of Europe to enter into a confederacy against us,
as adopting a system, viz., that of a monopoly of all
naval power, which would be at least as dangerous to

the liberties of Europe as that of Louis XIV. was, which drew almost all Europe upon his back." It was all the modern doctrine, so firmly insisted on by Clausewitz and so seldom recalled by our "idolaters of Neptune," that measures, however plausible, which tend to raise up fresh enemies do not increase the strength of our international position. So strongly did Bedford feel this truth that he even doubted the policy of excluding France from Canada. He dreaded our overloading ourselves with colonial possessions, as Spain had done to her ruin, but that was not the darkest outlook. "Indeed, my lord," he wrote to Newcastle, "I don't know whether the neighbourhood of the French to our North American colonies was not the greatest security for their dependence on the mother country, which. I feel will be slighted by them when their apprehension of the French is removed." How prophetic were both warnings we know. Both were destined to be fulfilled to the letter ere twenty years were gone.[1]

Such arguments as these could not but have weight. Indeed even for us to-day they would go far to condemn Pitt's attitude did we not know how strong and well founded was his conviction that the coalition which Bedford feared was already on foot. Too much had been done already to let Spain rest. Even Bedford grew doubtful whether France was in earnest for peace. The complaisance with which Choiseul accepted the basis of *uti possidetis* and the seizure of Belleisle, made him question whether she was not merely seeking to gain time in order to recover breath for a new and more dangerous war.[2]

---

[1] Bedford to Newcastle, May 9, *Newcastle Papers*, 32,922 ; same to Bute, July 9, *Bedford Corr.*, vol. iii. p. 24.

[2] Bedford to Bute, June 13, *Bedford Corr.*, vol. iii. p. 14.

Choiseul's proposals about the "compensations" had come. He suggested the return of Guadeloupe, Marie-galante, and Goree in exchange for Minorca; was ready to cede all Canada except Cape Breton, which, however, was not to be fortified by France, but merely used as a fishing station; and in return for the retention of the fishing rights she would give up all her conquests upon England's allies in Germany.

The dominant note of France, it will be observed, was the preservation of her sea power, and as the negotiations progressed it became more and more evident that it was upon this question they would turn. From this point of view Choiseul's proposal was very unsatisfactory, for it said nothing about the fate of Dunkirk, Ostend, and Nieuport. Still Pitt expressed himself ready to treat on this basis, and two Cabinets were held to discuss the answer. Under the pressure of the peace party he somewhat relaxed his attitude. The majority of the Ministers were clearly against insisting on the exclusive right of fishery, and Lord Granville, the President, with all the weight of his great reputation, strongly indorsed Bedford's arguments on the impolicy of doing so. He was for reviving the terms of the treaty of Utrecht both as to the Newfoundland fisheries and the fortification of Dunkirk. Pitt, in reply, drew attention to the obscurity and duplicity of Choiseul's note, as pointing to the insincerity of France. For himself he said he would rather risk another campaign than give way on the fishery question at all, but if the rest thought otherwise he would acquiesce. Bute was urgent for a shifty compromise by which we were "to make trial," that is, we were still to demand the exclusive fishery and give way if France stood firm. Pitt, much to Bute's annoyance, ridiculed the idea, and tried to persuade the King it was useless to "make trial" unless we meant what we said. Eventually it was left to Pitt to answer Choiseul, and his draft was to be settled in the Cabinet next day. After a renewed and somewhat heated discussion on Bute's compromise, Pitt's view was finally accepted in a modified form—that the fisheries " could not be given up except for some substantial compensation." [1]

So the words stand in the despatch which Pitt sent to Stanley in Paris, with the significant addition that the question of the "substantial compensation" could be discussed with that of Dunkirk. For the rest Stanley was to say the British court regarded Belleisle as an equivalent compensation for Minorca, and that if we ceded Guadeloupe and Mariegalante as well, France must immediately vacate all her conquests in Germany. As the minimum on which the King's intentions were "fixed and unalterable," he was to stipulate for all Canada and Cape Breton unequivocally: Senegal: Dunkirk to be unfortified on the footing of the treaty of Utrecht: the Neutral Islands in the West Indies to be evacuated, and Minorca restored. Finally he was to give Choiseul to understand, as delicately as might be, "that the most indispensable interests of Great Britain can never allow his Majesty to acquiesce in any views of acquisition which it has sometimes been surmised France might entertain with regard to Ostend and Nieuport." [2] In other words, the maintenance of the British naval position in the Narrow Seas as well as in the Mediterranean and America, was made a *sine qua non* of the continuance of the French sea power. It was on the question of Dunkirk and the Flemish ports that most difficulty was

---

[1] For what passed at these two meetings, *i.e.* June 24 and 26, see Newcastle to Devonshire, June 28, *Newcastle Papers*, 32,924.

[2] Pitt to Stanley, June 26, Thackeray, vol. i. p. 549.

expected, yet every one, even Bedford, felt this condition must be insisted on. " I have never myself," he said, "been much in apprehension of invasion of England . . . but, however, for the satisfaction of the nation, too great security cannot be taken to guard against any future alarms." [1]

Having clearly presented the British claims, Pitt took care not to relax for a moment the pressure necessary to force them home. The preparations for Martinique were pushed on without disguise, and Keppel was told to attempt some place on the French coast within striking distance of Belleisle.

Captain Stanhope, in pursuance of the commodore's directions to prevent the mobilisation of the Rochefort division, was already destroying for the third time the works on the Island of Aix, in spite of the French bomb vessels; but Keppel felt doubtful about the possibility of a descent on the mainland. L'Orient and Port Louis were tempting, he said, "but everywhere, as far down as Bordeaux, the alarm has caused a formidable concentration of troops." [2] This was of course well, so far as it went. It was part of Pitt's object, as before, so he assured Newcastle, to draw troops away from Westphalia, where the campaign was opening in form. [3]

The effect, however, in this direction seems to have been small. According to our intelligence a few regiments were moved down from Soubise's army, but the bulk of the coastal defence force came from the central provinces and from Languedoc and Provence. By these means Choiseul considered he rendered the coast safe,

---

[1] Bedford to Bute, July 9, and Bute's answer, July 12, *Bedford Corr.* vol. iii. p. 23 *et seq.*
[2] Keppel to Pitt, July 10, *Newcastle Papers*, 32,925.
[3] Newcastle to Devonshire, June 18, *ibid.*, 32,924.

and vowed that no landing in Oléron, Rhé, or any of the neighbouring French islands should induce him to recall a single man from Germany. He was even prepared to risk the Martinique expedition striking in Normandy rather than weaken Soubise's push for Hanover.[1] Still the pressure by the blockade alone was severe, and to add to it came the news that in the East Indies Pondicherry had fallen, and that in the West Douglas, with a force from New York under Lord Rollo, had seized Dominica.

Once more Amherst had shown his brilliant powers of organisation. Pitt's idea, it will be remembered, was to seize the islands of Dominica and St. Lucia before the hurricane season came on, so as to leave all clear for Martinique in the autumn. For this it was necessary that the expeditionary force should be on the spot by the end of May at latest. It was not, however, till January that he despatched the order, and he did not disguise from himself that it was only by a lucky passage of his despatch vessel and of the reinforcements that were necessary that the thing could be managed, and then only if Amherst had sufficient troops in a state of immediate mobility. Yet it was done. On June 4th, only a week or so late, Lord Rollo, with three of the line and as many frigates from the North American squadron, met Douglas at Guadeloupe, the appointed rendezvous. His military force was four battalions from Amherst's army, besides rangers and artillery, and not a moment was lost. Two days later they were before Roseau, which the French had made the capital of Dominica, and next day, though the inhabitants made a plucky attempt at resistance, it was seized by a *coup de main*.

The capture was one of naval value. Being a neutral

---

[1] "French Intelligence," July 2 and 3, *ibid.*, and July 14, *ibid.*, 32,925.

island under the treaty of Aix-la-Chapelle, and only recently occupied by the French, it was not intrinsically rich, but in Prince Rupert's Bay it could boast an un-rivalled roadstead admirably placed. It had, moreover, become a paradise for French privateers, and failing St. Lucia, which it was then too late to attempt, no island afforded a better strategical position, if war in the West Indies was to be renewed with Spain and France. This was all beside its political value at the moment—a value which Douglas was "minister" enough to understand. So soon as it was in his hands he sent a vessel home with the news, apologising that as they had heard many reports of a congress he thought it best to let the government know as soon as possible of their "little acquisition," as he called it.[1]

An extension of the war grew every day more certain, at least in Pitt's eyes, and the prospect of having to deal with Spain as well as France became more and more the dominant note of his war plan. Already, before the blow at Dominica had been struck, he had elaborated a scheme for pushing the operations in that quarter still further, and instructions had gone out to Amherst to have another large force ready by the time the hurricane season was over to go down to Barbadoes in order to take part in a great concentration against Martinique and all that the French had left in the West Indies. This order, as we shall see, was only part of his great scheme to render the intervention of Spain impotent when it came.

As the weeks went by the outlook at home served only to mark the wisdom of the precautions he was taking and the necessity for energetic action. By the third week in July no answer had come from Choiseul, and the

---

[1] Douglas to Admiralty, June 13, *Admiralty Secretary, In-letters*, 307. See also same to same, June 3 (with enclosures), *ibid.*

news from Westphalia was that Soubise and Broglie were actively engaged in a great combined movement to drive Ferdinand from the position he had taken up to cover Hanover on the line of the Lippe. As the two French armies amounted to nearly double that of Ferdinand the situation looked very ugly. Pitt's impatience and distrust of Choiseul increased every day, and so far infected his colleagues that it was decided to call a Cabinet on July 21st to consider his suspicious procrastination. Every one felt something must be done and done quickly, "the affected slowness in the negotiations on the part of France," as Pitt said, "combined with the vivacity of her operations in the field . . . being too dangerous to the sum of affairs, and too interesting to his Majesty's honour, to be longer acquiesced in." [1]

It was while the atmosphere was thus highly charged that Choiseul's answer at last arrived. It reached London on July 20th, just in time to be considered by the Cabinet on the morrow. The new Memorial appeared to be a frank endeavour to meet the English views. Choiseul was ready to give up Minorca in exchange for Guadeloupe and Marie-galante; to evacuate the French conquests in Germany in return for Belleisle; to consent to the British occupation of the neutral island of Tobago if France might retain St. Lucia; to permit to England the choice between Goree and Senegal; to settle the relations of the two East India Companies on the basis of the *status quo ante bellum ;* and to refer the question of the prizes taken before the declaration of war to the British Court of Admiralty; but he resolutely insisted on the fisheries and the retention of Cape Breton for a fishing station as the price of guaranteeing to England the conquest of Canada. As to Frederick, France would withdraw all her auxiliaries from Austria if

[1] Pitt to Stanley, July 25.—Thackeray, vol. ii. p. 554.

England withdrew the German forces in her pay from
Prussia.   She offered also as the British forces were recalled from Westphalia to recall double the number of
her own.

So far there was a distinct advance towards an agreement, and had there been no more there was little reason
why an equitable arrangement should not have been
reached.   But unfortunately the counter-proposals were
accompanied by a "Private Memorial" which was as
soothing as the explosion of a mine.   It was nothing less
than a bare-faced proposal that Spain should be invited
to guarantee the treaty.   The Memorial stated that the
Spanish Court had communicated to Versailles its three
points of dispute with England, viz. the restitution of
Spanish ships captured during the war; the right to fish
on the banks of Newfoundland; and the demolition of
the British log-cutting settlements in Honduras.   Worse
still, it was declared that France regarded the settlement of these differences with Spain as essential to
the conclusion of a lasting peace with herself.   Alone
this was objectionable enough.   It was sufficient to open
the eyes of the most sceptical to the game France and
Spain were playing; and by a nation elated and confident with successful war it could only be regarded as
an insolent threat.   But to make matters still worse and
leave no room for doubt, Stanley informed Pitt that it
was only with difficulty he had persuaded Choiseul to
relegate the Spanish claims to a separate document, and
not to incorporate them in the articles proposed for the
treaty of peace.   Personally, he did not think that
France, having given up Canada, would be in a hurry
to go to war about logwood, and he had told Choiseul
plainly we were not to be frightened by Spain.   This
hopeful opinion, however, he modified by a later dis-

covery that he had made. It was that France and
Spain had come to an agreement as to joint action before
ever the present negotiations had begun, and that Spain
had offered to exchange Puerto Rico for Minorca.[1]

At the same time, to add fuel to the fire, Bussy, the diplomatic agent whom Choiseul had sent to London, presented
a note on the subject of Prussia. It was to the effect
that since the presentation of her first proposals, France
had received Austria's consent to the principle of a separate
peace, but on two conditions. One was that the Empress-
Queen should keep possession of all the Prussian territory
which her armies occupied, and the other that England
should cease to support Frederick either with her own
troops or those of Hanover and the subsidised allies.
France on her part was to withdraw her succour from
Austria. Bussy intimated that France had acquiesced
in these "natural and equitable" conditions, and that
she expected that England would do the same. In Pitt's
eyes it was no better than a shameless invitation for
England to break her solemn word to Frederick, and to
the high sense of honour which was one of his most
marked characteristics it was insolent beyond endurance.[2]

So on the morrow, in hot blood, the new counter-
proposals were considered by the Cabinet, and with one
voice condemned as insulting and inadmissible. Pitt,
indeed, appears to have had things entirely his own way,
and was permitted to frame an answer in his highest and
most dictatorial tone. Bussy received it face to face,
and that there might be no mistake he had it repeated
in a note next day. "It is my duty," wrote Pitt, "to
declare farther to you in plain terms, in the name of his

---

[1] Stanley to Pitt, July 14, *Newcastle Papers*, 32,925. See also under
July 20, *ibid.*

[2] Thackeray, vol. ii. p. 553.

Majesty, that he will not suffer the disputes of Spain to
be blended in any manner whatsoever in the negotiations
between the two crowns. . . . Moreover, it is expected
that France will not at any time presume a right of
intermeddling in such disputes between Great Britain
and Spain. . . . I likewise return to you, sir, as totally
inadmissible, the Memorial relative to the King of Prussia,
as implying an attempt upon the honour of Great Britain."
Nothing could well be stronger; and to Stanley Pitt's instructions were equally forcible.   To add to the heat of his
spirit news had just come in of the fall of Pondicherry and
the capture of Dominica.   Two days later, on July 22nd,
came tidings of even greater moment.   Ferdinand, beyond
all hope, had soundly defeated Broglie in his first attempt
to strike.   The general elation was scarcely less than
after Minden.   "All is triumph.   All is joy," wrote
Pitt.[1]   And no wonder.   The victory had been as unexpected as Minden, and again it had been won mainly
by the British troops.   Granby, indeed, had directed the
action, and, as Ferdinand handsomely stated, he had only
arrived on the field to be an ordinary spectator of his
lieutenant's admirable dispositions.   The result of the
victory was entirely to upset the combination of the two
French armies, and to give great hopes that Ferdinand
would be able to hold his position on the line of the Lippe.

The effect upon the whole balance of the war Pitt was
careful to point out to Stanley, and the despatch was
further seasoned with the information that the transports
which were to go out to America to fetch Amherst's
contingent for the Martinique expedition had received
their sailing orders.   He also told him that in the opinion

---

[1] *Grenville Papers*, vol. i. p. 377, July 22.   See also Jenkinson to Grenville, July 21, *ibid*, p. 376 ; and *Newcastle Papers*, 32,925, July 20 and
July 22 (Hardwicke to Newcastle).

of the British government France had now left no room
for doubt that her whole object from the beginning had
been merely to gain time to push her operations in
Germany, and that as for the French engagements with
Spain, the British government regarded them " to have
been as disingenuously suppressed as they were now in
the moment insolently produced." " In this view, therefore," he wrote, " and in consequence of the unanimous
opinion of the second council held yesterday, his Majesty
has commanded me to send you the enclosed paper
containing conditions of peace . . . to serve as an answer
to the French Memorial of the 13th, and as the ultimatum
on the part of Great Britain." Further, Stanley was " to
express without asperity, but with all firmness, a desire
for a categorical answer," intimating at the same time,
with politeness and regret, " that otherwise your stay in
Paris cannot probably be long." [1] The enclosed paper
which Stanley was to present as an ultimatum was a
counter-proposal which amounted practically to falling
back to the original terms suggested by the British
government in the spring, though Stanley was instructed
that he might give way a little about Dunkirk and the
west coast of Africa.

The justification of Pitt's high attitude comes from
Choiseul's own pen. About four years later, when all
was over, he drew up a long memoir for the King in
defence of his policy. As seen and presented by him at
that time his conduct of affairs, no doubt, possessed an
artistic roundness which it may have lacked in reality,
but still there is little doubt the memoir represented
fairly well what his aims had been.[2] From the moment

---

[1] Pitt to Stanley, July 25.—Thackeray, vol. ii. p. 554.
[2] " Mémoire présenté à Louis XV.," Feb. 1765, Soulange-Bodin, *La
diplomatie de Louis XV. et le Pacte de Famille.—Pièces Justificatives*, B.

that, at the end of 1758, he had superseded Bernis at the
Foreign Office, he had set himself to bring the maritime
war to an end.   The increased power of England upon
the seas he believed he could balance in Europe by
getting for France the Flemish ports, and above all by
placing her at the head of a Bourbon confederation which
would include Spain, Sicily, and the Duchy of Parma.
In 1759, when Charles was about to proceed to Spain, he
had nearly succeeded in arranging an interview at Lyons
between him and Louis, but the influence of the Spanish
queen Maria Amelia brought it to nothing.   In November 1760 he tried again—this time going so far as to
propose a naval coalition against the domination of
England which Holland was to be forced to join.   But
under the same restraining influence Charles replied that
his fleet was not as yet in a condition to make such a
thing possible.[1]

Early in the next year, however, when Choiseul was
appointed War Minister, and the Spanish queen died, he
thought he saw in the proposal for a Congress a better
opportunity.   Persuading his master that England was
not in earnest for a general peace, he obtained permission
to attempt once more some arrangement with Spain.   It
was at this time that the old Spanish ambassador was
recalled and Grimaldi put in his place.   Choiseul's plan
was, while the general negotiations for the Congress proceeded, to enter into separate negotiations with England.
To this course, he boasts with pardonable pride, he obtained the consent of Austria and the other allies of
France in spite of their suspicions.   There was certainly
room enough for suspicion.   He further says he knew Pitt's
character too well to expect success with him, but that
in his second interview with Stanley he became convinced

[1] Bourguet, *Le Duc de Choiseul et l'alliance Espagnol.*

that Pitt's position was growing precarious, and that Bute
and a strong party in England were eager to end the war
in order to destroy his dictatorship.[1] " I then," he says,
" proposed to your Majesty two games to play together :
one to keep up the negotiation with England in such a
way that if it did not succeed this time it would serve
from its simplicity as a base for the genuine negotiation
which must take place if Pitt fell before the influence of
Bute. At the same time—and this was the second game
which I thought essential—I entered into an exchange of
views with Spain, so devised that if we were to make
peace that crown would find it to its interest to support
us in the negotiation, and guarantee the stability of the
treaty. If, on the contrary, we failed in this, my plan
was that Spain should be drawn into the war, and that
France would be able to profit by the events which this
new complication might produce and repair her losses.
Finally, if the event proved unfortunate, I had in view
that the losses of Spain would lighten those which France
might suffer." A policy so Machiavellian, so astutely
selfish, compels a certain admiration, but it certainly
justifies Pitt's passionate instinct that it deserved nothing
but swift violence.

Choiseul's path had not been easy. To begin with, the
readiness with which Grimaldi seized the first opening to
propose an offensive alliance against England frightened
him.[2] It looked like a snare, and he believed the ambassador was ahead of his court. This was true, but
Grimaldi's arguments and dexterity soon brought Charles
up to the point of a defensive alliance, though he still

---

[1] This is one of Choiseul's artistic touches. He proposed the treaty on
May 12 (Bourguet, p. 207), before Stanley had started for Paris. The first
interview did not take place till June 7. See Stanley to Pitt, June 12,
Thackeray, vol. i. p. 514.

[2] Feb. 15, Bourguet, p. 188.

hesitated about making it offensive. Gradually, however, the suspicions on both sides were reduced. In May, just as Choiseul's arrangements for negotiating a separate peace with England were completed, Charles authorised Grimaldi definitely to propose a general treaty of alliance between France and Spain. Choiseul considered it was now safe to proceed, and forwarded to the Spanish court a counter-proposal. His suggestion was that two treaties should be made. One, which he proposed to call the *Pacte de Famille,* was to be a general and intimate alliance, amounting almost to a confederation, between the two courts, and having no relation to any other Power. The other would regulate their relations with the rest of Europe. The project was not well received. Wall considered the very title " Family Compact " would alarm Europe, and for Charles in his warlike mood it did not go far enough. Grimaldi, on his part, particularly objected that it avoided the main object in view, which was the concert of the naval forces of the two Powers. Choiseul could wish for nothing better. By this time it had become pretty clear to his mind that the mere threat of Spanish intervention was going to have little or no effect in England; and seeing it was safe to take yet another step, he proposed on June 2nd that the Family Compact should be supplemented by a Special Convention to meet the actual situation. His suggestion was that Spain should undertake to declare war on England on May 1, 1762, if by that time peace had not been concluded, and on this condition France was ready to include the settlement of the Spanish grievances in the separate negotiation that she was carrying on with England. It was, in fact, a proposal for a complete offensive and defensive alliance. Grimaldi sprang at the idea, and was for signing on the spot. But Choiseul held back. The fact was he had made up his mind not to commit himself until the result of the existing negotiation with London was known. So he told Grimaldi that he felt it would be improper for them to proceed further till the matter had been referred to Madrid and the King's consent obtained.

With the Family Compact as drafted by Choiseul the Spanish Court was delighted. Wall himself approved, or apparently approved, and knowing what to expect from Pitt if the secret leaked out, forthwith set about strengthening all the old scarred places on the coasts. By the end of June the matter was regarded by the Spanish court as settled, though some minor points were deemed to require adjustment.

With the " Special Convention," however, things were not so smooth. Wall penetrated Choiseul's game far enough to suspect that if, under the threat of Spanish intervention, France could get a favourable enough peace with England, she would certainly leave Spain and her grievances in the lurch. Choiseul's attitude was clearly wavering with the changing aspect of his negotiation with London. Charles himself began to grow suspicious again, and to bring matters to a head offered to send Grimaldi authority to sign the Family Compact at once. Wall, however, found it easy enough to suggest difficulties over the points that were still unsettled. He particularly called attention to the free hand with which France was dividing the West Indies with England without consulting Spain. Spanish feathers were on end in a moment : the position grew strained, and oddly enough it was intensified by what was regarded as the half-hearted and equivocal way in which Bussy had presented the Spanish claims to Pitt.

Such was the state of affairs when the British ulti-

matum reached Paris, and with it Bussy's account of
the haughty manner in which his note on the Spanish
claims had been thrown back in his face. The effect
was immediate.   Scarcely a hope of peace remained,
and Choiseul had to choose between the chance of Pitt's
fall and the nearer prospect of losing Spain.   There was
indeed no room for hesitation, and he forthwith sent
word to Madrid that Louis regarded the two treaties
as signed, and was sure that Charles must be feeling
as deeply wounded as himself at the insult of the
British minister.   In Spain the message was received
in the same spirit that it was sent.   By Pitt's instructions, Lord Bristol had just submitted Bussy's offensive
memorial to Wall, and asked whether it was authorised
by the Court of Spain.   On its being acknowledged, his
orders were to remonstrate on the unexampled irregularity of the proceeding, and, as it could only be regarded
as "a declaration of war in reversion," he was to demand
an explanation of the warlike preparations that were
being made in the Spanish arsenals.[1]   The effect of
Bristol's action was naturally to increase Charles's delight
at the communication from Paris.   The only trouble
was he was not yet ready for war.   Choiseul had told
him that it would be necessary for Spain to hasten her
declaration.   But Charles had to reply that he could
not possibly commence hostilities till the *flota*, or Plate
Fleet, came home from Havana, and he did not expect
it till October.   Every other point was rapidly agreed
upon, and on 15th August both the Family Compact and
the Special Convention were signed.

The Special Convention is what chiefly concerns us
here.   It was a military agreement by which a complete
and unreserved offensive and defensive alliance was

---

[1] Pitt to Bristol, July 28.—Thackeray, vol. i. p. 572.

formed between the two crowns for the period of the war; all plans were to be concerted, and no peace or truce was to be made without mutual consent. May 1st still stood as the date for the arrangement to come into operation. Louis engaged on that day to hand over Minorca to Charles. It was to be occupied during the war by a Spanish garrison, and if the arms of the two kings were successful, France was to use every effort to assure its cession to the Spanish crown at the peace. Then came a highly important article to the effect that Portugal was to be invited to become a party to the Convention, in order to close her ports and trade to the British, and it was understood that if she refused she was to be treated as a common enemy and an ally of England. Other maritime states that might wish to join the coalition should be permitted to do so; and, finally, if Spain were driven to begin the war before May 1st, the treaty was to come into force from the moment she commenced hostilities.

All these details were, of course, kept secret from England, but it was impossible to conceal entirely the fact that an arrangement of some kind had been come to between the two Bourbon Powers. Pitt, however, seems still to have regarded the *rapprochement* as a mere attempt to intimidate him into easier terms. In view of the four great successes he had just won—at Belle-isle, at Dominica, at Pondicherry, and in Westphalia—he believed that a firm attitude was all that was required to force France to give way, and that the resolute answer to Choiseul's memorandum, which had been sent on 27th July, would be accepted at Versailles.[1]

He was quickly undeceived. On August 5th Bussy handed him what was called an ultimatum in reply to

[1] Jenkinson to Grenville, July 28, *Grenville Papers*, vol. i. p. 380.

his own. It was, in fact, a defiant reply to the British ultimatum. Though most of Pitt's points were accepted, all the important ones were refused. France still insisted on her right to fish in the Gulf of St. Lawrence, as well as on the Newfoundland banks, and to have a fishing station reserved to her. She refused to exchange Belleisle for Minorca, as was only natural, since Minorca was promised to Spain; she went back on her undertaking to evacuate her conquests in Westphalia; gave no undertaking about Nieuport and Ostend, and finally revived more strongly than ever her demand for the restitution of the prizes taken by England before the declaration of war. At the same time a note, actually drawn up by Choiseul, was presented by Bussy in his own name resenting the tone of Pitt's last communication, and requesting an interview to discuss the new French proposal. Instead of granting it, Pitt laid the whole matter before the Cabinet.

Whatever doubts he may have entertained hitherto as to what was before him, he was now certain that France did not intend to make peace, and that war with Spain was inevitable. He had received from Stanley a despatch in which he said the whole tone at the French court had altered. The anxious air which till then he had noted in Grimaldi, as well as in the Austrian ambassador, had changed for one of exultation. He could not but see they had gained the upper hand of him, and that unless some unforeseen circumstance occurred he entirely despaired of accomplishing his Majesty's wishes for peace.[1] He had come to be convinced that the kernel of the situation was resistance to the maritime domination of England, and that the fishery difficulty was insuperable. Choiseul

[1] Stanley to Pitt, Aug. 6.—Thackeray, vol. ii. p. 571.

vowed he dared not give way. He would be stoned, he said, in the streets of Paris if he did, and all Stanley could suggest to Pitt was that, in hopes of arousing in the starving and exhausted French provinces a popular demonstration in favour of peace, he should be recalled and Bussy dismissed.

This letter, together with the French ultimatum and notes, Pitt laid before the Cabinet on August 13th. The peace party was for making one more effort. Pitt was as determined to break off the negotiations— to refuse even to discuss the ultimatum with Bussy. With Bedford at their head his opponents were able to make some impression. He was forced from his irreconcilable attitude about the fisheries, so far as to agree to test the sincerity of Choiseul by offering a port of refuge or *abri* on the Newfoundland coast. The little island of St. Pierre was suggested. So far, but no further, would Pitt go. On the morrow they met again to settle his draft answer to Choiseul. It was found to be drawn in a highly peremptory tone, and the peace party freely criticised its phrasing as objectionable and irritating. Pitt, having given up his darling point of excluding France from the Gulf of St. Lawrence altogether, and denying her an *abri* anywhere, was in no mood to bear criticism, and another scene occurred. To every amendment that was suggested, Pitt objected in his most overbearing manner. Not a word would he have altered. He would permit no one, he cried fiercely, to cobble his work, and the sitting ended in heat with a sullen acquiescence that the despatch should go as it stood. Both meetings lasted for hours. "Very stormy they were," wrote Hardwicke to his eldest son, "but we rid out the tempest. . . . After much altercation and some thumps of the fist on the table, it was at last carried (on my motion), that the conference should be had, but not without an answer to Bussy's letter."[1]

So far Pitt had his way, but it had been too fierce a struggle not to leave deep scars. The Duke of Bedford announced that he would not attend another Cabinet, and kept his word. Pitt's imperious manner of doing business was beyond bearing. Devonshire said as much, and Newcastle went so far in the same direction as his constitutional irresolution would let him. Could they have known the truth it might have been different. For on that very day, as we know, while Pitt, in his passion to make them see, was banging the table in their faces, Choiseul and Grimaldi at Versailles were quietly signing the two secret treaties.

Still the question was far from settled. There remained the instructions that were to be sent to Stanley with the new British ultimatum. Council after council was held, the Duke of Bedford stubbornly refusing to attend even at the King's urgent entreaty. The point was that the offer of the island of St. Pierre was to be regarded as a final test of France's sincerity, and Stanley had to be informed as to how far he was to go in meeting any alternative suggestions which Choiseul might offer. Pitt himself was against offering even St. Pierre. He said he was clearly against leaving any fishery rights to France except those allowed her on the Newfoundland banks by the Treaty of Utrecht, and in letting her into the Gulf of St. Lawrence he was only conforming to the opinion of others. Hardwicke thus summed up the result: "We had two meetings this week. The same persons present. All was calm and decent. The great points were liberty to fish in the Gulf of St. Lawrence and an *abri*. Many

---

[1] Hardwicke to Viscount Royston, Aug. 15, *Rockingham Memoirs*, vol. i. p. 27.

speeches. At last *both* agreed to by *all*. . . . It is also agreed to speak clearly about Dunkirk being put on the footing of the Treaty of Aix, and the liberty of fishing and drying fish in Newfoundland according to the thirteenth article of the Treaty of Utrecht. It has also been agreed with the *bonne foi* of the French king's declaration about Nieuport and Ostend [that is, that he had no intention of occupying them permanently], and that each side (after our particular peace made) may assist their respective allies in money only. Thus far is settled, and we meet on Monday to fix the particular place for the *abri*." [1] This meeting also went off calmly enough. It was agreed to offer St. Pierre, though Pitt persisted in his opinion that the whole concession was a mistake. He would not have given an inch, he said. He had no fear of Spain, and so far from being deterred by her threat of intervention, he vowed he would rather fight France and Spain together than France alone—his meaning being that the benevolent neutrality of Spain towards France was a greater evil than her declared hostility. [2]

Pitt's check in the Cabinet was all the more exasperating because he felt he had the general feeling of the country behind him. In the City the idea of war with Spain was popular—it meant rich prizes. Indeed, that all important factor in war, the spirit of the people, was a grave anxiety to the peace party, and made them more than half afraid of what they had done. Much as the nation desired peace, it was too much intoxicated with the recent recrudescence of victory to be willing to give up anything to secure it. " Mr. Pitt," as Bedford

---

[1] Hardwicke to Lord Royston, Aug. 22 (Saturday), *Rockingham Memoirs*, vol. i. p. 33.

[2] "Short Notes of the Meeting at St. James's, Aug. 24," *Hardwicke Papers (Add. MSS.)*, 35,570, f. 301.

VOL. II.

was told by his *alter ego*, Richard Rigby, "it is plain, does govern; and the worst of it is, he governs not only in the Cabinet Council, but in the opinions of the people too. . . . They will tell you in the same breath that you must keep everything which you have taken from the French, and have everything returned to you which you have lost by the war. Depend upon it, my Lord, this is the madness of the times, and there is but one cure for it, and that is a defeat of some one of our projects. Whilst we succeed and make conquests and bonfires, the value of the capture is no part of the consideration —fresh fuel is added to the delirium, and the fire is kept constantly fanned. . . . I should not be sorry to hear that Martinico, or the next windmill which you attack, should get the better of you."[1]

As Rigby wrote, the matter was settled. On the same day Pitt instructed Stanley that he was to present the new ultimatum as England's last word. If the French refused to accept the main points—that is, the fishery settlement, the entire cession of Canada, the restitution of everything in Germany, and liberty of each party to continue to assist its allies—he was not to await further orders, but to return home without taking leave.

With such a letter on its way the hope of peace was very remote. But worse was yet to come. As the decision was thus hanging in the balance, another cyphered letter, written by Grimaldi to Fuentes on August 31st, was intercepted. It was enough to open a blind man's eyes. "They have not given Lord Bristol the answer in writing," Grimaldi wrote. ". . . The fear of our Court, which is not ill grounded, is for the *Flota*. They want to gain time there till it has arrived at Cadiz, and they are secretly sending out twelve ships by way of convoy. . . .

---

[1] Rigby to Bedford, Aug. 27, *Bedford Corr.*, vol. iii. p. 42.

They have remained here [in Paris] entirely bound by the Family Compact and the Convention. . . . What your Excellency mentions is not to be feared . . . since both instruments were signed on the 15th, and I expect shortly the ratification." At the same time, moreover—apparently on the same day—came a despatch from Stanley, saying he had got sight of an article from some recent secret treaty, by which France engaged to support the interests of Spain equally with her own in the negotiation of the peace. This article was also referred to in Grimaldi's letter as ensuring that the French could not finish the war without the Spanish claims being settled.[1]

A day or two later came three more letters from Stanley respecting the result of his discussions with Choiseul on the last ultimatum. He could no longer hope that any concession that Choiseul seemed inclined to make would lead to peace. France was certainly not in earnest. He had come to a final conclusion that a reconciliation between the two Crowns was impracticable, and that it was time for him to return home without taking his leave. People, moreover, were everywhere asserting that Spain was about to declare war, and he had little doubt it was true. " I cannot answer," he said, " whether the convention between these two Crowns is actually authenticated; but I am assured that at least it wants only the last hand and signature." Finally, he confirmed the intelligence about the Spanish ships going out to meet the *Flota*, and added that Choiseul, though personally polite, had suddenly become extremely grave and full of anxiety.[2]

---

[1] *Chatham Corr.*, vol. ii. p. 139 ; *Newcastle Papers*, Aug. 31, 32,927.

[2] Stanley to Pitt, Sept. 4, 6, and 8, Thackeray, vol. ii. pp. 612–618. The letters came to hand on the 11th. Newcastle to Bedford, *Bedford Corr.*, vol. ii. p. 43.

For Pitt this was enough. Indeed, it was no more than he had long expected, and he was resolved to seize the initiative. The means was ready in his mind. Stanley must be recalled immediately, and a squadron sent down to Cadiz to intercept the expected *Flota*. There was apparently no difficulty about it. Keppel had now something like sixty sail under his broad-pendant; and on intelligence from Holmes that some rich French vessels were coming home under convoy from St. Domingo, he had spread his fleet as far down as Finisterre to intercept them.[1] Anson, moreover, furnished a memorandum, showing he had "within call" fifty-four of the line and fifty-eight frigates, besides the Mediterranean squadron.[2]

On September 15th the Cabinet met, and Pitt laid his drastic proposals before it. About their attitude towards France there was little difficulty. Hardwicke himself was for Stanley's recall, and though he was absent, at the death-bed of his wife, his influence prevailed. That night Pitt wrote to Stanley that he was to demand his passports forthwith. With the Spanish business it was different. For the peace party the continuance of the old war was as much as they could bear. To rush into a new one was midsummer madness. And here they had the powerful support of Anson. He had recently been promoted Admiral of the Fleet to fetch the new Queen

----

[1] Keppel to Admiralty, July 25, *In-letters*, 91.

[2] *Newcastle Papers, Add. MSS.*, 32,928, Sept. 15, and *Hardwicke Papers*, ibid., 35,870, f. 301. Anson gave the distribution of the fleet as follows: *Home Stations.*—Ships of the line: convoys and cruising, 5; Downs, 1; off Havre, 2; Keppel, 28; in port or under sailing orders, 20, less 2 just cast. Total, 56; frigates, 58. *Mediterranean.*—Saunders, "probably off Toulon," 11 of the line and 12 frigates. *Distant Stations.*—Ships of the line: East Indies, 14; Jamaica, 6; Leeward Islands, 8; North America, 6; other plantations, 2; convoys and cruising, 4. Total, 40. Grand total— Home and Mediterranean, 65 of the line and 70 frigates. In all, 105 of the line.

from Holland. Thither he had gone in high state with all the royal yachts, and had just returned in time for the council. It was the last time he ever flew his flag. He was approaching seventy, and the strain of his strenuous life, and, above all, of the last few years, had told its tale. He had set out on his stately mission when hopes of peace were high. He returned to find a new war before him. It was more than he could face, and with all the authority of his great name, he pronounced that it was impossible to support a war with Spain.[1]

The Cabinet met again for a final decision on the 17th, but so violent was the struggle that it had to be adjourned till the next day. Then it was Pitt laid before them Grimaldi's intercepted letter, but still they resisted. In vain he urged his point with all his eloquence and powers of exposition, and every one agreed he had never spoken better or more reasonably. He began by setting out all the varied evidence that pointed irresistibly to the existence of a Bourbon alliance. There was danger in his proposal, he admitted, but danger lay in any resolution they might take, and delay could only increase it. What was the "option of dangers"? he asked, in the words Wolfe had used about Rochefort. There was nothing between vigorous action and acquiescence. If there was danger now, how much greater would it be in the coming May, when Spain was to declare herself. Why not act at once? There was now but one House of Bourbon. Spain had grafted herself upon France, and her fleet must be regarded as the remnant of the fleet of France. "Spain," he added, "is France, and France is Spain."[2]

---

[1] *Newcastle Papers*, Sept. 15, 32,928.

[2] "Notes of Pitt's Speech, Sept. 18," *Hardwicke Papers, Add. MSS.*, 35,570, f. 304. In the margin his son and successor has written, "This was an able speech." And compare Newcastle's Notes, *ibid.*, 32,928.

But for all his force and eloquence the men of peace were unshaken. Supported by Bute, they urged, with the nicety of the *grands seigneurs* they were, that a blow before declaration could not be justified on knowledge obtained from intercepted letters. Spain, like France, must be put to fair trial. Before adopting the drastic course for which Pitt was on fire and well prepared, they argued that there were first three questions to be settled : was such a course justified ? was it within our naval and military strength ? and, lastly, was it expedient ? It was recalled by Lord Granville how Lord Torrington's instructions in 1718, which had resulted, in full time of peace, in the destruction of the Spanish fleet off Cape Passaro, had never been forgiven to that day. It was also urged that Boscawen's opening of the present war was no great argument for repeating the experiment. Let Bristol, therefore, be instructed to make a strong protest, and demand an explanation at Madrid, and, at the same time, give a handsome offer about Honduras. Let Saunders be strengthened in the Mediterranean, and Holmes and Douglas in the West Indies, and let care be taken against a sudden blow from Spain, either upon the British coasts or Ireland. Finally, Anson clenched the matter by declaring that the ships he had within call at home were nearly four thousand men short of their complements.

Such talk Pitt knew well, and it drove him, as always, to violent resistance. Seeing argument was no further use, he insisted on putting Bristol's immediate recall to the vote. In spite of his convinced vehemence, no one but his fiery brother-in-law, Lord Temple, supported his motion, and the decision was given against him. Furious at his check, but not yet defeated, Pitt fell back on the old device, which had served him so well before, of insisting that a minute of the vote should be drawn up that the King and country might know who was responsible. Nor was this all, for he went so far as to announce his intention of drawing up a protest against the decision for presentation to the King. Still the rest stood to their guns, and a minute of the proceedings was drafted. It was to the effect that Pitt's proposals had been rejected by the majority as both inexpedient and unjustified; that Bristol was to demand an explanation of the Spanish intentions, and to offer to evacuate Honduras if the right to cut logwood were guaranteed, and that three thousand men and seven ships of the line should be sent to Guadeloupe, and Saunders reinforced.[1]

For the peace party it was a Pyrrhic victory. In the heat of the debate Pitt had plainly hinted at resignation. Bute, at least, was seriously alarmed, and Newcastle, as of old, almost subdued. To defeat Pitt was one thing, to face the war and the excited country without him was another. On the morrow, therefore, Bute summoned his party to meet him at Devonshire House. If peace came, he said, Pitt might go or stay—it mattered not—but as war was practically certain they ought to make a great effort to keep him. He begged them, therefore, to meet again on the morrow, and consider Pitt's protest. This they did, all but Hardwicke, the death of whose wife deprived them of his sagacious and temperate counsel at the critical hour. In the end it was found they could not take the step Pitt demanded. It was agreed that before hostilities were commenced a notification, tantamount to a declaration of war, must be given to Spain, and Bristol recalled. The only concession they could

---

[1] *Newcastle Papers*, Sept. 15, 17, and 18, *Add. MSS.*, 32,928; *Hardwicke Papers*, ibid., 35,570, f. 304.

bring themselves to make was that naval preparations should go on as though war were certain.[1]

On September 21st Pitt presented his protest to the King. The King, to his surprise, refused to receive it. His Majesty, with Bute at his elbow, declared bluntly he would take no resolution with regard to Spain till Stanley came back to tell them all he knew. A Council was held directly afterwards to consider this last means of deferring a decision. Bute, Devonshire, and Newcastle approved it and held their ground. Mansfield was unsteady, but was inclined to side with them on the plea that he could not see what operations could be undertaken against Spain that would suffer by the delay. This gave Pitt his chance. At great length, and with studied politeness and candour, he laid before them the whole plan of war which he had already elaborated, showing how important was instant action, and how certain was success against the united House of Bourbon. He ended by declaring he would not set his hand to any other plan, and that was his last word. His eloquence shook Mansfield, who declared the statement put things in a very different light, and he "plainly made fair weather for Pitt." Temple followed hotly and rudely on the same side, but in the end there was nothing but an adjournment *sine die* till Stanley's return.[2]

With Mansfield's half conversion the crisis became acute, and a new meeting of the Opposition was called. Pitt's protest, which was also signed by Temple, was for them the alarming factor. It was a temperate document and difficult to meet. After reciting that the Spanish Government had acknowledged Bussy's action in pre-

---

[1] Minute of Meeting, Sept. 19, Newcastle to Hardwicke, Sept. 20. The Ministers present were Granville, Devonshire, Newcastle, Bute, and Mansfield. *Newcastle Papers, Add. MSS.*, 32,928.

[2] Newcastle to Hardwicke, Sept. 21, *Rockingham Memoirs*, vol. i. p. 37.

senting their claims, and his boast that the French King
was ready to support Spain if she took action, the
document proceeded, " This unjust and unexampled proceeding . . . and the full declaration and avowal at last
made of the union of counsels and interest between the
two monarchies of the House of Bourbon . . . call in-
dispensably on his Majesty to take forthwith such
necessary and timely measures as God hath put into his
hands." And therefore an order should be sent to Lord
Bristol to deliver a declaration to that effect, and come
away immediately without taking his leave. The protest,
it will be seen, though it hinted at action before declaration, did not demand it categorically. Nothing was
definitely insisted on but an immediate breaking off of
diplomatic relations tantamount to a declaration of war.
It might easily have been done before any blow was struck
at the Plate fleet.[1]

Scarcely had this step been taken when a new weapon
came to Pitt's hand. Yet another despatch from Grimaldi to Fuentes, dated September 13th, was intercepted
on the 22nd. In this letter Grimaldi said the treaty had
been ratified, and that in accordance with its provisions
Bussy had been instructed by Choiseul to sign nothing
that did not include an accommodation with Spain. Still,
what weakened Pitt's position was that the Spaniards
were plainly ill at ease. Grimaldi said he believed that
the French were ready to accept the British terms, and
that if the negotiations were broken off it would be
entirely on the account of Spain.[2] From this point of

---

[1] For the text of the protest or "Advice in Writing," see *Grenville
Papers*, vol. i. p. 386, and *Hardwicke Papers, Add. MSS.*, 35,570, f. 306.

[2] Grimaldi to Fuentes, Sept. 13, *Chatham Corr.*, vol. ii. p. 141. It was
intercepted apparently about a week later. Newcastle's copy is endorsed
as read, Sept. 23, *Newcastle Papers*, 32,928 ; Grenville saw it on Friday,
24th, *Grenville Papers*, vol. i. p. 391.

view, therefore, the letter might be said to tell in favour of trying to come to terms with Spain, rather than for immediate action.

Pitt, however, demanded that a Cabinet should be called forthwith to consider Grimaldi's despatch, but to no purpose.[1] A last letter had come from Stanley which served materially to strengthen the position of Bute and his friends. Stanley had had another talk with Choiseul, in which that accomplished diplomat protested warmly that he still desired peace, and that the affairs of Spain should not prevent it. And he added Spain could easily be dropped. On the other hand, Stanley also said that from information he had received an attack on Portugal must be expected as soon as Spain declared war. In a previous letter he had given warning that the tone of the Court was changing. There had been influences about the King which till lately had threatened to subvert Choiseul's domination. Now he said Choiseul was completely in the ascendant, and that he was convinced he wanted peace.[2] These letters made no impression on Pitt, who saw clearly through Choiseul's game. "Mr. Pitt," wrote Newcastle, "triumphs much on Grimaldi's letter and on that curious expression in Stanley's, ' When Spain declares war I expect an attack in Portugal.' " The King and Bute thought differently, and were supported by all the peace party. Another meeting was held at Devonshire House, at which they decided that Pitt's request for a Cabinet should be refused, since Stanley's letters made it absurd to take any step until he returned.[3]

---

[1] Jenkinson to Grenville, Sept. 29, *Grenville Papers*, vol. i. p. 391.

[2] Stanley to Pitt, Sept. 15, Thackeray, vol. ii. p. 623 ; Newcastle to Hardwicke, Sept. 23, *Rockingham Memoirs*, vol. i. p. 40.

[3] Newcastle to Hardwicke, Sept. 23 and 26, *Newcastle Papers*, 32,928, and part of the letter of the 23rd is printed in the *Rockingham Memoirs*.

So much was easy, but there still remained the thorny question of how to meet the protest of Pitt and Temple. To answer it in writing could only lead to a paper war. Hardwicke had warned Newcastle to bear in mind that the House of Commons might call for papers and Pitt would certainly support the motion.[1] To enter into a written controversy, therefore, would only be playing into Pitt's hand. It was his obvious game to appeal from the Cabinet to the people, and that was a proceeding they were not prepared to face. It was accordingly resolved, to Pitt's deep resentment, that each of them should go singly to the King and give his private opinion by word of mouth. So one by one they went—Mansfield, Anson, Ligonier, and all. Anson told the King he could not have a squadron ready for the coast of Spain for two months since Keppel's ships were so foul, and he promised to say so in the Cabinet so as to cut short any idea of immediate operations.[2] When Pitt found out what was going on, he had an audience too. But the effect was only to increase the King's growing antipathy. "The King," wrote Newcastle, "seems every day more offended with Mr. Pitt, and plainly wants to get rid of him at all events."[3]

On the last day of September Stanley had arrived from Paris, and a Council was forthwith called for three days later. His report once more swung opinion to Pitt's side. On being questioned it was found he could not or would not uphold the views expressed in his last letters. His talk tended all to war and not to peace, and he represented the whole situation in a light

---

[1] Hardwicke to Newcastle, Sept. 24, *ibid.*
[2] *Newcastle Papers*, 32,929, "Mem., Sept. 30."
[3] To Hardwicke, Sept. 26, *Rockingham Memoirs*, vol. i. p. 43.

favourable to Pitt.[1]   Even Hardwicke was shaken.   He
thought Stanley's report and Grimaldi's letter together
showed that Spain was more in earnest than they had
thought.   Still he was against declaring war without
first demanding an explanation, but Anson, he said,
had told him he had six clean ships of the line ready,
and these had better be sent at once to Saunders, with
orders for him to remain at Gibraltar ready to act the
moment Spain stirred.[2]

So before ever the Cabinet met the matter was settled.
Pitt made one more appeal, urging particularly Grimaldi's
last letter, and Stanley's warning about the danger of
Portugal.   It was useless.   The rest all held their old
ground.   Ligonier supported them in the strongest
manner, arguing plausibly enough that war with Spain
meant adding sixty thousand good troops to the army of
France.   Anson pronounced that the fleet was not ready
for any material operation against Spain.   Mansfield
dwelt on the danger from neutral maritime powers, who
would all suspect we meant to destroy them one after
the other.   To press the matter further was waste labour.
Temple took an angry farewell and left the room.   Pitt
declared his opinion unchanged.   The King and country,
he said, had received an indignity under which he could
not sit down.   " I have in my bag," he solemnly declared,
" so much matter as I think would be criminal matter
against any Secretary of State who let it sleep in his
office."   He reminded them how he had been called to
direct the war at a time when every one had abdicated,
how all or nearly all of his expeditions had been ridiculed
and thwarted, and what success they had won.   Now it
was clear all were against him and he must make an end.

[1] Newcastle to Hardwicke, Oct. 1, *Rockingham Memoirs*, vol. i. p. 44.

[2] Hardwicke to Newcastle, *Newcastle Papers*, 32,929, Oct. 1.

" I will be responsible," he said, " for nothing that I do not direct." [1]

Thus in his last words he formulated the doctrine which was at the bottom of the resistance he had raised. He undoubtedly believed that it was only by the complete responsibility of a War Minister that a constitutional country could hope to make war successfully. Such had been his position, and well had he justified the new theory. But it was one which the old Constitutional Whigs could not possibly accept or endorse. Granville, the personification of their political theories, broken as he was with his excesses, and at death's door, took upon himself to answer. " I find," he is reported to have said, " the gentleman is determined to leave us, nor can I say I am sorry for it, since he would otherwise have compelled us to leave him. But if he is resolved to assume the right of addressing his Majesty and directing the operations of war, to what purpose are we called to this Council? . . . However, though he may possibly have convinced himself of his infallibility, still it remains that we should be equally convinced before we can resign our understandings to his direction, or join with him in the measure he proposes." [2] Pitt's theory which the brilliant old statesman combated with the last flare of his genius has found to this day no real resting-place in English ideas of government. To the great political leaders of that day—the high priests of the English Revolution—it was little short of treason. Granville's declaration could only convince them that loyalty and

---

[1] " Notes at the Meeting of the Lords, Oct. 2," *Hardwicke Papers, Add. MSS.*, 35,370, f. 310 ; *Newcastle Papers*, Oct. 2, *ibid.*, 32,929 ; Newcastle to Bedford, Oct. 2, *Bedford Corr.*, vol. iii. p. 46.

[2] *Annual Register*, 1761, p. 44. The speech is not mentioned by Hardwicke or Newcastle in their notes of the meeting and it may be apocryphal, but it certainly represents the feeling which crushed Pitt.

patriotism demanded they should stand firm. So when
the President ceased to speak, the Council broke up un-
shaken and three days later Pitt resigned.

So fell the greatest war administrator England has
ever had, a victim to the disease which in a constitutional country is inherent in effective war-direction. His
words, " I will be responsible for nothing that I do not
direct," were taken hold of and harped upon with increasing resentment, and perhaps with justice and sound
intuition. Under a government like our own, it is probable that any form of real combined control in war
must sooner or later produce a pathological condition, so
obnoxious to the constitution that either the constitution
must perish or develop a paroxysm—as in one of Pitt's
own fits of the gout—in which it will throw off the disease
and rid itself of the morbid impurity. In Cromwell's
case, the constitution was not sound enough to engender
the healing paroxysm ; in Marlborough's and in Pitt's it
was, and with what diverse results we know.

In the present case the loss was indeed great—the
remedy severe—and yet, perhaps, the utmost good had
been already obtained from the strong wine of Pitt's
domination. Of Lord Hardwicke, the greatest of the
Chancellors, it is said that during his tenure of the
woolsack, he raised equity from a chaos of isolated
precedents to a reasoned system. Pitt had done the
same for the war, and afforded his country for all time,
if she had had the wit to understand, a complete system
of how to use the peculiar strength that belonged to her
and to no one else. He had done so triumphantly—too
triumphantly, indeed, for the security of the world—and
there lay cause enough for his defeat. In his vision of
England as sole mistress of the sea, he fell into an
error as enticing and as fatal as that which brought the

Grand Monarque and Napoleon to their ruin. Magnificent as was his strategy, it broke the golden rule. He pushed his action beyond the point where by drawing fresh force to the enemy it strengthens him more than it can hurt. In Pitt's defence it must be said he did give way. He was ready to make peace on terms below what he believed it to be in his power to enforce. His mistake was that in the pride of the power to which he had lifted his country he did not make sure of Spain. A liberal and timely concession in Honduras might well have kept Wall staunch, but he let the hour slip by and so played into Choiseul's hands. It is usually said his fall was due to the dislike and intrigue of the young King and his Court. It would be truer, perhaps, to regard it as a triumph of Choiseul's subtle policy. By the French Minister's own statement that policy was based on Pitt's fall, and by his clever balancing so long between a reasonable peace and an alliance with Spain Pitt's quarrel with his colleagues and the throne was brought to a head. But for the Spanish complication there would certainly have been a compromise between Pitt and the peace party, and France would have been compelled to make peace on the terms he last offered. It was on the question of an immediate attack on Spain, and on that alone that he fell.

On that question was he right or wrong? It is difficult to say even now when we know all that followed. No situation could better exemplify the extreme delicacy of disentangling politics from pure strategy. Being convinced that war with Spain was inevitable he was bidden by pure strategy to strike at once. Every war we had had with Spain had opened with an attempt upon the Plate fleet. One more such attempt could hardly have given us a worse reputation, especially as in this case it would probably have been preceded by the withdrawal of our ambassador. Yet was the game worth the candle? Assuming, as we well may, that the material difficulties raised by Anson were not insuperable, could we have gained enough to compensate for the odium which the contemplated blow would have entailed? It is very doubtful. There were other wavering neutrals, like Denmark and the Dutch, who would have felt the smart dangerously. It is strange that Pitt of all men should have been ready to run the risk. No one felt so strongly as he how weak and unready was Spain, and how easily she was to be beaten by open war upon the high seas. But the vice of permitting an almost declared enemy to commence hostilities at the moment that best pleases her seems to have been intolerable to his strategic sense. If war was inevitable Pitt was perhaps right; if it was not he was wrong. Pitt believed it was: his opponents still hoped. There was enough evidence to show that the main impulse came from France and not from Spain; that the union of the two countries was by no means stable, and that even at the eleventh hour Spain might be persuaded there was an easier way of obtaining her end than by burning her fingers for France. There was much to justify at least an attempt to stay her hand, and it is difficult to read the reasoned arguments of such a man as Hardwicke without feeling that the great majority of sagacious and experienced statesmen would have been, like Anson and Ligonier, on his side and the King's, and not on Pitt's.

CHAPTER VII

COMPLETION OF THE WEST INDIAN ATTACK—
MARTINIQUE

If there had been hesitation about commencing hostilities with Spain, there was none about a vigorous continuation of the war with France. Before Pitt resigned, he had been able to fire his last bolt against her, and to set in motion the third wave of the great attack, with which he meant to sweep her from her last footing in the West Indies.

The only effect of Choiseul's cunning had been to increase its intensity. In July the final orders had gone to Amherst and Admiral Colville, on the American station, for the despatch of ten battalions with artillery and engineers to Barbadoes, where they were to find their orders. At the same time Sir James Douglas, who was still in command in the Leeward Islands, was told to expect them at Guadeloupe by the end of October. He was also informed that the French were preparing two squadrons, one at Brest and one at Rochefort, each consisting of about seven of the line, which were intended for the succour of Martinique, and that if they escaped the home blockade he was to station a squadron off the island strong enough to deal with them. General Monckton, who was bringing the troops from America, was to command in chief ashore, and he was to arrange with him for a rendezvous. There Lord Rollo's troops and all that could be spared from the garrisons of Guadeloupe and Antigua were to be concentrated, and the

whole force would then amount to about eleven thousand
men.   Douglas would have about twelve of the line
available to act with the military force, and with these
he was to render them every assistance in his power.[1]

But for the possibility of Spanish intervention such a
force would have been ample for its purpose. But as the
horizon darkened, Pitt's intention was not bounded by
the mere conquest of Martinique.   It must also serve as
a secure foothold from whence he could spring upon the
Spanish islands the moment Spain stirred.   So far and
no further had Pitt persuaded the Cabinet to go upon
the road he knew they would have to tread.   It will be
remembered that at the famous meeting in September,
where he had exhausted all his vehemence in trying to
force them to strike a sudden blow at Spain and had
been outvoted, he had wrung from them a consent to
reinforce Saunders in the Mediterranean and to send out
three thousand fresh troops and seven more of the line
to Guadeloupe.   The very day after the meeting, when
the King refused to receive his protest, the orders were
issued—to Belleisle for four regiments to be sent off
immediately, and for Swanton and five other captains to
join Douglas, and finally to Rodney to hoist his flag and
proceed to Guadeloupe to take Douglas and the whole
naval force under his command.   This notable appointment, which became necessary owing to the increase of
the force and the danger, and which Rodney had well
earned by his indefatigable operations in the Channel
against the French flotillas, was the last Pitt ever made.
Even before the new commander-in-chief had hoisted his
flag, Pitt had resigned.[2]

---

[1] *Admiralty Secretary, Out-letters (Secret Orders)*, 1331, July 22.
[2] *Secret Orders*, ibid., Oct. 1 and 7. Rodney's Orders are dated Sept. 21.
He hoisted his flag on Oct. 9 at Portsmouth.

As thus from America, from Belleisle, and from home
the forces which his spirit continued to wield were
gathering to do his will, the new Ministers were making
the best of the more sober policy to which they had
committed themselves.   Newcastle still retained the
nominal leadership, but his reward for the part he had
played in unseating Pitt was to find himself more of a
nonentity than ever.   Eager to take the fallen leader's
place, he was for consulting Anson on a number of
vague projects, which showed all his old incapacity for
concentrated design.   Oléron, the French coast, the
Scheldt, Emden, America, India, all passed through his
mind, aimlessly, but no one gave him heed.   He complained that he was entirely neglected; that new regiments were being raised every day, of which he knew
nothing; that the King was doing everything; and his
letters to all his old correspondents and allies—Bedford,
Devonshire, Hardwicke, and the rest, who were as much
out in the cold as himself—were filled with sarcasms
upon the Ministers who had his ambitious Majesty's ear.[1]
The truth was that the blow they had struck in the
name of the Constitution and of Cabinet responsibility
was raising the worse devil of autocracy.

The real head of the new government was Bute, whom
we know for a well-meaning mediocrity, full of high
ideas of kingship.   Ignorant as yet of what government
meant, he still thought, like Phaeton, he could drive the
horses of the sun.   "Young king, young nobility," was
his motto.   For him Newcastle was but a "crazy old
man," whom it was convenient to permit to "tide over a
year or two more of his political life."[2]   To Bute and
the King, whose brains were buzzing with Stuart theories

---

[1] *Newcastle Papers*, 32,929–30 *passim*.
[2] "Heads of Lord Bute's Letters," *Grenville Papers*, vol. i. p. 395.

of monarchy, the old minister represented, with the Russells, the Cavendishes, and the rest, the aristocratic oligarchy that had dominated the throne ever since the Revolution. Their power was to be broken, but, for the present, concessions had to be made and places provided for them in the Government. Bedford himself, who at this time was entirely devoted to Bute, was made Privy Seal. Devonshire received no office, probably because he was regarded as too entirely under the influence of Fox.

It was an influence which seriously added to the greatest difficulty of the new administration. The crux was the management of the House of Commons, where Pitt's terrible figure would still be supreme. For this arduous task Bute pitched on his intimate friend, George Grenville, who had held the lucrative office of Treasurer of the Navy almost continuously since the beginning of the war. Though brother to Lord Temple, and consequently brother-in-law to Pitt, he had not tendered his resignation with the rest of his family, and Bute pressed him to accept the seals which Pitt had laid down. This, however, Grenville protested was too much for his "delicacy." He begged to be made Speaker, but neither the King nor Bute would listen, and eventually he was induced to retain his old office and accept the leadership of the House. Under this arrangement it was, of course, necessary to keep Pitt's successor out of the Commons. Beyond all question, if ability were to decide, Fox was the man who should have taken up the reins. But Grenville absolutely refused to do business with him, and he himself was content to continue amassing a fortune as Paymaster of the Forces. At Grenville's suggestion, therefore, Pitt's cloak was fastened on the shoulders of Lord Egremont, whose sister he had married, and by this means, the Navy and the Foreign Office continued to be as intimately connected as before.[1]

The Spanish question was by no means the end of the false position which the new Government had taken up in regard to the war. To justify a policy founded on the good intentions of Spain was bad enough, but behind it lay the equally thorny questions of the German war and the militia. The annual treaty with Frederick and the term for which the militia had been raised were both about to expire. The King wished to renew neither. His passion to be an English king set his mind obstinately against using the resources of the country for the defence of Hanover. He hated the place—the wits said he could never find it on the map. Could he but withdraw his troops from the Continent there would be no need of the militia, and in his eyes the militia, being in the hands of the territorial aristocracy, was the great danger to the royal prerogative which he was determined to enhance.

Such were the difficulties which Grenville had to face at the start. The new Parliament, the first of the new reign, was to meet early in November, and every one was looking to the King's Speech for light on the burning questions. The country was in a highly excitable condition. After a few days' resentment at Pitt's accepting a pension for himself and a peerage for his wife at the King's hands it had worked itself into a fury of sympathy and admiration for the fallen Minister. It had begun again to rain upon him addresses and gold boxes; and on Lord Mayor's Day, on the occasion of the King and Queen visiting the City, there had been a riotous demonstration against Bute and in Pitt's favour. Three days earlier the King's Speech had been delivered, and it was

---

[1] "Grenville's Narrative," *ibid.*, 409–12.

silent on all that the country wanted to know.   Neither the German war nor the militia were mentioned, and far from there being a word about the insult which the country regarded itself to have suffered from Spain, the *Gazette* had vaunted the pacific disposition of the offending Court.

On November 13th the Address was moved, and led to a great deal of violent invective on both sides.   Above all was heard a loud note of arraignment of the German war.   Frederick had recently suffered a serious reverse at Sweidnitz, and in spite of Ferdinand's victory Germany was again in bad odour.   Loyalty to Frederick forced Pitt at last to his feet.   He did not wish, he said, to defend his conduct then, but he could not let the post go abroad without a word being said in that House in support of England's allies.   So he fell into an explanation of all the German war had meant in his system.   Recalling the old scare under which he had come to power, he reminded them that it was nothing but the spectre of an invasion that had frightened us out of Minorca.   The Ministers of that day, he said, had not had constancy enough to look it in the face, and so it would be again if the troops of France found themselves at liberty to quit Germany. He had known five thousand French occasion our recalling seventy or four-score thousand to confront them (alluding probably to what had occurred in 1745).   The way to peace was not by abandoning our efforts.   England was equal to both wars, the American and the German ; and if they were continued, nothing but conquest would follow—all owing to the German war.   If we abandoned our allies, God would abandon us.   When we had spent a hundred millions, should we throw away the fruit rather than spend twelve more.   Let a man so narrow-minded stand behind a counter, and not govern a kingdom.

Then he made his famous declaration, "America has been conquered in Germany." Forced from its context it was much ridiculed at the time, and since has led to serious misconception of what Pitt's system really was. It will be seen that it must not be taken as a scientific statement of the principle on which his war-plan was framed, but as a defence of the principal containing or defensive operations, without which his main attack could not have been made, and if made, must in the end have been fruitless. He ended by solemnly repudiating the accusation that he had courted war with Spain, protested he would divulge nothing it was his duty as a Privy Councillor to conceal, but would leave it to the House to judge when all the papers, including his own protest to the King, were produced, how patient and long-suffering he had been. With that he sat down, and Grenville did not venture to answer him.

The conclusion at least was very difficult to answer. A fortnight after Pitt's resignation another despatch from Grimaldi to Fuentes in London had been intercepted, which made the intentions of Spain look less pacific than ever. Bussy, so Grimaldi said, had just returned to Paris, and then added, " We shall see one another shortly, be it a little sooner or a little later. The moment is not yet fixed." Meanwhile Fuentes was to send advices of any expeditions and warlike preparations that were on foot in England.[1] It was clear Spain was only waiting till she was ready to commence hostilities, and in the course of the week the Cabinet hardened its heart to instruct Lord Bristol at Madrid to ask in a friendly way for the communication of the Franco-Spanish treaty, and to intimate with all politeness that although the new Government

[1] Grimaldi to Fuentes, Paris, Oct. 5, received Oct. 16, *Newcastle Papers*, 32,929.

was prepared to negotiate liberally on the Spanish claims, the granting of his request was to be a condition precedent to the negotiation. The day after the debate on the Address Bristol's reply arrived. He had seen Wall, and asked him if the rumour of the alliance was true. Wall had answered with long and angry abuse of England and all her ways. At a second interview Bristol had continued to press his point, till at last Wall acknowledged that the Family Compact had been renewed, but absolutely refused to say whether any further treaty existed. Bristol concluded his despatch by saying that the Plate fleet had got home with enormously rich cargoes, and he assumed that this, coupled with the recent French successes towards Hanover and those of Austria in Silesia, accounted for Wall's startling change of tone.[1]

It would have been thought that the game of Spain was now clear enough, and that the obvious course was not to leave her to declare war at her own time. That there was any hope of averting it no man could really believe; yet the Government could bring themselves no further than to send an ultimatum. Bristol was instructed to demand an explicit and prompt answer as to whether or not it was the intention of Spain to ally herself with France against England. If he failed to obtain a satisfactory answer he was to come from Madrid forthwith, without taking leave, and repair to Lisbon. But first, when all hopes were at an end, he was to send word of his approaching departure to Saunders and Keppel, and to repeat the information the moment he reached the Portuguese frontier. He already had been told to disabuse the Spanish Government of any idea they might have conceived that the resignation of Pitt meant that the whole spirit of the war was subsiding. " The example

[1] *Ibid.*, Nov. 2, received 14th ; Beatson, vol. iii. p. 313.

of the spirit of the late measures," Egremont had written, " will be a spur to his Majesty's servants to persevere, and to stretch every nerve of this country towards forcing the enemy to come into a safe, honourable, and, above all, a lasting peace."

It is no more than justice to say that the action of the new Government did not belie this spirited declaration. On November 20th, the day after the ultimatum was received, seven of the line and two frigates, which Anson by this time had been able to get ready, were ordered to reinforce Saunders, whereby the Mediterranean fleet would be brought up to nineteen of the line and a dozen frigates, and at the same time Keppel was ordered to send him three bomb-vessels. All cruisers on the Portuguese coast were ordered into Lisbon to be ready to receive the news of the result of the ultimatum and to carry it to all stations. Next day, moreover, the Admiralty issued warnings in every direction that the ultimatum had been sent, and that it was expected that Bristol would leave directly. The moment the commanding officers heard from him that he intended to do so they were to commence hostilities, but not before. Saunders's attention was specially directed to the ships that were in Cadiz, and he was impressed with the importance of dealing a severe blow at once.[1] Grenville's admiration for Pitt's energy and thoroughness had always been high. His first act, as Horace Walpole tells, had been to add to Hardwicke's sober draft of the King's Speech " some of Mr. Pitt's *sonantia verba*." The old spirit had not ceased to glow. Anson was still at the helm, and the intimacy between the Admiralty and the Foreign Office left nothing to be desired.

The following day, November 22nd, Rodney, ignorant

---

[1] *Admiralty Secretary, Out-letters (Secret Orders)*, 1331.

of the turn things had taken, reached Barbadoes. He
was alone. His squadron had been scattered in a gale
and foul winds had seriously delayed its passage. In
Carlisle Bay was Douglas waiting for him. He had been
there all the month with cruisers watching Martinique
and his battle squadron ready to sail, according to his
previous orders, the moment he heard of the escape of a
squadron from Brest or Rochefort. He had made up his
mind, when he still believed he was to be in command of
the attempt against Martinique, that the first thing to do,
so soon as Monckton arrived from America, was to make
feints in various parts of the island.[1] The idea apparently commended itself to Rodney, for directly he had
communicated with Douglas he despatched him to
blockade St. Pierre, the capital of the island, and to
destroy the batteries there, although it was not his real
objective.

Then followed a long wait while his scattered forces
gathered. Rodney employed it hiring and fitting out
ten local sloops to supply his weakness in small cruisers,
and these he sent, partly to search the creeks of Martinique
and partly to watch St. Eustatius, and prevent the Dutch
sending supplies to the enemy. It was not till December
9th that all his own squadron joined, being three of the
line, with two cruisers and three bomb-vessels. On the
14th arrived the *Téméraire* and a frigate, with the transports from Belleisle, and ten days later General Monckton
and the North American contingent, escorted by three of
the line and a forty-gun ship from Colville's squadron.
Lord Rollo, with the troops from Guadeloupe and Antigua,
joined shortly afterwards, and the force was then complete. With Douglas's squadron Rodney had now at
his disposal eighteen of the line, a score of cruisers, and

[1] Douglas to the Admiralty, Nov. 5, *In-letters*, 307.

four bomb-vessels, while Monckton had over thirteen
thousand troops, besides about a thousand volunteers and
negroes raised by the authorities at Barbadoes.[1]

After a few days, required to water the fleet, they sailed,
and on January 8, 1762, anchored in St. Pierre's Bay.
There they found Douglas had silenced the batteries,
though with the loss of the *Raisonnable*, a " sixty-four,"
which a clumsy pilot had run aground as she was
leading-in for the French forts. But, as has been said,
there was no intention of proceeding further. " Having,"
says Rodney, " by the motion of the fleet and army taken
possession of an excellent harbour, and secured a landing
in the northernmost part of the island, which might be
made tenable at any time, and likewise thereby greatly
alarmed the enemy, at General Monckton's request I
despatched Commodore Swanton with a squadron of
ships and two brigades to the Bay of Petite Anse, in order
to take post there." Petite Anse d'Arlet was in the
extreme south-west of the island, below Fort Royal, the
naval station which was the real objective. The influence
of the operations at Quebec is clear. Under Wolfe and
Saunders, Monckton had learned the bewildering power
that is the strength of troops afloat, and full use of it was
being made. To confuse the enemy still further a
squadron of five large frigates was sent to La Trinité, a
port almost opposite St. Pierre, on the windward side of
the island, with orders to threaten a landing, and Swanton
was directed to fly a flag similar to the Admiral's.
Rodney himself, so soon as these detachments were away,
took the mass of the fleet round Swanton, and came to
anchor in St. Anne's Bay, in the extreme south of the island.

[1] Rodney to the Admiralty, Jan. 19, 1761.—Mundy, *Life of Rodney*, vol. i.
p. 69. Monckton to Egremont, Dec. 31, 1762, *S.P. Colonial* (*America and
West Indies*), 102.

Here the little batteries were quickly silenced and the troops landed, for from this point it was intended to make the real attack on Fort Royal over-land. A direct attack from the sea was impossible, for in the mouth of the Bay, on its south side, stood a high rocky island known as Isle des Ramiers, or Pigeon Island. It was crowned by a battery of heavy guns, which effectually barred the entrance to a hostile fleet. Consequently the reduction of this work was regarded as the first step to be taken. The idea was to land the troops at a point known as St. Luce, on the southern shore of the island, close to St. Anne's road. Hence in distance it was but a day's march to Fort Royal Bay. This method of getting at Pigeon Island, therefore, looked feasible enough; but no reconnoitring had been done in advance, and they were quite unaware that the country over which they meant to pass was so deeply scored with ravines and rocky ridges as to be impassable for artillery. The first reconnaissance revealed the ugly truth, and it was obvious that, if Pigeon Island was to be reduced, a landing much nearer Fort Royal Bay must be used. It was resolved, therefore, to try again to the westward, where Swanton had been operating at the Petite Anse d'Arlet. The troops were accordingly re-embarked and the St. Anne's fort blown up.

At the new point a footing had already been established by Brigadier Haviland, the same who had commanded the central column against Montreal. The indefatigable Hervey, too, was there—the hero of Hawke's inshore squadron off Brest, who, always in the thick of the work, had come out with Swanton from Keppel's Belleisle squadron. After Swanton had silenced the batteries at Petite Anse d'Arlet, he had sent Hervey on the 10th, the same day that Rodney had anchored at St.

Anne's, into the adjoining Grand Anse, which lay immediately to the north and nearer still to the objective. There, with his wonted energy, he had promptly silenced the battery and occupied it with his marines. Troops quickly followed from Haviland in support, and, marching inland, they seized Gros Point, immediately opposite Pigeon Island. But here it was the same story. The officer in command reported the country quite impracticable for artillery, and suggested his return to Haviland and Swanton's ships. While waiting for orders, he was attacked by troops sent from Fort Royal across the Bay; but he easily drove them off, and eventually retired unmolested. It was unpleasant news for Rodney and Monckton when they arrived. There was obviously nothing left but failure or a direct attack, and on the morrow, the 14th, the whole fleet anchored in the mouth of Fort Royal Bay.

Rodney and Monckton immediately proceeded to make a fresh reconnaissance, and ugly the project looked. The whole country appeared a kind of natural fortification, and, in spite of the various feints which had been made, it seemed to be swarming with irregular troops exactly adapted to the warfare in hand. The shores bristled with batteries, deep in the Bay sat the formidable citadel towering on a rocky height, and above it, a little inshore, rose, like great outworks, three lofty hills—the Morne Tortensson, the Morne Garnier, and the Morne Capuchin, all strongly entrenched. A landing within the Bay was clearly impossible, but next day a likely place was found, just to the north of it, at Cas Navires, close to where Moore and Hopson had tried two years before. Like every other possible point, it was defended by batteries, and the country between it and Fort Royal looked as bad as ever. But it was this or nothing. Accordingly, on the 16th, the whole fleet stood in, silenced the batteries, and at sunset Monckton was able to establish himself ashore unopposed, with a strong advanced guard. Their bewildering activity had been rewarded by an effective surprise, and, shortly after daybreak next morning, the whole army, including marines, had disembarked without the loss of a man. Swanton himself, with Hervey and Shuldham of the lost *Raisonnable*, conducted the three divisions of boats; and so well practised by this time was such amphibious work, that all had gone like a clock. The whole study of the war tells how difficult and dangerous are these operations to a force that is unfamiliar with them, and how easy and formidable when both fleet and army are at home with the work, and schooled for it, hand in hand, by constant and well-ordered practice.

So soon as the footing was made good, something like a regular approach was commenced against Morne Tortensson and Morne Garnier, the two nearest heights. Of what followed a picture has survived which is too vivid to lose : " As soon as we were all safely disembarked," wrote an officer of Scott's Light Infantry, " our engineers were immediately set to work in raising batteries, as well to establish our footing on the island as to cover our approaches to dislodge the enemy from their posts. For this purpose all the cannon and other warlike stores were landed as soon as possible, and dragged by the ' Jacks ' to any point they [the engineers] thought proper. You may fancy you know the spirit of these fellows : but to see them in action exceeds any idea that can be formed of them. A hundred or two of them with ropes and pullies will do more than all your dray-horses in London. Let but their tackle hold, and they will draw you a cannon or a mortar on its proper carriage up to any height, though the weight be never so great. It is droll enough to see them tugging along with a good twenty-four pounder at their heels; as they go, huzzaing and hallooing, sometimes up hill, sometimes down hill; now sticking fast in the brakes, presently floundering in the mud and mire; swearing, blasting, damning, sinking, and as careless of everything but the matter committed to their charge as if death or danger had nothing to do with them. We had a thousand of these brave fellows sent to our assistance by the admiral, and the service they did us both on shore and on the water is incredible." [1]

But though the bluejackets revolutionised the ideas of the army officers as to what ground was practicable for a siege train and what was not, the work of the troops was equally determined and brilliant. True their force was overwhelming compared with that of the French, but the country was extraordinarily close and difficult, a paradise for irregular troops. It was not till a week after the landing that the batteries against Morne Tortensson were complete, and early on January 24th a general assault was ordered. It was most brilliantly done. On the right Colonel Rufane's brigade and the marines, supported by a thousand seamen in flat boats rowing along the shore, had to take battery after battery. In the centre the massed Grenadier companies, supported by Lord Rollo's brigade, found an endless succession of works in their path, and scarcely could have succeeded but for Scott's Light Infantry, who, with the third brigade in support, outflanked the position and forced the enemy slowly back. Almost every yard had to be won; yet by nine o'clock all was over, and the troops were cheering in the formidable and well-armed redoubt on the summit of Morne Tortensson.

Before the overwhelming pressure of the well-nourished

[1] Mundy, *Life of Rodney*, vol. i. p. 74, *note.*

attack the enemy had retreated to the still higher Morne
Garnier, across an almost impassable ravine. So completely did it command the captured position that it was
seen it must be taken before batteries could be erected
against the citadel upon the ground they had won. Haviland, who now had the extreme left and had already
seized a footing across the ravine, was ordered to establish
batteries there. On the 27th he began the work; but
no sooner had he broken ground than the enemy resolved
to dislodge him, and towards evening made a desperate
attack in force. But the troops seasoned in the Canadian
wilds and the Highlanders he had with him withstood
the shock, and not satisfied with repulsing their enemy,
pushed on after them as they retreated, and by nightfall
were in possession of all the batteries on the lower slopes
of Morne Garnier. Still they were not content. Major
Leland, with a detachment of light infantry on the
extreme left flank, still crept on through the darkness.
Feeling nothing in front of him he climbed higher and
higher, till at last he found himself in the deserted redoubt on the summit with a loaded mortar and eight un-
spiked guns in his possession. He was quickly supported
from below, and thus as the contemporary narrator says,
" by a happy presence of mind was a defensive advantage
improved in the nick of time to a successful attack." [1]

The fact was that the French governor, M. de la
Touche, after leaving a garrison of about a thousand men
in Fort Royal, had retired with the bulk of his force to
St. Pierre. A garrison so abandoned has seldom great
resisting spirit. So soon as the governor's back was
turned the regulars retired into the citadel, and the
militia dispersed to their homes. A day or two later,
while the citadel was bombarded from Morne Tortensson,

[1] Beatson, vol. ii. p. 524.

the third position, Morne Capuchin, which was the nearest to Fort Royal, was occupied without opposition. It was but four hundred yards from the citadel, and Monckton immediately prepared to establish a new and more effective battery upon its summit. But the garrison would stand no more. Further resistance was indeed hopeless. On February 3rd they beat the *chamade*, and next day Fort Royal was in Monckton's hands. The garrison that marched out was but eight hundred men all told, but none the less the extraordinary physical difficulties and the precision and dash with which they had been overcome made the whole exploit a fine feat of arms. The strength of the French preparations, which they had had so long a time to make, may be judged by the fact that over a hundred and seventy pieces of artillery fell into Monckton's hands, with a vast quantity of ammunition. Added to this Rodney received the surrender of Pigeon Island on summons, and fourteen fine privateers that were lying in the harbour.

Immediately Fort Royal had surrendered Hervey, with a small squadron, was sent round to support the frigates at La Trinité. There he promptly landed five hundred seamen and marines to seize the place, and the whole district at once made its submission. It was the end of the operations. M. de la Touche could resist no further the pressure which the inhabitants brought to bear upon him. Rodney was in the act of moving on against St. Pierre when a proposal for capitulation arrived, and on February 15th Martinique was a British possession.

At last the power of the French in the West Indies was completely broken. It remained but to gather in the lesser islands. Swanton with a brigade was despatched to Grenada, where he quickly forced the governor to surrender. Hervey, with an insignificant detachment,

was sent to St. Lucia and St. Vincent. His orders
were to attack St. Lucia if he found it not beyond his
strength, and if it were he was to report to the admiral.
On arriving before the place he found he could not make
sure whether it was beyond his force or not. The entrance was so narrow as to block the view, but as usual
he was equal to the occasion. He resolved to send in a
summons to the governor, and after his own peculiar
manner accompanied the flag of truce dressed as a mid-
shipman so as to see for himself. His visit satisfied him
that the task was not beyond his strength. The place
was defended by a single fort, and he assured himself
it was possible to run right in and lay his ships close
enough to knock it to pieces. This plan he accordingly
proceeded to put in execution the next day, but no sooner
were his ships seen standing for the harbour than a
capitulation was sent to meet him. It was thus, as it
were, single-handed, this intrepid officer had the honour
of adding to the British possessions that famous naval
base, which in the future was destined to be the key of
our position in the Caribbean Sea. No doubt St. Vincent
too would have been added to his score, but in his absence
an event had happened which changed the whole situation. As he was in the act of proceeding to carry out
the rest of his instructions he received an urgent order
from Rodney to rejoin him with all expedition.

CHAPTER VIII

THE INTERVENTION OF SPAIN

WHILE Rodney had been engaged in breaking the last of the French power in the West Indies, the situation in Europe had been developing with equal energy. As the new Ministers in London waited for the result of their ultimatum in Spain their situation grew daily more difficult. Their efforts to curb the momentum which Pitt had given the war in his last weeks of power had no effect but to mark the divisions that hampered them. The army estimates had involved them in a damaging debate on the German war. Charles Townshend, the general's brother, who had succeeded Barrington at the War Office, moved for sufficient forces to continue to support Prince Ferdinand on the previous scale. In the course of his speech he justified the continental operations as the bed-rock defence from which the whole of our conquest had been pushed forward. He urged that the harmonious co-ordination of offence and defence, "the totality of the war," as he called it, had been one of the great causes of its success, and he ended with a well-reasoned panegyric on what he termed " Mr. Pitt's divine plan." The Court dared not permit its views on the subject to be seen too openly, but Rigby, Bedford's man, had no such scruples, and he denounced the whole continental system from beginning to end. Grenville was more guarded. It was France's lack of seamen, he said, and not the German war which had prevented her sup-

porting her operations in America or invading England ;
yet he protested Ministers were bound by treaty to continue the continental war against their will.   Such a
speech was tantamount to a declaration that they meant
to desert Frederick so soon as they could find a decent
occasion, and it brought Pitt to his legs once more.   In
temperate language he defended his system.   The German
war, he said, had been forced upon him against his will by
the breach of the Convention of Kloster Zeven, but even
so he had only agreed to it after every other service had
been provided for.   Having had to undertake it, he
claimed that he had managed it in such a way that he
had thereby annihilated the French power both in the
West and the East Indies.   As Germany had formerly
been handled, it had been a millstone round our necks,
but he had made it a millstone about the neck of France,
and he vowed, though he stood alone, he would divide
the House against deserting our allies.

The debate closed without a division, but next day the
trouble was renewed by a private member's motion for
papers on our relations with Spain.   Grenville could only
resist it by a high assertion that the power to negotiate
belonged to the Crown.   The debate grew angry, the
House lost its temper, and Pitt magnanimously inter-
vened.   Too loyal and too deeply convinced of the value
of his cherished view of sound war administration to go
back on it for a tactical advantage, however tempting, he
claimed for Lord Egremont "the right to guide his own
correspondence."   He himself, who, he' hoped, had not
lessened his country, had always claimed the right.   It was
no question, he said, of "sole Minister," and in thus dis-
tinguishing between his idea of ministerial responsibility
and the spectre of dictatorship, he seized the opportunity
of repudiating the stories that were and still are current

about his despotism. In the Treasury, he said, in the
Military, and in the Navy he had never assumed or
claimed any direction : he had never spoken to the King
on these heads, but had always applied to the Ministers
of the several departments. Then, having vindicated his
theory of war direction, he proceeded moderately to
support the motion for papers on the ground that their
production could only strengthen the King's hands by
showing how patient we had been, and that it was
impossible for the House to judge what supplies were
necessary till it knew how we stood with Spain. Yet he
protested he would not press the motion if told by
authority it was premature. He concluded by saying
that he had secret information which placed it beyond
doubt that Spain meant war, and by pointing out how
weak and unready she was.[1] A gross and violent
personal attack by truculent Colonel Barré was his
reward. Disdaining to answer, he dismissed the insult
with a jest about Red Indians and tomahawks. Eventually, on a suggestion that an express from Spain was probably even then on the road, the motion was negatived
without a division.[2]

An express was indeed on its way not only to England,
but to all the ends of the earth. While they debated
the crisis had come. The King's messenger had reached
Madrid with the ultimatum on December 5th. Bristol
saw Wall next day, and repeated his demand for a dis-

---

[1] These frequent allusions of Pitt to information in his possession leave
little doubt that he had evidence of Spain's intentions beyond that which
was known to the Cabinet from the intercepted Fuentes-Grimaldi correspondence. The common explanation is that he had obtained it under
seal of absolute secrecy from George Keith, the attainted Earl Marischal,
who in 1759 was Frederick's ambassador in Madrid, and that the Earl's
pardon was his reward. His pardon, however, was signed on May 29,
1759, and his attainder reversed the following year.

[2] Walpole, *Memoirs of George III.*, vol. i. p. 91 *et seq.*

closure of the treaty. Wall was polite and conciliatory, so Bristol said nothing about leaving. Misled by Fuentes's reports of the infirmity of the new Government in London, decisive action was the last thing Wall expected. Two days later he calmly presented Bristol with the King's reply, which was to the effect that no further answer could be given beyond a memorial which had been despatched to Fuentes for delivery to Egremont. Then Bristol plainly declared what his instructions were—to demand whether Spain meant to join France, and if an answer were refused to leave at once. Wall was astounded. He could scarcely believe his ears, and requested Bristol to put his demand in writing. This he did, and next day received a categorical refusal. On the same day, the 10th, orders were sent out to seize every British vessel, man-of-war or merchantman, in the Spanish ports, with an embargo on all Spanish ships, so as to prevent the news of the seizure getting abroad. Bristol immediately set about carrying out his secret instructions, but he found it no easy matter. Every difficulty was thrown in the way of his communicating with the admirals. Post-horses were even refused him, and it was not till he reached the Portuguese frontier, nearly at the end of the month, that he was able to send forward warning to the fleet.

Saunders was at Gibraltar crouching for a spring. In the middle of November he had sent to Anson a project for dealing a death-blow to the French Mediterranean trade by raiding Marseilles under cover of a feint on Minorca. In view of war with Spain, it was accompanied by another plan for a similar blow on the ships at Cadiz, and for the capture of Oran as an equivalent for Minorca if that island were handed over to Spain. He regretted that never having seen either Marseilles or Cadiz he could not give a decided opinion as to the practicability of his proposals, but he was ready to try so soon as he got the word. His information was that the Spaniards had ten of the line in Cadiz. He himself, besides his detached ships, had fifteen of the line in Gibraltar Bay ready to sail at a moment's notice. At the end of the year two more joined him with some fireships, but still there was no word from Lord Bristol. It was not till January 4th that the ambassador's letter, which he had written on December 11th to say he was leaving, reached him. It was forwarded by Hay, our Minister at Lisbon, and with it unhappily came news that ever since the middle of December the Spaniards had been hard at work putting Cadiz in a state of defence, and that the ships had been withdrawn into the inner harbour. Saunders sadly recognised that his chance was gone. Seeing at once that the only method of performing his containing functions, was to assume a purely defensive attitude, he wrote home to say he had decided the attack was impracticable and that he must confine himself to preventing any concentration of the scattered divisions of the allies, and particularly to keeping apart the divisions within the Straits and those in the Atlantic. His main preoccupation was the Toulon squadron, and his dominant object to prevent its getting out of the Mediterranean. For the present, however, he knew it was not ready for sea, and felt he could attend to the scarcely less important object of preventing a junction between the enemy's Atlantic divisions. So soon, therefore, as the wind would permit, he moved up to the westward to blockade Cadiz, so as to prevent its squadron getting out, or anything from the northward getting in.[1]

So far, then, as Saunders was concerned, the Spaniards

---

[1] Saunders to the Admiralty, Dec. 8, 16, 18, 24, 1761, Jan. 8 and 21, 1762, *In-letters*, 384.

had certainly managed well in preventing his striking
the rapid blow which would so greatly have eased the
difficulties of his containing position. Elsewhere, however, owing to the enterprise of an obscure naval officer,
they were not so successful. It happened that a certain
Captain George Johnstone, of his Majesty's sloop *Hornet*,
had just captured a smart French privateer off the coast
of Portugal, from whom he learned of the order of
December 10th for the seizure of British shipping. He
immediately carried her into Lisbon, where a few days
later he ascertained that Spain had declared war. Thereupon, on his own responsibility, he manned and victualled
his prize, placed her under the command of his master,
and sent her away express to Rodney with the news.[1]

London was equally fortunate. In spite of the Spanish
precautions, Bristol's advices of his departure reached
home in less than a fortnight, and on Christmas Eve
orders were issued to all stations to commence hostilities.
Two days later the *Gazette* announced a state of war with
Spain, and on the 29th Sir Peircy Brett, the officer who
since 1759 had had charge of the northern section of the
Channel blockade, was sent down with two more of the
line and another frigate further to reinforce Saunders.

The latest information that Bristol had sent home was
that there was a squadron of eleven of the line in Ferrol
ready for sea, and that fifteen hundred troops had
marched to that port to embark for the West Indies.
In Cadiz were five battalions awaiting final orders for the
same destination. One regiment had already gone to
Majorca, and another was on its way, and two vessels
laden with arms and ammunition had sailed for the West
Indies from Barcelona. The movement to Majorca might
of course be merely defensive, or it might indicate a

[1] Beatson, vol. ii. p. 531 ; and see *infra note*, p. 235.

Spanish occupation of Minorca. The intention of the Ferrol squadron was still more uncertain. The general belief, however, both in England and Spain, was that it threatened a descent on Ireland.[1] To Choiseul, however, it meant something much more ambitious. He was forming in his mind a grandiose plan for a combined invasion of England on the familiar lines which have failed so often. His complete plan, however, was not presented to the Spanish Court till the following April, and may be considered later.

The immediate anxiety of the British Government was a squadron of seven of the line and four frigates which was lying in Brest ready for sea with some three thousand troops on board, and known to be destined for the West Indies, and it was believed that the ships in Rochefort and the Charente were intended to steal round and join it. The Brest squadron was being watched by a division of Keppel's fleet consisting of thirteen of the line under Captain Matthew Buckle. On December 5th word came home from him that he feared it had given him the slip, and warning was at once sent out to Rodney to be on his guard. If the escaped squadron appeared towards Jamaica he was to send Douglas with at least six of the line to reinforce Holmes, an order which must be remembered as it came to have considerable importance. If, on the other hand, it came his own way he might call on Holmes for assistance.[2] Next day orders were despatched to Keppel recalling five more regiments from Belleisle, which with artillery and the dragoons made up four thousand five hundred men. He had previously told the Government that four of the line and a few cruisers would be enough to co-operate with the garrison that

---

[1] Duro, *Armada Española*, vol. vii. p. 40.
[2] *Admiralty Secretary, Out-letters (Secret Orders)*, 1331, Dec. 5.

would remain, and he was ordered in consequence to leave such a squadron on the station and proceed himself to take command off Ushant.[1]   At the same time, since the combined operations in which he had been engaged were at an end, he was told henceforth to receive his orders from the Admiralty and not from the Secretary of State.

The reported escape of the Brest squadron was soon known to be a false alarm, but Keppel was by no means easy about the blockade.   He had been pressing the Admiralty with his opinions on the vital necessity of speed, pointing out the error of setting foul ships to intercept clean ones.[2]   He knew the Rochefort ships were ready to sail, and doubted the possibility of the slugs at his command preventing their junction with those that were still in Brest.   His mistrust of the blockade with the material at his disposal was too well founded.   On December 23rd, before ever he could crawl up to his new station, the whole Brest squadron, under Monsieur de Blénac, gave the slip to Captain Spry, who had succeeded Buckle off Ushant, and had made straight for the West Indies.[3]   Even when Keppel reached the station he could not hold it.   The weather proved quite beyond the endurance of his worn squadron, and the second week of January a terrific gale sent the whole of his ships flying for any Channel port they could reach, and for the time he was practically off the board.

Once more it was proved, as was to be shown so often in the future, how weak a form of war is a prolonged close blockade; how the wear and tear of ships, and the consequent loss of speed and endurance, even in sailing days,

[1] *Ibid.*, Dec. 6, 1761.
[2] Keppel, *Life of Keppel*, vol. i. p. 336, Keppel to Buckle, Oct. 17, 1761.
[3] Rodney to the Admiralty, March 24, 1762.—Mundy, *Life of Rodney*, vol. i. p. 76.

inevitably gives the enemy his chance sooner or later. For a short time it is well. It would serve to keep the enemy in and the sea clear for covering or preventing a definite oversea operation—that is, for a temporary and local command. For permanent command it must always be doubtful whether it can compare with an open blockade conducted from a good interior position by a fleet that can retain its speed and fitness for action, without the demoralisation of absolute inactivity.

It was these events which had recalled Hervey in the midst of his little career of conquest. Rodney had already received by Captain Johnstone's prize a copy of the embargo order, and news that a state of war had been declared in Spain on December 15th. The transformed French prize had all the qualities of her class, and had made an extraordinarily quick passage, so that Rodney received the warning some time in the middle of February, a fortnight or more before an official intimation reached him. The news was quickly confirmed by a British transport bringing out infantry drafts, which, having put into a Spanish port on the way, had narrowly escaped seizure herself. Thereupon Rodney threw out his cruisers, and before the end of the month Captain Ourry, of the *Actæon* frigate, had captured a "register ship" laden with arms and military stores, presumably one of those which Bristol had reported as sailing from Barcelona. On the last day of the month all doubt was removed by the arrival from Antigua of a frigate from home with the Admiralty orders to begin hostilities.[1]

[1] Beatson (vol. ii. p. 531) says M'Laurin, the *Hornet's* master, made the passage in twenty-three days, and delivered Johnstone's letter to Rodney on Jan. 18, that is, just after the landing at Cas Navires. This may well be true, though Rodney sent home a despatch next day, and another on Feb. 10, without saying a word about it. In his next, however, dated Feb. 28, he says he had received the news some time back, and had already captured a valuable Spanish prize; and the *Actæon's Log* mentions

Still Rodney did not think it necessary to interrupt the work of organising his new conquest in which he was engaged off St. Pierre, or to call in his scattered squadrons. Within the week, however, the whole situation was changed. On March 5th, three more frigates reached him with despatches. One was direct from home, and another from Saunders with copies of the orders already received. The third had a different and less pleasant tale to tell. She was straight from Ushant, sent off in hot haste by Spry to inform him of Blénac's escape. Since the first false alarm had reached him Rodney had had a chain of frigates to windward the whole length of the Caribbee Islands, on the look-out for the Brest squadron as well as for Spanish prizes, and he now repeated to them his orders for the utmost vigilance. It was now, too, he despatched his urgent order recalling Hervey, and at the same time sent word to Swanton, who was down at Grenada with seven of the line, positive orders to attack Blénac if he appeared on his station. As Fort Royal, however, was Blénac's probable destination, Swanton was further directed, if he had already taken Grenada, to join the flag at once with five of the line, so as to enable Rodney to form two squadrons each strong enough to engage the enemy whether he tried to reach his goal by the north or the south end of Martinique.

Blénac, however, was too clever to do either. Having no mind to thrust his head into the lion's mouth, he warily made the windward side of Martinique near La Trinité, and on March 8th sent an officer ashore for intelligence. Here, early on the 9th, he was sighted by the very frigate by which Spry had sent the warning.

the capture of a Spanish ship, bound to La Guayra from Cadiz on Feb. 4. —*Admiralty Secretary, In-letters,* 307 ; *Captain's Logs,* 2. Johnstone and M'Laurin were both made post for the service, and Johnstone governor of Pensacola in 1763.—Hardy, *List of Captains,* 1673–1783.

The same afternoon she was seen from Rodney's flagship off St. Pierre, flying the signal for an enemy's fleet,
and the admiral immediately signalled to weigh. Unhappily it fell calm and he could not stir. The frigate-
captain came on board and reported that at eight o'clock
that morning the enemy's squadron, thirteen sail strong, of
which eight were of the line, were off La Trinité standing
south.

The information indicated that it was Blénac's intention to reach Fort Royal round the southern point of
the island. There Douglas was cruising with a weak
detachment, and his position was critical. Fortunately
the wind had now sprung up, and Rodney, who had with
him six of the line, crowded all sail to the rescue.
Swanton and Hervey had been given the same point for
rendezvous, and he made no doubt Blénac was delivered
into his hands. But he was doomed to disappointment.
After joining Douglas he sailed round the island on the
windward side, but without finding a trace of his opponent. When Blénac had been seen by the British frigate
he had already ascertained that the island was in British
hands, and was now on his way northward, heading for
Cap François. His board to the south which the frigate
had seen had probably been only a ruse. After lying-to
till midday on the 10th he put before the wind, warned
perhaps from the shore of Rodney's movement, and after
running so close to La Trinité that the officer in command
made ready for an attack, he held away northward towards Dominica. A day or two after came news from
Guadeloupe that he had been seen from there steering
to the westward. There could no longer be room for
doubt that he was making either for Jamaica or Cap
François, with the probable intention of effecting a pre-
concerted junction with the Spaniards. Rodney thus

found himself confronted with a strategical situation which called for all his sagacity and readiness to take responsibility.

In Havana he knew that a formidable naval concentration had been going on for some time. It was said that fourteen of the line were already there, and others were on the station. He felt, like Saunders at the other side of the ocean, that at all hazards the allied squadrons must be prevented from getting together. To stop Blénac reaching Cap François was now impossible, and Swanton and Hervey having by this time joined he resolved to return to St. Pierre for victuals and water with all speed, and then to proceed to the succour of Jamaica. His orders under the circumstances that had arisen, it will be remembered, did no more than authorise his detaching Douglas to Jamaica. But they had been issued before the Spanish declaration of war, and like the fine officer he was in his prime, he determined to take the responsibility of leaving his station for the point of danger.

As in hot haste he was watering at St. Pierre the crisis was intensified, and the course on which he had determined made clearer. An urgent express came in from the governor and council of Jamaica, to say they had learned from intercepted letters that the island was to be attacked by the combined forces of Spain and France, and the French officers who were to command were on board Blénac's fleet. Blénac had reached Cap François on the 15th, that is about the same time that Rodney had returned to water at St. Pierre. Captain Carteret of the *Merlin* sloop had been watching the port as usual, when that night he suddenly found himself close to the French fleet. Some of them gave chase, and seeing no escape Carteret, as a last hope, began signalling with lights and guns, as though the British battle-fleet were within call.

Trite as was the device, it succeeded. It was no part of Blénac's game to fight single-handed. He was fortunate enough not to find the Jamaica squadron barring his entrance to Cap François. The chasing ships were recalled, and the squadron went crowding into port in such a hurry that a sixty-four took the ground and was lost.[1]

Thus threatened, the Jamaica authorities felt compelled to urge Rodney and Monckton to send them relief. To add to the trouble, their demand was accompanied by a letter from Captain Forrest, the senior officer on the station, to say that his admiral, the gallant and resourceful Holmes, was dead—a loss which may have accounted for Cap François having been left open.

All shadow of doubt as to what his duty was was now removed from Rodney's mind. Not only did he resolve to move at once to the Jamaica station with every ship that could be spared from the Caribbee Islands, but he pressed Monckton to let him take a body of troops as well. In spite of the admiral's importunity, Monckton in great distress refused. He did not, he said, consider himself sufficiently authorised to detach troops from his command without orders from England. For this refusal he was afterwards blamed by his commander-in-chief, Amherst, who wrote to him that he ought to have assented, in view of the Spanish concentration at Havana. In the general's defence, however, it must be said, that whereas Rodney had definite orders to make a detachment to Jamaica if it were threatened by Blénac, Monckton had not. Still, with this evidence of what was in the mind of the Home Government, Monckton, had he been a less commonplace officer than he was, might well have decided " to march to the sound of the guns." Still, for all his fine soldiership, he would not be persuaded,

[1] Beatson, vol. ii. p. 535.

and Rodney went off with practically his whole fleet. "I flatter myself," wrote Rodney in his despatch, "their lordships will not be displeased with me if I take the liberty to construe my instructions in such a manner as to think myself authorised and obliged to succour any of his Majesty's colonies that may be in danger; and shall therefore hasten to the succour of Jamaica with ten sail of the line, three frigates, and three bombs." And he concluded by saying that it was his intention, unless he received orders to the contrary, which he obviously expected, to return to his station before the hurricane months, leaving a sufficient force behind him for the protection of Jamaica. After making all deductions, it was a fine resolve, and should live as a classical example of a seamanlike interpretation of orders, and of the true spirit of command.[1]

When Rodney penned his despatch, he had already reached Antigua. By the division of his force which he intended to make, he would, with Holmes's squadron, have perhaps twenty of the line, a force about equal to the combined squadrons of the enemy, and amply sufficient by defensive action to prevent an oversea military expedition. At the same time he would be able to send back Douglas with eight of the line, which would be sufficient to deal with Blénac if he doubled back, or with the Rochefort squadron if it came out. To Forrest, as acting commander on the Jamaica station, he wrote that he was to meet him with his whole squadron at Cape Nicholas in the Windward Passage, as it was his intention to get between the enemy's squadrons and blockade Blénac wherever he found him. This done he

---

[1] Rodney to the Admiralty, March 24, *In-letters*, 307 (Printed by Mundy, i. p. 80); Amherst to Egremont, May 12, *S.P. Colonial* (*America and West Indies*), 97; and *cf.* Beatson, vol. ii. p. 530 *et seq.*

went on to St. Christopher's, where he meant finally
to divide his force. He reached it on March 26, but
only to suffer another bitter disappointment, for there
he was met by Captain Elphinstone, of the *Richmond*
frigate, with fresh orders direct from home.

They told him that a secret expedition was coming out
by the middle of April under Sir George Pocock of
Indian fame and the Earl of Albemarle. He was to
be superseded in the supreme command, but with a
handsome apology it was explained that the importance
of the enterprise demanded an officer of high rank at
its head. The actual objective was not disclosed. Rodney
was merely informed that the intention was to make an
impression on the Spanish colonies and everything must
give way to it. Even if Martinique were not entirely
conquered, all further operations must be suspended.
Rodney himself was to be under Pocock's orders, and was
to devote himself to preparing for the " grand expedition."
He had strict orders himself to repair to Martinique to
prepare transports for Monckton's force to take its part,
and to organise a division of ten of the line, whose
captains were junior to Swanton, for special service with
the expedition. To leave no room for independent judgment, the order concluded in the most stringent form.
" As you must be sensible of the great importance of these
orders it is unnecessary for us to add any motives to
enforce the most punctual and expeditious obedience
thereto." [1]

Even so it was beyond Rodney's nature to obey. Strict
as were his orders, he could not bring himself to abandon
his move, and at this point his conduct, which up to then
most men will praise, becomes more doubtful. There was
within his knowledge something upon which the Home

---

[1] *In-letters (Secret Orders)*, 1332, Feb. 5.

Government had not counted.   The Brest squadron was in Cap François, bent on forming a junction with the Spaniards at Havana.   Strategy cried aloud with a voice that seemed to drown all other considerations that it should be kept there, and Rodney could not shut his ears.   On the other hand, he certainly should have remembered that there was much in the mind of the Government which was concealed from him, and he knew they were not unaware of Blénac's escape.   There was a new war plan on foot, the details of which had been kept from him, and to which he was strictly enjoined to make himself subservient.   Under such circumstances it may be doubted whether an officer is ever justified in acting on his own initiative, however plausible it may appear on the spot, when such initiative involves a clear departure from the main lines of the war plan, so far as it is disclosed to him.   Yet this is what Rodney did.   For him to leave his station himself was now impossible.   The orders were too imperative for that.   But in spite of his plain instructions to have a squadron under Swanton ready for Pocock when he arrived, he decided that Douglas should still go on in accordance with the discretion his original orders allowed.   While he, therefore, returned to Martinique, Douglas, with ten of the line and Hervey for his second, held on for Jamaica.

In Port Royal, which Douglas reached on April 12, he found nine sail.   Here, too, he heard that the Brest squadron, now reduced to six of the line and three frigates, was in Cap François, and that any intention there may have been of an attack on Jamaica from Havana had been abandoned, owing, it was believed, to the dispositions which Rodney had made.   He also heard that more troops were expected down from North America to join the " grand expedition," and had sight of the orders which had been sent to Holmes, in view of the coming expedition. In these the dead admiral was ordered to assist in raising five hundred negroes to act with Albemarle's troops and to await Pocock's instructions at Port Royal with all his squadron ready to sail. The orders ended with the same stringent clause as Rodney's.[1] But Douglas was as little affected as his chief. The danger of the American contingent seemed to him to justify the freest interpretation. Instead, therefore, of obeying he took a leaf out of Rodney's book, and immediately sent Hervey away with seven of the line and two frigates to take station at Tortuga, an island which lies just to leeward of Cap François, so as to cover the passage of the North American transports, and deal with Blénac if he attempted to come out.[2]

Rodney himself returned to St. Pierre. There he found Monckton had been concentrating every man that could safely be recalled from the island garrisons. The unhappy admiral likewise busied himself with transport arrangements according to his new instructions. Still he could not be content to see his squadron idle, and in spite of the order to undertake no new operations, and his special directions about Swanton, he despatched him with the greatest part of his remaining ships to cruise on the Spanish main.

It may be that the chance of rich prizes was not without influence in this decision.[3] There was, however, a good strategical reason which was quite in accord with his other dispositions. For in Cartagena lay a Spanish squadron of three of the line and a frigate, which might well be

---

[1] *Secret Orders*, 1332, Feb. 5.

[2] Douglas to the Admiralty, May 8, *In-letters*, 307.

[3] Rodney to the Admiralty, May 31.—Mundy, vol. i. p. 92. There he only says, "Mr. Swanton has rejoined me from the Spanish main, where I sent him to cruise for some time, but without success."

destined to form part of a general concentration against Jamaica, and which, therefore, had to be watched as well as Blénac in Cap François.[1]   Even if we assume this to have been his intention, and he nowhere says so, the responsibility he took in sending a squadron so far to leeward was very serious.   He was still further scattering the fleet he had been told to concentrate, and surely without sufficient justification.

Such cases are very hard to judge.   Nothing is more admired with us than a fearlessness of responsibility and a sagacious readiness to interpret orders in the light of actual conditions on the spot.   Yet nothing is more dangerous.   Where is the line to be drawn?   It is impossible to say.   Yet the present case would seem to indicate that it lies somewhere between Rodney's first resolution and his second.   His first impulse to protect Jamaica it is difficult not to applaud; but what of his second after his new orders were received?   He knew that he was to be superseded, and superseded because of his inexperience and the impossibility of his knowing what was in the mind of the Government.   So much he was plainly told.   He knew, moreover, that he was to be subservient to a new plan of campaign for which another man was responsible, and which had not been disclosed to him.   Even the objective he could only guess.   It may well be doubted whether, under such circumstances, any local considerations could justify the wide liberty Rodney took with his plain orders.   Surely he should have considered that what he knew of the local conditions to justify his action was insignificant compared with his almost entire ignorance of the new plan of campaign.   The special knowledge of the

---

[1] Duro, *Armada Española*, vol. vii. p. 43.   There is no actual evidence that Rodney knew of this squadron.

Admiralty was out of all proportion greater than his own, and, in such cases, simple obedience like Monckton's seems the better course. At best, Rodney's conduct on this occasion must stand for an example of latitude of interpretation being stretched to its extreme limit.

CHAPTER IX

THE ATTACK ON SPAIN—HAVANA

IN the attitude which each officer had chosen to assume, Rodney and Monckton awaited the coming of the "grand expedition." Its objective, as none could doubt, was Havana. It is said the conception was Pitt's, and that, like Drake in 1585, he was bent on stabbing Spain at once in the heart of her colonial power and wealth. However this may be, the general design was certainly Anson's, founded on information furnished by Admiral Sir Charles Knowles, whom we have met with as second in command of the Rochefort expedition. During the late war, he had himself conducted operations against Cuba, had made an unsuccessful attack on Santiago, and had fought an indecisive action before Havana. Since then he had been for four years governor of Jamaica, and, as late as 1756, in the last year of his office, had visited Havana and been entertained by the Spanish governor. Having kept his eyes open, he was able to provide a detailed report on the defences and general condition of the place, and to indicate exactly the points at which it was most easily assailable. To his report he added a strong opinion as to the feasibility of the enterprise, and the unparalleled advantages that must ensue from its success.[1]

---

[1] *Add. MSS.*, 23,678. This unnoticed document is in the form of an anonymous pamphlet, but apparently Knowles never published it. He says that after all was over the *Journal of the Siege* was submitted to him to revise before publication. He seized the occasion, after his cross-

Thus fortified, Anson had little difficulty in over-coming the resistance in his way.   In spite of the determined opposition of Bedford and the half-hearted doubts of the Newcastle set, the new Government took up his idea with commendable promptitude.   It was only at Christmas, as we have seen, that Bristol's departure was known in London, yet, by the first week in January, at a meeting of the Secret Committee to settle the war plan, all was decided.   Bedford, who was in open opposition to continuing the war at all, was not summoned.   There were present Devonshire, Anson, Ligonier, Grenville, and Newcastle, with the two Secre-taries of State, Bute and Egremont.   "We began," wrote Newcastle, "with my Lord Anson's project of attacking Havana, and, after hearing the facility with which his lordship and Lord Ligonier apprehended there was in doing it, we all unanimously ordered the undertaking." [1]

grained manner, to draw up an intemperate invective on the whole conduct of the operations and Anson's plan of campaign, being particularly bitter against the soldiers.   No great importance need be attached to it.   For all his many good qualities he was constitutionally wrong-headed and quarrelsome, and by this time he was thoroughly embittered and a con-firmed pamphleteer.   After Vernon's failure at Cartagena in 1741 he had written a similar attack on the army ; his action off Havana had led to an unprecedented crop of duels and court-martials ; and, after Rochefort, he had perversely taken upon himself to defend General Mordaunt, and so offensive was the pamphlet he wrote both to Pitt and Anson that he was deprived of the command of the "Grand Fleet," which he then held, and was no more employed at sea.

The work submitted to Knowles for revision was An Authentic Journal of the Siege of Havana, by an Officer, 1762.   It is from the military point of view, and is the chief authority for the expedition.   With Knowles's MS. there is another Journal by "the chief engineer," Patrick MacKellar, who had served in the same capacity at the taking and the defence of Quebec, and at Martinique, and as second at Louisbourg.   It was published in the Gazette, Sept. 1762.

[1] Hardwicke clearly attributed the design to Anson.   In the notes of his speech on the Peace, where he reaches the question of Havana, he writes, "Stop a little, and here do justice to Lord Anson."—Parliamentary History, vol. xv. p. 1254, note.   Cf. also post p. 261, note.   Writing to Newcastle,

Then Egremont brought up Colonel Draper's design for taking Manilla with the troops already in India in concert with the East India Company. This also, "in a manner," says Newcastle, was agreed to. Then followed the thorny question as to whether it was possible, in view of the demands of the new war, to continue the war in Germany. On this point no agreement, even "in a manner," was possible. It was destined, indeed, in a few months to break up the Government.[1]

The new offensive movement, once decided on, was pushed forward with energy. Anson was still at his post, spilling the last drops of his devoted life in the service of the country which owed him so much. He had always protested the fleet was unequal to a war with both France and Spain. With the last glow of his energy, as it smouldered out, he proved it was not; but the effort killed him. Pocock's final orders were issued on February 18th, and they were the last he ever signed. After that he broke up, and, early in June, before he could know the result of his work, he was dead.[2]

Pocock's appointment was certainly his work. As we shall see, the plan of campaign demanded for its conduct a man of the highest powers, not only as a fighting admiral, but as a navigator and seaman, and from both points of view no better choice could have been made. Boscawen was dead; Hawke was wanted for the Channel

Oct. 2, on receiving news of the fall of Havana, he says: "It does the greatest honour to the memory of poor Lord Anson, who had so great a part in the formation and direction of it."—*Newcastle Papers*, 32,943.

[1] Newcastle to Hardwicke, Jan. 10, *Newcastle Papers*, 32,933.

[2] Writing on July 22 a private letter to Anson, Rodney begins: "It was with infinite concern I heard of your lordship's bad state of health, and I most sincerely hope ere this it is perfectly restored."—Mundy, vol. i. p. 93. He had been ill since the beginning of the year.—Walpole, *George III.*, vol. i. p. 130, and *Newcastle Papers*, ibid. passim.

Fleet; Saunders could not be spared from the all-important Mediterranean command; and, after them, no one could show so fine a record of fleet actions as Pocock, and he had served as commander-in-chief on the Leeward Islands station during the late war. Keppel, though still only a commodore, was selected for the second post, as he richly deserved, and was given a special commission to be second-in-command and Pocock's successor in case of his death. It was not quite fair to Rodney, whose knowledge of the theatre and well-earned success should have marked him for the second post. But his success was not yet known, and, besides in Keppel's appointment, though as an old "Centurion" he was probably a *persona grata* to Anson, we perhaps see traces of an influence which was flagrantly evident in the military command.

At the War Office there was no Anson to resist court and political favouritism. The Duke of Cumberland was again in the ascendant. The young King had a high regard for his uncle, and, though he held no office, he was the real military adviser of the throne. So the unhappy game, which Pitt had stopped with so much difficulty, began again. The old Duke was incorrigible. After the Martinique expedition had sailed, he had told Newcastle he approved of the design, but not of the admiral, the general, or the number of troops.[1] Whether he thought the troops were too many or too few is not clear, but what he meant about the general became painfully evident. In his eyes no one could be fit for such a command who had not been on his staff. He believed, no doubt honestly enough, that his "family" embraced all the real military talent in the country, and highest in favour in his "family" stood Keppel's eldest brother,

[1] Newcastle to Devonshire, Oct. 31, 1761, *Newcastle Papers*, 32,930.

the young Earl of Albemarle. He was not yet forty, and had been a member of the Duke's household ever since he was sixteen, and had served on his staff at Fontenoy and Culloden. Whatever his hereditary abilities for command, he had never held one, and whatever knowledge of his profession he had acquired as the Duke's aide-de-camp he had never proved it. By Wolfe, with all his admiration for the Duke, Albemarle was set down as a parade officer, whose soldiership consisted in a taste for showy uniforms.

For second in command there was General George Eliott, better known as Lord Heathfield, the famous defender of Gibraltar. His record during the war was very high. In the expedition against Cherbourg and St. Malo, he had been remarked for his soldier-like efforts to set right the mistakes of the incompetent quarter-master-general,[1] and ever since he had been commanding his regiment in Germany and winning golden opinions from Prince Ferdinand. The two divisional generals were La Fausillé and Albemarle's younger brother, William Keppel. Thus no less than three of that favoured family were given the chance of a lion's share in the enormous booty that was confidently expected from the expedition, while the men on the spot, like Haviland and Rollo, who had borne the heat and burden of the day and made themselves masters of amphibious warfare, had to be content with brigades. The only redeeming feature in the staff, besides Eliott, was the appointment of Colonel Guy Carleton to the important post of quarter-master-general. He had been Wolfe's favourite officer, and, in spite of the old King's vehement opposition, Pitt had insisted on his having him in the same post for the Quebec expedition. He was fresh

---

[1] *Stopford-Sackeville MSS. (Hist. MSS. Com.)*, IX. iii. 72a.

from the successful command of a brigade at Belleisle, and, as he also had been of the Duke's family, there was now no difficulty about it.

It is usually said that considerable delay occurred in getting the expedition away. It is certainly true that, owing to the hesitation of the new Government in declaring war, preparations began a little late. But the truth is that when once the decision was taken, the matter was pushed through with an energy and success that Pitt himself could not have surpassed. The feat of the new administration is all the more remarkable if we consider the difficulties it had to overcome from the nervousness of the older Ministers and the vastness of the whole plan, of which the Havana expedition was only a part. Newcastle soon became alarmed at the scale on which it was being prepared, for it was becoming every day more evident that assistance of some kind would have to be sent to Portugal. In every war we had had with Spain the security of our ancient ally had always been a serious preoccupation. Apart from the importance of our commercial interests, which the famous Methuen treaty had set up, Lisbon was almost essential to maintaining our naval position in the Mediterranean, and especially so since the loss of Minorca. At the moment, owing to the earthquake at Lisbon and other causes, Portugal was particularly weak, and one of the motives which had hardened the heart of Spain to declaring war was always supposed to be the prospect of seizing it, as the Duke of Alva had done for Philip II. in 1580. Choiseul quite approved the idea. In the eyes of both France and Spain, Portugal was little better than a British colony, and it seemed obviously to offer the necessary scope for bringing military pressure to bear upon the common enemy in exactly the same way that Hanover did in Northern Europe.

So certain was the Court of Lisbon of what to expect that Mello, who was then Portuguese Minister in London, was already pressing for assistance. What he asked was twelve thousand foot, three or four thousand horse, guns and arms for the whole Portuguese army, and a complete staff to organise and command it. Such a succour was quite out of the question, at least for the present; but he had been promised half the foot he asked, a regiment of light horse and twenty thousand stand of arms. Mello was not content, and protested if the whole did not come before May, his master must submit. Newcastle pressed the point on Bute, and Bute would only say that he would probably be able to do what was wanted, as he had no intention of supporting the war in Germany. This, of course, shut Newcastle's mouth. It was a price he was not prepared to pay, and in the old feeble spirit he began to tease to have the Havana expedition diverted to Lisbon. His suggestions were treated almost with contempt. " A most expensive, hazardous expedition to the Havana," he wrote in despair, " when both ships and men are wanted elsewhere. A wild-goose chase (as I now understand), afterwards after Mexico, St. Augustine and God knows what, and the whimsical plan of expeditions going on faster than ever. Portugal is also to be defended at a vast expense. God knows from whence and how." [1]

The strain of this aspect of the war must have been very great, but Grenville at least was too good a pupil of Pitt's to allow anything to distract his attention from the main attack. He and Bute had quite got the upper

[1] *Newcastle Papers*, Jan. 10, 32,923, and Feb. 11 and 12, 32,934.

hand, and, so far from relaxing their concentration on
Havana, they persisted at all hazards in massing upon it
every man which Cumberland and Ligonier considered
necessary to ensure success.   Important as it was to
control the Bay of Biscay and to attract French troops
from the Spanish frontier, they resolved to reduce the
garrison of Belleisle to its lowest defensive point, and
even, if necessary, to abandon it altogether.   Early in
December, as we have already seen, five more battalions
had been called home to take the place of an equivalent
number added to Albemarle's force.   Thus when at last
they sailed, Albemarle had with him over four thousand
men.[1]   Nor was this all.   Immediately after the troops
arrived from Belleisle, orders were despatched to Amherst
in America to provide a further contingent, and to Colville to arrange for their transport and escort to Cape
St. Nicholas, where they were to meet Pocock, or to
Havana if he was not there.[2]   In this way it was calculated that, with Monckton's men already on the
spot, the force available in the West Indies would be
some sixteen or seventeen thousand men, which, after
providing for the garrisons of the islands, would give
Albemarle about fourteen thousand for the main attack.
Finally, Pocock got away on March 6, a month later
than it should have been, but still well in time.   He
took out five more of the line, and, though this was two
less than was intended, it would bring the whole naval
force in the West Indies up to thirty-four of the line,
and about as many cruisers.

Even this great effort did not exhaust the energy of

[1] The troops were recalled on Dec. 6, *Admiralty Secretary, Out-letters*,
1331.   Hodgson arrived at Spithead with them on Jan. 10.—Hodgson to
Townshend, Jan. 10, *W. O. In-letters.*   Only one of the Belleisle regiments,
the 9th (Whitmore's), went out with Albemarle.

[2] *Admiralty Secretary, Out-letters (Secret Orders)*, 1332, Jan. 13, 1762.

Grenville. Colonel Draper's project for the capture of Manilla, which Newcastle thought had been only "in a manner" agreed upon, was put in motion without any further regard to him. At all costs the new men were determined to recover the mistake they had made by rivalling the exploits of the man they had supplanted. Before January was out the necessary orders had been signed, and Draper was taking them out to Steevens. His instructions were to arrange a joint expedition with the King's and the East India Company's officers for the capture of Manilla. The idea was still commerce destruction. The Ministers' aim apparently was to paralyse Spanish trade at both its main sources, and thus induce the new enemy to see the wisdom of abandoning her ally. Permanent conquest was certainly not in contemplation; for Steevens was instructed, after taking Manilla, to establish a settlement in the independent island of Mindanao, at the opposite extremity of the Philippine group, "which could be kept after the peace."[1] The point, though generally overlooked, is of some importance, not only for a correct understanding of the nature of the war in the Far East, but also for rightly judging the manner in which Manilla was dealt with in making peace.

Vast and wide-flung as were these offensive movements, they were not permitted to prejudice the defensive part of the plan to which Pitt had always attached so much importance. Grenville, with Anson's devoted help, was equal, in spite of the strain upon the resources of the country, to covering the whole with a series of blockades extending from Dunkirk to Gibraltar. The system upon which it was done is of the highest interest, as representing the developed ideas of naval strategy which had

[1] *Secret Orders*, 1332, Jan. 25.

ripened during the war. It is the last word of Anson's school, and the full consideration it deserves can best be given when we come to consider the counter-strokes which the enemy contemplated, and which the blockade was designed to prevent. For the present it is enough to remember that it existed, while we follow the fortunes of Pocock and Albemarle.

On April 20, forty-five days out, but well up to time, Pocock reached Barbadoes with his five of the line, thirty transports, and nearly as many store-ships. Here he learnt of the capture of Martinique, and that Rodney, according to instructions, had appointed Cas Navires Bay as the best point for the rendezvous. Stores were also ready, which enabled him to complete to six months victuals. Having taken them on board he sailed at once, and reached Cas Navires Bay on the 25th. Monckton's transports were all there ready to sail with the troops on board, but fleet there was none, and Pocock's feelings may easily be imagined.

As instructed by his secret orders, he had of course expected to find Rodney's whole squadron, with a special division of ten of the line, under Swanton, ready to join his flag.[1] What he did find was nothing but Rodney's own flagship, the *Marlborough*, with three other ships of the line, and three "fifties" whose condition demanded their being sent home to refit with the next convoy. It was no more than the security of the island required, and Pocock was aghast. To add to his vexation, Rodney sent off word that he was down with fever at St. Pierre and could not come off to pay his respects. The anger of the new commander-in-chief was pardonable; for, in consequence of what Rodney had done, he found himself

---

[1] *Secret Orders*, 1332, Feb. 18; Rodney to the Admiralty, May 31.— Mundy, vol. i. p. 88.

confronted with a situation which must have looked almost desperate.

The information awaiting him was that in Havana the Spaniards had a fleet of twenty of the line, and that the Brest squadron had got into Cap François, but whether it was still there or not was unknown. He had therefore to conduct a combined expedition over an uncommanded sea actually in the face of two fleets, with the least of which he was barely equal. Nor was this all. The anxieties of commerce protection were almost as great. For at St. Kitts lay some fifty sail of the outward-bound Jamaica convoy, with two more of the line waiting to proceed across the danger zone under his protection, while at Kingston was gathering the first homeward-bound convoy, which he was charged to see safely on its way. The problem presented was about as difficult as a man could have to face, and Rodney had entirely upset the design as it had been planned at home. Anson had based the whole operation regularly on a naval concentration outside the danger area, but, as the harassed Admiral wrote home, Rodney had scattered his units so widely that it was impossible to order them to close upon him at Martinique. Rodney had committed him to a concentration at Cape St. Nicholas, and from this there was no escape. The way in which he finally solved the problem presents one of the most instructive strategical combinations in the whole war.

There was one important consideration—and Anson had certainly counted upon it to some extent—which rendered the problem less difficult than it appeared, and went far to justify Rodney's distribution. A concentration of the allied fleets was by no means a simple matter. In the first place, two allied squadrons are seldom, if ever, the same thing strategically as two divisions of one fleet.

It will rarely happen but that they have opposing interests drawing them in opposite directions, and hardly ever is it easy for them to agree as to which of several risks is the lesser one to accept. This was markedly so in the present case. Both the hostile admirals, and particularly Blénac, who had express orders on the subject, counted upon a concentration, but each was naturally anxious that it should be effected at a point which would best cover the interests of his own country. Blénac, who had left France before war with Spain was declared, or immediately expected, had come to save what he could of the French islands. Don Juan de Prado Porto Carrero, the Spanish Captain-General, on his part, was strictly charged with the defence of Havana. He had with him not twenty of the line, as reported to Pocock, but twenty sail, of which only twelve were of the line. There were also three of the line at Santiago at the opposite end of the island, and one or two at Vera Cruz, the port of Mexico. They were all under the command of Don Gutierre de Hevia, Marqués del Real Transporte, who had come out with Prado as commander-in-chief of the American squadrons. His orders were, after the true Spanish model, to keep the Havana squadron concentrated and within the port ready for any emergency, and not to risk needless sorties.[1] These at least were the last instructions which he and Prado had received, and they were nearly six months old. When war was certain, later orders had been sent out, but, owing to Captain Johnstone's smart warning to Rodney, he had been able to intercept them. The *Milford*, of 16 guns, fell in with the *Aviso*, that was carrying them, off Cape Tiburon, the westernmost point of St. Domingo, and after fighting her all day he forced her to strike. The commander, of

[1] Duro, vol. vii. p. 43. They were dated Nov. 24.

course, sunk his despatches, and nothing ever reached Havana except a copy of the Madrid *Gazette* containing the declaration of war.[1]

Added to these considerations there was in the way of a concentration the further difficulty of the prevailing weather conditions, and on these Anson certainly counted. Though it was easy enough for Blénac to run down to Havana, it was very difficult for Hevia to beat up to Cap François. Rodney and Douglas, of course, thoroughly appreciated the situation, and, knowing there was little chance of Hevia's attempting to get to Blénac, had taken care that Blénac should not get to Hevia. When Prado and Hevia came out from Spain they had a squadron of six of the line, and Blénac had securely expected them to call at Cap François. Keenly disappointed, he was now urging them to come to his help. He informed them that Hervey's squadron was before the port, and that if Hevia would only come it might easily be surprised and destroyed. Then together they might take the offensive and strike an important blow. But Prado and Hevia, entrenched in their defensive orders, would not move.

Under these circumstances a concentration at Cape St. Nicholas, although within the theatre of operations, was scarcely beyond the limit of legitimate risk. In any case, it had to be done, and the day after Pocock reached Martinique he sent off an express to Douglas to meet him there with all the Jamaica squadron, which, according to his instructions, he believed was awaiting his orders in Port Royal. There was plenty of time, for Monckton's arrangements did not please Albemarle, and he spent the best part of a fortnight reorganising

---

[1] *Ibid.*, p. 45. Beatson (vol. iii. p. 531) says the British vessel was "tender to the *Dublin*," which was Douglas's flagship. If so, she must have been sent on special service into these waters.

the whole of the transport disposition that had been made, getting more troops from Dominica and fitting out horse transports. It is clear every one was in a bad temper over what had been done. Pocock found relief for his feelings in taking away Rodney's flagship. Owing to the scattering of the fleet, so he informed the Admiralty, he could not possibly do without the *Marlborough*, and to Rodney's intense disgust he bundled all his staff into a sixty-four. By this means, with the two ships of the line which were waiting at St. Kitts, he was able to bring his own battle squadron up to eight sail, that is, superior to what he believed Blénac's to be, and on May 6th, after having sent forward orders for the convoy to meet him at Basse Terre Road, in St. Kitts, he sailed on his perilous enterprise.

The reason why the final concentration was to be at Cape St. Nicholas, that is, in the Windward Passage between St. Domingo and Cuba, brings us to the most brilliant point in Anson's design. It was not, of course, on the ordinary route from the Windward Islands to Havana. That lay dead to leeward, past Jamaica and through the Yucatan Channel, with an easy beat back of some two hundred and fifty miles with the current along the north-western end of Cuba. The natural plan, therefore, and the one the enemy would expect, was a concentration at Port Royal, with a squadron held back off Cap François to blockade Blénac and cover the line of passage from North America as Hervey was then doing. It was indeed a strategical certainty that so long as the Spaniards saw no concentration at Jamaica they would be lulled into comparative security.

Now, surprise is of the essence of the class of operations to which the present one belonged, and had there been any doubt of it there was the fine old precedent of

Drake's attempt on San Juan de Puerto Rico in 1595, the last and perhaps boldest of his dazzling career. That master of daring expedients had not been content to reach his objective by the ordinary route from the westward through the Mona Passage, but, in order to effect a surprise, had performed what was then regarded as the incredible feat of carrying his whole force through the uncharted labyrinth of the Virgin Archipelago, and had sprung upon his prey from the eastward. Anson, whose name had been made in reviving Drake's glory in the South Sea, must have known the story well. Indeed, a declaration of war with Spain had always been the signal for reopening the pages of Drake's life, and Anson knew that here was a chance of repeating his exploit at Puerto Rico.

To Havana, as to Puerto Rico, there existed another route from the eastward and windward. It lay through the Old Bahama Channel, and as the similar route through the Virgins had never been used till Drake sounded his way through it, so the Old Bahama Channel, from its intricacies and dangers, was regarded as impracticable for the unweatherly fleets of those days, and was never used by the Spaniards except for quite small craft. But Anson had in his possession—booty probably of his adventurous youth—an old Spanish chart of it, and it convinced him that under such a man as Pocock, a British fleet could pass. It was at least too fine a stroke of strategy not to try. Not only would the line of advance be wholly unexpected, but it would be quicker. It involved no beat back, it was before the wind the whole way, and it was much shorter. While, therefore, it would ensure a surprise, it would also mean a great gain of time before the hurricanes set in. And, over and above all this, it would permit a sudden

and unlooked-for concentration interposed between the
two bases of the enemy; it would provide for the rapid
junction of the American contingent, and it would probably prevent the Spanish and the French fleets joining
hands. Whether Rodney had divined this brilliant conception is not clear. It was certainly not communicated
to him in the orders he received to prepare for it. But
it will be seen that the dispositions he had made did not
really prejudice its execution. So far as they had gone
they indicated an attack on St. Domingo rather than
Havana, and they had prevented the allied junction,
which it was an integral part of the design to stop.[1]

Such, then, was the adventure on which Pocock was
proceeding. In two days he was off St. Kitts, where
the two ships of the line and the Jamaica convoy were
awaiting him, and he found himself in charge, all told, of
some two hundred sail. In the transports Albemarle,
besides military stores, and his artillery and engineers,
had five brigades of infantry, numbering nearly twelve
thousand men, and over two thousand more were to
come from North America and Jamaica.[2] With this
unwieldly armada the admiral proceeded without stopping, and reaching through the Mona Passage, so as to
keep to windward of St. Domingo, made Cape St. Nicholas
on May 17th. Here was awaiting him a letter from
Douglas, saying that his orders had been received, that
he was about to join him with nine of the line, and that

---

[1] Sir Charles Knowles roundly condemns what he calls Lord Anson's
"obstinacy" in persisting in his approach by the Bahama Channel.
Thereby, he contends, he gravely imperilled the whole force merely to
save a week's time. He entirely ignores the advantage of surprise and
interposition between the Spanish and French fleets.

[2] In his despatch from St. Nicholas, May 26, Pocock says he had 160
sail of transports, &c., 46 of the Jamaica convoy, and 13 of his own
squadron. It is possible he meant that 160 included them all, but the
sense seems rather as stated in the text.—*In-letters*, 307.

he had also given the rendezvous to Hervey, who with seven was blockading Cap François. He had secured pilots for the Old Bahama Channel, but as they seemed very incapable, he had despatched Captain Elphinstone in the *Richmond* frigate to survey it as far to leeward as Cay Sal, where the five hundred miles of danger came to an end.

On the morrow Hervey, with whom Pocock had already got in touch as he passed, joined him, and reported Blénac still in Cap François. Douglas sailed the same day, and joined on the 23rd. It was Pocock's intention to detach the Jamaica convoy under his command. As Douglas had leave to go home, he was also to take charge of the homeward-bound convoy, which Pocock intended to get away through the Yucatan and Florida Channels if Blénac remained at Cap François. This of course could be done safely, so soon as he had made sure of the Spanish fleet in Havana. The only trouble was the troops from America. On the 26th he heard from Amherst that they were just about to sail when his despatch left. Pocock no doubt expected them to join in a day or two. But in any case by his secret orders he was instructed not to wait for them, and on May 27, after detaching Douglas and the convoy to Port Royal, he sailed with his whole fleet, leaving the American transports to take their chance with Blénac.

This was the weak part of his design, but Rodney's action in sending Swanton to the Spanish main, and the information available, left no alternative. The latest intelligence Douglas had obtained was that there were sixteen of the line in Havana. Pocock had but nineteen—all, except two, of the lower rates. To divide his fleet was therefore impossible. Moreover, Douglas had received a credible report from a vessel that had

been in Cap François that Blénac was bitterly disappointed on finding that Hevia, when he brought out
Prado with his six of the line, had gone on to Havana
instead of joining him, and that he had declared his
intention, if the Spaniards made no move to unite forces,
to go straight home with the French trade.[1]

To the men of Quebec, who had made light of the
St. Lawrence, the Old Bahama Channel can have presented few terrors. The pilots proved as useless as
Douglas had feared, but fortunately, owing to his fore-
sight, Elphinstone met them the day after they sailed.
He had been right up to Cay Sal and back again, and
was able to produce a complete survey of the channel,
with sketches of the land and Cays on both sides, and to
report that Anson's chart was correct. He was therefore in a position to lead through, and the main cause
for anxiety was at an end. Following the method
Saunders had adopted on the St. Lawrence, Pocock
organised the transports into seven divisions, each with
its conducting men-of-war. The way in which the
escort was distributed deserves notice. Contrary to
what would naturally be looked for, there was no regular
vanguard or rearguard—the whole of the navy ships
being allotted to the various divisions. With the first
division were four of the line under Pocock; with the
second was Keppel's ship alone; and with the third were
again four of the line, the idea being apparently to provide for a concentration of nine of the line in the van or
the centre. The next two divisions had between them
only two of the line and a fifty, but the sixth had three

---

[1] Douglas to Pocock, May 6, enclosed in Pocock's despatch of May 26,
In-letters, 307. Besides his nineteen of the line he had one forty-four, five
frigates, two sloops, and three bomb vessels.—"List of the Fleet," *ibid.*
He was subsequently joined at Havana by four more of the line and one
or two cruisers.—Beatson, vol. iii. p. 394.

of the line and a fifty, and the last division five of the line
and a fifty.　The main anxiety, it will be seen, was an
attack from the windward upon the rear by Blénac, and
provision was thus made for a rearguard of eight of the
line and two fifties to deal with him effectively if he
made the attempt.[1]　But Blénac had less mind than
ever to burn his fingers for the Spaniards, whom he
regarded as having deserted him.　He remained passive,
and the fleet proceeded without interference.　Elphinstone performed his duty admirably.　No hitch of any
kind occurred.　The narrowest and most dangerous part
of the channel between Cay Lobos and Cay Comfite was
actually passed at night by means of fires burning upon
the rocks, and by the evening of June 5th, that is a week
after leaving Cape Nicholas, the whole fleet was clear of
Cay Sal, and in sight of Matanzas, less than a hundred
miles from its objective.

Meanwhile the authorities at Havana were resting in
blind security.　Though it was a little more than a year
since the captain-general and the admiral had come out
with two French engineers and elaborate directions for
repairing and improving the defences of the place, next to
nothing had been done.　The weak point of Havana was
a rocky ridge known as the Cabaña Hill, which ran along
the east side of the harbour opposite the city.　It was
high enough to command all, or nearly all, the defences
as well as the city itself and the harbour.　The official
scheme of defence provided for its occupation by a powerful redoubt at its inner and landward termination, the
famous Morro Castle being at the other.　But the work
had only been talked about until the copy of the *Gazette*
announcing war had been received.　Then they began to
clear the site, but some troops and labourers sent for

---

[1] See organisation of the fleet in Keppel's *Life of Keppel*, vol. i. p. 346.

from Mexico had introduced an outbreak of yellow fever
and the work had been abandoned. In the eyes of the
authorities there was really nothing to fear. Prado fully
believed that owing to the other preparations he had
made the British would not think of attacking them,
and cheerily assured his sovereign that if they were so
rash they would certainly break their heads. Nothing
could shake the captain - general's complacency. As
Pocock lay at Cape St. Nicholas waiting for Douglas to
join, a travelled-stained man had rushed into his antechamber demanding an instant audience. He was a
Spanish merchant from Jamaica who had got away to
Cape Antonio in a boat, and had ridden night and day
with news of what was in the wind. The captain-general
would not listen. No one, indeed, would admit the possibility of a fleet coming through the Old Bahama Channel.
A fortnight later, on June 6th, Pocock's sails were seen
from the top of Morro Castle, and an officer hurried
across the harbour to tell the news in the city ; but only
to be reprimanded for spreading false alarms. The fleet
could be nothing, he was told, but the regular Jamaica
convoy homeward bound. Finally it was not till fresh
messengers reported that a fleet was standing in a little
to the eastward with flat-boats in tow that the miracle
could be believed. Then all was alarm. Then and not
till then the garrison was mobilised, the militia called
out, and horses sought for the dragoons. Anson's clever
device had entirely succeeded. The surprise was complete.[1]

It was on the evening of June 6th, as the old First
Lord lay dying at home, that the alarm was given. On
that day Pocock had arrived off the Coximar river, about

[1] Duro, *Armada Española*, vol. vii. pp. 46–9. His main authority is the
report of the official Spanish Court of Inquiry.

five leagues east of the Morro. Before sailing he and
Albemarle had been furnished with a copy of Knowles's
report. It indicated the sandy bay where the river falls
into the sea as the only possible landing-place, since on
the further or city side of the harbour the coast was
supposed to be all foul ground. Here then the admiral
dropped the transports and a division of six of the line
under Keppel to destroy the two forts which they found
guarding the bay, exactly as Knowles had stated, and to
cover the landing. Pocock himself with the remaining
thirteen of the line and the bomb-vessels went on to
blockade and threaten the city. It was all on the regular
lines that Drake had laid down, and it went with
practised precision. Pocock in the orthodox way got his
marines into the boats and made a feint of landing on
the further or western side of the city. At the same
time Keppel, having quickly destroyed the forts, was
getting the troops ashore in the usual three divisions
under Captains Hervey, Barton and Drake at a point on
the east side of Coximar Bay which Knowles had advised,
and it was done without the loss of a man.

Here, however, Knowles's plan began to be departed
from. From the point where the landing was made a
path led through the bush to the inner end of the
Cabaña ridge where the redoubt had been planned, and
Knowles had recommended that an immediate advance
should be made along this track and the position seized.
For some reason this was not done, probable because the
soldiers considered that the Morro Castle rendered the
ridge untenable. This formidable work stood at its seaward end upon a somewhat isolated rock, and formed
the main defence of the harbour entrance. It was to
be assumed that it enfiladed the Cabaña ridge. Knowles
seems to have thought it did not: and, moreover, had

satisfied himself that from the Quarry Hill, in which the ridge terminated towards the sea just short of the Morro, the Castle could be attacked on its weakest side. The soldiers apparently were of a different opinion. At all events, though an immediate advance was made, it was not made upon the ridge. The soldiers preferred to make direct for the bastioned front of Morro. They therefore advanced along the shore, Keppel scouring the beach and woods before them with his small cruisers, With this help they had passed the last obstacle between them and their objective before night.

Still no attempt on the Cabaña ridge was made. Instead a corps was detached next day under Eliott with orders to force his way through the woods below it, and endeavour to seize the village of Guanabacoa, which lay in the open country beyond at the head of Havana Bay. Driving a considerable body of troops before him, he successfully accomplished his task. The idea of the operation seems to have been to secure horses and fresh provisions, and to cut off the communication of the city with the interior on that side, and to cover the siege. The whole movement is roundly condemned by Knowles, and it must be said with some show of reason. It had the effect, as he points out, of permanently dividing the army, and of preventing Eliott's corps taking any part in the subsequent siege operations. It appears also as the first indication of Albemarle's incapacity for the kind of operation entrusted to him. A *coup de main* is the method to which such combined attacks peculiarly lend themselves, and which above all in such a climate they particularly demand. Pocock had handed the general a complete surprise for the purpose, yet he was proceeding by the text-book rules for continental warfare in Europe, and every hour was letting his chances slip. There

may, of course, have been military reasons of which we
are unaware, still we cannot but endorse Knowles's comment. "Experience," he says, "in former expeditions
might have taught them that whatever is to be effected
in the West Indies must be done as expeditiously as
possible." But it is all part of a large and vital question
on which clearer light will fall as we proceed.

To see how fine was the chance which Albemarle was
missing, we have but to look within the city walls.
During all this time the Spanish Council of War was
sitting in distracted debate. An order had been immediately issued to complete the unfinished redoubt which
had been designed for the shore end of the Cabaña ridge,
so as to enfilade the whole; for the truth was that by
this means alone could its occupation by the enemy be
prevented. A thousand sailors from the fleet were set to
drag up guns to arm it. Knowles's view of what was
the vulnerable spot is certainly endorsed by the Spaniards'
alarm for its safety. In their eyes the point which the
British had chosen for their landing indicated the Cabaña
as the first objective. But in the panic that prevailed no
one thought of covering the working parties by abattis or
other temporary expedients such as the difficult ground
afforded in abundance. The consequence was fatal. The
following night Carleton pushed a reconnaissance towards
the enemy's works. The excited Spaniards took it for an
attack in force, and took to their heels. The panic spread
to the Council, and in spite of the direct and elaborate
orders from Spain they hastily decided to spike the
twelve heavy guns which the sailors had got up, and to
abandon the position as untenable. But still Albemarle
let it alone.

In the city they almost gave themselves up for lost.
With all the warning they had had, and the years Spain

had been preparing for war, the regular force in the place, according to the official return, was under three thousand, including marines and available seamen, and the militia and volunteers amounted to less than six thousand.[1] Without the help of Hevia's crews, therefore, they regarded the place as untenable, and the depressing step was taken of paralysing the fleet by devoting its life to the land defence. But even here the panic-brewing did not stop. Close off the mouth of the harbour lay Pocock threatening attack. The entrance to the splendid haven was but half a mile wide. It was defended in the strongest manner. Besides the Morro Castle and two heavy batteries below it on the water's edge, there was on the opposite or western side the formidable Punta Fort and the city batteries, denying all access. Yet even so the timid and startled Council could not rest at ease, and the insane resolution was taken of sinking three ships of the line to block the entrance. So, for no possible good, they imprisoned their own fleet and rendered Pocock free to assist the army. The British had been presented gratuitously with the absolute local command of the sea, and the admiral was able to perform the last part of his special task, and send word to Douglas that all was clear for him to pass the convoy homeward.

On the 11th, under cover of a diversion which Pocock made to the westward, Carleton seized the end of the

[1] The total, according to Captain Duro, given by the official returns which were put in at the Court of Inquiry, were:—Regular troops, sailors, and marines of the squadron, 2800; militia and *paisanos voluntarios*, a little more than 5000; arsenal hands, 250; freed slaves, 600. See *Armada Española*, vol. vii. p. 50 *note*. English authorities, of course, place the total much higher. Beatson, vol. ii. p. 543, gives a return, apparently the report of a prisoner, three times greater—Dragoons, 810; infantry, 3500; artillery, 300; sailors and marines, 9000—total regulars, 13,610. Militia and people of colour, 14,000. Grand total, 27,610. This may have been on paper the whole force in the island. Probably it was the judicious exaggeration of a prisoner.

Cabaña ridge adjoining the Morro with hardly any resistance, but no use was made of the lodgment. The idea was merely to prevent interruption of the siege works which were now opened against the Morro. Thus several days had been lost to no purpose, and of the rest of the proceedings the best that can be said is that they continued to afford an unhappy example of the unwisdom of committing such work to a general without experience of combined expeditions, and with no genius for amphibious warfare.

That he landed where he did cannot be laid to his charge. It was Knowles's idea that he should do so and proceed to attack the Morro as being the key of the place. Where he failed was in not shifting his ground so soon as it was found how far beyond the range of a *coup de main* the capture of the castle was. From first to last it seems never to have entered his head to try elsewhere. In spite of what Saunders and Wolfe had proved so well at Quebec; in spite of its endorsement by Keppel and Hodgson at Belleisle, and by Rodney and Monckton at Martinique, the peculiar strength of the force at his command was a sealed book to him. Bred in the rigid school of Cumberland, he had no notion of how to avail himself of the mobility of an amphibious force. He could do nothing more original than sit down before the Morro in solemn Low Country form. Yet on the other side of the harbour lay the city, his real objective, so weakly defended that, seeing the state of panic and confusion that prevailed, it could scarcely have resisted a vehement assault from troops steeped in victory like those at Albemarle's command. To the men who had climbed the Heights of Abraham and the cliff of Belleisle, and had rushed the Morne Garnier at Martinique, there would have been no thought of repulse.

Such at least was the opinion of many officers in both services, and of the Spaniards themselves. The city walls were low and old, designed merely for defence against buccaneers; in several places they had crumbled down and half-filled the ditch, and whatever loss a bold assault in the early days would have cost it must have been far less than that which Albemarle's pipeclay tactics involved.

It is true he had the excuse that, according to Knowles's information, a landing on the city side was impossible, owing to there being all foul ground off the shore. But Pocock quickly found out that it was not so, and in a day or two he had anchored off the Chorera river, a little to the westward, and seized the village at its mouth as a watering place. Good anchorage was found all along the coast, but it made no difference to Albemarle. Knowles's general comment is worth recording. "When a general," he says, "is sent abroad upon a particular enterprise, in which he is to co-operate with another corps [meaning a fleet], both are obliged to make use of their joint force for the accomplishment of that object, for it differs widely from his having an unlimited power in an enemy's country during the continuance of a war." But it is a difference of which Albemarle was unable to grasp the significance.

Not even when the formidable nature of the task he had set himself was fully apparent were his eyes opened. The work of conducting a regular siege under the conditions that prevailed proved murderous, and the labour was severely increased by Eliott's corps being too distant to share it. The soil was too thin for proper approaches to be made; the whole ground was a tangle of dense and sickly bush, through which roads had to be cut, and so rocky was the surface that the moving of stores and guns was beyond measure arduous. And overhead burned the pitiless June sun, under which not

even a Cuban can work with impunity. Finally, and
worst of all, there was no water to be found ; every drop
had to be brought by the seamen from the other side of
the Bay. Yet Albemarle clung stolidly to his false
position, and, the word being given, soldier and sailor
strove merrily together to make the best of it. But in
spite of the confident spirit that prevailed, they began
quickly to drop at their work, struck down in ever
increasing numbers by the insufferable heat and thirst.
For three weeks the deadly toil went on without a single
effort to turn the surprise to advantage. Colonel Howe,
it is true, had been sent to the other side to occupy
the village of Chorera, but the object was merely to cut
the enemy's communications to the westward, to interrupt
his water-supply, and to protect our own.

It was not until the end of the month that the
breaching batteries were complete. On July 1st they
were to open, and Albemarle's limited ideas of combined
operations were fully displayed. Having no higher grasp
of the possibilities of the force at his disposal than to use
the fleet as an artillery reinforcement, he requested the
Admiral to batter the castle from the sea, so as to take
off some of the fire from his batteries. It was madness.
The Morro was too high for ships to touch ; but Hervey,
after his wont, volunteered to try. He was given three
of the line, and in the morning stood in. The leading
ship of the devoted squadron could not face it, and her
captain was afterwards cashiered for not going close
enough. Hervey took his place, and held on until he
ran aground with his broadside bearing. So, in chorus
with the shore batteries, he continued firing ferociously
till two in the afternoon—one of the hottest fires ever
seen, it was said. " I am unluckily aground," he wrote
presently to Keppel ; " but my guns bear. I cannot per-

ceive their fire to slacken. . . . I am afraid they are too high to do the execution we wished. I have many men out of combat now, and officers wounded; my masts and rigging much cut about, and only one anchor. I shall stay here as long as I can and wait your orders." Every minute he expected to hear the army was advancing to the assault, but no word came, and in the heat of the fire he wrote again, asking for assistance to get off. "The smoke," he said, "makes it impossible to see the effect we have had or likely to have, nor can we tell when the army will advance," and, still cheery as ever, he signed himself "often duller, and ever yours, A. Hervey." But the army could not advance. The new battery, as was usual with our engineers at that time, had been badly placed. Hervey's bombardment, so the soldiers say, did so far distract the enemy's fire seawards that it enabled them to dismount most of the guns on the land front of the Morro, but the fire of its sea bastion was not dominated sufficiently to permit an assault. At two o'clock Albemarle decided to abandon the attempt and signalled to the ships to that effect. By that time Hervey's squadron had nearly two hundred men killed and wounded, including Captain Goostrey of the *Cambridge*, and he drew off at last, cut to pieces, and with another brilliant bit of daring to his record.

The fact was they had miscalculated the resistance they were to meet, as was only natural in view of the pusillanimous opening of the defence. The arrangements were all those of Hevia, the Spanish Admiral, who, making up in truculence what he lacked in military insight, completely dominated the captain-general and all his council.[1]

---

[1] Pezuela, *Historia de Cuba*, vol. ii. p. 474, quoted by Captain Duro, with many other authorities, in his Appendix. " Datos y juicios de la rendición de la Habana."—*Armada Española*, vol. vii. p. 71 *et seq.*

So it happened, curiously enough, that his faint-
hearted treatment of the fleet turned to the Spaniards'
greatest advantage.   For, having resolved to devote
his force to the defence of the city, Hevia insisted on
turning out all the enervated local officers and committing the important posts to the captains of his ships.
The Morro had been given to the famous Don Luis
Vicente de Velasco, a veteran captain of the old war, who
still lives as one of the national heroes of Spain.   The
castle mounted about seventy guns, and for garrison he
was allowed three hundred infantry, fifty seamen and fifty
gunners, with three hundred negro labourers, who were
relieved every third day.   In testimony of the spirit that
was in him, he began by walling up the gate of the
castle, and leaving no communication with the outside,
except by hanging ladders.   The fire he kept up was
beyond all control, and, not content with mere defence,
he kept urging the authorities to sally out and attack
the works which the British were so painfully rearing.
The example which he and his fellows set put new heart
into the place, reinforcements began to come in from the
interior, and the heroism of the defence proved in striking
contrast to the nerveless plan on which it was designed.

Still the odds against him were enormous.   Hervey's
diversion had enabled General William Keppel, who had
charge of the siege, to make some little impression, and
next day the bombardment was continued more furiously
than ever.   Several of the batteries were manned and
armed from the fleet, and the way the seamen served
their guns is said to have filled the soldiers with astonishment.   "Our sea folks," wrote one, "began a new kind of
fire unknown, or, at all events, unpractised by artillery
people.   The greatest fire from one piece of cannon is
reckoned by them from eighty to ninety times in twenty-

four hours, but our people went on the sea system, firing extremely quick and with the best direction ever seen, and in sixteen hours fired their guns one hundred and forty-nine times."[1] Nothing could stand such work, and by next evening Velasco had only two guns in action. All promised a speedy success, but, unhappily, the fury of the seamen's fire was equally disastrous to their own works. The fascines, scorched to tinder under the burning sun, kept taking fire — water was not to be had, and scarcely any earth—and just as the destruction of the Morro defences seemed nearly complete, the principal battery was almost entirely destroyed. In a few hours the labour of seventeen days and hundreds of men was consumed, and all had to begin again. It was a mortifying stroke, for in the suffocating air the hardships of the siege were growing beyond human endurance. The food got worse and worse, the water scarcer, and the air more pestilential. Over five thousand troops and three thousand seamen were down already with wounds and sickness, and scores were dying daily. No reinforcements had come from America, and the hurricane season was getting alarmingly near. Still Albemarle clung stolidly to his conventional plan, and the Spaniards were left almost as completely undisturbed from the sea, as though Havana was the heart of a continent.

Meanwhile Pocock had thoroughly established his position at Chorera on the other side, and had his whole fleet comfortably berthed in the new anchorage he had found. Since the Spaniards had relieved him of the pains of blockading, he had practically nothing for his battle squadron to do except to assist the troops with shore parties, and to keep a small division in the offing to intercept any reinforcements that might appear. This

[1] *Life of Keppel*, vol. i. p. 357.

precaution was still necessary. So soon as Hevia had regained his senses and discovered that effective resistance was made possible by Albemarle's mistake, he had sent far and wide through the Indies for help. Pocock's information still was that in Santiago there were three of the line, at Cartagena three more, besides two others cruising in Campeachy Bay. These vessels constituted a menace to our local control, remote it is true, but they had to be watched. Besides this preoccupation, Pocock had to cover the passage of the Jamaica convoy and the arrival of the American division, and both of them were daily expected. He therefore threw a chain of frigates out to the Bay of Florida, and kept a cruiser squadron off Matanzas to the eastward, and another off Cape Antonio to the westward to watch the Yucatan Channel, and, though the enemy's squadrons never appeared, he was rewarded by a number of prizes.

It was on June 15th—that is, three days after the harbour was finally blocked—that he had landed at Chorera, by Albemarle's request, two battalions of marines and the detachment of infantry which the general sent across with Howe. This looked more like the proper thing, but nothing came of it. Albemarle could not rise to anything better than a commonplace diversion. With such a man as Wolfe or any of his pupils in command it is impossible to believe nothing more would have been done. In a single night, as at Quebec, sufficient troops could have been thrown across to Pocock's side to rush the defences of the city itself, while Eliott's corps replaced them before the Morro. At least the possibilities of a successful surprise were great enough to have made it under the circumstances almost criminal not to have tried.

Yet for three weeks more after the first failure the

work went on just as before on the Morro side, where new batteries had to be established in a better position, with the same appalling sacrifice of life. The walls of the castle seemed to be all in ruins, but yet Velasco kept up his fire as vigorously as ever. This he was well able to do, because no attempt was made to interrupt his periodical relief from the city, although, so Knowles says, this could easily have been done with a gun or two on the Quarry hill, which Carleton had seized. The situation grew more critical and hopeless every day, and still nothing was heard of the American troops. Yet, to the credit of all concerned, there was no thought of letting go their hold, even though the hurricanes might burst upon them in a few weeks. After the failure of the attack on the Morro, Pocock devoted himself to preparing for the worst. Some thirty miles to the westward lay the excellent natural harbour of Mariel. This he seized with a number of vessels, including two royal frigates that had sought shelter there, and thus provided himself with a refuge where the whole fleet could lie in perfect security and water.

Ashore the work slowly progressed, in spite of every difficulty. On July 12th Douglas appeared with the Jamaica convoy on its homeward voyage. He came to drop some hundreds of negroes whom Albemarle had purchased for labourers, and the occasion was seized to buy a number of cotton bales to form the approaches and batteries. Then things began to go better. In a fortnight we had twenty guns against only five or six of the enemy's. Velasco, seriously wounded, had had to leave his post. In a day or two more the Morro's fire was entirely silenced, or at least there was but a gun or two fitfully firing. The sap could now be pushed along the edge of the coast towards the sea bastion of the castle, and by the 20th the miners reached the face of the rock on which it stood. The ditch was seventy feet deep, and could only be passed in single file by an exposed ridge that had been left to prevent its being entered from the sea. Yet it was done with the loss of only three or four men, and a mine was commenced under the bastion. At the same time a shaft was sunk in the counter-scarp opposite, in order to throw it into the ditch and form a way for the stormers to cross. That same night, further to mark the lack of enterprise in the pedantic general, a sergeant and his party scaled the sea face and found the guard asleep. They stole down again for support, but ere they could return the alarm was given and the chance lost.

Still the mining went on, and Velasco, as he lay in hospital, could not rest. Though himself condemned to inactivity by his wound, he persuaded his chiefs that a passive defence could no longer save them. A second sally in force was ordered and excellently planned. It was in two divisions—one against Carleton's post on the Cabaña ridge, the other directly against the sap. But at such work the Spaniards were no match for Albemarle's seasoned veterans, sick and exhausted as they were. Carleton, who had replaced Lord Rollo, invalided home, was brigadier of the day. He was everywhere, and, thanks to his energy and the staunchness of the troops, both sorties were quickly repulsed with heavy loss. All hope of stopping the British work was given up, and Velasco left his bed to return to his doomed post. Four days later, on the 28th, to make matters worse, the first division of the American contingent appeared.

The moral effect was excellent, but the force which Burton brought was but a fragment of the whole that was expected. The weak point in Pocock's disposition had told. To begin with it was no more than the first division, and in the Caicos Passage it had encountered a division of Blénac's squadron, under M. Fabre, consisting of two of the line, two frigates, and half-a-dozen smaller cruisers. Its escort was but one ship of the line and a frigate. The French gave chase, cut off five or six transports and captured them, with 350 regulars, 150 provincials, and a quantity of stores.[1] The rest the escort saved, but only to lose in their hurry the frigate and four more transports on the Cayo Comfite, in the narrowest part of the Old Bahama Channel, for want of a guide. Pocock immediately sent off Elphinstone, with some transports and sloops, to rescue the wrecked crews and bring on the second division.

The failure of the whole American contingent to arrive was particularly unfortunate, and may to some extent account for Albemarle's inactivity on the city side. Though the slender reinforcements which Burton brought appeared in the nick of time to enhearten the army for the supreme effort, the rest were sadly wanted. By this time the Morro mines were ready, and it had been decided to attack the city the moment it fell. Preparations were already well advanced, and Burton and his troops were landed at Chorera in readiness for the contemplated attack. On the morrow the mines were to be sprung. Velasco saw that all was over, and sent to his chiefs for orders whether to abide the assault, or evacuate and save the garrison. The council of war, irresolute to the last, sent word back that he was to act as he saw best according to circumstances.

To a man of Velasco's punctilious honour such an order was a condemnation to death. Alive to its folly, and broken-hearted for his devoted garrison, he sent again

[1] Pocock to Admiralty, Aug. 16.

next day for precise orders. The answer never came.
At the hour of siesta, when the British camp seemed
sunk in rest under the blazing sun, a terrific explosion
was heard which shook the castle like an earthquake.
The garrison sprang to arms, but only to find the narrow
and almost impracticable breach swarming with British
grenadiers. Counter-guards had been erected in plenty,
but there was no time to man them. Velasco himself, as
he rushed to the ramparts, fell shot in the breast. In a
few minutes all was over, and the Morro had fallen.

The defence had been brilliant as the end was sudden.
The British officers were far more deeply impressed with
Velasco's achievement than with their own. Their first
care was for his life, and at his own request he was sent
across the harbour to be treated by the Spanish surgeons.
Night had fallen, and, as there might be a difficulty
about his being landed, one of the general's aide-de-
camps was sent with him, with orders that if admittance
could not be had he was to bring the wounded man back
to Albemarle's own camp, " that he might be treated with
all the care and homage that was due to an officer who,
with so much glory, had known how to uphold his trust
and the honour of his Prince's arms." [1] He was admitted, but all care was unavailing, and two days later
he died, spared the knowledge of the final act.

Albemarle now lost no time in doing what, in the
opinion of many, he ought to have done at first. He
went over to reconnoitre the west side, leaving his
brother to form heavy batteries on the shore end of
the Cabaña ridge, which could now be reached from the
Morro by water, and to prepare the Morro batteries
for bombarding the city and Fort Punta. The reconnaissance proved his mistake up to the hilt. A road

---

[1] Hevia's Diary, quoted by Duro, vol. vii. p. 67.

was found leading almost up to the weak defences, and covered, the greater part of the way, from the fire of Fort Punta. Even now it was only stopped by abattis, and had a bold advance been pushed home at first, in the midst of the panic and under cover of a bombardment of Fort Punta by the fleet, it could scarcely have failed to succeed. So untenable was the place on this side that, although the second American division arrived safely on August 2nd, Albemarle would not waste life in an assault, assured that, according to the rules of his art, the city must surrender when the Cabaña and Morro batteries and those he was making on the western side were complete. The difficulties of the ground were almost insuperable, but the Admiral solved them by making the fleet carpenters saw up one of the prize frigates for gun platforms. On the 10th all was ready, and Albemarle sent in his summons. It was refused in handsome style, and next day at dawn all the new batteries opened. Before ten o'clock Punta was silenced, and by noon there was scarcely a Spanish gun firing. Shortly afterwards all was silence, and white flags were flying from every point. Havana had decided to surrender. On August 14th, after two days' wrangling, the gates were delivered into our hands, and what was left of the garrison marched out with the full honours of war.

So after a two months' siege fell the Queen city of the Indies. For over a hundred and fifty years, since Drake first sailed out against it, it had baffled our every effort even to approach its virgin walls. It had come to be regarded as impregnable, the inviolate symbol of the power of Spain. The moral effect of such a blow at the outset of the new war was incalculable. As always, it had been the hope of Spain, in challenging England,

that she would recover the gate of the Mediterranean.
Instead, she had lost the gate of the Indies, and we had
won another Gibraltar in the West. Such a gain was
well worth perhaps its terrible cost. The day after the
capitulation, the return showed eighteen hundred dead,
besides thousands of sick and wounded, who were dying
daily. And that was only the beginning. The sickness
continued to rage unabated all the autumn. Early in
October the return showed five hundred and sixty killed
or dead from their wounds, and no less than four thousand
seven hundred dead from disease. This alone was well
over a third of the whole force, and it took no count of
the hundreds who died afterwards in England or America,
or only recovered to drag out a crippled and decayed
existence. Albemarle himself was a sick man for the rest
of his life. This terrible loss by disease was the real cost
of refusing Pitt's importunity to begin the war at the
proper season, and of the delay that was caused by the
hesitation of the new Ministry and their general's lack of
experience.

Yet when all the carnage is reckoned, the fact remains
that probably no conquest, at once so rich, so decisive,
and of so high a strategical value, was ever made against
a civilised force at so small a cost. Over and above the
moral and strategical effect, the actual booty was enormous, and the direct loss to Spain even greater still.
With the city were surrendered nine ships of the line,
besides the three that had been sunk and two nearly
finished on the stocks. It meant a fifth of the whole
Spanish navy. Added to these were half-a-dozen royal
frigates and despatch vessels captured either in the port
or outside at various times, a ship of seventy-eight guns
and six more frigates belonging to the great trading
corporations, and nearly a hundred merchantmen. The

booty was further swelled by over a hundred brass guns,
quantities of warlike stores, and an immense amount of
merchandise. The actual sum of prize-money divided
equally between the navy and the army was nearly
three-quarters of a million. Unhappily, according to
the evil old precedents, it was divided wholly in favour
of the senior officers. Each commander-in-chief received
a third of the moiety allotted to his service, and the
commodore and divisional generals a fifteenth. Thus
Pocock and Albemarle each received over £122,000,
and the three Keppel brothers between them over
£150,000, or more than a fifth of the whole. Pocock's
share was at least well earned, if only because with Clive he
had given us the Indian empire; but Albemarle had spent
the years of stress as Lord of the Bedchamber to the
Duke of Cumberland. And it was not even a general's
victory. Success had been won by the indomitable
staunchness of rank and file, the devotion of the subordinate officers, and the co-operation of the men of
both services forcing a bad plan through by sheer pluck
and endurance. It was the men who had borne the
heat and the burden, and their reward was to every
private £4, 1s. 8½d., and to every bluejacket £3, 14s. 9¾d.[1]

It was Hervey whom Pocock selected to carry home

---

[1] The division of the prize-money is often spoken of as though it were
contrary to precedent. This was not so. Before sailing Pocock was
given "Additional Instructions" to enable him to adjust the division
with Albemarle. For this purpose they were furnished with three precedents:—1. *The expedition of Commodore Wilmot and Colonel Lillingston
to the West Indies in 1694–5 (William III.)*—Commanders-in-chief, $\frac{1}{3}$, the
rest to officers and men. Of the Navy share, officers had $\frac{1}{8}$; warrant
officers, $\frac{1}{8}$; petty officers and men, $\frac{2}{8}$. 2. *Naval Orders under Anne*, 1702
—Queen and States-General (*i.e.* the Dutch Government), $\frac{2}{3}$; of the re-
maining $\frac{1}{3}$—admirals, $\frac{3}{15}$; vice-admirals, $\frac{1}{15}$; captains and lieutenants, $\frac{4}{15}$;
the rest, $\frac{7}{15}$. 3. *The Order of 1740 (George II.)*—Commanders-in-chief by
land and sea, equally between them, $\frac{6}{15}$; generals and flag officers, in proportion to their salaries, $\frac{2}{15}$; commissioned officers, $\frac{3}{15}$; rest of the force, $\frac{9}{15}$.

the glorious despatch, and richly had he deserved it. In Spain the honours of the fine defence rested on the hero of the Morro. While the captain-general and the Marqués del Real Transporte were both disgraced, his family was ennobled with the title of the place he had held so well, and the King issued a decree that for ever afterwards there should be a ship in the Spanish navy named *Velasco*.

CHAPTER X

BETWEEN WAR AND PEACE—THE BOURBON
COUNTER-ATTACK—PORTUGAL

By the time Havana fell Bute and the King had succeeded in dragging their unwilling country to the brink
of a nerveless peace. So far, indeed, had they gone, that
Hervey reached home with the glorious news only just in
time to prevent them flinging away the priceless advantage that had been won, and all the blood and devotion it
had cost.

With Bute, such things weighed but light. He had
come to power to make peace, and to make it at the
lowest price an abiding fear of impeachment would let
him. Within ten days of Pitt's fall he had begun his
task by taking secret steps to reopen the negotiations at
the point where they had been broken off. The inter-
mediaries he employed were his old friend the Comte de
Viri, Sardinian ambassador in London, and his colleague
in Paris, the Bailli de Solar, and the correspondence was
conducted apparently without the knowledge of any
other person except the King. It began with a letter
from Viri to Solar on October 17, 1761, in which he
speaks of Pitt's fall as a great surprise, and says a certain
person of credit wishes it had taken place before Stanley
and Bussy had been recalled.[1]

[1] *Lansdowne House MSS.*, *Viri-Solar Corr.*, vol. i. The three volumes,
for access to which I am indebted to the kindness of the Marquis of
Lansdowne, contain a complete copy of the correspondence which led to
the peace. Except when otherwise stated, the letters quoted in the text
are to be found there. See also Lord Fitz-Maurice's *Life of Shelburne*,
vol. i. p. 137 and *note*.

Upon this hint the delicate work was begun, and in a month's time, just when our ultimatum was sent to Spain, negotiations were actually on foot. According to Lord Chesterfield they were managed on the English side by Viri, since Bute was entirely without experience in diplomacy, a statement which the correspondence itself fully endorses. On December 13th Choiseul formally accepted the Sardinian mediation, but there is no trace of Bute's having communicated the affair to the rest of the Cabinet before the end of January, when Newcastle saw a cold letter from Choiseul to Solar expressing grave doubt of the sincerity of the overture.[1] Viri, however, was clever enough to keep the matter going, and early in February another "most secret" letter to him from Solar was shown to Newcastle, intimating that Choiseul was willing to make peace.[2] From this point the negotiations appear to have passed into Egremont's hands, to whose province they properly belonged, and early in March Choiseul began to communicate directly with him. By March 21st, only a fortnight after Pocock and Albemarle had sailed, he had got so far as to send to Viri, for Solar's information, the terms on which England was ready to treat. It must be, he said, on a basis of *uti possidetis*. Of the neutral West Indies we should require St. Lucia and St. Vincent, in Africa Goree, and on the knotty point of the Newfoundland fisheries we were ready to grant a French police post in the island of St. Pierre.[3]

This negotiation was by no means the only one in which the new Government was groping for a way out of its troubles. At the same time Newcastle was urging Yorke

[1] Choiseul to Solar, Jan. 23, and Newcastle to Hardwicke, dated Wednesday (? Jan. 27), *Rockingham Memoirs*, vol. i. pp. 97-9.

[2] "Substance of a most secret letter, &c.," *Newcastle Papers*, 32,934, Feb. 5.

[3] Egremont to Viri, March 21, *ibid.*, 32,936.

at the Hague to persuade the Dutch to come in, on the ground that if they did not we should have to withdraw from the Continent and leave them to the mercy of the Bourbon coalition. It was a suggestion after Bute's own heart. He himself was telling Yorke to persuade the Dutch to let their Scots brigade serve in Portugal, and he endorsed Newcastle's scheme cordially.[1] Hardwicke shook his head over it all. He did not believe, he said, in secret negotiations, and feared they would only make France think we were " knocking at every door for peace." [2]

Still they went on, and had he but known to what further lengths they were being carried he would have shaken his wise head more dubiously still. With the airy self-confidence of a novice Bute had undertaken on his sole responsibility no less a task than the restoration of the system of William III.—the old Triple Alliance which the war had upset. Newcastle's idea of bringing in the Dutch therefore exactly hit his fancy. His own part had been a characteristically amateurish attempt to come to a secret understanding with Austria. So hopeless a misconception of the trend of European politics, on which Kaunitz's great coalition had been founded, is almost inconceivable. For Austria, the dominant factor in the world was the rise of Prussia as a rival for the hegemony in Germany. Yet Bute in his blindness believed that he could raise in its place the old bugbear of the Bourbon alliance, and bring Europe back to what it was before the days of the great Elector and Frederick's unpardonable seizure of Silesia.

It is not to be denied that there was much in the actual situation of affairs to tempt a sanguine novice to try such an overture. But even so, an older hand

---

[1] Newcastle to Yorke, Jan. 8 ; Bute to same, Jan. 12, *ibid.*, 32,933.

[2] Hardwicke to Newcastle, March 21, *ibid.*, 32,936.

would have known it was the worst possible moment to
make it. The heart of the matter lay in the military
situation. For our own army on the Lower Rhine, the
campaign of 1761 had ended satisfactorily enough. It
was in its old position on the line of the Upper Ems,
and the British contingent was wintering at Münster and
Osnabrück. The French had withdrawn their left for
the winter behind the Rhine, with their headquarters at
Cassel, so that neither side had gained any ground during
the campaign, and the defence of Hanover if not of
Hesse was still good. With the central armies things
were in the same unchanged condition, but in the Eastern
or Prussian theatre they were as bad as they could be.
After a desperate defensive campaign Frederick had only
just been able to hold his front. He had secured it,
however, at the last moment by winning the battle of
Torgau in Saxony, which had practically decided the
campaign in his favour and enabled him to maintain
his headquarters at Breslau: still, for the first time in
the war, the Austrians were wintering in Silesia. But
worst of all was in his rear. There the Russians, after
raiding Berlin, had turned into Pomerania and captured
the important seaport of Colberg. Their success had
been achieved by combined operations with a fleet in the
Baltic, and Frederick could not help harping on the
naval help he had confidently expected when he began
the war. "Give my compliments to the good Mitchell,"
he wrote to his Minister in Berlin, "and tell him, but
with no kind of reproach, that with six English ships of
the line Colberg would have been saved."[1] It was a
crushing disaster. Russians as well as Austrians were
able to winter in Prussian territory, and worse still they

[1] Frederick to Finchenstein, Dec. 27, 1761, *Politische Corr.*, vol. xx.
p. 144.

had a sea base from which in the next campaign they could deal Frederick a blow in the back which he had no means of resisting. Once more he fell into a black fit of despair, feeding the dregs of his hope on the chimerical chance of getting the Tartars to make a diversion against Russia and the Porte against Austria. It is even said he took to carrying poison, determined never to fall into the hands of his enemies or to sign an ignominious peace.

If Bute, too, thought the game in Germany was lost beyond redemption, it is scarcely to be wondered. The news of the fall of Colberg reached London on January 4th, just when Mello was pressing the Government to come to the rescue of Portugal. Our annual treaty with Frederick had expired; negotiations for its renewal were on foot; but in view of the secret communications with France, there was a difficulty about renewing it on precisely the old terms, for it contained a proviso that neither party should treat with the common enemy without the knowledge of the other. Further hesitation was caused by the fact that with the defence of Portugal added to our burden it seemed scarcely possible to continue to give Prussia any assistance that could avail to save her. It was just at this time, moreover, that the Cabinet had been in the throes of a final decision about Havana. In the eyes of the Court party the whole situation was beyond our resources, and although after the fall of Colberg a renewal of the Prussian treaty had been promised in general terms, Parliament had not been asked to vote the subsidy. Instead, therefore, of anything definite about the renewal being said, Bute wrote off to Mitchell in Berlin to tell him that Frederick must make peace on the best terms he could get; for in the face of the new war, and our having to defend Portugal, we could go on in Germany no longer.[1] It is conceivable under these circumstances that Bute really believed the only possible way of helping Frederick out of his difficulties was to try to come to terms with Austria, though the ruling motive was undoubtedly his own and his master's detestation of the whole German embroilment. In the rawness of his inexperience he does not seem to have stopped to consider what the effect on Frederick's darkened mind would be should the Austrian overture come to his ears, nor of the disastrous effect on our prestige if it failed. He could think of nothing but tearing himself and the country free from the hopeless situation at any cost.

Yet scarcely had he taken his blundering step, when the whole prospect changed by one of the most dazzling tricks of fortune even in Frederick's career. The very day after the fall of Colberg was known in London the Czarina Elizabeth suddenly died. Her successor was Peter, Duke of Holstein-Gottorp, who had been serving under Frederick as a general of horse, and idolised him as devoutly as Elizabeth had detested him. He at once intimated a complete change of policy. At his first levée he had come up smiling to Keith, the British ambassador, and whispered in his ear he hoped he would be pleased with him, for he had sent an order to stop the Russian advance into Prussia. Immediately afterwards Keith was informed that orders had been issued for an armistice, and for the withdrawal of the Russian troops from the Austrian army.[2] Thus at the very moment when Bute was deciding to abandon Frederick to his fate, the danger which threatened Prussia with extinction vanished with magical suddenness, and the great coalition of Kaunitz,

---

[1] Bute to Mitchell, Jan. 8, *Newcastle Corr.*, 32,933; same to same, May 26, *Mitchell Memoirs*, vol. ii. p. 294.

[2] Keith to Bute, Jan. 8, *Newcastle Papers*, 32,933.

on which our obligations to Frederick were founded, was broken in pieces at a stroke. " I can only compare my situation," wrote Frederick to Ferdinand, "to that of Louis XIV. at the end of the War of Succession. What the disgrace of Marlborough's party was to him, the death of the Empress of Russia is to me." [1]

Unfortunately it was impossible for the startling news to reach London till the end of the month, and in the meanwhile Bute's clumsy activity had had time to do all the harm it could. Yorke, according to his orders, had got into communication with Vienna, and Bute's overture in due course found its way to Kaunitz. As was only to be expected, it was treated by him with the haughtiest disdain. He would not even vouchsafe to reply. In the most contemptuous manner in which such an application can be met, he merely wrote to Yorke's secret agent, reminding him that in the original negotiations in 1755, on the eve of the war, Austria had already put forward her apprehension of her danger from a new Bourbon coalition, but that England, absorbed in her own ends, refused to listen. " Under these circumstances," he concluded, " I must confess to you that his Imperial Majesty and his Minister cannot understand what the confidential overture of the English really means, and consequently it is easy to see that we do not find ourselves here in a position to return an answer." [2]

To the prestige of a country about to treat for peace as a conqueror, no rebuff could be more damaging. But even this was not the worst. Kaunitz took care to spread the story all over Europe, and Frederick quickly got to know that an overture of some kind had been made to his

---

[1] *Politische Corr.*, vol. xxi. p. 256, Feb. 17.
[2] Kaunitz to Baron de Reischach, Vienna, March 3 ; Adolphus, *History of England*, vol. i. p. 493, *Appendix II.*

arch-enemy behind his back. There can now be no doubt
that Bute's unfortunate idea was no worse than the well-
intentioned blunder of a self-confident and incapable man
without diplomatic experience, and that it went no further
than his actual written instructions to Yorke. Without
doubt he foolishly believed that Austria could be induced
to take a new view of the situation, and turn her energies
against the Bourbon coalition instead of consuming them
on Frederick. It would be best for every one if she did.
But there were interested parties who took care that
the whole transaction should be given a very different
colour. To complete Bute's folly, although he kept
the matter secret from Frederick, he was moved to
impart it to Galitzin, the Russian ambassador in London,
who was about to leave. Now Galitzin was a convinced member of the powerful Austrian party which,
of course, still existed at the Russian Court, and he
took care that his conversation with Bute should reach
Frederick's ears in so garbled a form as fairly to astound
the unhappy British Minister when he heard of it.
Galitzin in his report to the Czar said that Bute wished
to warn Russia to be on her guard against encouraging the
chimerical projects of Frederick against Austria. Bute
had also expressed a hope that Peter would not desert his
old ally for the new one, and had declared he could not do
better for Frederick than induce him to save himself from
destruction by making peace even at the sacrifice of some
of his territory. According to the report, Bute further
suggested that the best way to keep a hand over the King
of Prussia and accelerate a general peace was not to withdraw the Russian troops from the Austrian army. Peter
lost little time in communicating the news to his friend,
and Frederick was naturally furious. Bute with trans-
parent sincerity absolutely and vehemently denied having

said any such thing, but the relations between England and Prussia at the moment were so uneasy that Frederick could only believe the worst.[1]

At the end of the previous year, when the last news from Germany was the favourable winter position of Ferdinand and Frederick's victory at Torgau, Parliament had agreed without a division that all the German subsidies should be continued for another year. Two millions had been voted for Ferdinand's army, but still no call had been made for Frederick. At this time Bute and the King seemed resolved to abandon him altogether rather than renew the treaty on the old terms. It is true that when news came of the new Czar's attitude they had made a desperate effort to recover their mistake. Bedford, in spite of every pressure that could be brought to bear on him, had insisted on moving in the House of Lords for the suppression of all the subsidies and the immediate recall of our troops. Bute had seized the opportunity to make a handsome speech against the motion, in which he declared that "a steady adherence to our German allies was now necessary for bringing about a speedy, honourable, and permanent peace." Bedford was beaten by an overwhelming majority, but it did nothing to satisfy Frederick. It was peace, not war, that was clearly in Bute's mind. Instead of proceeding at once to settle the payment of the Prussian subsidy, he intimated that in view of the changed attitude of Russia his master hoped that the money would be used for securing peace rather than for continuing the war, and begged to know what Frederick's plans were to that end. Absorbed in the obvious advantage of replacing England

[1] "Extrait d'une dépêche du Prince Galizin," London, Jan. 26, forwarded to Frederick from St. Petersburg, March 13.—Frederick to Goltz, March 23, *Politische Corr.*, vol. xxi. pp. 311–12.

by Russia as his main ally, and as yet uncertain how his overtures to St. Petersburg would go, Frederick was at a loss what to reply. Week after week he maintained what in England could only be regarded as an almost insolent silence. When at last a letter did come from him to the King, it contained nothing but exultation over his new friend and exhortations for a vigorous continuation of the war. The Prussian Ministers in London were at the same time pressing importunately for the subsidy to be settled. Bute and the King lost temper, and the Prussians got for an answer a sharp protest to the effect that not a penny would be paid till Frederick explained his ideas on the subject of peace.

It was just at this time that Frederick got wind of the perverted version of Bute's overtures to Vienna, and to make matters worse, he himself was taking an equally unfortunate step. Peter had told Keith shortly after his accession that he would be glad to receive an envoy from Frederick. Keith quickly arranged the matter through Mitchell, but before the officer who was sent had been in St. Petersburg many days, our vigilant ambassador discovered that some negotiations were going on which were being kept secret from him. It was nothing less than a suggestion from Frederick to the new Czar for coming to terms at the expense of Denmark. Since Peter was Duke of Holstein-Gottorp, his position as heir to the Russian crown raised the eternal question of the duchies. By the terms of the original sub-infeudation by the King of Denmark, they could not be severed from the Danish crown. In the danger that thus threatened the integrity of Denmark Frederick had seen a chance of getting from her the assistance he most needed, and up to the moment of the Czarina's death he had been contemplating an offer to guarantee to the Danish Court the sovereignty

of the Schleswig-Holstein duchies in return for a Baltic
fleet to recover Colberg.   As soon, however, as the new
Czar ascended the throne and began making his friendly
overtures, the versatile King turned round.   The special
envoy, whom Peter had invited, carried with him to
St. Petersburg instructions to say that if the Czar would
evacuate Prussian territory, and also, if possible, guarantee
him Silesia, he was ready to guarantee Holstein to his
crown.   He was even ready to sign an act of neutrality
in view of Russia making war on Denmark, but it must
be " most secret," and above all, be concealed from the
British ambassador.[1]

Mitchell in Berlin also got wind of the affair.   He
believed, like Keith, that the arrangement extended to
Schleswig, and added a rumour that Frederick was making
preparations to seize the free city of Lübeck in order to
facilitate the execution of his plan.   Considering that the
Prussian mission to the Czar, and indeed the whole
rapprochement, had been arranged by the good offices of
the British representatives at Berlin and St. Petersburg,
the secrecy in which the Danish intrigue had been
wrapped could only raise the gravest suspicions.   For of
all the Courts in Europe, that of Denmark was the one
to which our own was most closely allied by blood.   The
Queen of Denmark was actually a daughter of George
the Second, and what made matters still worse was that
England and Russia were two of the Powers which had
guaranteed the Danish sovereignty of Schleswig.   It is
true that at first Frederick's proposal did not go beyond
Holstein, but even so, it was a considerable strain on the
loyalty of his harassed ally.   King George was naturally
indignant.   In a personal letter he accused Frederick of

---

[1] " Instruction pour le Baron de Goltz," Feb. 7, *Politische Corr.*, vol. xxi.
p. 234.

intending to use the subsidy not for making peace but for spreading the war still further, and Bute instructed Mitchell to say that if the King of Prussia had made any engagement about Schleswig it would cost him his subsidy, and if he had not, his denial of all such intention must be a condition of the grant.[1]

This letter was written in April, and just a week after news had come in of the capture of Martinique.   Every one was in high spirits about the Spanish war, and even the most timid were now confident that Havana would share the fate of the French island.   On the 8th the Cabinet had met to settle the three vital questions of the hour—that is to say, the formal opening of negotiations with France, the amount of assistance that could be given to Portugal, and the continuance of the Prussian subsidy. Grenville and Bute were openly for making no further payments, even for Ferdinand's army, and would stop the war in Germany altogether.   On this point no firm decision was taken, but on the question of Portugal it was otherwise.   Though at first Frederick had admitted our duty of protecting her even at the cost of neglecting Ferdinand's army, he had recently changed his tone, and was now doing his best to get us to desert our old ally. Not, of course, openly; but "in confidence" he told his Minister in London that the case of Portugal was hopeless, and that the King had better retire to Brazil.   The following week, again, he suggested that the threatened invasion of Portugal was a mere parade designed to cover a Spanish descent on Ireland, or even on England itself.[2]

[1] See the correspondence in Adolphus, vol. i. Appendix II. ; also Mitchell to Bute, Jan. 30 and March 2, 7, and 25, *Mitchell Memoirs*, vol. ii.

[2] Frederick to Knyphausen, Feb. 8 and 13, *Politische Corr.*, vol. xxi. pp. 239–50.

At the moment such an attitude on the part of Frederick in regard to Portugal was quite enough to bring the British Cabinet to unanimity in the opposite sense. The main trouble was that it was agreed we could spare no more than six thousand men, and it was doubtful whether so small a force could be of any use. To settle the question, Lord Tyrawley, the old friend of the Portuguese Court, had been sent out, at Mello's request, with some other officers on a secret mission to report on the situation, and to arrange a plan of defence. It so happened that his report just now came to hand, and it was to the effect that the available force would probably be sufficient to enable Portugal to hold her own. For the Cabinet this was enough, and without further hesitation it was decided to issue orders for six thousand men to proceed to Lisbon at once. To mark further the complete breach with Frederick, Bute, as the result of the meeting, sent his defiant despatch on the question of the Danish duchies and the subsidy, and Egremont wrote formally to Choiseul proposing a revival of the negotiations on the basis of the last "two ultimatums," and intimating our readiness to attend a congress to settle the war in Germany.[1]

Within a week of the despatch being sent, Choiseul had penned a favourable reply, and on the very same day, like the resolute statesman he was, he had sent to Spain his elaborate war plan for a final effort to bring England to reason.[2] At the same moment Anson, as though, on the brink of the grave, he was inspired with a vision of Choiseul's mind, was preparing a plan for the

[1] Newcastle to Hardwicke, April 1 and 10; same to Bedford and to Barrington, April 8; Egremont to Choiseul, April 8, *Newcastle Papers*, 32,936–7; Viri to Solar, April 8, *Lansdowne House MSS.*, i.
[2] Choiseul to Egremont, April 14, *Newcastle Papers*, 32,937; Duro, *Armada Española*, vol. vii. p. 53.

defence of the coasts. The force that remained available for the purpose was slender to the last degree, and he was urging that Hawke must hoist his flag in the Channel fleet at once. On April 12th Bute went to see him. The same day the Cabinet considered his proposals, ordered them to go forward, and the dying admiral, at the end of his strength, was carried down to Bath.[1]

It had been the hope of Bute and the peacemakers that their work ere this would have made sufficient progress to render needless the opening of a new campaign. Ferdinand had been held back, fretting and inactive, till the last moment, but now the time had come when "aye" or "no" must be pronounced, and the air, which should have been mild with peace, was highly charged with war. The diplomatic tangle was too dangerous for any man to trust. The British Ministers could feel Pitt's spirit burning round them throughout the country. They dared not flinch if they would—Choiseul would not if he could. The word was peace, but sword in hand. On both sides the war plans had to be set in motion; and to turn to them from the misguided and trothless diplomacy of the hour is a welcome relief. They at least were marked on the French side by the grandiose mind of a great War Minister, and on our own by the skill and comprehensive grasp which Pitt's administration had bred in every department concerned.

The original proposals of Spain bore no such stamp. Penetrated, like Napoleon, with the idea that England's power rested entirely on her commerce, she anticipated him in suggesting to France the formation of a "continental system" for the exclusion of British trade from

[1] Bute to Newcastle, April 10; Newcastle to Devonshire, April 13, *Newcastle Papers*, 32,937.

European ports. Choiseul was to get the adhesion of Russia, and she herself would manage the Mediterranean Princes. Choiseul, more far-sighted than Napoleon, at once refused, on the ground that such a method of meeting England would be as costly as it was dangerous. "Commerce," he observed in his reply, "is a kind of torrent. Its course can only be changed with difficulty, and if you try to cut it off suddenly, it destroys the banks where you stop it." The military operations which Spain had to propose were of the usual nature—an attack on Gibraltar by sea, a descent in Ireland, the conquest of Jamaica, and the invasion of Holland by France on the old plan of securing an indemnity against the British conquests beyond the sea.[1] But Choiseul would have none of these things. Methods so trite were below the starting-point where his creative mind began to think. He was bent on Spain's concentrating the whole of her home energy on Portugal, enforcing his advice with the reflection that the Portuguese Court was resting secure and inactive in the confidence of neutrality. In this belief—if it really was a belief—we know Choiseul was wrong. Portugal was already awake and busy securing British protection.

In order to afford Spain no pretext for attack, the affair was being conducted with the utmost secrecy by Mello in London. Not even Hay, our minister in Lisbon, was informed of it officially. Oeyras, the famous Portuguese dictator, was in power. As early as November 1761 he scented what was in the wind, and he was determined at all costs that no sign of his moving should give Spain the handle she wanted. It was in the middle of December that Mello had made his application for

[1] Flassan, *La Diplomatic Française*, vol. vi. p. 456, citing a despatch of the Duc d'Ossun, the French Ambassador in Madrid, dated Jan. 18.

Lord Tyrawley. By January 7th Egremont had been instructed to give the desired assurance. A month later the regiments that were available had been warned for service, and Tyrawley appointed to command, and given his secret instructions for the confidential report.[1]

Whether or not it was Choiseul who first suggested the shameless violation of Portuguese neutrality is difficult to determine. It is certain, however, that he was for Spain's striking an immediate blow while the victim, as he supposed, was still asleep and before England could act. This, however, was a length to which the chivalry of the Spanish King would not permit him to go. He insisted on proceeding more honourably by diplomatic means. He would first present a demand to Portugal, in accordance with his original plan, that she should close her ports to British trade, and detach herself altogether from the British interest. If she accepted, she was to be guaranteed against attack; if she refused, she would be regarded as an ally of the common enemy. She must choose between one side and the other—neutrality was impossible; but until she had made her choice Charles declined to act, and Choiseul had to consent. He was careful, however, to send a special envoy to Lisbon to conduct the negotiation in conjunction with the Spanish Minister, and to see things went the right way.[2] It must further be remembered that an intrigue to create in Portugal itself a reaction of popular sentiment against England had been an undercurrent of French policy since the beginning of the war, and that under Choiseul's administration the French Minister at Lisbon had been fomenting a campaign in the press to that end. The affair had ended in failure, and by the

---

[1] Egremont to Hay, Feb. 9, *S.P. Foreign (Portugal)*, 54.
[2] Flassan, *Diplomatie Française*, vol. vi. p. 458.

end of 1761 it was clear that nothing but force could overcome the stubborn loyalty of Portugal.[1] But what is most significant of all is that an attack on Portugal, and the diversion of British attention to its defence, was a point upon which Choiseul's whole war plan turned.

As we have seen already, this war plan in its final form was not delivered to Spain till after the Havana expedition had sailed, and news had come of Rodney's success at Martinique. It is also important to note that Choiseul had just been officially informed that Sweden was going to follow the lead of Russia, and make her peace with Frederick.[2] All chance, therefore, for France to obtain in Hanover the long-sought guarantee for a favourable peace was gone, and it was the moment when Choiseul had decided to re-open negotiations with Bute.

To aggravate the situation for him Spain was still hanging back from the final step. In the middle of March the joint ultimatum of the two powers had been presented in Lisbon, and an answer demanded in four days. It was given without shrinking, in terms of brave and pathetic dignity. Honour and justice would not permit the King's joining them against England. He deplored the quarrel of his friends, and, after expressing his willingness to mediate, appealed to Charles to have pity on the miserable state of his country. Charles was moved, and his emotion was sharpened by the unwelcome news that Martinique was lost. For the moment nothing was done. " I see well," wrote Choiseul to the French ambassador in Spain, " that at Madrid they are not used to disasters. It is a difficult habit to acquire when you are engaged in war; but these are just the situations

---

[1] Wheeler, *The " Discours Politique," attributed to Pombal [then Count of Oeyras].—English Historical Review*, vol. xix. p. 128.

[2] Havrincourt to Choiseul, March 26, *Newcastle Papers*, 32,936.

that call for the highest courage." [1]   But even as he
wrote the die was cast.   A second threatening ultimatum
had been presented to the King of Portugal, and he had
rejected it passionately, exclaiming, " It would affect him
less to let the last tile of his palace fall, and see his
faithful subjects spill the last drop of their blood, than to
sacrifice the honour of his crown and all that Portugal
held most dear." It was four days after this high
answer was penned that Choiseul sent off his war plan.

Whatever may be said of it, it cannot be denied the
quality of courage.   With England still advancing from
success to success beyond the seas, and all hope of coun-
tervailing advantages on the Continent gone, Choiseul
found himself driven, as a counsel of despair, to deliver
a counter-stroke at his enemy's heart, and deliver it by
invasion over an uncommanded sea.   This condition was
the absorbing difficulty.   He did not disguise from himself that for the success of his scheme local and temporary command was essential.   For it was no mere raid
that he had in contemplation, but a continuing operation
in successive waves.   He frankly faced the situation that
such a command could only be obtained by diversion—
by working, that is, for a dissipation of the English naval
defence, and the deflection of the enemy's attention from
his theatre of operation.   With this postulate as the
essential condition of success, he argued that it was impossible to throw across the whole force required in one
body.   The concentration of the troops, and the collec-
tion of sufficient transport, would at once put England on
her guard.   Concealment was only possible by suddenly
seizing a *pied à terre* with a small body of troops that
could be passed over in local craft, and reinforcing them
as rapidly as possible.   The obvious drawback of the

[1] Choiseul to d'Ossun, April 5.—Flassan, vol. vi. p. 466.

method was, that it involved securing a local control of
the sea of considerable duration, but Choiseul made up
his mind that this was the lesser risk.

In the memorandum then, in which he communicated
his plan, he began by pointing out that if the two
crowns decided to send an army to England, it would
be necessary to arrange a combination, so as to secure
" the command of the Channel and a superiority in that
sea for at least five weeks." In view of the force they
had available this was by no means easy. According to
Choiseul's information there were in Brest 6 of the line;
in Rochefort, 10; in Ferrol, 8; in Cadiz, 14; in Cartagena, 4; and in Toulon, 10. In all there were 52 of
the line, but, as he observed, they were distributed in a
manner that by no means lent itself to concentrating and
carrying them in one fleet into the Channel. The ten
sail in Toulon could easily join the four in Cartagena, but
they would together form a squadron too weak to force
the Straits in the face of Saunders, and the attempt to do
so would probably end in giving the enemy a decision
in the Mediterranean. It was only possible, therefore,
to count on the thirty-eight that remained in the various
Atlantic ports, and from these must be deducted the
ten in Rochefort, which could not move so long as
the British held their blockading position at the Isle of
Aix. There remained, then, no more than the twenty-
eight in Brest, Ferrol, and Cadiz; and as it would be
necessary to leave at least six of these for the defence of
the Cadiz waters, the striking fleet could not amount to
more than twenty-two of the line. With such a force
an open bid for the command of English waters was
impossible, but, seeing how widely the British fleet was
distributed, it might be possible, by diversion, to seize
the Channel and hold it for the five weeks needed before

the enemy could concentrate a sufficient force to drive them off.

For such a method to succeed he insisted that two things were necessary: firstly, absolute secrecy, and, secondly, operations to throw the enemy off his guard and lull him to security at home. The primary object, therefore, must be to induce him to send the greatest possible number of vessels away from his own seas, and to denude the British Islands of troops. The means to this end were the war in Germany, the war in Portugal, a demonstration of besieging Gibraltar, and across the Atlantic a threat to recover Martinique and Guadeloupe, and to seize Jamaica, for which operations the two crowns had already thirty of the line in the West Indies. These diversions must be made with promptitude and vigour; for the moment the enemy got wind of the real object of the allied squadrons, they would gather a force together which would never lose sight of them, and be certain to ruin the plan. "Well do we know," wrote Choiseul, "that, in spite of the wide distribution of their fleet which they have maintained throughout the war, they have always shown themselves in a position to face every danger with which France threatened them." In the European theatre he thought that Gibraltar would afford the best means of diversion, as being furthest away from England. A feint of besieging it was to be made, and, to give it reality, thirty French battalions would be sent down from Marseilles, and landed at Estrepona. If, at the same time, the operation was accompanied by movements of the Toulon and Cartagena squadrons, it would certainly fix the bulk of the British strength in the Straits.

Meanwhile France would quietly be making the necessary preparations for passing troops across the

Channel. The originality of Choiseul's plan was that no more than eight small vessels were to be collected between Dunkirk and Calais, enough to enable him to establish a footing in England, and rapidly to support it during the four or five weeks the allied fleet would be masters of the Channel. So small an assemblage of transports, he repeated, would not arouse suspicion, and the English would be certain to take the substance for the shadow. The real difficulty would be the formation of the corps of invasion. To assemble a sufficient force on the coast would be to betray the whole secret. But he believed it could be managed in another way. By organising the corps between the Meuse and the Lower Rhine, it would acquire the colour of a reserve for the Westphalian army, and at the last moment it could be moved by forced marches to the coast in échelon as required. It was to consist of a hundred battalions, or about 50,000 men.

Then follows the method in which he hoped to manage the naval concentration without revealing its object. The rendezvous must be Ferrol, as being the point calculated to make the enemy most uneasy about Gibraltar, and also as being outside the actual theatre of operations, so as to admit of the allied fleet reaching the Channel without fighting. To Ferrol, then, France must send eight of the line from Brest, and Spain eight from Cadiz, and the junction must be made without meeting the enemy. This might reasonably be counted on because the English would naturally believe the concentration was intended to form a combination with the fourteen ships of the Mediterranean squadrons and establish the siege of Gibraltar, and they would therefore prefer to hold the Straits to blockading Ferrol. Consequently it was to be expected that the English would take up a position somewhere between Cape Gata and Cape St. Mary, that is either within or without the Straits, so as to "attend the motions" of the allies and be superior to either wing of the combined fleets. That this would be done could be counted on with certainty, for so favourable for the British was the position indicated that with a score or so of the line they could contain the whole of the available thirty-six of the allies. Such a trap would be all the more certain to catch them because, while they would see active operations ashore against Gibraltar, there would be no sign of movement at Calais or Dunkirk. Further to ensure the deception, the King of Spain must withdraw all his troops except ordinary garrisons from Galicia, since even a small force on that coast, with a fleet in Ferrol, would indicate a raid on Ireland, and tend to reveal to the enemy all that it was most essential to hide. It would turn their attention to Ferrol, and they would take up a position off the port which would make it impossible for the allied fleet to get out without fighting. An action would ruin the whole plan, for, even if victorious, the combined squadron must suffer so much damage that the English would be able to retain command of the Channel with a mere handful of ships. It was indeed essential that the combined squadron in Ferrol should be ordered to defer its sailing till there was nothing in its path.[1]

It will be seen at once how vital to the scheme was a diversion against Portugal. Within a week Solar sent over to Viri a report of what was in the wind. Falling straight into Choiseul's trap he warned Viri that the chief obstacle to securing peace would be Spain and

[1] "Project for the invasion of England, formed by the French Ministry, and remitted April 14, 1760," Duro, *Armada Española*, vol. vii. p. 53, *Appendix.*

Grimaldi, and that England's best chance of spoiling
their game was to support Portugal with all the troops
she could.   Portugal, he said, and not Hanover, was to
be the main object of the year's campaign.[1] Clearly
what Choiseul was aiming at—and what Viri unwittingly
was doing his best to bring about—was to throw into confusion the covering or containing system which Pitt had
used with so much success throughout the war.   Anything
like a conquest of England was not in his mind.   The
military force at his disposal was not great enough, and
if it had been he could not have got it across.   But if
only the enemy's home defence force could be temporarily
reduced to a low enough point, he trusted that his fifty
thousand men would be able to deal to England a blow
which would rush her into accepting reasonable terms.
The attack on Portugal was the only means of securing
such a reduction; for Gibraltar was fully garrisoned, and
in view of the condition of affairs in Germany, and the
fate of Martinique, no reinforcements were likely to be
drawn away to either of those theatres.

The whole plan, though suffering from an excess of
subtlety and elaboration, was undeniably well conceived
in view of the actual situation.   It cannot be said it had
no chance of success, and it was certainly simpler and more
firmly knit than any of those which Napoleon afterwards
adopted.   A scheme very like his last—so like, indeed,
that it is obviously the origin of Napoleon's idea—had
actually been submitted to Choiseul amongst many others
at this time.   A squadron was to leave Toulon in the
winter, and, after recapturing Goree, was to return to Ferrol
in July the following year.   Two other squadrons, leaving
Brest and Rochefort in the same way, were to rendezvous at Martinique, recapture Guadeloupe, and threaten

---

[1] Solar to Viri, April 16, *Lansdowne House MSS.*

Jamaica. In July they were to meet the Toulon squadron in Ferrol, and then the three in company were to set free a fourth squadron in Brest, seize the command of the Channel, and cover the passage of an invading army. This project, which was drawn up before the Family Compact was signed, became even more attractive when the Spanish co-operation was available; but Choiseul rejected it in favour of his simpler scheme, founded directly on a combination with the Spanish fleet, and the fresh possibilities of diversion arising from the shift in the balance of the war.[1]

The manner in which the danger of this scheme was detected and met by England, and the system on which, in spite of it, she maintained her covering position for the main attack on Havana, are of high interest. Let us turn first to the Straits—the southern area, where for the defence the situation was most critical and difficult. There, it will be remembered, Saunders, having found that from unavoidable delays his chance of striking a blow at Spain was lost, had correctly decided to assume the defensive. Clearly appreciating that his function in the British plan was discharged by keeping the Mediterranean and Atlantic divisions of the enemy apart, he would permit nothing to distract him from holding the Straits and setting up the strategical deadlock which Choiseul had recognised to be insoluble. We left him before Cadiz, whither he had gone at the earliest possible moment, hoping for a chance to attack. Though he at once recognised there was nothing left for him but the defensive, it was by no means easy to decide how best to

---

[1] See Lacour-Gayet, *Marine sous Louis XV.*, p. 354. The author is of opinion that Napoleon consulted this memoir as well as the subsequent projects of the Duc de Broglie drawn up in 1763–65, *ibid.*, 422 n. He does not, however, mention the project which, according to Captain Duro, Choiseul actually forwarded to the Spanish Court as his final plan.

perform his function. The force at his command was eighteen of the line, and though all were small except his own flagship, he had nothing to fear from any probable concentration of the allies, provided he could maintain an interior position between their Mediterranean and their Atlantic divisions. But it was essential for him to make sure of being able to deal with either concentration singly, if the Atlantic divisions tried to join those in the Mediterranean, or *vice versa*. There was, of course, an obvious temptation to endeavour to improve the situation by blockading Cadiz, so as to prevent the Atlantic divisions getting together at all. But his fine strategical insight and his masterly grasp of the essential conditions quickly convinced him that this would be an error. It would be trying too much at the risk of losing everything. A position which would enable him to blockade Cadiz, and at the same time make sure of barring the Straits, was not to be found. In his despatch to the Admiralty we have his exact appreciation of the position. If, he says, with the wind easterly he remained in the Gut to prevent the exit of the combined Mediterranean divisions, he left Cadiz open for a concentration of the Atlantic divisions. If, on the other hand, to prevent this he cruised west of the Gut and within striking distance of Cadiz, the first Levanter would probably drive him so far to sea that the Mediterranean division would be able to pass out untouched, and slip by inshore of him round Cape Trafalgar into Cadiz. To his broad grasp of essentials this was the greater danger, and he decided that the position which his function in the war plan indicated was to secure the Gut and ignore the minor risk of leaving Cadiz open.

So much was plain to him, but it happened that this dilemma, which he solved so sagaciously, did not exhaust the strategical complexity of his position. For, no sooner had he reached Cadiz and realised the problem before him, than he had received an urgent and mysterious summons from Hay for three or four ships to be sent to Lisbon immediately, if he could possibly spare them. No explanation was given, but it was requested that they should drop in one by one, as though by hazard. As yet there was no sign of movement at Toulon, which his frigates were watching from the Savoyard port of Villa-franca. An immediate occupation of the Gut, therefore, was not necessary, and on February 4th he decided to send up three of the line to the Tagus "to see what was the matter there."

The matter was that Oeyras had just let Hay into the secret of the Franco-Spanish designs. The Paris *Gazette* had arrived with an acknowledgment of the Family Com-pact, and with it news that O'Dunn, Choiseul's special envoy, was on his way to force Portugal to declare war for or against the alliance. Oeyras also said that British protection had been claimed, and that Mello had been promised the succour he asked in London, and pending its arrival they were making the best defensive arrange-ments they could. For the present, at least, so completely disorganised was the Portuguese army, there could be no thought of holding the frontier. The only way was to make a stand at Lisbon, where they could hold out for three or four months. The immediate need was to keep the Tagus open till the sea-forts were repaired, and the few ships they had could be prepared for its defence. It was with this object that he had begged Hay to send the message to Saunders. But Oeyras still attached so much importance to giving no colour of provocation to Spain, that he begged Saunders should not be told the reason. The move was very happily timed, for it so happened that the very day O'Dunn reached Lisbon the three battleships came sailing into the Tagus and quietly requested victuals and water.

Though Saunders was too good a "minister" to refuse an urgent diplomatic request, if he could possibly assent, he did not like it. The officer in command of the detached division brought a letter from him to Hay, saying that the call left him with only fifteen of the line, and that the French and Spaniards had twenty-eight between Toulon and Cadiz. He was, therefore, not to keep the ships a moment longer than was necessary. But so soon as the detachment had parted company, Saunders seems to have repented his decision, for the next day he wrote again to say that he could not employ the ships of his squadron without knowing what service they had gone on, and they must be sent back at once. Hay in great distress went to Oeyras and begged to be allowed to tell Saunders everything. Oeyras consented, and the admiral was informed that succours were coming from England, and that his ships were wanted in conjunction with the Lisbon squadron to keep the port open from an attack from Ferrol till they came. Hay, therefore, begged they might stay a little longer. By the time the new request reached Saunders, Sir Peircy Brett had joined him as second in command, with two more of the line, and he had heard that the French and Spanish force east of the Straits was only seventeen. Recognising, therefore, the importance of the mysterious service, he gave his consent, and the first week in March he moved down to take up his Gibraltar position and do his best with the force he had left.[1] The whole episode has long

[1] Hay to Egremont, Jan. 17, Feb. 9 and 20 ; Saunders to Hay, Feb. 4 and 5 ; Hay to Saunders, Feb. 19, *S.P. Foreign (Portugal)*, 54 ; Hay to Saunders, Jan. 18 ; Saunders to the Admiralty, "Off Cadiz," Jan. 18, Feb. 2 and 22, and "Gibraltar Bay," March 4, *Admiralty Secretary, In-letters*, 384.

been forgotten, with so much else that stands to Saunders's credit. But it is well worth rescuing from oblivion as a fine example of an admiral weighing with sagacity and ripe understanding the political object against the purely strategical, and deliberately choosing to run the risk of a strategical failure for the sake of securing a great and certain political advantage. Let us see with how clear a head and sure a grasp he held the high line he had chosen.

His new position, as he had said, left Cadiz open; but it could not be helped. At Lisbon there was no apprehension of an attack from that quarter, and his own observation convinced him the Cadiz squadron did not intend to move unless and until it was joined by the squadrons in Toulon and Cartagena. There was little, therefore, to deflect his clear view that, having done what was wanted for Portugal, he could rightly devote himself to his primary object of preventing a junction of the enemies' Mediterranean and Atlantic divisions.[1] With this intention he began cruising in the Gut between Europa Point and Ceuta. In a few days, however, a frigate arrived from Villafranca to report that the Toulon squadron was not nearly ready for sea. Whereupon, seeing he was still free to attend to his minor object of thwarting a concentration of the Atlantic divisions, he returned immediately to Cadiz, and there he was rejoined by his Lisbon detachment.

Oeyras had done with it. Early in March he had informed Hay that the Tagus forts were complete, and that with his own ships he had now no fear of anything the Spaniards had ready to send out of Ferrol. Moreover, though the Spanish army was slowly massing on the

[1] Saunders to the Admiralty, "Gibraltar Bay, March 4," *In-letters*, 384.

frontier, O'Dunn had made no move. Oeyras believed
he was waiting till the arrival of the British troops gave
him an excuse for acting, and the Minister, anxious to
remove all shadow of such excuse, desired that the ships
should be returned at once to Saunders, with a warm
expression of gratitude.[1]

The position with which Oeyras had to deal is well
worth noting, for it must almost necessarily recur
where a neutral state is in the position that Portugal
found herself. Though determined not to break with
England, her main desire, prostrate as she was with
misfortune, was to preserve her neutrality. She wished
to give all her preparations the colour of being made as
much against one belligerent as the other. Consequently
when, on March 12th, Tyrawley arrived on his delicate
mission, he found it in spite of his cordial reception very
difficult to do anything owing to the nervous desire for
secrecy that obtained. "They cry aloud for the King's
assistance," he wrote home, "and are afraid to avail themselves of it."[2] It was a situation, however, that had to be
accepted, and Tyrawley went quietly to work to ascertain
and report the real necessities and possibilities of the
case. Still his movements could not be concealed, and,
in the belief of the Portuguese Government, they brought
down the crisis on their heads.[3] At all events, about a
week after the arrival of Tyrawley and his staff of British
officers, O'Dunn and his Spanish colleague presented
their joint ultimatum and Oeyras presented his temporising answer. It was long, he told Hay, but would
have been much shorter if the troops as well as the
officers had arrived from England.

[1] Hay to Egremont, March 12, *S.P. Foreign (Portugal)*, 54.
[2] Tyrawley to Egremont, March 12, *ibid.*
[3] Hay to Saunders, March 29, *ibid.*

But there was yet long to wait. The British Government was still standing fast for Tyrawley's confidential report. Its tenour we have already seen. Contrary to the insidious suggestions of Frederick, it was to the effect that the six thousand troops and a regiment of dragoons that were available would in all probability save the situation. There was, of course, no certainty in the matter, but, as he observed, the value of the Portuguese trade was worth the risk, for the force specified was too insignificant to affect materially the safety of the British dominions. He urged, however, that if it was to come, it could not come too soon.

The truth was that the hesitation of Bute for a while exposed Portugal to serious danger. Since the ultimatum had been delivered and answered a state of war practically existed, and the invasion might begin at any moment. There was a special anxiety for the southern or Algarve coast, which lay open to a blow from the opposite shores of Andalusia. Hay therefore promptly warned Saunders of what had occurred, and begged he would have a care for the threatened coast.[1] But Saunders was already moving away from Cadiz. He had heard that the naval force of the allies within the Straits was going to concentrate at Cartagena, and, never taking his eyes from what he called his " principal object," he returned to Gibraltar. Here Hay's request reached him. He was at his wit's end for cruisers, but he still kept his hold on the master thread, and, without hesitating, he spared two or three for the Algarve coast, telling Hay at the same time that the Portuguese must form a coast defence flotilla under their protection. It was all he could do, and, come what might, he was determined thenceforth to hold his

---

[1] Hay to Egremont, and Tyrawley to same, March 22 ; Hay to Saunders, March 29, *ibid.*

position in the Gut and close the Straits.[1] The admiral's
concentration of purpose was excellent, but at the same
time it should be observed how well Choiseul's plan for
confusing the British defence was working. It remains to
be seen how, nevertheless, it entirely failed to bring about
the situation at which he had aimed, and for this we
must turn to the northern area of the covering operations.

It is clear that if Anson had not penetrated Choiseul's
design from the first, he at least considered that our
defensive system was incomplete without providing against
some such counter-stroke at home as the French Minister
had suggested to Spain. When, on Jan. 24th, Blénac
eluded Spry's blockade and got out of Brest, immediate
steps were taken to see whether it was not the first movement of a concentration for counter-attack. Ferrol was
open, and the Spanish force there was being watched by
only a small cruiser squadron. It was the chief source of
anxiety, and there was an obvious probability that it was
Blenac's destination. His intention might be, after joining
hands with the Ferrol squadron, to return either to attack
Commodore Denis, who had succeeded Howe in the Basque
Roads with nine of the line, or to cover a blow at England
itself, or both. Orders, therefore, were hurried off to Denis
to proceed to Ferrol and ascertain the truth.[2] Before the
result of his reconnaissance could be known, definite warning came from our agents in France that an invasion was
intended from Dunkirk. The French, so the information
ran, were far from thinking themselves capable of making
a conquest, but their object was to throw England into
confusion, and destroy her credit, so as to prevent her maintaining her army in Germany.[3] It was, of course, soon

---

[1] Saunders to the Admiralty, April 9 and 29 and May 10, *In-letters*, 384 ;
Hay to Egremont, *S.P. Foreign (Portugal)*, 54.
[2] *Secret Orders*, 1332.   [3] *Newcastle Papers*, 32,934, f. 357.

known that Blénac had gone to the West Indies, but, as our cruisers reported twelve of the line in Ferrol nearly ready for sea, the place continued to cause grave anxiety. The usual cruisers and flotillas, supported by a small battle squadron under Moore in the Downs, were watching Dunkirk and the Breton ports to see that no transports crossed, but for Ferrol there was nothing but the Channel Fleet, which was not yet available.

The tension was soon increased by the news that France and Spain had presented their joint ultimatum at Lisbon, and that it had been rejected. The tidings reached London from Hay on April 6th, together with Oeyras's remark about " a short answer," and Tyrawley's urgent report. It was then the Cabinet met, as we have already seen, to make a final decision as to what troops were to be sent to Lisbon. It was clear that action must be taken at once; and it was then, too, that Anson presented his scheme for coast defence, and told Bute plainly it was absolutely necessary for Hawke to get the Channel Squadron to sea without a moment's delay.[1] At all costs the necessary succour for Portugal must be passed to Lisbon in face of the Ferrol squadron. Steps for her assistance had already been taken on the strength of an informal note which Oeyras had dictated to Hay in the middle of January. Arms, tents, and equipments were already at Portsmouth, and transports had gone to Cork, under convoy of two ships of the line, to pick up two battalions of infantry. Their line of passage to Lisbon involved little risk; they could easily steal across unperceived; but with the rest of the troops it was different, and for them, seeing where they were to come from, more serious precautions had to be taken. When Frederick first heard of the Spanish movement against Portugal he had not yet been alienated

[1] *Newcastle Papers*, 32,936, April 8 to 10.

by Bute's tricks, and he had immediately suggested that
it could be met, without prejudice to the war in Germany,
by throwing into Portugal the garrison of Belleisle.[1] His
advice was now adopted. Indeed, the dragoons and the
rest of the infantry that Tyrawley's report called for
could come from nowhere else, and from Belleisle, at
least, the course lay past the jaws of Ferrol, and the
movement could not be concealed.

On April 8th Hawke received his commission, and on
the 27th hoisted his flag. For second in command he
had to take Prince Edward, Duke of York, but Howe
had been summoned back to be the royal admiral's flag
captain. Hawke did not get to sea at once. There was
no great hurry. Portugal still had a faint hope of preserving her neutrality. For some reason, partly because
the allies were not ready and partly because, on a strange
hint from the Spanish ambassador, the Portuguese Queen
was interceding with her brother, the King of Spain, a
declaration of war did not follow the ultimatum immediately. It was not till May 3rd, as the stores from England
began to arrive, that the Spaniards crossed the north-
eastern frontier, and seized the border town of Miranda.
Three days later the Irish regiments came in, and as soon
as it was known they were in the Tagus, but not till
then, war was declared. The seizure of Braganza followed
immediately, on May 15th, and the Spaniards began to
advance down the Douro on Oporto. But this mattered
little. The procrastination had been so great that in the
middle of April Hay had been able to report that the
Spaniards had lost their chance, for Lisbon was now safe
from a *coup de main*.[2]

[1] Frederick to Ferdinand, Feb. 3, *Politische Corr.*, vol. xxii. p. 221.
[2] Hay to Egremont, April 13 and 27, *S.P. Foreign (Portugal)*, 54 ; same
to same, May 6, *ibid.*, 55.

Meanwhile, at Portsmouth, till the Belleisle transports were ready, Hawke was devoting himself to organising the plan of home defence which Anson had worked out with the last dregs of his strength. He was dying down at Bath. Lord Halifax was acting in his place, with Admiral Forbes for his chief adviser—a capable officer, whose health had denied him all active service since he had fought well, twenty years before, in Mathews's action off Toulon, and who had served on the Board throughout the war. The new chief, not content to let Hawke make his own arrangements, began bothering him with detailed orders. The interference, which certainly seems to have been excessive, was naturally resented by a man of Hawke's temper, who always considered, in common with other wise heads, that he should have worn Anson's cloak. He was at all events conscious of a unique experience in the work that was required. Under Pitt and Anson such annoyance never occurred, and before the admiral had flown his flag a week he was driven to forward a formal request that he might be left a free hand in disposing the ships under his command. A week later, in answer to some further nervous suggestions, he was informing the Board he considered the passage of the troops to Portugal the most important part of his duty. At the end of May he told them he had reorganised the blockade of Dunkirk on the plan approved by Anson before he left town, so as to insure that the French should at once encounter a superior squadron if they came out. Under the old system, he explained, the cruisers were scattered in such small groups that if the French moved they could not attack at once, but must fall back and inform Moore in the Downs. The reply was that he was to maintain the old system until they warned him there was danger.

So far the Admiralty was probably within its function. It was a question of Home defence, and they had the information. But the interference pursued him when he sailed to cover the passage of the Belleisle troops. He had worked out the problem with the utmost care, but he merely informed the Board his rendezvous would be ten leagues north-west of Finisterre. Failing to fathom his strategy, they were seriously alarmed, and immediately sent down to press upon him a crude plan of their own founded on a series of ingenious pictures they had been making for themselves. In their minds the Ferrol squadron was given so many dangerous possibilities that, on the eve of Hawke's sailing, they had been contemplating ordering an attack upon it. With our own fleet only just of sufficient strength to perform its covering functions such a design, of course, involved a wholly unjustifiable risk, and a departure from the defensive attitude at home on which Pitt's whole system had been founded. The idea, which presumably arose out of a false analogy with Pitt's own expeditions against the French coast, was abandoned, but only, it would appear, from political reasons, on the ground that it was unwise to provoke Spain further, now that direct negotiations were on the point of opening.[1] Still their nervousness about Ferrol was such that they could not feel safe unless Hawke planted himself immediately before the port. This was the effect of their orders, but before they could reach Spithead Hawke was gone.

Arrived off Ushant, he despatched two sixty-fours to Belleisle with orders for the troops to sail at once under their convoy. He himself held on for his chosen station, and reached it on July 1st. A chain of cruisers was then thrown out to Ferrol, and in this position he waited,

---

[1] *Grenville Papers*, vol. i. pp. 443–5, May 20.

certain of securing the safe passage of the troops. By
good fortune his line of reasoning is known to us exactly,
for at the end of the week the Board's correction reached
him, and in his testy but dignified way he once more
practically told them to mind their own business. " I
had maturely considered," he wrote, " every circumstance,
both with regard to the enemy and the transports to
come from Belleisle. As to the first, not the least
fear of them being at sea filled me either with distrac-
tion or irresolution. The enemy themselves could never
suppose me so absurd as either to appoint a rendezvous
for the convoy from Belleisle or the commander of it to
shape his course for any port within the Cape, as thereby
he would run the risk of being embayed with a westerly
wind. The course from that island with a fair wind is
west-south-west by compass, which will fall in with Cape
Torrinana [just north of Finisterre], and consequently
with my rendezvous." The conductor of the convoy, he
pointed out, would certainly in common prudence keep
outside that line. " Under these circumstances," he concluded, " I should not think of being nearer Ferrol than
I am. Had I shown myself off that port I must have
come here at once for fear of westerly winds, Ortegal
being improper. The enemy cannot get out with a
westerly wind, and if they come out on an easterly I
must have intelligence, and they can't get in again.
When the army arrives I shall see it safe round the
Cape, and proceed with the last part of your orders." [1]
To his own disposition, therefore, he clung. What the
new orders were we shall see.

To the southward the covering combination was completed by Saunders. All through May and June he had

[1] Hawke to the Admiralty, June 25, " Off St. Helen's," and July 9,
" Finisterre, 9 leagues," *In-letters*, 92.

been cruising in the Gut, held there by so much of
Choiseul's war plan as had been realised. Early in June
the Cartagena squadron put to sea. It returned in a
week, but no sooner did Saunders hear it was in port
again than he received intelligence that the Toulon
squadron was about to sail, and that troops were concentrating in the port. Their real purpose was to reinforce the French garrison in Minorca, since it was
impossible to tell that Port Mahon was not the objective
of the British force coming from Belleisle. A report,
however, was spread that Gibraltar was to be besieged,
and at the end of June the Toulon squadron did actually
put to sea. Saunders was thus held more firmly than
ever. But he was not without reward. Prizes came fast,
and among them one of the most famous in our annals.
This was the treasure ship *Hermione,* that had sailed from
Lima before the declaration of war was known. On May
15th she was met and captured off Cape St. Mary, on
the Algarve coast, only a day's sail from home, by two
of Saunders's cruisers—the *Active* (28) and *Favourite*
(18), Captains Sawyer and Pownal. So enormously rich
did she prove that, after deducting all expenses, more
than half a million sterling was distributed in prize-
money.[1]

The Toulon squadron was still out when Saunders heard
the Belleisle troops were moving. For the moment, in
his clear appreciation of the position, their safe passage
into the Tagus overrode all other considerations, and
he did not hesitate to leave the Gut and move up to
blockade the Cadiz squadron. The result of the com-

---

[1] Saunders to the Admiralty, June 16, *In-letters,* 384. Saunders and
the two fortunate captains had about £65,000 each, and the share of
every seaman was nearly £500. The commissioned officers had £13,000
each.—Beatson, vol. iii. p. 419.

bination between him and Hawke was an entire success. The Toulon squadron, after landing the troops which Saunders had heard of at Minorca, returned to Hyères and made no attempt to come out; the Belleisle transports passed into Lisbon without interruption either from Ferrol or Cadiz; and within a week Saunders had resumed his position in the Gut.[1]

Once arrived, the British troops lost no time in getting to work. Lord Loudoun, called from his long retirement, was in command as second to Tyrawley; Townshend was third; Burgoyne, of American fame, had a brigade; and with them came a number of officers to organise the Portuguese army, and three naval captains for their fleet. With this assistance they were able to hold their own. At Oeyras's request the British Government had sent out Count zu Lippe-Brückeberg, one of Prince Ferdinand's ablest lieutenants in Westphalia, to take supreme command. Under him the defence was conducted with great skill and spirit, and though the French sent a dozen battalions to the Spaniards' assistance, they were never able to do more than capture a few unimportant places on the frontier. Oporto was for a moment in danger, but Lisbon was never even approached; and Saunders, maintaining his watch on the Algarve coast, successfully prevented any attempt to penetrate the country from the south.[2]

The fresh orders which Hawke had received, with the shallow criticism of his strategy, instructed him, as soon as he had seen the troops in safety, to cruise between Finisterre and the south of Ireland for a month to en-

---

[1] Saunders to the Admiralty, July 21 and Aug. 17, *ibid.* He was off Cadiz on July 15. Hawke parted with the transports on the 14th.

[2] For a detailed account of the campaign see Pajol, *Guerres sous ouis XV.*, vol. vi. ch. iv.

deavour to intercept Blénac on his return. Accordingly, after parting with the transports on July 14th,
he made for Cape Clear, confident that Blénac would
steer for Brest. In three weeks he was standing back
again, and having made Ortegal without any sign of
his quarry he bore up for England, according to orders,
and struck his flag for the last time at Torbay on
August 23rd. So to the end his ill luck dogged him.
It is true that, like Saunders, he had a number of fat
prizes to his credit, but Blénac had not moved from Cap
François.

Hawke was immediately relieved by Sir Charles Hardy.
The Government was once more nervous about the Brest
squadron. Mann was off Ushant with seven of the line,
but that did not content them. They had certain news,
moreover, that Blénac was bringing home the French
trade, and our own East and West India fleets were due.
Hardy was therefore to take every ship he could lay
hands on and cruise in the Soundings for six weeks, but
he had no more luck than Hawke.[1] Blénac, arriving
with the now familiar happy gale which opened Brest,
got safely in, and the French took no action in the
Channel. The war was indeed over, and nothing came
of Choiseul's grandiose projects for a counter-stroke but
an idle raid on Newfoundland.

Still it must be said that from a naval point of view the
operation was very brilliantly conducted, and it successfully diverted a force more than double its own. Its
hero was the Chevalier de Ternay, who had served as a
lieutenant in Conflans's action with Hawke. Since then,
with another lieutenant, the Comte d'Hector, he had
highly distinguished himself at various times by getting
no less than five ships of the line and a frigate out of

[1] *Secret Orders*, 1332, Sept. 2.

the Villaine and into Brest in spite of the vigilance of the British blockading squadrons.   For this both officers were given post rank, and on May 8th, 1762, by Choiseul's orders, Ternay, who had just brought in the last of the ships he saved, adroitly slipped out of Brest with two of the line, both of which he and his friend had rescued, two frigates, and a military force under M. de Haussonville.

Reaching Newfoundland on June 20th they quickly captured St. John's, seized a sloop in the harbour, and proceeded to destroy the fisheries and plunder the colony. They claimed to have destroyed nearly five hundred craft of all sizes, and to have inflicted damage to the extent of a million sterling, before they were interrupted.   Nothing was known of the raid in England till the end of July, when orders were despatched to Colville on the North American station to see to it, and Captain Hugh Palliser with three of the line was sent to reinforce him.   But Colville was already at work.   When Ternay arrived, the governor, Captain Graves, the well-known admiral of the next war, was away with his ship at Placentia on the western side.   He immediately sent off to New York to warn Amherst and Colville, and remained where he was to defend the port.   Colville reached Placentia in person about August 20th with his flagship and a frigate, and after landing some of his marines to strengthen the garrison, he sailed with Graves for St. John's.   As yet he had no troops, and could do little but prevent further depredations.   But inferior as he was he boldly blockaded Ternay.

Owing to the efforts Amherst had made for the Havana expedition, no troops were available except those in the garrisons of Nova Scotia.   They took some time to collect, but by September 11th fifteen hundred of them, a force only just equal to Haussonville's, reached Colville under Colonel Amherst, the general's brother. Graves had a plan of action ready which Colville at once adopted as better than his own, and in less than a week the enemy were driven from their advanced posts, and St. John's was invested. On the 16th, under cover of a dense fog, Colonel Amherst was able to make his final arrangements for attacking the place. Ternay saw all was lost, and he did not doubt a moment what to do. He had not brought his ships out of the Villaine, he said, to take such a place as St. John's, and he was determined to save them or make Colville pay dear for their capture. He too, therefore, seized the opportunity of the fog, as he had done so often before, towed out with his boats, stole quietly past Colville, and was far away beyond pursuit before the fog lifted. By good luck he just missed the superior squadron of Palliser, which arrived a day or two later, but on the 18th, before it could appear, Haussonville surrendered. Ternay, it is pleasant to relate, after being chased off the coast of France by two British divisions, found refuge in Coruña.[1]

But the dreams of Ternay and his like of the *jeune école*—dreams of attempting one more bid for the command of the sea—were not to be realised. For France to recover her broken navy from the blows which Hawke and Boscawen had dealt was beyond the national power so long as the war lasted. Choiseul knew it too well— the study of revenge was all that was left, and for that peace must be had. Though fresh alarms arose, Ternay's raid, to which the ambitious invasion project had dwindled, was the last effort of Choiseul to secure

---

[1] Lacour-Gayet, *Marine sous Louis XV.*, p. 364; Beatson, vol. iii. p. 576 *et seq.*; *Secret Orders*, 1332, July 31; Amherst to Egremont, Aug. 15, *S.P. Colonial (America and West Indies)*, 97.

by force endurable terms.   Spain had failed him; everywhere upon the sea the British fleet held him fast; and there was nothing to look to except the negotiations. To these we must now return, and follow them to the end.

CHAPTER XI

BUTE'S PEACE

IT was at the beginning of April, as we have seen, that the secret negotiations which had been conducted through the Sardinian ambassadors reached a stage when direct and official communication with the French Court could begin. It was just at this time that our relations with Frederick were strained to breaking-point. Towards the end of March, it will be remembered, Frederick had received from the Czar Galitzin's report of his conversation with Bute. Aghast at what he naturally regarded as the shameless perfidy of the British Ministers, he practically decided to have no more to do with them. In the first heat of his indignation he wrote to his envoy in St. Petersburg to agree at once to military co-operation with Peter in Holstein in return for a Russian corps to assist him against Austria, and on no account was a word to be said to Keith. To Denmark, who was growing uneasy and had appealed to England, he wrote a friendly letter to lull her into security, and immediately afterwards to St. Petersburg again to ascertain if Peter wished to extend his operations to the conquest of Schleswig. Frederick pointed out that it was a perfectly safe operation, and with an expression of his own readiness to assist, he enclosed a complete war plan for the purpose.

If we would judge Frederick fairly for this unscrupulous step, if indeed we would form anything like an impartial estimate of the whole unhappy quarrel, which even yet has

not ceased to embitter Anglo-Prussian relations, one con-
trolling consideration must not be forgotten. For purely
geographical reasons alone a Russian alliance was, and
must always be, of higher value to Prussia than a British
alliance. At the moment also, it must be borne in mind,
the very existence of Prussia seemed to hang on the
possibility of gaining the friendship of Russia, and
Frederick could see no way in which it was to be purchased except by the sacrifice of the Danish duchies. It
meant offence to England, but he had to choose between
the old ally and the new, and seeing how desperate was
his position he could not hesitate in the choice. With
the best will in the world to do him justice, it is
impossible to miss, both in his conduct and his utterances
at this time, symptoms of an uneasy conscience—it is
impossible to avoid a suspicion that a plausible reason
for breaking with England was not unwelcome. When
Mitchell afterwards taxed him with his knowledge of
Galitzin's notorious French and Austrian sympathies he
could make no reply. He simply passed by what he
obviously felt was a very weak link in his case; and yet to
the end he never ceased to justify his grievance against
England, on the very point with which he always shirked
to deal. The truth seems to be that while his direct and
unvarnished political methods determined him rightly
enough to let no tenderness for England and her engagements stand in the way of binding Russia to his cause,
he was at the same time anxious to go on using England,
or if that were impossible, to throw the whole odium of
the change of front upon her. "I laugh at the friendship of England," he said, even in the darkest hours of
his fortunes, "if it is no use to me." [1] Bute's clumsiness
had given him just the handle he wanted, and whether

---

[1] *Politische Corr.*, vol. xviii. p. 630, Nov. 12, 1759.

or not he really believed the Galitzin story, it would be absurd to blame him for taking a quick hold and making the most of it. That he was playing a double game is as certain as that he had a very pretty excuse for doing so.

To any soothing representation from Knyphausen and Michel, his Ministers in London, he would not listen a moment, but fell to scolding them in a manner which well betrays his state of mind. "I think, gentlemen," he said, "you are Bute's clerks. You don't seem to be Prussians. Your father, Knyphausen, used to take money from France and England, and was broken for it. Has he bequeathed the habit to you?"[1] Poor Knyphausen was meanwhile doing his best. That same day he presented Bute with a formal demand for the communication of the overtures to Vienna. Bute immediately showed him his correspondence with Yorke. It was innocent enough, as we know, and all there was to show; and Bute, not content with defending himself, chose in his clumsy way to proceed to counter-attack. He caused the King, as we have already seen, to send his indignant personal protest to Frederick for having vouchsafed no reply to his request for the Prussian views about peace, and he instructed Mitchell to desire that Knyphausen should be reprimanded for sending libellous reports about the Vienna overture.[2] Nothing could have been more illadvised. Mitchell was even then writing to say that peace between Prussia and Russia was on the point of being concluded, and it was of the utmost importance to treat Frederick tenderly, so as to share the advantages of the new coalition. He urged, therefore, that for the

---

[1] *Politische Corr.*, vol. xxi. pp. 312, 316–8, March 23–5; despatch to Goltz, March 28, pp. 323–7.
[2] Bute to Mitchell, March 26 and 30; George III. to Frederick, March 30.
—Adolphus, vol. i. p. 488 *et seq.*

moment at any rate the excuses about the Duchies which
he would certainly make should be accepted, and on no
account should his temper be spoilt by dealing with him
as a pecuniary dependent.   In spite of the sound advice, as
we know, Bute demanded a categorical disavowal of the
Schleswig-Holstein intrigue, on pain of the subsidy being
stopped.[1]

Bute and Frederick were now at arm's length, and each
went the best way to widen the breach.   Frederick, after
his manner, took a clear view of the situation, and proceeded to act upon it.   He convinced himself that the
suspicious attitude of the British Ministers was solely
due to the mess they had got themselves into with the
Spanish war, and the defence of Portugal that it involved.
"All the same," he wrote to General Goltz, his envoy in
St. Petersburg, "it would be doing the English nation an
injustice to attribute to them a proceeding of this nature.
It is the Earl of Bute and the Duke of Bedford who are
the sole authors of this pretty scheme, and the nation,
with the Chevalier Pitt at its head, would be as much
revolted by it as I have cause to be, if they came to
know of it."[2]   Such expressions constantly recur in his
correspondence.   So far he had measured English sentiment with perfect accuracy, and saw that if he still hoped
to get anything out of it his only game was to upset Bute
as Choiseul had upset Pitt.   Knyphausen and his colleague
were therefore directed to approach Pitt.   After informing
him of the whole "perfidy," they were to consult him as
to the propriety of their making a declaration to the King
that they could no longer negotiate with such a minister
as Bute, and of communicating his conversation with

---

[1] Mitchell to Bute, March 25, *Mitchell Memoirs*, vol. ii. p. 279 ; Bute to
Mitchell.—April 9, Adolphus, vol. i. p. 491.
[2] *Politische Corr.*, vol. xxi. p. 320, March 27.

Galitzin to Frederick's friends in both Houses. Frederick gave them further to understand that if nothing was to be done in this direction they were to consider that, though he did not actually recall them, they only held their place in order to watch Bute's tricks.[1]

The whole series of his despatches to London since Pitt's fall had been full of the same kind of insulting expressions as had embittered his relations with the Czarina Elizabeth, Maria Theresa, and the Pompadour. Many of them reached Bute's ears, and they inflamed his antipathy, and that of the Court, to burning-point. The consequence was that when Pitt was consulted by Knyphausen he could only say that Frederick's plan was impracticable. He was, in any case, too good an Englishman to permit, or even encourage, foreign interference with home politics. He therefore put the Prussians off by saying that the subjection into which Bute had reduced the King made any denunciation of him useless, and as for Parliament, the Court party was now so strong that nothing could be done there."[2] Pitt was of course absolutely right, and Frederick did not for a moment question his advice. He was contented to accept the situation, and instructed Knyphausen to devote himself to keeping a strict watch, and to fomenting the discord between Bute and Newcastle.

Meanwhile the French proposals had been forwarded to Viri, and were being considered by the British government. Choiseul declared himself ready to persuade Spain to settle her three points in a manner acceptable to us. The question of prizes taken during the war was to be left to our courts; we were to destroy our fortified

---

[1] *Ibid.*, pp. 365 and 425; Newcastle to Yorke, May 14, *Newcastle Papers,* 32,938.

[2] *Politische Corr.*, vol. xxi. p. 469 and *note*.

posts in Honduras, and to retain our right to cut logwood; and as for her right of fishing in Newfoundland waters, it was pointed out that in the last century she had only sent two ships. The claim was a mere point of honour, and Choiseul suggested the matter might well be left as it was. For herself, France was ready to acknowledge Canada as conquered, but was not satisfied with St. Pierre as an *abri*. She must have more, but was willing that England should take precautions to secure that no fortifications were erected. On the West Coast of Africa she merely wanted one station for the slave trade, Goree or Senegal. In India England could propose a settlement. In Europe she would restore Minorca, and evacuate the territory of the King of England and his allies. This, Choiseul considered, could be done without difficulty by finding a formula which would remove all suspicion of deserting their respective allies. Belleisle he regarded, so he said, as too trivial a conquest even to mention, well knowing that this view was shared by most of Pitt's political opponents. It was in the West Indies the crux of the settlement lay. The news of the conquest of Martinique and the Grenadines, with the rest of the neutral islands, had just come home, and he said he should have to add to the old demand for Gaudeloupe and Mariegalante the restitution of Martinique and an equitable division of the neutral islands.

The proposals arrived on April 22nd. On the whole they were well received. It was easily agreed to add the Island of Miquelon to St. Pierre as an *abri* for the fisheries, but the West Indian demands staggered every one. Cabinet after Cabinet was held and Viri worked hard. The general feeling was that, if we gave up

---

[1] Choiseul to Solar, with the accompanying proposal, April 15, *Lansdowne House MSS.*

Martinique, we ought to have something substantial in return. Gaudeloupe or Louisiana were regarded as reasonable equivalents, and so strongly was this opinion supported, particularly by Grenville, that Egremont was instructed to draft his reply accordingly. It was not until the last moment, when an extraordinary Council was summoned finally to settle the draft and Grenville was too ill to attend, that Bute seized the moment to intervene.[1] "When we met again," he wrote to the Duke of Bedford, "to hear Lord Egremont's despatch read over, I ventured to fling out the following opinion : that on weighing attentively the offer we had made for restoring Martinique on the French ceding Guadeloupe or Louisiana, I frankly owned I saw no probability of peace. They certainly would not accept these terms, and if so war must be continued." To avert this he proposed that we should demand instead "the neutral islands and the Grenada, and that, to prevent all further disputes in North America, the Mississippi should be the boundary between the two nations." The compromise was probably the suggestion of Viri ; but whoever was its inventor, it was certainly ingenious. For while the Mississippi line had the colour of being a mere method of securing a natural geographical boundary, it would give us the ports of Mobile and New Orleans in the Gulf of Mexico, or all there was worth having in Louisiana. Newcastle and Devonshire, Bute says, heartily agreed.

So the matter was settled, and they went on to discuss the explosive question of the Prussian subsidy. Newcastle, Hardwicke, and Devonshire would not budge from their position that it must be continued. Mansfield would say nothing, but "the other Lords," Bute says,

[1] *Grenville Papers*, vol. i. p. 450.

" thought it highly improper to continue it under the load of evidence we have of the most determined enmity of that Prince and under our own necessitous circumstances." [1] Considering that Frederick's representatives at the moment, with the obvious intention of wrecking the peace, were trying to induce the city to petition against the retrocession of Martinique, it must be owned that Bute and " the other Lords" had some grounds for their attitude.[2]

So deep, indeed, was the exasperation of the Court party at the way Frederick was behaving, as they honestly believed without any just provocation, that Bute made up his mind that the interval of waiting for the French answer must be used in getting rid of the old Prussian party in the Cabinet. He accordingly commenced an intrigue which rapidly brought his discord with Newcastle to a head, and saved the Prussian Legation the pains of fomenting it.

Newcastle's loyalty to Frederick had always gone far to redeem his career from mere political opportunism, and he was now using all the weight of his powerful connection in a last desperate effort to secure a renewal of the Prussian Treaty. Parliament, having been prorogued a month before, had just been summoned for the purpose of obtaining a supplementary grant. Bute proposed to ask for no more than a million, and to earmark it for Portugal. Newcastle was for demanding two millions and not restricting the expenditure to Portugal, and he was warmly supported in the Cabinet by Devonshire, Hardwicke, and Mansfield. Bute regarded so large a

---

[1] Bute to Bedford, May 1, *Bedford Corr.*, vol. iii. p. 75.

[2] Viri to Solar, May 4, *Lansdowne House MSS.* This is a separate letter from that of the same date in which Viri communicated the results of the Cabinets.

sum as beyond our resources. Newcastle, as head of the Treasury, pronounced that we could easily afford it. Bute, however, was not to be beaten. He went behind Newcastle's back, and secretly got a declaration from the Treasury officials that no more than a million could be raised. An irregularity so offensive was more than even Newcastle's tenacity of office could endure. "I send your lordship," he wrote to Hardwicke on May 10th, just as Parliament was reassembling, "direct proof . . . of such a behaviour in my lord Bute to me in my office, as hardly any gentleman ever acted towards another, let him be ever so insignificant."

Three days later Grenville moved in the House of Commons for a million for the defence of Portugal. Pitt in one of his best speeches supported the motion, but he declared himself not content with it. He implored the ministers to ask a larger sum, that we might do our duty to the King of Prussia. It was but ten days since Knyphausen had brought him Frederick's appeal for help, and he did his best to honour it; but still, true to his principles, he would not stir a finger to encourage his royal admirer in his ill-judged interference with British politics. He would not move himself, he told the House, for a continuation of the Prussian subsidy, because he did not think it became him to oppose the King's servants. But if such a motion were made he would support it. He earnestly begged, if a cloud arose between London and Berlin—and he knew too well how black a cloud there was, and how much Frederick was to blame for it—that the situation might be handled without temper and for reconciliation. In his peroration he made one more passionate appeal to lift his country from the degradation to which Bute was dragging it, and to inspire his supplanters with something of his own heroic statesmanship.

Recalling our long succession of victories in all parts of the world, and how favourable was our situation since the break up of Kaunitz's coalition, he called on them to act now "upon a great system while it was in their power." "A million more," he said, "would be a pittance to place you at the head of Europe, and enable you to treat with efficacy and dignity. Save it not in the last critical year! give the million to the war at large, and add three, four, or five hundred thousand pounds more to Portugal, or avow to the House of Bourbon you are not able to treat at the head of your allies."[1]

His lofty appeal made a great impression on the House, but on the ministers it was thrown away. One million only was voted, and voted for Portugal, and next day Newcastle tendered his resignation. None of his friends followed his example—indeed, he had begged them not to do so. He fell alone and unregretted, a feeble victim of the blunderer for whom he had betrayed Pitt. But pitiable as was the figure he cut, he was not yet defeated. There still clung to him the intangible force of political aptitude which had enabled him so long to control the machinery of State. Every one felt it. Bute and the King did their best to get him to accept some favour as Pitt had done, but with a courage and dignity that touches his fall with light, he firmly refused every offer either for himself or his family, and retired into the country to nurse the forces of opposition which began at once to gather round him.[2]

But for the time Bute was master, and the power of the old oligarchy was broken. The triumphant favourite

[1] From Horace Walpole's Report, *Memoirs of George III.*, vol. i. pp. 163–6.

[2] For a detailed account of the whole affair by Newcastle, see his "most secret" letter to Yorke, May 14, *Newcastle Papers*, 32,938.

became First Lord of the Treasury. Grenville took his place as Secretary of State, and with Egremont they had complete control of the negotiations. Before leaving the Foreign Office Bute was careful to send to Berlin a detailed defence of his conduct, which amounted also to a declaration of the policy he meant to pursue. Parliament rose again in a few days without having granted a subsidy to Prussia, and Bute felt he must explain why it was withheld. Shortly the new policy was based on the new situation. "We," wrote Bute in the pith of his despatch, "have a very powerful additional enemy to contend with; His Prussian Majesty has a new and very powerful friend. The weight of Spain is thrown into our opposite scale; that of Russia, and Sweden too, is taken out of his. The King of Prussia had Pomerania and Brandenburg to defend, besides Saxony and Silesia: the two former are no longer in danger. We had, on our part, a most expensive land war to support in Germany: we must now provide for another in Portugal." [1]

The British case was perfectly good if Bute had had the sense and candour to put it to Frederick at the first. There was ample reason for discontinuing Frederick's subsidy. We were in no way bound to provide it when the danger on which it was originally based disappeared. We were doing Frederick no wrong. He did not even pretend we were. The negotiations had been regularly communicated to him from the moment they were officially on foot; he had had copies of the material documents, and had been invited to express his views. [2] What we were doing in the matter was much what he himself had proposed to Pitt. He knew as well as any one that the

[1] Bute to Mitchell, May 26, *Mitchell Papers*, vol. xvii., *Add. MSS.* 6820, and printed by Adolphus, vol. i. p. 493, and Bisset, vol. ii. p. 294.

[2] Bute to Mitchell, April 9 and 30, *Mitchell Papers*, vol. xvii. p. 6820.

only way to bring the war to a speedy end was for us to come to terms with France. The main issue once decided, the subordinate continental war, which had attached itself to the imperial struggle, must collapse. Under Pitt, therefore, he had fully endorsed the policy of a separate negotiation with France. His grievance now and till the end was not that, but that he could not trust Bute. He had made up his mind that he was going to be betrayed, and Bute did his worst to confirm the impression. He was hand-in-glove with Frederick's arch-enemy, the Duke of Bedford, and actually had selected him to go to Paris as British Plenipotentiary so soon as the negotiations were sufficiently advanced. The most ardent French patriot could not have invented a better scheme for weakening our hand. Bedford, by his exaggerated behaviour, had stamped himself as an advocate for peace at any price. Choiseul could scarcely conceal his delight at having such a simpleton as Bute to deal with. He was as eager to keep him in power as Frederick was to get rid of him. Indeed, during the late ministerial crisis he had become so much alarmed for the security of Bute's position that he solemnly warned Solar to let the King of England know that unless Bute remained in power he would have nothing more to do with the negotiations. "I would rather go and row in the galleys," he said, "than have to discuss any kind of peace with Mr. Pitt."[1]

On Bute's becoming First Lord of the Treasury he was reassured, and the negotiations could proceed. Bute, fooled and flattered by Choiseul's expressions of regard, was like clay in the hands of the accomplished veteran.

[1] Choiseul to Solar, May 13, *Bedford Corr.*, vol. iii. p. 84. " Nous avons eu une peur effroiable du changement du Ministère," same to same, May 25. —*Lansdowne House MSS.*

He was beaten at every turn, and had it not been for Grenville's stiffness, and the awe of Pitt in which Bute stood, there is no knowing to what lengths of unstable concession he would not have gone.

The first and decisive trial of strength took place, as before, over the question of naval position. It was inevitable that it should be so, seeing that the whole war was a struggle for maritime empire. Directly Grenville's despatch reached Paris with the British reply to the terms Choiseul had proposed, Solar sent over a warning that France would never abandon all the neutral islands. The crux was, of course, St. Lucia. We have seen the importance which English strategy had come to attach to it as the commanding naval position of the Windward Islands. Choiseul was equally aware of its value, and on this he took his most determined stand. He was not, indeed, satisfied with St. Pierre and Miquelon as *abris* for the fishery. He wanted Cape Breton Island too, but as he must have known this would not be granted he intimated he would be satisfied with a drying station on its shores. It was St. Lucia that he refused to swallow. "The restitution of Martinique," he wrote, "will be a precarious restitution if England blockades it to leeward and to windward by keeping St. Lucia and Dominica. There would be nothing left for France but to renew the war as soon as she was able."

The whole despatch is characteristic of his method. He stated his position with the assumption of an almost cynical candour. There was, he said, no example in history of a victor retaining all his conquests beyond the sea, and this for three good reasons. Firstly, such acquisitions were very costly at the outset to the metropolitan country; secondly, it made an enduring peace impossible; and thirdly, because, as the case of Spain herself proved, such conquests were extremely difficult to maintain. For these reasons, he said, he intended to persist in his attitude, as knowing that its inherent and fundamental strength made it impossible for us to resist. With equal candour he explained that his claim was of the essence of his colonial policy. On principle he objected to the whole American system. He did not believe in colonies—better far, he thought, for a country to devote its strength to developing its own resources. There were, however, certain luxuries, like coffee and sugar, which had become necessaries to the French people, and which they could not produce at home. Colonial possessions, therefore, for the production of such articles, he regarded as legitimate and even necessary. That was the simple extent of his ideas of Colonial expansion—he wished nothing more, but so much he must have, and could not leave at the mercy of the British navy. For India, on the same principle, he would be content with simple factories in Bengal and on the Coromandel and Malabar coasts, but he must retain Mauritius and Bourbon. He therefore reiterated his demand for Guadeloupe, Mariegalante, and Martinique, with the addition of St. Lucia, but in return he was ready to give us Mobile and the line of the Mississippi, but not to the sea. It must diverge at La Belle Rivière to Lake Pontchartrain, so as to leave New Orleans to France.

Having thus clearly defined his position beyond the seas, he attacked the German question. Here the only real difficulty was Cleves, Wesel, and Gueldres, with the rest of the Prussian territory on the Lower Rhine. These he intimated he was willing to evacuate with the rest of Germany, but in that he was bound by his alliance to regard them as Austrian conquests he could not do so without the consent of Vienna. This, he urged, would take time and delay the peace. He therefore proposed that the Prussian Rhenish towns should be held by French or Austrian troops till a general peace was secured, and that England should give an assurance that no part of Ferdinand's army in her pay should join Frederick.

His Memoir was accompanied by a note from Choiseul to Solar, in which he explained that Grimaldi, whom he detested for an ill-mannered braggart, objected violently to any concession to England in the Gulf of Mexico, and was talking very big. The little Spanish successes in Portugal had turned his head, and he was confident that the British expedition to Havana would end in disaster. But Choiseul was not afraid of his bragging. "I cajole M. de Grimaldi," he said, "as though I were his own heart's dupe." The importance of a rapid settlement, he urged, was that Russia must be prevented from upsetting all Europe with her Tartars under Frederick's direction; but he could not secure it at the price of St. Lucia. "I tell you frankly, my dear ambassador," he wrote, "if England persists in wanting it I shall advise the Council to break off negotiations." He was ready, however, to give up the Grenadines. "I don't mention Belleisle in my Memoir," he added. "I have always maintained that it was a folly England committed in undertaking that conquest."[1]

In England the Memoir produced so bad an impression, especially by what most of the ministers regarded as the French *chicanerie* about St. Lucia and the *abris*, that it was a month before an answer could be sent. The period of silence that the delay entailed could only increase Frederick's mistrust. His military position had

---

[1] "Memoire du Duc de Choiseul," May 25, and Choiseul to Solar, May 27, *Lansdowne House MSS.*

been materially improved. A victory of Prince Henry had given him back Freyburg, and with growing elation he was ordering his ministers in London to attach themselves to the opposition which was forming round Newcastle under the patronage of the Duke of Cumberland, till they saw a chance of " breaking the neck of a minister so little versed in affairs, so inconsequent and without system." " It is astounding," he said, " to see Lord Bute not only acting against all rules of good faith, prudence, and even politics, but playing the game so clumsily that if he loses, it can only cost his master the confidence of the nation. As for me, I will not confound this minister with the King and the nation." [1]

It was a strange coincidence that immediately after the French Memoir was received, and peace was seen to turn on our future naval position in the West Indies, Anson, who best knew the strategical value of St. Lucia, died. " Who will succeed him ? " wrote Newcastle. " Some say Hawke, but I hardly believe they will do so right a thing." They did not. Halifax was confirmed in his appointment, and according to Barrington, who had succeeded Grenville as Treasurer of the Navy, it was with the full approval of Pitt and Cleveland, the veteran secretary.[2] In any case it made little difference to the burning question. For Grenville, too, with his long experience at the Admiralty, knew St. Lucia's value well enough, and continued violently to oppose the concession. A Cabinet to settle the matter was held on June 21st. Bedford and Bute were both for giving way, but the feeling was too strong for them, and a tart reply agreed

---

[1] Frederick to Knyphausen and Mitchell, June 10, *Politische Corr.*, vol. xxi. p. 523.

[2] Newcastle to Devonshire, June 10, *Newcastle Papers*, 32,939 ; Barrington to Newcastle, June 21, *ibid.*, 32,940.

to. Displeasure was frankly expressed at France's not accepting the extra *abri* offered, and some resentment at the refusal of the whole Mississippi line after the large concessions we had made, and especially at the demand for St. Lucia. To this they said it was impossible to agree, nor could they consent to the proposed arrangement about Wesel and Gueldres without consulting Prussia, but they were ready to fall back on the old plan of both sides retiring from German territory altogether. To smooth matters a little Viri was informed that Bedford would go as plenipotentiary when the time came; but in the same breath Egremont warmly expressed to him his surprise that France could have so much regard for her treaty with Austria and so little for ours with Prussia. Egremont further said we were not to be frightened by a Russian bogy—in fact, we looked upon a Russo-Prussian alliance as an excellent counterpoise to the Family Compact.[1]

So far, then, it will be seen there had been little giving way and no disloyalty to Prussia. Bute, however, as though bound to commit every mistake within his reach, made no further communication to Frederick as to how the negotiations were proceeding. The natural inference was that we had something to hide, whereas the truth was that so far from deserting Frederick we had taken up so strong an attitude in his interest that, in the opinion of most people, a continuation of hostilities was inevitable. Orders indeed were now issued to Ferdinand for a new campaign in Westphalia. There was as yet no word from Spain or news from Pocock and Albemarle. Even Ligonier grew nervous that what he had divined of Choiseul's war plan would be carried out. He saw forty-

---

[1] Egremont to Viri, June 20 (enclosing the British Memoir); Viri to Solar, June 27, *Lansdowne House MSS.*

five thousand men cantoned along the opposite coast. Hawke was taking the Channel Fleet to Ferrol, and there were neither troops nor ships enough at home, in his opinion, to stop an invasion if it were intended. His fear was that the Channel Fleet might be overwhelmed by a Franco-Spanish concentration, unless Saunders and Hawke had orders to unite. He hoped they had, but did not know.

Hawke and Saunders, as we have seen, had no such instructions, and they knew better than to club their fleets in a lump. They had passed beyond such crude ideas of naval concentration, and as we know had arranged between them a subtler and more elastic combination, which rendered impossible the concentration Ligonier feared. Still he was none the less anxious. Like so many of our best soldiers before and since, so long as he saw across the water troops in sufficient strength to make an invasion, he thought invasion possible. He told Newcastle, however, that he could not get any one to listen to him, and in a kind of heroic despair that if anything happened he meant to gather the flower of his troops round London and do his best.[1]

As it happened his apprehensions were groundless, even on military grounds. The danger, such as it ever was, had already passed. In view of the unpromising nature of the French reply, it had been decided as we have seen, to hold Ferdinand's hand no longer. Granby went over to his command, and both sides were already mobilising for a fresh campaign. D'Estrées and Soubise had been ordered to join hands, and had advanced northward from Cassel towards the Diemal

---

[1] "List of the French Army in Flanders under M. de Heronville," May 21, *Newcastle Papers*, 32,939; Newcastle to Hardwicke, June 28; same to Devonshire, June 29, *ibid.*, 32,940.

behind which Ferdinand was at work. The French
Marshals appear to have thought the war was over.
Soubise, so it was said in the City, was at this time
making immense purchases in the English funds, and the
French Court was following his example.[1] The Marshals
at any rate made the loosest dispositions, took no precautions against surprise, and Ferdinand, with his usual
promptitude, seized the chance. Secretly concentrating
his force, he suddenly passed the Diemal, and after a
night march flung himself upon the French camp. There
was a hard struggle. The French had seventy thousand
men to Ferdinand's forty, but in the end they were driven
back in confusion under the walls of Cassel. The exultation in England was great; for again a large share of
the glory had fallen to Granby and the British troops.
He had executed a difficult and well-sustained flank
attack that had proved decisive, and more than half the
allies' loss was in his corps. The relief was immediate.
News quickly came that the French army of the Lower
Rhine had marched to the support of the defeated Marshals; that the Maison du Roi, which was at Dunkirk, had
orders to hurry in the same direction; and that the force
which Ligonier was watching so anxiously was to be
broken up.[2]

It was in the midst of the rejoicings over the victory
that the next communication arrived from France. It
amounted to nothing, however, but their last proposal

---

[1] Newcastle to Yorke, June 25, *ibid.* Later he reported that Walpole, a
well-known broker, and Vanneck, his partner, had received from De Borde,
"a creature of Choiseul's," £100,000 to invest in the Funds. Same to
Cumberland, July 11, *ibid.* This is to some extent confirmed by Solar,
who wrote to Viri on Aug. 22 that everything was being told to "M. de la
Borde, the Court banker," apparently for him to use the information. He
was sending expresses everywhere, and had probably sent Vanneck to
London.—*Lansdowne House MSS.*, Aug. 22.

[2] Hague Advices, July 9, *ibid.*

reduced to formal articles and regularly signed on behalf of France and Spain by Choiseul and Wall, whose general assent to treat had at last reached Paris. It was accompanied by another note from Choiseul to Solar explaining that Austria had expressed herself as ready to agree to any settlement France might make with England, provided she sacrificed no territory and steps were taken to extinguish the war in every part of Europe. To this end she was ready to assent to a revival of the abortive Congress and to an armistice, and she desired that Frederick's views should be obtained through the British Court.[1]

Bute now found his position very delicate. Since Ferdinand's victory on the Diemal, Grenville and others who thought with him were naturally more determined than ever, but Bute and Egremont had taken a step behind their backs which made further resistance on the main point practically impossible. While waiting for the French answer they had told Viri, without saying a word to their colleagues, that if the reply were otherwise favourable St. Lucia should not stand in the way of peace.[2] The deception of course had to be kept up. To keep Grenville and his followers quiet, Egremont was obliged to present to Viri formal observations on the French articles in which the original British attitude was firmly maintained. It was impossible, he repeated, after sacrificing Guadeloupe and Martinique, to give up St. Lucia too, nor did loyalty to Prussia permit them to accept the proposals about Wesel and Gueldres without Frederick's consent.

Viri was now almost in despair. " You can't tell,"

---

[1] " Projet des Articles de Paix dressé par le France," and Choiseul to Solar, June 28, *Lansdowne House MSS.*

[2] Viri to Solar, June 28, *Lansdowne House MSS.*

he wrote to Solar, "how Grenville bothers us. He may be sound at heart but he wants popularity, and the worst of it is Egremont sometimes gets the same idea into his head." Since his last letters from Paris naturally referred to Bute's secret concession it was impossible to show them to Grenville. Viri told him they contained a definite declaration that if the British claim to St. Lucia and New Orleans were not abandoned the negotiations would be broken off. He had talked with him for six hours, but was sure six hours more would not make him give up St. Lucia, and Egremont was with him on New Orleans. He warned Solar, therefore, that France had better be careful and not make difficulties about the Mississippi line, for there was serious danger brewing from the gathering opposition. No one but Bute and Egremont yet knew of the offer about St. Lucia, and the only course, he said, was to send at once an answer to the last British Memoir which must reveal nothing of the secret, so that it could be shown to the Cabinet. St. Lucia should be insisted on as a *sine qua non*, and a new line excluding new Orleans be proposed. It would also be well to offer a joint Anglo-French occupation of Wesel and Gueldres, but it must be understood that England had so far committed herself to her last suggestion for reciprocal evacuation of all German territory as to refer it to Frederick for his consent. Lastly, there was no need to worry about Portugal, for until Spain had evacuated it, England would simply not stir from Cuba.[1]

The Cabinet had in fact decided to break its long silence with Berlin, and to communicate the exact state of the negotiations, so far as they knew them, to Frederick, together with the Austrian proposal for a Congress and British mediation. All the documents were sent to

[1] Viri to Solar, July 12.

Mitchell, including the French proposals about Rhenish Prussia, and he was instructed to ask for a special interview with Frederick to ascertain his views.[1] In this we undoubtedly see the determination of Grenville to deal loyally with our ally.

No sooner, however, had this straightforward despatch gone off than Bute received a secret intimation from Paris that if St. Lucia were given up Choiseul would let nothing stop him concluding peace.[2] But he pressed for a speedy settlement. In view of a growing anxiety in France lest Prussia and Austria should settle their differences first, he urged that plenipotentiaries should be exchanged to sign the preliminaries at the earliest moment. The effect upon Bute was to determine him to push the matter through at all costs. On July 19th he sent for Bedford and told him of the last French assurance. France, he said, had agreed to everything except New Orleans and the Prussian towns, which she declared must be given over to Austrian garrisons. She had also undertaken that Portugal should be evacuated, and that peace should be signed with Spain either in Paris or Madrid, as we preferred; and in view of the importance she attached to plenipotentiaries being exchanged at once, the King hoped Bedford would be able to set out in the middle of August. Bute further explained that in consenting to the French proposal they would have fulfilled all their engagements to Prussia, and, as Bedford thought, was obviously anxious to make peace on the basis proposed by France.[3] A day or two later the French answer on the lines Viri had suggested was received. St. Lucia and New Orleans were insisted

---

[1] Grenville to Mitchell, July 14, *Mitchell Papers, Add. MSS.* 6820.
[2] Solar to Viri, July 11.
[3] *Bedford Corr.*, vol. iii. p. 88.

on. As to Gueldres and Wesel, Choiseul protested he could not give them up without the consent of Austria, but undertook to propose nothing in regard to their final disposition which could be deemed contrary to His Britannic Majesty's loyalty to his allies.[1]

For Bute this was enough, and the Cabinet was called for July 29th to make the final decision. Since the resignation of Newcastle, Hardwicke had ceased to be summoned and Devonshire had refused to attend. Mansfield, still recalcitrant, had gone on circuit to be out of the way. Still the obstacles in Bute's path were great. Egremont only gave way on peremptory orders from the King that he was to hasten peace. Granville and Bedford were specially called up from the country, but the former proved unexpectedly obstinate. Bute had meant to talk to them both before the meeting, in order probably to let them into his secret understanding with Choiseul, but they arrived too late. Granville had been in secret concert with Egremont and Grenville, and at the Cabinet he took a strong line against Bute. Not only did he refuse to give way on St. Lucia, New Orleans, or the German article, but he protested we must come to terms with Spain before agreeing with France, since Grimaldi's language was still impossible on the question of our admittance into the Gulf of Mexico.[2]

Seeing how formidable a political figure Granville still was and that he was universally regarded as the highest authority on foreign affairs in the kingdom, Bute was at his wits' end. In fear of his head, he did not dare to act without him. With difficulty he secured an adjournment. Viri, who naturally could not estimate the importance of the naval questions involved, assured himself that the obstinacy of Grenville and his friends was solely due to

[1] *Lansdowne House MSS.*, July 20.   [2] *Ibid.*, Aug. 1.

fear of the gathering opposition. If so, it was not only they who were afraid. Within living memory, Harley had been sent to the Tower for his share in the Peace of Utrecht on a charge of high treason. It was but five-and-twenty years since Walpole had narrowly escaped impeachment for preserving an unpopular neutrality, and it was Pitt who had voiced the national outcry. Bute could not forget it, or that it was mainly Newcastle's influence that had saved the fallen minister. In the midst, therefore, of his struggle with the Cabinet he made a desperate effort to re-open relations with his old chief, but only to encounter an icy rebuff.[1]

With Grenville and his recalcitrant supporters in the Cabinet he was more successful. In concert with the King and Viri he worked hard to bring them round. By July 31st they had been so far dominated as to pass a despatch to Choiseul, practically accepting the French terms, except those relating to Rhenish Prussia. The King, so Egremont was made to say, would give up New Orleans and St. Lucia, though with deep regret. He would also at once proceed to exchange plenipotentiaries. But on the question of Gueldres and Wesel, Bute had not been able to carry them so far. On that point Egremont had leave to say the King had already gone as far as he could without breaking faith with his ally, and Grenville wrote off to Mitchell to tell Frederick that we had decided to hold firm to our simple proposal of a general evacuation of German territory on both sides.[2] So far, therefore, the Cabinet was perfectly loyal; but, as the matter was not finally settled, it still to some extent

---

[1] *Rockingham Memoirs*, vol. i. p. 118.
[2] Egremont to Choiseul, July 31 ; Viri to Solar, Aug. 1, *Lansdowne House MSS.* ; Grenville to Mitchell, Aug. 2, *Mitchell Papers*, vol. xvii., *Add. MSS.* 6820.

rested in the hands of Bedford, and if Frederick still
believed he was being betrayed by Bute he certainly had
good reasons.

The day after the decisive Cabinet, Mitchell saw
Frederick at his headquarters in the field to make the
formal communication of the negotiations and the Austrian
proposal. Unfortunately he as yet knew nothing of the
final decision to stand by Frederick on the question
of Wesel and Gueldres, and it was otherwise a bad
moment. A few weeks before, a revolution had taken
place at St. Petersburg. Peter III., mainly for his violent
Prussian sympathies, had been deposed. The great
reign of the Czarina Katherine had begun, and her
first step had been to withdraw the Russian contingent
from Frederick's army, and her Marshal had forced the
Prussians under his jurisdiction to take the oath of fidelity
to her crown. How much more was to come could not
yet be told. Mitchell consequently found the King cold,
though still personally cordial. Frederick began by
explaining to the ambassador the Russian revolution, and
told him Peter had just died under suspicious circumstances. Colberg, however, had been given up, the
Marshal's action disavowed, and his troops ordered to
evacuate Prussian territory. He also said that that very
morning he had received a formal notification of the
Czarina's intention to confirm the late peace, but not the
offensive and defensive alliance. Mitchell then communicated the negotiations and his master's desire to
have Frederick's views upon the terms suggested, as
showing the friendly disposition of the English Court, and
affording an opening for British mediation with Vienna.
At the mention of Vienna Frederick immediately froze,
and the interview ended abruptly. Next day Mitchell
handed the King the papers he had received from London,

but could obtain no answer. Frederick protested he was too much occupied with his military operations to consider the matter, and must refer it to his Minister in Berlin.[1]

This he did, with instructions to return Mitchell a polite and straightforward answer, insisting on his desire for an honourable peace, but pointing out that in the proposal to permit the French to occupy Wesel and Gueldres till a general peace, while evacuating the rest of Germany, he had reason to detect an intention to sacrifice his interests in breach of the most solemn engagements between him and Great Britain. Had he known that the British Cabinet had just rejected this proposal, his answer might have been different. As it was, he felt he could only refuse the British offer of mediation. The matter, he bluntly said, was one that could only be treated directly between Vienna and Berlin; at present he was waiting for Austria to begin. But even here his sardonic spirit would not permit him to stop. He must needs instruct his Minister that, in declining British mediation, he was to hint, " in the most gentle and delicate manner," that Prussia would not trust her interests to the British government as at present constituted. " Finally," he wrote, " you will easily grasp that your answer must be decent and agreeable to the present situation, but illusory, so as to gain time for me to see more clearly into my affairs and the success they may have." " It is useless worry," he concluded ; " it will all lead to nothing but haggling, of which I am surfeited." [2]

Considering what Frederick's knowledge was at the time his unhappy reply had much to excuse it, but the step with which he followed it up was unpardonable and

---

[1] Mitchell to Grenville, Aug. 6, *Mitchell Memoirs*, vol. ii. p. 322.
[2] Frederick to Finckenstein, Aug. 2, *Politische Corr.*, vol. xxii. p 103 ; same to Knyphausen, Aug. 5, *ibid.*, p. 114.

disastrous. His constitutional fondness for underhand
means was too much for him. A day or two later, before
Grenville's second despatch could arrive with the formal
decision of the Cabinet, he received from Knyphausen a
report, dated July 23rd, of what was going on in London,
and immediately instructed him "to lose no opportunity
that might occur in secretly inciting and embittering the
nation against Bute and his administration, and to cast
upon him the odium of any regrettable incidents that
might occur, as arising from mismanagement." "Finally,"
he concluded, "you will even incite, so far as possible,
the authors of the current pamphlets to decry the conduct of this minister, so as to come constantly nearer to
hurling him from his place."[1] This letter, as usual, was
intercepted and read, and naturally with the worst consequences. Following upon Frederick's dilatory answer
and his abrupt rejection of British mediation, it could
only deepen Bute's exasperation and disgust Grenville.
It had already been found necessary to administer to
Knyphausen and his colleague a sharp rebuke for their
previous efforts in the same direction, which amounted
practically to breaking off relations with them. On
August 5th, Grenville, by the King's orders, had formally
declared to them "that until such time as the King of
Prussia had Ministers who abstained from meddling in
matters that concerned the interior of the kingdom, his
Majesty judged it proper to make no communications to
the King of Prussia except through his own Ministers at
the Prussian Court."[2]

To aggravate the situation Bute was growing more
and more alarmed at the increasing feeling in the country

---

[1] Frederick to Knyphausen, Aug. 7, *Politische Corr.*, vol. xxii. p. 117,
and *Grenville Papers*, vol. i. p. 467, *note*. The two copies have verbal
differences which have no importance.   [2] *Ibid.*

against him, and at the growing strength and coherence
of the opposition. The pamphleteers, with Wilkes at
their head, were pouring upon him and his policy a flood
of scurrility such as not even the Treaty of Utrecht had
called forth. The most biting suggestions with which
Frederick continued to ply his legation in London were
harped upon with ever-growing venom, and how much
Knyphausen had to do with it could not be told. In
London Bute could scarcely appear in public. In the
country his name became a byword. At the Guildford
Assize dinner, for instance, the solicitor to the Treasury
had proposed his health. The sheriff and over a hundred
of the county gentry were present, but every man got up
and refused to drink it. Such an insult to a Prime
Minister was unheard of.[1] It was at this time, moreover,
that the popular excitement against the peace was further
inflamed by the arrival of the *Hermione* treasure. Laden
in twenty wagons and decorated with British colours flying
gaily over those of Spain, it reached London on August
12th while Havana was in the act of surrendering, and
was escorted by dragoons and martial music in a stirring
procession down Piccadilly, past St. James's Palace, and
so through the city to the Tower, "amidst the acclama-
tions of a prodigious concourse of people." [2] Then within
a week came news, obtained by a West Indian merchantman from one of Pocock's cruisers, that a landing had
been effected at Havana, and that by July 1st the siege
of the Morro was well advanced.[3] Every day, therefore,
tidings were looked for that the Gate of the Indies had
fallen, and the exultation was increased by continued
news of military successes on the Continent.

[1] Newcastle to Hardwicke, Aug. 11, *Newcastle Papers*, 32,941.
[2] Beatson, vol. ii. p. 588.
[3] Halifax to Newcastle, Aug. 18, *Newcastle Papers*, 32,941.

Thus passed the month of August while Bedford made ready for his mission, and in this atmosphere he received his last instructions from Bute. Nothing but details remained except on two points, Havana and the Prussian Rhineland. Bute told him that if news came of the capture of Havana, Egremont and Grenville insisted on further compensation being demanded from Spain, and he, with apparent reluctance, instructed him accordingly. As to Wesel and Gueldres, our understanding was they were to be evacuated to the first comer, the French giving notice to Austria and we to Prussia —an arrangement which for military reasons must certainly result, if loyally carried out, in Frederick's seizing them both.[1]

This did not content Grenville. His suspicion was kept alive by a despatch from Paris in which was dropped all mention of reciprocal evacuation, and the final understanding was stated to be that " the two crowns have taken as the basis of their conciliation to propose nothing which is contrary to their honour and their engagements, and to establish a perfect reciprocity in their conduct to their allies." Now Grenville, in view of Bedford's departure, had drafted a circular to all the German powers concerned, including Prussia, based on the British idea of complete evacuation on both sides, and the King had approved it. He begged, therefore, that its terms should be clearly explained to Bedford before he started. " Your lordship," he wrote to Bute, " will see that the whole depends on the repeated declarations made to the King of Prussia of his Majesty's resolution not to depart from the measure of withdrawing the troops on both sides as soon as the preliminaries shall be signed ; and consequently if this letter be sent, no other expedient

---

[1] *Bedford Corr.*, vol. iii. p. 96.

can be taken." [1]   Distasteful as the despatch must have
been to Bute he dared not stop it, and it went forward.
After expressing to Mitchell the resentment felt by the
British Court at Frederick's blunt refusal of their mediation, Grenville proceeded to say they meant, nevertheless,
to stand by him in the matter of the Rhineland.   They
had informed France finally that "she must withdraw
from all Prussian territories as well as from every other
country and place in the Empire whereof she had got
possession in the course of the war."   Mitchell was further
instructed to point out that the King was surprised at
the silence Frederick had kept in face of our repeated
requests for his views, and at his not having sent a word
in acknowledgment of our loyalty to his cause, or of the
fact that we had not stipulated anything in regard to his
interests without his knowledge.[2]

Unfortunately the despatch had to conclude with an
official intimation that Bedford was to be our plenipotentiary.   In Frederick's eyes, in spite of all Grenville
could honestly say, it could only be regarded as a triumph
for Bute's policy, and as such it was angrily recognised
throughout the country.   The City especially, so Newcastle told Devonshire, was in the highest rage with
Bedford, and with Fox as Bute's adviser.[3]   Every Englishman who was not in the Court Camarilla regarded his
mission as meaning a betrayal of our heroic ally, and
the feeling against Bute rose higher and higher.   But in
truth the struggle was far from over.   The King himself
sent for Newcastle to try to assuage the anger of the
Opposition.   He told him Choiseul had declared, "No

---

[1] *Grenville Papers*, Sept. 1, vol. i. p. 465 ; Comte de Choiseul to Egremont, Aug. 26, *Lansdowne House MSS.*, vol. iii.

[2] Grenville to Mitchell, Aug. 31, *Mitchell Papers, Add. MSS.* 6828.

[3] *Newcastle Papers*, 32,942, Sept. 4.

St. Lucia, no peace." Newcastle only replied, that when he was in the Cabinet they had agreed to insist on all the neutral islands in exchange for Martinique. Passing to Germany, the King said he could do nothing but leave Frederick to himself, since he flatly refused his mediation and would open nothing. Newcastle was unconvinced, and told the King he ought at least to ask something more for our successes this year. The King merely thanked him for explaining the views of the Opposition, and dismissed him with nothing done.[1]

Bute now stood almost alone. Even Egremont was growing hostile. The Duc de Nivernais had come over as the French plenipotentiary, and was making various suggestions on his own account, all of which had been rejected already. He was particularly pressing about putting neutral garrisons into the Rhenish towns, and Egremont stubbornly refused to listen. It was a fortnight since Bedford had reached Paris, and not a word had come from him. Egremont grew anxious. " Pray come to town soon," he wrote to Grenville ; "you may be wanted." And indeed he was. Two days later a long and complacent despatch came from Bedford. Egremont sent it on immediately to meet his colleague on his way to London. " You will see," he wrote, " that headstrong silly wretch has already given up two or three points in his conversation with Choiseul, and that his design was to have been signed without any communication here. I have seen Lord Bute this morning and had much talk with him. Some I did not like, but I have not given way in anything : nor shall in the attack I expect from the Superior." [2]

---

[1] Interview with King, Sept. 11, *Newcastle Papers*, 32,942.
[2] Egremont to Grenville, Sept. 24 and 26, *Grenville Papers*, vol. i. p. 474.

The points that Bedford had let go were really of little importance. They related merely to the inspection of the fishery stations, Dunkirk, and the status of the factories to be restored to France in India. Still they gave ground for suspecting the Duke's constancy; but quite groundlessly, as his next despatch proved. It followed close on the heels of the other, and its contents raised still greater alarm. At his second interview with Choiseul, Bedford, to his dismay, found that no arrangement whatever had been made with Spain. Choiseul had not even dared to tell Grimaldi that he had agreed to let us into the Gulf of Mexico, or that we should require fresh concessions if Havana were taken. He had not so much as settled for the evacuation of Portugal, and he implored Bedford not to say a word to Grimaldi. Bedford, however, insisted on seeing him at once. The Spanish ambassador talked like a madman. "Either he or his Court," wrote Bedford, "have lost their senses." In vain the two Choiseuls, Solar, and the Pompadour herself tried to smooth the anger of the indignant Englishman, and get him to give way. He would not budge an inch, and insisted on referring the whole matter home.

The immediate effect was to inspire every one but Bute with a conviction that France was false. "I do not suppose," wrote Egremont to Grenville, "that ever there existed such a specimen of falsehood, inconsistency, insolence, &c., &c., as these papers exhibit: and I do not see almost how the negotiation can proceed. The Duke of Bedford is in consternation about it himself. . . . The King comes to town to dinner. Lord Bute is at Kew. For God's sake come up to town." [1]

With both King and Cabinet a panic ensued at the risk they had run in entrusting Bedford with plenary

---

[1] Egremont to Grenville, Oct. —, *Grenville Papers*, vol. i. p. 476.

powers.   There was a feeling they must be curtailed, so
that he should not have authority to sign anything till it
had been referred home.   Grenville went so far as to
press that the preliminaries should be submitted to Parliament before anything was done.   Bute was obstinate.
To revoke Bedford's powers was to annul the symbol of
his success.   A desperate struggle for the mastery ensued,
which brought both the peace and the Cabinet to the brink
of wreck.   Grenville threatened to resign.   Bute begged the
King for leave to abandon a position for which at last he
felt himself wholly inadequate ; but at the bare suggestion
of his desertion his distracted master would sit " for hours
together leaning his head upon his arm without speaking."
Bute felt he must stay.   But he quite lost his head.
His advisers in the City, whose language he pathetically
confessed he could not understand when they came to
talk finance, were declaring it would be impossible to
raise money so long as he was in power.   The war could
not go on, and Bute in despair proposed to accept the
last French terms, and demand no equivalent if Havana
were taken.   Grenville utterly refused to listen.   He
would not give way : Bute could not let him go : and not
a ray of hope was to be seen in the darkness.

To increase the blackness of the outlook, Frederick was
continuing his amiable instructions to his Ministers in
London. He told them that if Bute dared to do anything
against the sentiment of the nation he would assuredly
risk his head, and that they were to do their best to add
to the risk—not only by tampering with the press, but
by getting some of the great cities to petition against the
shame which the Ministers were bringing on the Crown
and country.   They were to leave no stone unturned to
fling Bute down, and, in particular, were to inspire the
Opposition press with remarks upon the misery royal

favourites had always brought on England ; a hint which the pamphleteers developed with shameless and ingenious fertility.[1] Bute felt the danger only too keenly. Viri told Solar plainly that Choiseul must remember Bute could not keep Harley's fate out of his head. He could not make war : he dared not make peace. What would have happened it is impossible to tell, but the very afternoon that the deadlock pronounced itself Captain Hervey sprang boisterously upon the scene with the glorious news that Havana had fallen.[2]

He came like a flash of light into the gloom, and with a lusty breeze from the west that cleared the situation like magic and fanned the whole country once more into flames of triumph. The bells and the bonfires left no two words to be said. Within an hour of the news being told Grenville and Egremont both declared that they would sign no such peace as Bute desired. At their backs was rising a cry, loudest in the City, that no peace should be made till Spain denounced the Family Compact. There was nothing for it but to bend before the storm. Bute dared not face Parliament, on which Frederick based his hope. It was to meet next week, but was hastily prorogued. He dared not even face a Cabinet. Without any meeting being called Bedford's plenary powers were revoked, and he was told to expect a new "Project of Peace" as England's last word.

But Bute, with courage worthy of better ends, was only bending. Already he was at work to get rid of Grenville's opposition. With such a man at the Foreign Office and leading the House of Commons, he could not go on. Grenville, moreover, was pressing for Newcastle

---

[1] Frederick to Kynphausen, Sept. 10, *Politische Corr.*, vol. xxii. p. 207.

[2] *Newcastle Papers*, 32,943, Oct. 3. Note of his interview with Cumberland. Hervey arrived on Sept. 29.

and his friends to be called back to council, and Halifax, who had supported Bute throughout, was in favour of the coalition. The King sanctioned an overture, but Halifax's well-meant efforts were met with a blunt refusal from Newcastle and his friends. Bute was now free to go his way. He had made up his mind to fall back on Fox, whose unpopularity was second only to his own; still he was the only man who could hope to face Pitt. Indolent and satiated as he was with the wealth he had acquired as Paymaster during the war, he was persuaded to accept the leadership of the House of Commons, without office but with almost despotic powers.[1] Grenville was forced to go to the Admiralty, and Halifax took his place as Foreign Secretary for the North. Nor did Bute stop there. It had been decided in principle that the "New Project" should adhere to the English plan of a general evacuation of Germany and Portugal, that Florida or Puerto Rico should be demanded for Havana, and that no variation of the material articles would be permitted. The moment it was settled Bute secretly informed Viri of what was coming, in order that he might prepare the Court of France, and told him that on no account must Bedford or Spain be informed.

He might well have saved himself the last piece of treachery to the constitution. The Court of France needed no preparation. Havana had done its work; Choiseul himself had taken alarm; Paris was as clamorous for peace as London was violent for higher terms, and the long-headed French Minister knew the time had come to close. Havana, he said, "had stopped Grimaldi's cackle"; Frederick had taken Sweidnitz, the main objective of his campaign; Ferdinand was expected any day

---

[1] For the best and most authentic account of Fox's intervention see Lord Fitzmaurice's *Life of Shelburne*, vol. i. p. 153 *et seq.*

to capture Cassel; and Choiseul resolved at all costs to force the English terms down Spain's throat. On October 22nd and 25th the reconstructed Cabinet met to pass the draft of the "New Project." Grenville was still for demanding St. Lucia, but it was not brought up, and the Project as it stood was passed unanimously.[1] It reached Paris by the end of the month. Hard as the terms were, Choiseul, with characteristic decision, did not flinch. He saw, as was only fair, that France must pay the price for Havana, and as the payment could be made to clear his country of the "American system" altogether, he could do it with a light heart. All, therefore, of Louisiana that was not already promised to England was offered to Spain if she would give up Florida. Spain accepted, and on November 3rd the long-fought Preliminaries were signed at Fontainebleau.

On only one material point had Bedford given way, and this unfortunately was in the article relating to the Prussian Rhineland. By the English Project France was to evacuate Cleves, Wesel, and Gueldres immediately after the ratification of the Preliminaries, and neither side was to furnish succour of any kind to their respective allies. In this form the article was communicated to Frederick;[2] but when, a few days later, he received the whole text of the Preliminaries it was found the article had been altered. Not only was France merely to evacuate his territory "as soon as it can be done," but there was attached a declaration that she was to be permitted to pay all arrears of her subsidy to Austria. It was the last false stroke of Bute and Bedford, and Frederick

---

[1] Grenville to Egremont, and Egremont to Grenville, *Grenville Papers*, vol. i. p. 492, Oct. 24; Jones to Newcastle, Oct. 23, 24, and 26, *Newcastle Papers*, 32,943–4.

[2] Halifax to Mitchell, Nov. 9, *Mitchell Papers*, vol. xvii., *Add. MSS.* 6820.

was naturally more convinced than ever he was betrayed. He saw in the variation a clear intention of letting Austria into the disputed towns. He had suspected so much already, and was deep in a scheme for persuading either the Dutch or Ferdinand to seize them on his behalf as soon as the French left. He now redoubled his efforts, made preparations to lay hold of other Westphalian territory by way of security, and sent a firm and indignant protest to London, which Knyphausen was ordered to have printed and scatter broadcast.

There was still hope that the obnoxious article might be given a proper turn. Grenville's insistence and Bute's memories of Harley and Walpole had so far prevailed that the Preliminaries were to be submitted to Parliament before a definitive treaty was proceeded with. As the terms leaked out the anger of the nation blazed hotter and hotter. The King, by an insult to Devonshire, had alienated all the best of the nobility, and they were resigning their offices every day; and worst of all, Pitt and the Newcastle group were meeting in the Duke of Cumberland's house. But all was of no avail against the able and not too nice generalship of Fox. Having put his hand to the plough he let no indecency of reward or punishment turn him aside. Never had bribery been so open and drastic, or proscription so heartless and searching. By the time Parliament met both Houses had been purged and poisoned to the core. It was on December 9th the great debate took place. In the Lords Hardwicke rent the peace to tatters with unanswerable logic. To the Commons Pitt, swathed in flannel, was carried from a bed of sickness, and, suffering agonies from the gout, unable to stand, at times hardly able to speak, he denounced it for three hours and a half. Outside a turbulent crowd roared in concert, but not even their shouts could replace the fire his pain had quenched. At his best, perhaps, he could not have availed to undo Fox's insidious work. As he ended and was carried from the House it was clear the game was lost. Newcastle passed the word for his men not to vote. In the Lords the peace was agreed to without a division. In the Commons it was carried by an overwhelming majority.

The Government had triumphed, but the temper that had been displayed in the attack and which continued to rise in the country could not be ignored. The desertion of the Protestant hero had been the point that had pricked the deepest, and it might yet kill. Thus it was that righteous and justifiable as was Frederick's anger, he quickly found it was uncalled for. Halifax, at least, was a man of too high character to purchase peace, much as he loved it, at the price of national honour. He had already set on foot a scheme by which Frederick should receive all he wanted. It took the form of a joint effort by France and England to induce all the princes of the Empire to declare their neutrality and withdraw their contingents from Austria. To complete the pacification he also proposed a convention by which all Frederick's territory in Westphalia and on the Rhine should be restored to him, and that as a counterpoise France and England should jointly guarantee the neutrality of Holland and the Austrian Netherlands. This statesman-like scheme was so well received that by the time Frederick's impassioned protest arrived Halifax was able to assure Knyphausen there was nothing to fear. So soon as the plan was conveyed to Frederick he accepted it with alacrity. "As I find this measure," he wrote to Knyphausen, "to be in complete conformity with my interests, my intention is that you declare . . . that I am willing to put my hand to it and conclude the proposed convention under the guarantee of the two Courts." [1]

So in the end he was not betrayed, and England, at the cost of the great sacrifice of her interests that had been forced on her in the East and West Indies and on the African coast, had fulfilled to the letter every engagement to her ally. On February 10th the definitive treaty was signed at Paris by Bedford, the Comte de Choiseul, and Grimaldi, and the great imperial war was at an end.

But by this time it had reached to the farthest ends of the earth, and there it still continued to rumble like passing thunder. In the West Indies Keppel swept up prize after prize, and in the far East, Admiral Cornish and General Draper were doing no less. On October 6th they had taken Manilla, and the eastern fountain of Spanish wealth was as completely in our hands as the western. But, though the capitulation had been made before the Preliminaries were signed, the news did not reach Europe till after their ratification ; and as no mention of the conquest was made in the treaty, all had to be restored without equivalent. Even the ransom bills which had been extorted, the Spaniards refused to pay. It required but this to complete the popular exasperation. The rage against Bute knew no bounds, and two months were not passed before he fell, crushed under the weight of his own peace.

[1] *Politische Corr.*, vol. xxii. p. 483, Jan. 26, 1763.

CHAPTER XII

CONCLUSION—LESSONS OF THE WAR

A CONTEST so prolonged and waged with so much ability as the Seven Years' War could not but leave its mark upon the naval art. It may indeed be said to have effected the transition from the ideas of the seventeenth century to those of the eighteenth. No definite formulation of the revolution in thought is known to exist, but in the change that came over the organisation of the fleet it is very clearly expressed. It is impossible to examine these changes without feeling ourselves in contact with a new and more scientific conception of naval warfare. We can see growing up a clearer analysis of the various services required; a germ of their classification into battle, scouting, and inshore work; and side by side an attempt to organise the fleet upon a corresponding threefold basis of battleships, cruisers, and flotilla. The process accompanied the effort to improve our naval architecture in accordance with the French models captured by Anson and Hawke in 1747. That process is well known.[1] The subtler strategical development is of even higher interest, and deserves wider recognition than it has hitherto received.

Up till the end of the war of the Austrian Succession the classification of our ships had become purely arbitrary, corresponding to no philosophical conception of the duties of a fleet. In the first rate were 100-gun

[1] Charnock, *History of Marine Architecture*, 1801-3, vol. iii. pp. 158 *et seq.*

ships; in the second 90-gun ships—all three-deckers. So far there is nothing to criticise. It is in the third rate the lack of system becomes apparent. It was headed by 80-gun ships of three decks, and the bulk of the rest were 70-gun ships of two decks. In the fourth rate was a weak class of 60-gun and 50-gun ships also of two decks. This class was the largest of all, numbering no less than seventy. Their multiplication, so Charnock believed, was due to the increasing area our trade was covering, and we can only assume it was due to a desire to combine battle and commerce-protection properties in one type—that is, they were hybrids between a weak battleship and a powerful cruiser without any clear recognition of an intermediate type. In any case, in spite of their known battle weakness, they were regarded primarily as battleships, and until nearly the end of the Seven Years' War were all classed as ships of the line. Below these came the fifth rates, which were cruisers, but in no way did they differ from ships of the line except in size. They were all cramped two-deckers of 44 and 40 guns, and had no distinctive class-name. No doubt they were to some extent an expression of the fundamental need of an intermediate type for cruiser support, but being merely small battleships they had no special adaptation for acting with cruisers. The true cruiser was represented by the sixth rates, which comprised small and weakly armed 20-gun ships, and between them and the "forties" there was nothing. Below these, but again without any clear differentiation, came the unrated sloops.

Thus it will be seen that not only was there no logical distinction between the large and the small type of battleship, but there was none between the battleship and the cruiser or between the cruisers and the flotilla. It is impossible to detect any strategical or tactical theory of class functions to which the classification will correspond. The only conceivable explanation is that the system was a decrepit survival of the earliest days of warfare under sail. In the whole gamut of rates there is nowhere a distinct gap except between the two-decked "forties" and the 20-gun cruisers. A special characteristic of these vessels and the sloops was that they could be moved by oars, and we are therefore driven to the conclusion that the rating of the middle of the eighteenth century was purely arbitrary, with no scientific foundation beneath it except the obsolete classification of the fleet into true sailing ships and vessels with auxiliary oar propulsion. It was the classification on which Henry the Eighth had originally founded the sailing navy, and which was at the bottom of the Elizabethan distinction between ships and pinnaces. In other words, it is the last trace of the hybrid ship and galley navies of the Middle Ages.

If we turn now to the Navy List as it existed at the end of the Seven Years' War, after Anson's long spell of office, we find all this is changed. Whether or not it was done as the conscious expression of a scientific conception of naval warfare is unknown, but it is none the less interesting if it was due to the silent pressure of strategical law acting through hard experience upon a creative mind, and forcing the fleet into the shape it demanded.

To begin with we find, eliminating foreign prizes introduced into the service, that the three-deckers or fleet flagship type are confined to the two highest rates, and three-deckers of less than 90 guns have ceased to be built. Similarly there is a tendency to confine the two-deckers—the rank and file of the line of battle—to the

third and fourth rates, and at the same time their size
was increased to make them really fit for their special
function. A new class of 1500-ton 74's was begun in
place of the older 70's, and a class of 1200-ton 64's in
place of the older 60's. In both cases there was an
advance of about 300 tons, and it was regarded, even at
the end of the century, as a "grand stretch of mechanics."
Still the fermenting aspirations of the new school were
unsatisfied, and in 1758 were laid down two 74's of
a still larger design, which had been in contemplation
ever since Anson and Hawke had captured their models
in 1747. They marked another "grand stretch" of
300 tons, or of no less than one-third over the old
class of 70's. But somewhere, possibly due to Anson's
death, the courage of conviction was wanting, and for
many years to come these two vessels were regarded as
experimental, and not repeated. In all ten 74's were
added during the war, besides three French prizes and
the seven large Spanish 70's taken at Havana.

Coming to the fourth rate we see it still comprising
ships of from 60 to 50 guns, but with a highly significant difference. A hard line is drawn between the 60's
and the 50's, and the 60's only are classed as ships of
the line. Charnock tells us that even so their retention
as battleships was nominal, and that they were no longer
regarded as really fit to lie in the line against the powerful rank and file of France and Spain. The interesting
point, however, is not so much the status of the 60's as
that of the 50's. For in the fact that though increased
in power and still included in the fourth rate they were
no longer classed as battleships, we seem to get the first
clear recognition of the need of an intermediate type—a
type, that is, whose function is to act as a supporting
ship to stiffen the cruiser line—and for this purpose

they were almost invariably used in the later years of the war. As flagships of cruiser squadrons, for convoy work and for commerce protection generally, they found their chief employment, and the tendency was for the old 60's that remained to sink to the same category, while no less than twelve 60's and eight 50's were broken up during the war.

In the cruiser class we find the advance in thought no less strongly marked. During the war, besides units that were lost, ten 40's were broken up and eighteen 20's sold. The 40's ceased to be built, and their numbers had fallen from thirty-eight to twenty-one. In their place are no less than thirty-two 32-gun frigates, the first of the new type of cruiser which was to prove so effective, and to clothe itself with so much renown. Added to these were four of 36-guns, of which one was a French prize. In the same way there appears in the sixth class twenty-two new 28-gun frigates. A few more of the old 20-gun type had been completed, which kept the numbers up to forty-four, but at the same time a comparatively new experimental class of 18-gun frigates had been disrated and relegated to the flotilla.[1]

If, then, we summarise broadly, eliminating instances of confusion caused by the incorporation of prize ships, the tendency becomes clear. It is towards simplification and specialisation of the three main types. The battle-ships remain as at the beginning of the war, one hundred and forty in number, with a proportion of one-seventh three-deckers for flagships, while the two-deckers, largely

[1] The frigates actually added during the war were four 36's (one French), two 30's (one bought and one French), twenty 32's (two French), sixteen 28's (two French), one 26 and one 24, both French.—*Charnock*, vol. iii. p. 198.

increased in force, are condensing to two types only, 74's and 64's. Between them is a wide gap to the 32 and 28-gun cruisers, filled, however, by the intermediate 50's, which are no longer classed as battleships. Then the 40-gun class is dying out, leaving a distinct cruiser class of true single-decked frigates, while an equally well-marked gap is forming between the frigates and the sloops, that is, between cruisers and flotilla.

Such was the revolution which was carried out practically in ten years. When we consider that in those days 74's took, as a rule, nearly four years to complete, and that the *Royal George* (100), the first ship laid down on the improved French lines, took nearly ten, "revolution" seems not too strong a term. It is noteworthy, moreover, that unlike the similar sweeping reform which was inaugurated by Sir Thomas Hardy in 1830, it was carried out in high time of war, and as a result of the actual experience of a previous war. Anson, a true fighting admiral as well as a great administrator, is the personality to whom we must credit the great advance; but in honouring him we must not forget the name of Sir Thomas Slade, who, as Surveyor of the Navy from 1755 to 1771, was directly responsible for the creation of this true modern fleet.

In tactics no such advance was made. In the army the improvement was great, but the nature of the struggle at sea robbed the admirals of that day of the necessary stimulus of general actions. That it was not a period of actual stagnation in thought is proved by the official introduction of the new Additional Instructions which have been noticed in their place. It was practice and the need of tactics that were wanting. How little practical attention was given to the subject, we have seen in Anson's complaint of the ignorance and slackness

of battle tactics which he found on taking over from
Hawke and Boscawen the main fleet in 1758. Indeed,
it is not too much to say, that although, from the
conditions of the war, there was little tactical fruition,
Anson was the true begetter of a better state of things.
Men who knew him well acclaimed his appointment as
First Lord as heralding a new era. " How seldom,"
wrote one of them, " have we had one man at the
Admiralty who . . . made the improvement of discipline
(*i.e.* tactics) any part of his care! . . . I expect a great
deal from you, and if I am deceived will never again
hope to see . . . any real improvements made, but conclude we are to go on in the old stupid tracks of our
predecessors, leave all to chance, and blunder on *ad
infinitum* without any regular system of discipline. . . .
I hope you will give another turn to affairs, and form
a society for the propagation of sea-military knowledge.
I think you had formerly such a scheme." [1]

This scheme he never realised, but the fact that it
had been in his mind suggests that the great reforms he
made were the outcome of a reasoned apprehension of
the principles of his art and not the mere intuitions of
hand to mouth experience. But of all this scarcely a
glimpse remains. " The silent son-in-law of the Chan-
cellor," as Horace Walpole called him, seldom spoke and
never wrote a word more than he could help. His friends
cherished his few letters as the rarest of possessions,
and affectionately reviled him as the worst of correspondents. For him, as for his disciple Saunders, silence
was golden. Yet how great a loss it cost the service can
never be known, for it meant the minds of both were
buried with them.

The reason why Anson and his admirals were denied

---

[1] Barrow, *Life of Anson*, p. 405.

the chance of putting his tactical ideas to the test brings us to another permanent lesson of the war. No great action took place, because the weakness of the French at sea and the exigencies of their war plan forced them to adopt a naval defensive. It was their wise policy to avoid a decision at sea, and to keep the command in dispute as long as possible, while they concentrated their offensive powers upon the army ashore. It was exactly the reverse of Pitt's system, and how nearly it came to defeating it is one of the great facts of the war.

The essence of the defensive is waiting for an opportunity to pass to the offensive, and we cannot look back upon the struggle which the French attitude so skilfully prolonged without a shudder to see how nearly they were rewarded. Had Ferdinand, the Anglophile king of Spain, died a year or two sooner than he did, Spain would certainly have joined our enemy before we had attained our object in America. As it was, the French, by preserving their fleet from a decision, prevented us for five long years from completing that easy conquest which we looked to settle in one campaign. With the Spanish fleet to help them dispute the control of the American communications, there is no saying how much longer the labour would have lasted. Again, if the Czarina Elizabeth had survived one more campaign it is impossible to see how Frederick could have maintained his position. On all the chances of war we must have been crushed; Hanover, and Holland, and the Netherlands would have been at the mercy of France, and the treaty of peace could scarcely have been on a better basis for us than the *status quo ante bellum*.

There is no clearer lesson in history how unwise and short-sighted it is to despise and ridicule a naval defensive. Of all strategical attitudes it is the most difficult to meet and the most deeply fraught with danger for the opposing belligerent if he is weak ashore and his enemy strong. The prolongation of war at sea tends to raise up fresh enemies for the dominant power in a much higher degree than it does on land, owing to the inevitable exasperation of neutrals. In the long run and by itself the defensive cannot, of course, lead to a final attainment of the command of the sea. But it can prevent its attainment by the other side, and this, taken in concert with a powerful offensive ashore, may well secure a final triumph. The real lesson of the war is not that we should treat a naval defensive with contempt, just because in this case it failed by the chance prolongation of two human lives; but that we should note the supreme necessity and difficulty of crushing it down before it has time to operate its normal effect. The primary and all-absorbing object of a superior naval power is not merely to take the offensive, but to force the enemy to expose himself to a decision as quickly as possible. One of the rare glimpses we have had into Anson's mind showed us how deeply he was impressed with this preoccupation. In his heart he never approved of Pitt's coastal operations. Great as he was as a master of naval warfare, there is no sign he ever rose to Pitt's larger conception of combined strategy. It was only because Hardwicke's broad mind grasped and approved the policy, that his silent son-in-law held his tongue and loyally gave an outward assent. We have seen that the sole use he could find in coastal expeditions was a means of forcing a decision at sea, and so far and no further he believed them justified. Much has been said of the first function of the British army being to assist the fleet in obtaining command of the sea. We may take it that in Lord Anson's opinion there was no better way in which this function could be performed than by operating over the uncommanded sea, and tempting the enemy's battleships into the open.

There remains to consider the lessons of commerce destruction. Though actual statistics are hard to come by, there seems no doubt that the French claim to have captured a greater number of vessels than we did is justified. The value of the captures is less certain. Very little harm was done to our convoys, less still by the enemy's cruisers. The bulk of the havoc was amongst small vessels and coasting craft by the enemy's privateers, and the results afford a poor precedent as to what is likely to happen now that privateering is supposed to be abolished. This, however, is not the important point. The fact of permanent value is that successful as were the French operations, they did very little to injure our credit, and that is the main strategic value of commerce destruction. Money was freely obtainable, at least until the end of Pitt's administration, and then any tightness there was was entirely due to mistrust of Bute's capacity. On the other hand, the credit of France was effectively destroyed, and her finances reduced to the direst straits.

The truth seems to be that the bulk of our commerce was so great that the mere pelagic operations of our enemy, though they absorbed in the end almost the whole of her vitality at sea, could not make a sufficient percentage impression to produce any real warlike advantage. Such an advantage, it would appear, is only to be obtained by a practical stoppage of trade communications and the capture of the oversea depots. When the volume of commerce is so vast and its theatre so widespread as ours was even in those days, pelagic operations against it can never amount to more than nibbling. They may produce inconvenience, but cannot paralyse finance. To injure credit to such an extent as to amount to a real consideration of war, operations against trade must be systematically carried on by land and sea till its main sources and the possibility of transit are practically destroyed. Then, and then only, can it become a material factor in securing the ultimate object —a favourable peace. That, at least, is the moral of the Seven Years' War.

With regard to the merits of the peace itself, though it was the most triumphant we ever made, it can only be said that, as Boscawen began the war, so Bute ended it. What we did was either too little or too much. That we were in a position to extract still harder terms than we did is certain. Pitt would have done so, and was minded by crushing the French navy, body and soul, to put it out of her power ever to retaliate. Whether this was possible or not there were many wise heads who thought it impolitic; better, they argued, to be easy and rest content with a situation which would be endurable to a chivalrous enemy. To this end we sacrificed much, and all to no purpose. We had gone already far beyond what so great and proud a nation could accept; and even while Choiseul was pressing for terms mild enough to secure a lasting peace, he was planning the revenge which was to fall so heavily and so soon.

APPENDIX

DEFINITIVE TREATY OF PEACE BETWEEN GREAT BRITAIN, FRANCE, AND SPAIN

1763

. . . .

Peace.—Art. 1. There shall be a Christian, universal, and perpetual peace, as well by sea as by land, and a sincere and constant friendship shall be re-established between their Britannic, most Christian, Catholic, and most Faithful majesties, and between their heirs and sucessors, kingdoms, dominions, provinces, countries, subjects, and vassals, of what quality or condition soever they be, without exception of places, or of persons: so that the high contracting parties shall give the greatest attention to maintain between themselves and their said dominions and subjects, this reciprocal friendship and correspondence, without permitting, on either side, any kind of hostilities, by sea or by land, to be committed, from henceforth, for any cause, or under any pretence whatsoever, and every thing shall be carefully avoided which might, hereafter, prejudice the union happily re-established, applying themselves, on the contrary, on every occasion, to procure for each other whatever may contribute to their mutual glory, interests, and advantages, without giving any assistance or protection, directly or indirectly, to those who would cause any prejudice to either of the high contracting parties: there shall be a general oblivion of everything that may have been done or committed before, or since, the commencement of the war, which is just ended.

Treaties Confirmed.—Art. II. The treaties of Westphalia of 1648; those of Madrid between the crowns of Great Britain and Spain of 1667 and 1670; the treaties of peace of Nimeguen of 1678 and 1679; of Ryswick of 1697; those of peace and of commerce of Utrecht of 1713; that of Baden of 1714; the treaty of the Triple Alliance of the Hague of 1717; that of the Quadruple Alliance of London of 1718; the treaty of peace of Vienna of 1738; the definitive treaty of Aix la Chapelle of 1748; and that of Madrid between the crowns of Great Britain and Spain of 1750, as well as the treaties between the crowns of Spain and Portugal, of the 13th February 1668; of the 6th February 1715; and of the 12th February 1761; and that of the 11th April 1713 between France and Portugal, with the guarantees of Great Britain, serve as a basis and foundation to the peace and to the present treaty; and for this purpose, they are all renewed and confirmed in the best form, as well as all the treaties in general, which subsisted between the high contracting parties before the war, as if they were inserted here word for word, so that they are to be exactly observed, for the future, in their whole tenor, and religiously executed on all sides, in all their points, which shall not be derogated from by the present Treaty, notwithstanding all that may have been stipulated to the contrary by any of the high contracting parties: and all the said parties declare, that they will not suffer any privilege, favour, or indulgence, to subsist, contrary to the treaties above confirmed, except what shall have been agreed and stipulated by the present Treaty.

Exchange of Prisoners.—Art. III. All the prisoners made, on all sides, as well by land as by sea, and the hostages carried away, or given during the war, and to this day, shall be restored without ransom, six weeks, at latest, to be computed from the day of the exchange of the ratification of the present treaty, each crown respectively paying the advances which shall have been made for the subsistence and maintenance of their prisoners, by the sovereign of the country where they shall have been detained, according to the attested receipts and estimates, and other authentic vouchers, which shall be furnished on one side and the other: and securities shall be reciprocally given for the payment of the debts which the prisoners shall have contracted in the countries where they have been detained, until their entire liberty. And all the ships of war and merchant vessels which shall have been taken since the expiration of the terms agreed upon for the cessation of hostilities by sea, shall be likewise restored *bona fide*, with all their crews and cargoes ; and the execution of this article shall be proceeded upon immediately after the exchange of the ratifications of this treaty.

Nova Scotia and Canada. — Art. IV. His most Christian majesty renounces all the pretensions which he has heretofore formed, or might form, to Nova Scotia, or Acadia, in all its parts, and guarantees the whole of it, and with all its dependencies, to the king of Great Britain : moreover, his most Christian majesty cedes and guarantees to his said Britannic majesty, in full right, Canada, with all its dependencies, as well as the island of Cape Breton, and all the other islands and coasts in the gulph and river St. Laurence, and, in general, every thing that depends on the said countries, lands, islands, and coasts, with the sovereignty, property, possession, and all rights acquired by treaty or otherwise, which the most Christian king, and the crown of France, have had, till now, over the said countries, islands, lands, places, coasts, and their inhabitants, so that the most Christian king cedes and makes over the whole to the said king, and to the crown of Great Britain, and that in the most ample manner and form, without restriction, and without any liberty to depart from the said cession and guaranty, under any pretence, or to disturb Great Britain in the possessions above mentioned. His Britannic majesty, on his side, agrees to grant the liberty of the Catholic religion to the inhabitants of Canada ; he will, consequently, give the most precise and most effectual orders, that his new Roman Catholic subjects may profess the worship of their religion, according to the rites of the Romish Church, as far as the laws of Great Britain permit. His Britannic majesty further agrees, that the French inhabitants, or others who had been subjects of the most Christian king in Canada, may retire, with all safety and freedom, wherever they shall think proper, and may sell their estates, provided it be to subjects of his Britannic majesty, and bring away their effects as well as their persons, without being restrained in their emigration, under any pretence whatsoever, except that of debts, or of criminal prosecutions : the term limited for this emigration shall be fixed to the space of eighteen months, to be computed from the day of the exchange of the ratifications of the present treaty.

Fisheries.—Art. V. The subjects of France shall have the

liberty of fishing and drying, on a part of the coasts of the island of Newfoundland, such as it is specified in the 13th Article of the Treaty of Utrecht; which article is renewed and confirmed by the present treaty (except what relates to the island of Cape Breton, as well as to the other islands and coasts, in the mouth and in the gulph of St. Laurence); and his Britannic majesty consents to leave to the subjects of the most Christian king the liberty of fishing in the gulph of St. Laurence, on condition that the subjects of France do not exercise the said fishery, but at the distance of three leagues from all the coasts belonging to Great Britain, as well those of the continent, as those of the islands situated in the said gulph of St. Laurence. And as to what relates to the fishery on the coasts of the island of Cape Breton out of the said gulph, the subjects of the most Christian king shall not be permitted to exercise the said fishery, but at the distance of 15 leagues from the coasts of the island of Cape Breton; and the fishery on the coasts of Nova Scotia or Acadia, and everywhere else out of the said gulph, shall remain on the foot of former treaties.

Fishing Stations.—Art. VI. The king of Great Britain cedes the islands of St. Peter and Miquelon, in full right, to his most Christian majesty, to serve as a shelter to the French fishermen: and his said most Christian majesty engages not to fortify the said islands; to erect no buildings upon them, but merely for the convenience of the fishery; and to keep upon them a guard of 50 men only for the police.

The Mississippi Line.—Art. VII. In order to re-establish peace on solid and durable foundations, and to remove for ever all subject of dispute with regard to the limits of the British and French territories on the continent of America; it is agreed, that, for the future, the confines between the dominions of his Britannic majesty, and those of his most Christian majesty, in that part of the world, shall be fixed irrevocably by a line drawn along the middle of the river Mississippi, from its source to the river Iberville, and from thence, by a line drawn along the middle of this river, and the lakes Maurepas and Pontchartrain, to the sea; and for this purpose, the most Christian king cedes in full right, and guarantees to his Britannic majesty, the river and port of the Mobile, and everything which he possesses, or ought to possess, on the left side of the river Mississippi, except the town of New Orleans, and the island in which it is situated, which shall remain to France; provided that the navigation of the river Mississippi shall be equally free, as well to the subjects of Great Britain, as to those of France, in its whole breadth and length, from its source to the sea, and expressly that part which is between the said island of New Orleans, and the right bank of that river, as well as the passage both in and out of its mouth : it is further stipulated, that the vessels belonging to the subjects of either nation, shall not be stopped, visited, or subjected to the payment of any duty whatsoever. The stipulations, inserted in the 4th Article, in favour of the inhabitants of Canada, shall also take place, with regard to the inhabitants of the countries ceded by this Article.

Restoration of French Islands.—Art. VIII. The king of Great Britain shall restore to France the islands of Guadaloupe, of Marie Galante, of Desirade, of Martinico, and of Belleisle; and the fortresses of these islands shall be restored in the same condition they were in, when they were conquered by the British arms; provided that his Britannic majesty's subjects, who shall have settled in the said islands, or those who shall have any commercial affairs to settle there, or in the other places restored to France by the present treaty, shall have liberty to sell their lands and their estates, to settle their affairs, to recover their debts, and to bring away their effects, as well as their persons, on board vessels, which they shall be permitted to send to the said islands, and other places restored as above, and which shall serve for this use only, without being restrained on account of their religion, or under any other pretence whatsoever, except that of debts, or of criminal prosecutions : and for this purpose, the term of eighteen months is allowed to his Britannic majesty's subjects, to be computed from the day of the exchange of the ratifications of the present Treaty; but, as the liberty, granted to his Britannic majesty's subjects, to bring away their persons and their effects, in vessels of their nation, may be liable to abuses, if precautions were not taken to prevent them; it has been expressly agreed between his Britannic majesty and his most Christian majesty, that the number of English vessels, which shall have leave to go to the said islands and places restored to France, shall be limited, as well as the number of tons of each one; that they shall go in ballast; shall set sail at a fixed time; and shall make one voyage only, all the effects, belonging to the English, being to be embarked at the same time. It has been further agreed, that his most Christian majesty shall cause the necessary passports to be given to the said vessels; that, for the greater security, it shall be allowed to place two French clerks or guards, in each of the said vessels, which shall be visited in the landing places, and ports of the said islands, and places, restored to France, and that the merchandise, which shall be found therein, shall be confiscated.

Islands Ceded to England.—Art. IX. The most Christian king cedes and guarantees to his Britannic majesty, in full right, the islands of Grenada, and of the Grenadines, with the same stipulations in favour of the inhabitants of this colony, inserted in the 4th Article for those of Canada; and the partition of the islands, called Neutral, is agreed and fixed, so that those of St. Vincent, Dominica, and Tobago, shall remain in full right to Great Britain, and that of St. Lucia shall be delivered to France, to enjoy the same likewise in full right; and the high contracting parties guaranty the partition so stipulated.

Goree and Senegal.—Art. X. His Britannic majesty shall restore to France the island of Gorée, in the condition it was in when conquered: and his most Christian majesty cedes, in full right, and guarantees to the king of Great Britain, the river Senegal, with the forts and factories of St. Lewis, Podor, and Galam; and with all the rights and dependencies of the said river Senegal.

India.—Art. XI. In the East Indies, Great Britain shall restore to France, in the condition they are now in, the different factories, which that crown possessed, as well on the coast of Coromandel, and Orixa, as on that of Malabar, as also in Bengal, at the beginning of the year 1749. And his most Christian majesty renounces all pretensions to the acquisitions which he had made on the coast of Coromandel and Orixa, since the said beginning of the year 1749. His most Christian majesty shall restore, on his side, all that he may have conquered from Great Britain, in the East Indies, during the present war; and will expressly cause Nattal and Tapanoully, in the island of Sumatra, to be restored; he engages further, not to erect fortifications, or to keep troops in any part of the dominions of the subah of Bengal. And in order to preserve future peace on the coast of Coromandel and Orixa, the English and French shall acknowledge Mahomet Ally Khan for lawful nabob of the Carnatic, and Salabat Jing for lawful subah of the Decan; and both parties shall renounce all demands and pretensions of satisfaction, with which they might charge each other, or their Indian allies, for the depredations, or pillage, committed, on the one side, or on the other, during the war.

Minorca.—Art. XII. The island of Minorca shall be restored to his Britannic majesty, as well as Fort St. Philip, in the same condition they were in, when conquered by the arms of the most Christian king; and with the artillery which was there, when the said island and the said fort were taken.

Dunkirk.—Art. XIII. The town and port of Dunkirk shall be put into the state fixed by the last Treaty of Aix-la-Chapelle, and by former treaties. The cunette shall be destroyed immediately after the exchange of the ratifications of the present Treaty, as well as the forts and batteries which defend the entrance on the side of the sea; and provision shall be made, at the same time, for the wholesomeness of the air, and for the health of the inhabitants, by some other means, to the satisfaction of the king of Great Britain.

Germany.—Art. XIV. France shall restore all the countries belonging to the electorate of Hanover, to the landgrave of Hesse, to the duke of Brunswick, and to the count of La Lippe Buckebourg, which are, or shall be occupied by his most Christian majesty's arms; the fortresses of these different countries shall be restored in the same condition they were in, when conquered by the French arms; and the pieces of artillery, which shall have been carried elsewhere, shall be replaced by the same number of the same bore, weight, and metal.

Time for Evacuation.—Art. XV. In case the stipulations, contained in the 13th Article of the Preliminaries, should not be completed at the time of the signature of the present treaty, as well with regard to the evacuations to be made by the armies of France of the fortresses of Cleves, Wesel, Gueldres, and of all the countries belonging to the king of Prussia, as with regard to the evacuations to be made by the British and French armies of the countries which they occupy in Westphalia, Lower Saxony, on the Lower Rhine, the Upper Rhine, and in all the empire, and to the retreat of the troops into the dominions of their respective sovereigns; their Britannic, and most Christian majesties promise to proceed, *bona fide*, with all the dispatch the case will permit of, to the said evacuations, the entire completion whereof they stipulate before the 15th of March next, or sooner if it can be done; and their Britannic and most Christian majesties further engage and promise to each other, not to furnish any succours, of any kind, to their respective allies, who shall continue engaged in war in Germany.

Spanish Prizes before War.—Art. XVI. The decision of the prizes made in the time of peace, by the subjects of Great Britain, on the Spaniards, shall be referred to the courts of justice of the admiralty of Great Britain, conformably to the rules established among all nations, so that the validity of the said prizes, between the British and Spanish nations, shall be decided and judged, according to the law of nations, and according to treaties, in the courts of justice of the nation, who shall have made the capture.

Logwood.—Art. XVII. His Britannic majesty shall cause to be demolished all the fortifications which his subjects shall have erected in the bay of Honduras, and other places of the territory of Spain in that part of the world, four months after the ratification of the present treaty; and his Catholic majesty shall not permit his Britannic majesty's subjects, or their workmen, to be disturbed, or molested, under any pretence whatsoever, in the said places, in their occupation of cutting, loading, and carrying away logwood: and for this purpose, they may build without hindrance, and occupy without interruption, the houses and magazines which are necessary for them, for their families, and for their effects: and his Catholic majesty assures to them, by this Article, the full enjoyment of those advantages, and powers, on the Spanish coasts and territories, as above stipulated, immediately after the ratification of the present treaty.

Spanish Fishery.—Art. XVIII. His Catholic majesty desists, as well for himself, as for his successors, from all pretension, which he may have formed, in favour of the Guipuscoans, and other his subjects, to the right of fishing in the neighbourhood of the island of Newfoundland.

Restoration of Cuba.—Art. XIX. The king of Great Britain

shall restore to Spain all the territory which he has conquered in the island of Cuba, with the fortress of the Havana, and this fortress, as well as all the other fortresses of the said island, shall be restored in the same condition they were in when conquered by his Britannic majesty's arms; provided, that his Britannic majesty's subjects, who shall have any commercial affairs to settle there, shall have liberty to sell their lands, and their estates, to settle their affairs, to recover their debts, and to bring away their effects, as well as their persons, on board vessels which they shall be permitted to send to the said island restored as above, and which shall serve for that use only, without being restrained on account of their religion, or under any other pretence whatsoever, except that of debts, or criminal prosecutions: and for this purpose, the term of eighteen months is allowed to his Britannic majesty's subjects, to be computed from the day of the exchange of the ratifications of the present treaty: but as the liberty, granted to his Britannic majesty's subjects, to bring away their persons, and their effects, in vessels of their nation, may be liable to abuses, if precautions were not taken to prevent them; it has been expressly agreed, between his Britannic majesty and his Catholic majesty, that the number of English vessels, which shall have leave to go to the said island restored to Spain, shall be limited, as well as the number of tons of each one; that they shall go in ballast; shall set sail at a fixed time; and shall make one voyage only; all the effects belonging to the English being to be embarked at the same time: it has been further agreed, that his Catholic majesty shall cause the necessary passports to be given to the said vessels; that, for the greater security, it shall be allowed to place two Spanish clerks, or guards, in each of the said vessels, which shall be visited in the landing-places, and ports of the said island restored to Spain, and that the merchandise which shall be found therein, shall be confiscated

Florida.—Art. XX. In consequence of the restitution stipulated in the preceding Article, his Catholic majesty cedes and guarantees, in full right, to his Britannic majesty, Florida, with Fort St. Augustin and the bay of Pensacola, as well as all that Spain possesses on the continent of North America, to the east, or to the south-east, of the river Mississippi. And, in general, everything that depends on the said countries, and lands, with

VOL. II.

the sovereignty, property, possession, and all rights, acquired by treaties or otherwise, which the Catholic king, and the crown of Spain, have had, till now, over the said countries, lands, places, and their inhabitants; so that the Catholic king cedes and makes over the whole to the said king, and to the crown of Great Britain, and that in the most ample manner and form. His Britannic majesty agrees, on his side, to grant to the inhabitants of the countries, above ceded, the liberty of the Catholic religion : he will consequently give the most express and the most effectual orders, that his new Roman Catholic subjects may profess the worship of their religion, according to the rites of the Romish church, as far as the laws of Great Britain permit : his Britannic majesty further agrees, that the Spanish inhabitants, or others who had been subjects of the Catholic king in the said countries, may retire, with all safety and freedom, wherever they think proper; and may sell their estates, provided it be to his Britannic majesty's subjects, and bring away their effects, as well as their persons, without being restrained in their emigration, under any pretence whatsoever, except that of debts or of criminal prosecutions : the term, limited for this emigration, being fixed to the space of eighteen months, to be computed from the day of the exchange of the ratifications of the present treaty. It is moreover stipulated, that his Catholic majesty shall have power to cause all the effects, that may belong to him, to be brought away, whether it be artillery, or other things.

Evacuation of Portuguese Territory.—Art. XXI. The French and Spanish troops shall evacuate all the territories, lands, towns, places, and castles, of his most Faithful majesty, in Europe, without any reserve, which shall have been conquered by the armies of France and Spain, and shall restore them in the same condition they were in when conquered, with the same artillery, and ammunition, which was found there : and with regard to the Portuguese colonies in America, Africa, or in the East Indies, if any change shall have happened there. all things shall be restored on the same footing they were in, and conformably to the preceding treaties which subsisted between the courts of France, Spain, and Portugal, before the present war.

Restoration of Archives.—Art. XXII. All the papers, letters, documents, and archives, which were found in the countries, territories, towns, and places, that are restored, and those belonging to the countries ceded, shall be respectively and *bona fide*, delivered, or furnished at the same time, if possible, that possession is taken, or, at latest, four months after the exchange of the ratifications of the present treaty, in whatever places the said papers or documents may be found.

Unknown Conquests.—Art. XXIII. All the countries and territories, which may have been conquered, in whatsoever part of the world, by the arms of their Britannic and most Faithful majesties, as well as by those of their most Christian and Catholic majesties, which are not included in the present treaty, either under the title of cessions, or under the title of restitutions, shall be restored without difficulty, and without requiring any compensation.

Epochs.—Art. XXIV. As it is necessary to assign a fixed epoch for the restitutions, and the evacuations, to be made by each of the high contracting parties; it is agreed, that the British and French troops shall complete, before the 15th of March next, all that shall remain to be executed of the 12th and 13th Articles of the Preliminaries, signed the 3rd of November last, with regard to the evacuation to be made in the empire, or elsewhere. The island of Belleisle shall be evacuated six weeks after the exchange of the ratifications of the present treaty, or sooner, if it can be done. Guadeloupe, Desirade, Marie Galante, Martinico, and St. Lucia, three months after the exchange of the ratifications of the present treaty, or sooner if it can be done. Great Britain shall likewise, at the end of three months after the exchange of the ratifications of the present treaty, or sooner, if it can be done, enter into the possession of the river and port of the Mobile, and of all that is to form the limits of the territory of Great Britain, on the side of the river Mississippi, as they are specified in the 7th Article. The island of Gorée shall be evacuated by Great Britain, three months after the exchange of the ratifications of the present treaty; and the island of Minorca, by France, at the same epoch, or sooner, if it can be done: and according to the conditions of the 6th Article, France shall likewise enter into possession of the islands of St. Peter, and of Miquelon, at the end of three months after the exchange of the ratifications of the present treaty. The factories in the East Indies shall be restored six months after the exchange of the ratifications of the present treaty, or sooner, if it can be done. The fortresses of the Havana, with all that has been conquered in the island of Cuba, shall be restored three months after the exchange of the ratifications of the present treaty, or sooner, if it can be done : and, at the same time, Great Britain shall enter into possession of the country ceded by Spain, according to the 20th Article. All the places and countries of his most Faithful majesty in Europe, shall be restored immediately after the exchange of the ratifications of the present treaty : and the Portuguese colonies, which may have been conquered, shall be restored in the space of three months in the West Indies, and of six months in the East Indies, after the exchange of the ratifications of the present treaty, or sooner, if it can be done. All the fortresses, the restitution whereof is stipulated above, shall be restored, with the artillery and ammunition which were found there at the time of the conquest. In consequence whereof, the necessary orders shall be sent by each of the high contracting parties, with reciprocal passports for the ships that shall carry them, immediately after the exchange of the ratifications of the present treaty.

King George as Elector.—Art. XXV. His Britannic majesty, as elector of Brunswic Lunenbourg, as well for himself, as for his heirs and successors, and all the dominions and possessions of his said Majesty in Germany, are included and guaranteed by the present treaty of peace.

Mutual Guarantee.—Art. XXVI. Their sacred Britannic, most Christian, Catholic, and most Faithful majesties, promise to observe, sincerely and *bona fide*, all the articles contained and settled in the present treaty ; and they will not suffer the same to be infringed, directly or indirectly, by their respective subjects ; and the said high contracting parties, generally and reciprocally, guaranty to each other all the stipulations of the present treaty.

Ratification.—Art. XXVII. The solemn ratifications of the present treaty, expedited in good and due form, shall be exchanged in this city of Paris, between the high contracting parties, in the space of a month, or sooner if possible, to be computed from the day of the signature of the present treaty.

In witness whereof, we the underwritten, their ambassadors extraordinary, and ministers plenipotentiary, have signed with our hand, in their name, and in virtue of our full powers, the present definitive treaty, and have caused the seal of our arms to be put thereto.

Done at Paris the 10th of February, 1763.

(L.S.) Bedford, C.P.S.
(L.S.) Choiseul, Duc de Praslin.
(L.S.) El Marquis de Grimaldi.

SEPARATE ARTICLES.

Saving Titles.—I. Some of the titles made use of by the contracting powers, either in the full powers, and other acts, during the course of the negotiation, or in the preamble of the present treaty, not being generally acknowledged ; it has been agreed, that no prejudice shall ever result therefrom to any of the said contracting parties, and that the titles, taken or omitted, on either side, on occasion of the said negotiation, and of the present treaty, shall not be cited or quoted as a precedent.

French Language.—II. It has been agreed and determined, that the French language, made use of in all the copies of the present treaty, shall not become an example, which may be alleged, or made a precedent of, or prejudice, in any manner, any of the contracting powers ; and that they shall conform themselves, for the future, to what has been observed, and ought to be observed, with regard to, and on the part of powers, who are used, and have a right, to give and receive copies of like treaties in another language than French ; the present treaty having still the same force and effect, as if the aforesaid custom had been therein observed.

Portugal.—III. Though the king of Portugal has not signed the present definitive treaty, their Britannic, most Christian, and Catholic majesties acknowledge, nevertheless, that his most Faithful majesty is formally included therein as a con-tracting party, and as if he had expressly signed the said treaty : consequently, their Britannic, most Christian, and Catholic majesties, respectively and conjointly promise to his most Faithful majesty, in the most express and most binding manner, the execution of all and every the clauses contained in the said treaty, on his act of accession.

The present Separate Articles shall have the same force as if they were inserted in the treaty.

In witness whereof, we the underwritten ambassadors extraordinary, and ministers plenipotentiary, of their Britannic, most Christian, and Catholic majesties, have signed the present Separate Articles, and have caused the seal of our arms to be put thereto.

Done at Paris the 10th of February, 1763.

(L.S.) Bedford, C.P.S.
(L.S.) Choiseul, Duc de Praslin.
(L.S.) El Marquis de Grimaldi.

INDEX

A

Abercromby, Gen. James, his command, 1758, 306–7 ; his disaster, 330–3 ; superseded, 397

Abraham, Heights of, 270, 419, 452, 456, 464 ; ii. 110–11

Abreu, Marqués de, Spanish Ambas. in London, 48

d'Aché, Anne Antoine, Comte (Chef d'Escad.), 160, 338–40, 344–50 ; ii. 120–6, 129–30, 133–4

Achilles, ii. 25

Acrias, 249

Active, ii. 321

Actæon, ii. 52, 235–6

Additional Instructions. *See* Fighting Instructions

Africa, West Coast of, 337, 362, 366 ; ii. 183

Aiguillon, Emanuel Armand, Vignerot - Duplessis - Richelieu, Duc d', Governor of Brittany, 299–300 ; ii. 11, 18–9, 21, 45, 49, 50, 56, 70 ; his overtures to Howe, 73, 76, 168

Aix, Island of, 211–4, 217, 221, 223, 261–2, 269 ; ii. 176

Aix-la-Chapelle, Peace of (1748), 11, 17, 64, 82 ; ii. 178, 192

Albany (New York), 175, 306 ; ii. 106, 114

Albemarle, George Keppel, 3rd Earl of, ii. 157 ; C. - in - C. against Havana, 241, 250, 253, 258, 261, 266–73, 275–83

Albemarle, William Anne Keppel, 2nd Earl of, Ambas. in Paris, 10, 16, 27, 30

Alcide, 55, 65, 260

Aleppo, ii. 140

Algarve, ii. 314, 321–2

Alleghany, mountains, 13 ; river, 14

Aller, river, 193, 233–5, 238, 245–6

Almeria, 132

Alva, Duke of, cited, ii. 95 *n.*

Ambleteuse, ii. 18

Amherst, Gen. Jeffrey (afterwards Lord Amherst), 254, 315 ; C.-in-C. at Louisbourg, 320–31 ; C.-in-C. in N. America, 397–9 ; his orders, 1759, 404–5 ; his campaign, 423, 442, 445, 452–3 ; in Montreal campaign (1760), ii. 105–7, 111, 113–8 ; his instructions (1761), 143, 154, 177–8, 209, 239, 253, 262 ; relieves Newfoundland, 324–5

Amherst, Capt. John (afterwards Admiral, brother of above), 114

Amherst, Col. William (afterwards General, brother of above and father of William Pitt, Earl Amherst), ii. 324–5

Andrews, Capt. Thomas, 114

Anson, Adm. of Fleet, George, Lord (First Lord of Admiralty), his character, 34–6, 42, 47, 49 ; his relations with Hardwicke, 51–2, 85, 179 ; 58–9, 86 ; his responsibility for Minorca, 97, 102–3, 133–5 ; resigns, 138, 150 ; returns to office, 179–82 ; his relations with Pitt, 191, 232 ; ii. 11–13, 100, 103 ; hoists his flag (1758), 267, 269, 273, 275, 289–91, 297, 373–5 ; at Admiralty (1759), 403 ; his home defence, ii. 9, 21–4, 27, 44, 46–7, 49, 54, 73, 315–6 ; on Baltic squadron, 79 ; on Belleisle, 98, 100, 131 ; 102 ; on war with Spain, 196–8, 203–4, 208 ; his design against Hanava, ii. 246–9, 254–5, 259–60, 261 *n.*; dying, 297–8, 318 ; dead, 342 ; his influence on the navy, ii. 366–73 ; his strategical opinions and practice, i. 265 *n.*, 270, 273, 290, 311–3 ; ii. 374 ; on fleet tactics, i. 274–5 ; his pupils, i. 400 ; his influence as First Lord, i. 51, 56 ; ii. 366–73 ; letters of, i. 129–30